Identity, Mediation, and the Cunning of Capital

Critical Insurgencies
A Book Series of the Critical Ethnic Studies Association

Series Editors: Jodi A. Byrd and Michelle M. Wright

Critical Insurgencies features activists and scholars, as well as artists and other media makers, who forge new theoretical and political practices that unsettle the nation-state, neoliberalism, carcerality, settler colonialism, Western hegemony, legacies of slavery, colonial racial formations, gender binaries, and ableism, and challenge all forms of oppression and state violence through generative future imaginings.

About CESA   The Critical Ethnic Studies Association organizes projects and programs that engage ethnic studies while reimagining its futures. Grounded in multiple activist formations within and outside institutional spaces, CESA aims to develop an approach to intellectual and political projects animated by the spirit of decolonial, antiracist, antisexist, and other global liberationist movements. These movements enabled the creation of ethnic studies and continue to inform its political and intellectual projects.

www.criticalethnicstudies.org

Identity, Mediation, and the Cunning of Capital

Ani Maitra

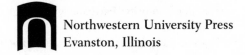
Northwestern University Press
Evanston, Illinois

Northwestern University Press
www.nupress.northwestern.edu

Printed in the United States of America

10 9 8 7 6 5 4 3 2 1

Library of Congress Cataloging-in-Publication Data

Names: Maitra, Ani, author.
Title: Identity, mediation, and the cunning of capital / Ani Maitra.
Other titles: Critical insurgencies.
Description: Evanston : Northwestern University Press, 2020. | Series:
   Critical insurgencies | Includes bibliographical references and index.
Identifiers: LCCN 2019023376 | ISBN 9780810141797 (paperback) |
   ISBN 9780810141803 (cloth) | ISBN 9780810141810 (ebook)
Subjects: LCSH: Fanon, Frantz, 1925–1961—Criticism and interpretation. |
   Cha, Theresa Hak Kyung—Criticism and interpretation. | Djebar, Assia,
   1936–2015—Criticism and interpretation. | Identity (Psychology) and
   mass media. | Identity (Psychology)—Social aspects. | Identity politics—
   Social aspects.
Classification: LCC P96.I34 M35 2020 | DDC 302.23—dc23
LC record available at https://lccn.loc.gov/2019023376

For Ma, Baba, and Matt

CONTENTS

ACKNOWLEDGMENTS

This book took shape on three different continents, with unflinching support from family, friends, professors, and colleagues in Bangalore; Cranston, Rhode Island; Hamilton, New York; Kolkata; London; Mumbai; New Delhi; New York; Oliveri, Italy; Providence, Rhode Island; Seattle; and Toronto. I am so incredibly grateful to all of you.

My undergraduate and graduate years at Jadavpur University in Kolkata have influenced the book in countless ways. My professors in the English and Comparative Literature Departments—especially Paromita Chakravarti, Supriya Chaudhuri, Nilanjana Deb, Ananda Lal, and Kavita Panjabi—taught me to think within and beyond disciplinary formations with a critical restlessness, or a hopeful pessimism, that is at the heart of this project. Jadavpur remains very special also because of Trina Banerjee, Nandini Das, Shuktara Lal, and Debosmita Majumder, everyday interlocutors during those five years and now cherished lifelong friends.

The project that would eventually become *Identity* started when I was a Ph.D. student in the Department of Modern Culture and Media at Brown University. People at Brown who made this project possible include all the professors who offered me invaluable guidance and mentorship, and especially Rey Chow, Wendy Hui Kyong Chun, Mary Ann Doane, Lynne Joyrich, Jacques Khalip, Philip Rosen, and Elizabeth Weed; the department administrators, Liza Hebert and Susan McNeil, who made me feel like family from the moment I arrived; and my very dear friends and interlocutors in the program, Kenneth Berger, Michelle Cho, Maggie Hennefeld, Rijuta Mehta, Matt Noble-Olson, Pooja Rangan, and Julie Levin Russo. The book owes a very special debt to Rey and Rijuta. Rey's intellectual presence will be fairly obvious to the reader, but I have also learned so much from her through our conversations and collaborations at and beyond Brown. And Rijuta was the kindest and most incisive reader as I turned the dissertation into the book. The final manuscript would not have been the same without her untiring emotional and intellectual support.

I am extremely fortunate to have the most thoughtful and encouraging colleagues at Colgate University, my home institution. I am especially grateful to the following people for taking the time to offer precious feedback on writing in progress: Hélène Julien, Nimanthi Rajasingham, Nagesh Rao, Lynn Schwarzer, Mary Simonson, and Emilio Spadola. My theorization of *mediation* and the *cunning of capital*—two key concepts in this book—crystallized only after several stimulating conversations with Emilio; Mary's and Lynn's mentorship and constant support allowed me to move past the moments of self-doubt with which my fellow first-time authors may be very familiar. The long hours spent in my office in Little Hall finishing the manuscript would have certainly felt longer without the warmth and kindness of my department administrators, Angela Kowalski and Lois Wilcox. The book also owes a lot to my students, especially those in my Global Cinema courses at Colgate.

Several other mentors, readers, and friends have contributed to the completion or the revision of individual chapters. The introduction gained clarity after very perceptive feedback on the project from Amelie Hastie and Lakshmi Luthra. Chapter 1, which began as a final term paper in a graduate seminar on psychoanalysis with Mary Ann Doane, unfolded through a series of conversations with Elizabeth Weed as well as very constructive suggestions from peer reviewers for the journal *differences*. Chapters 2 and 3 benefited immensely from comments from Bishnupriya Ghosh and Monique Roelofs, intellectual powerhouses whose scholarly contributions have also been indispensable to the project. And research for chapter 4 was significantly enriched by my conversations with Vikram Phukan and his warm hospitality during my trip to Mumbai in the summer of 2017.

I would also like to thank the following people for all the support that made it possible for me to transform the manuscript into a printed and bound book available to my readers: Jodi A. Byrd and Michelle M. Wright for including the project in Northwestern University Press's Critical Insurgencies series; Gianna Francesca Mosser, Trevor Perri, and Patrick P. Samuel for guiding me through the acquisition, review, and revision process; Maia M. Rigas and Melody Negron for overseeing the copyediting, typesetting, proofreading, and indexing; Brian Bendlin for the careful copyediting; JD Wilson for directing the marketing strategies; and Marianne Jankowski for directing the cover design as well as the interior layout.

Finally, *Identity* could not have been conceived or completed without the love, patience, and care that I have been incredibly lucky to receive from my mother, Anuradha Maitra, and my partner, Matthew Papino.

Sections from two chapters originally appeared as journal articles. Sections from chapter 1 were originally published as "Aberrant Narcissisms in Dolto, Lacan, and Fanon: Notes on a Wounded Imaginary," *differences* 28, no. 3 (2017): 93–135; copyright, 2017, Brown University and *differences: A Journal of Feminist Cultural Studies*; all rights reserved; republished by permission of the copyright holder, and the present publisher, Duke University Press, www.dukeupress.edu. A brief section of chapter 4 was originally published as "Touching Hearts: The Uncertain but Strategic Politics of KASHISH 2015," *Film Quarterly* 69, no. 2 (2015): 60–65; all rights reserved; republished by permission of the copyright holder, and the present publisher, University of California Press, www.ucpress.edu.

Identity, Mediation, and the Cunning of Capital

Identity in between Media

We go back to *ce qui reste*, fragments of essences to reckon with. . . .
Fragments of essences to reckon with rather than preserving myself from
essences. If you see this as an antiessentialist project, I start
running the other way again.
  —Gayatri Chakravorty Spivak, *Outside in the Teaching Machine*

Fractal personhood suggests a networked materiality in which consumers
are neither simply swallowed up by the objects they incorporate within
them . . . nor singular agents acting freely on commodities. . . . Rather,
they live a shadow life of objectified personhood dispersed into the world
of objects that seemingly are external to them.
  —Bishnupriya Ghosh, *Global Icons*

In late March 2017, African American artist and activist Parker
Bright posted a video on Facebook to protest a painting on display at
the Biennial in the Whitney Museum of American Art in New York
City.[1] The painting in front of which Bright protested for two days
was Dana Schutz's *Open Casket*, an oil on canvas based on a photograph of the mangled face of Emmett Till, a fourteen-year-old African
American lynched in Mississippi in 1955. The painting clearly intends
to avoid iconic resemblance. While it depicts Till as he appears in the
photograph—lying in a coffin in a black suit—and from the camera's
point of view, the artist blends thick strokes of brown and black on
her canvas to create a highly abstract, inchoate, and yet arresting vis-
age. It would appear that Schutz is not aiming for resemblance but
reminiscence, asking viewers not to see but to recollect the terrifying dis-
figurement of Till's face captured by the iconic photograph. And yet,
in his protest video, Bright stands in front of *Open Casket* with his

3

arms crossed, partially blocking the painting from our view, and drawing the viewer's attention to the words BLACK DEATH SPECTACLE written on the back of his T-shirt. Soon after the images of Bright's demonstration appeared online on Facebook and Instagram, several other artists joined him to object to what they deemed to be the commodification of black suffering by a U.S. artist for a primarily white audience at an elite museum in Manhattan. Echoing Bright's position, the black-identified biracial British artist Hannah Black penned an open letter to the curators and staff of the Biennial, calling for not just the removal but the destruction of Schutz's painting to prevent it from being exhibited or sold. In the letter, Black and her cosignatories argue that the very existence of the painting is a cold and hurtful testament to the normalized practice of converting "Black suffering into profit and fun."[2] Claiming that the painting's "subject matter is not Schutz's," the letter's authors insisted that black trauma, when represented by "non-Black" people, can only be exploitative. Literary critic Christina Sharpe, who also signed the letter, suggested elsewhere that the protests in front of *Open Casket* need to be seen as a kind of "wake work" where the protestors putting their own bodies in front of the painting were "keeping watch with the dead, practicing a kind of care."[3] This wake work *by* black bodies *for* other black bodies, she further noted, was also a protest against Schutz's abstract (i.e., nonrealist) representation of Till's maimed face in a nonphotographic medium. For Sharpe, the painting is a decontextualization of Till's murder, one that obfuscates the violence of lynching and white supremacy indexed more transparently by the original photograph. Thus, Sharpe, Bright, and the other protestors sought to assert or reclaim black identity through the photographic image of Till's body. Identity, in their argument, appears to be something that can be and must be guarded by a politics of cultural safekeeping, by protecting Till's image from aesthetic appropriation.

This necessarily identitarian rejection that also became a symbolic reappropriation of *Open Casket* did not go unchallenged. Schutz responded to her detractors by noting that the painting was never meant to be sold. Her primary intention was to engage with this image "through empathy with his [Till's] mother," Mamie Till-Mobley,[4] who had invited an African American magazine to publish the photograph of her son's corpse to draw public attention to the brutality.[5] Siding with Schutz, Cuban American artist and scholar Coco Fusco argued that the call to destroy Schutz's painting was, in fact, a form of moral policing that naturalized racial differences from an "essentialist position." Instead, Fusco urged viewers to read *Open Casket* through an informed "aesthetic understanding" that can move past moral judgment toward "interracial cooperation."[6] Such an antiessentialist approach, she noted, requires the viewer to participate in a "reasoned assessment" of the painting on its own terms, using "nuanced evaluative criteria" that are able to distinguish between an "individual artist's single, non-mass-produced artwork" and "the coercive power of an advertising campaign or a Hollywood blockbuster." Fusco's position can, therefore, be summarized as follows: Viewers need to be properly trained to be able to immerse themselves in the specificity of Schutz's artwork and situate it in a longer tradition of antiracist art. It is this informed and immersive mode of aesthetic engagement that can replace essentialism and antiaesthetic moralism with a "universal antiracist consciousness."[7]

Identity, Mediation, and the Cunning of Capital (henceforth *Identity*) troubles both the positions outlined above—the cultural reclamation of identity on the one hand, and the antiessentialist prescription of an aesthetic remedy on the other—that come into view through but are by no means confined to the *Open Casket* controversy. The book argues that identity politics cannot, in fact, be redeemed or transcended by cultural or aesthetic means—specifically through immersion in a particular aesthetic medium—to achieve equality under racialized capitalism. This is because, as a subjective and social experience, identity is a *multiply mediated* process, a continually unfolding aesthetic mechanism that is orchestrated and manipulated by capitalism. Identity can be neither consolidated nor undone through media aesthetics because it is produced and maintained between shifting forms and levels of technological and socioeconomic mediation. The main contention of the book, then, is that the global politics of identity as marginalized difference—which emerges in and mutates through colonial modernity—is also a politics of capital-bound mediation that requires sustained aesthetic analysis rather than attempts to transcend capitalism through aesthetic experience.

In order to track the continuities as well as discontinuities in identity production between the era of decolonization and the present, the book analyzes a range of aesthetic texts, heterogeneous in their global origins and their media. I move from anticolonial polemics to twentieth-century Asian American literature to postcolonial Algerian feminist cinema to LGBTQ+ media from contemporary India to argue that the global dominance of capitalism needs to be understood through the persistence of identity as a "media effect" or mediation, by which I mean a subjective and social fragmentation *between media* that includes but also far exceeds the effects of singular media technologies. In other words, mediation is here a function of capitalism, where powerful agents such as a colonial state, a private corporation, or a neoliberal regime of labor operate through but remain irreducible to language- and/or image-based technologies and hence cannot be circumvented through commercialized or more radical experimental media. Or, as Emilio Spadola puts it, mediation must be understood not just in terms of media technologies and infrastructures but also "the social and political hierarchies in which these are embedded, and the repeated practices by which people come to inhabit and identify with them."[8] Crucially, my argument about identity emerges through my readings of aesthetic texts—literary, cinematic, and literary-visual—that rethink their own medium specificity in terms of the coaction of several kinds of mediation through which capitalism controls the production of minoritized difference in both its colonial and neocolonial avatars. These readings demonstrate that the global dominance of capitalism also needs to be understood in terms of relentless aesthetic mediations of imbricated categories of difference—such as race, class, ethnicity, gender, and sexuality—that are inexorably sustained by and sustain the capitalist commodity. Thus, the book builds an archive to trace an aesthetic reflexivity that is also a transnational and transdisciplinary *method* of attending to the geopolitically distinct mediations of identitarian difference at the intersection of human and nonhuman capital.[9]

To sum up the book's intervention in terms of the *Open Casket* controversy, I argue that culturalist reclamations of identity as championed by Bright and others overlook how identity is produced and disciplined as a mediated fragment that ultimately bolsters the capitalist system of exchange and value production. At the same time, I demonstrate that the aesthetic antiessentialism—advocated by Fusco and others—relies on an idealized view of subjectivity, where the subject's immersion in a privileged aesthetic medium is offered as a more radical alternative to identity politics. In other words, in my view, current arguments for and against identity politics are insufficient until (1) we reframe the very notion of identity in terms of the complex work of aesthetic mediation and (2) we theorize these mediations as the *cunning of capital*—that is, as subservient to its fundamentally unequal relations of production and commodity logic. A crucial element of this cunning, I argue, is capitalism's ability to nurture competing notions of aesthetic resistance even as the aesthetic remains thoroughly implicated in its mediated logic of commodification.

I open *Identity* with the *Open Casket* controversy not only to highlight the opposed stances to the painting but also because the protests serve as a very helpful illustration of a multimodal production of black identity that is overlooked by the protestors as well as the defenders. "The 'content' of any medium is always another medium," wrote Marshall McLuhan in 1964.[10] McLuhan's generalization, however, acquires a chilling historical specificity when we note that what the protestors found to be both absent and present in Schutz's painting was the widely circulated photograph of Emmett Till's open-casket viewing. If Schutz's abstract painting at once interpellated and alienated the black protestor (as the symbolic guarding and "wake work" suggest), it was because the artwork's formal abstraction did not fail to evoke that photograph as well as the violent capitalist abstraction that is the photograph's condition of possibility.[11] It is vital not to ignore the historical and affective reasons for this eruption of the photograph in the reception of the nonphotographic painting.[12] In her book *Dead Matter*, Margaret Schwartz argues that, by circulating in a network of black magazines and newspapers after Till's memorial in Chicago, Till's photograph acquired the status of a "relic that holds us back from burying the corpse" such that readers encountering the image bore witness "to the suffering of one black body as the suffering of any and all black bodies."[13] In particular, black readers' embodied identification with Till—as well as their wounded physical awareness of themselves as black subjects—were inseparable from the white supremacy indexed by the photograph. Furthermore, the horror of viewing blackness as a maimed corpse also emerged from other starkly different photographs of Till displayed at the memorial next to his corpse. As Schwartz reminds us, in these other photographs, taken when Till was alive, "a grinning child dressed in his best suit leans against a television (at the time a luxury item) in a clearly middle-class home—supposedly, the security that first emancipation and then the Great Migration had won" (58). The illusion of successful black integration into U.S. democratic capitalism offered by these images was precisely what was shattered by the photographs of Till's mangled face in 1955. The profound disillusionment and sense of abjection produced by Till's murder and photographs were, in part, constitutive of African American identity on the eve of the civil rights movement.[14]

For poet and scholar of the black radical tradition Fred Moten, there is also a nonvisual, *sonic* dimension that structures the aesthetic and political force of Till's photograph. Both alongside and outside the visual depiction of the mutilated body, the photograph can be "heard" as a moan, or what Moten calls "mo'nin'," referring to a phonographic materiality of the cry of the lynched black body. This cry of the photograph is devoid of meaning or a single traceable origin. But it does carry and transmit to many spectators the profoundly historical echo of Till's last whistle or stuttered speech that was construed as flirtation with a white woman and that led to Till's murder as revenge for her violated honor. That is, Till's photograph pricks or wounds not just because of what it shows but also because it shouts, screams, and moans for and with Till.[15] This aural dimension becomes, in Moten's view, the basis of a blackness that is simultaneously essential and improvisational (*In the Break*, 255), at once derived from but not confined to the black individual.

Thus, while Schutz's *Open Casket* may not be entirely mimetic, it is possible to see how even its nonrealist evocation of Till's relic-image and its phonic materiality might elicit blackness as a collective wound and sentiment, one that is not quite reducible to what Wendy Brown calls the "fixed" narcissistic wound of ressentiment.[16] Blackness is necessarily split between what is on the canvas, the protestor's self-perception as a black body, and the absent-present photograph's cry against American capitalism's horrific devalorization of the black body. If, by "mediation," media theorists often mean the effects of a recursive and historically specific set of conventions considered proper to an aesthetic medium,[17] then *Open Casket* elicits a blackness that cannot be confined to the properties of its own material substrate, that of the canvas. The dissenting spectatorial body, the absent-present iconic photograph, and the abstract painting all work as discrete and yet enmeshed media, producing and keeping suspended *between* them a fragmented blackness, oscillating between identification and alienation. Blackness is, in this sense, an unstable intermedial fragmentation.

But that's not all. There are at least three other levels of mediation that require our attention in this scene of identity production. First, the Whitney Museum itself functions as a mediating exhibition space that attempts to reconcile racioeconomic disparities by promoting antiracist art. To follow the logic of this reconciliation, we need to think of *mediation* beyond individual media technologies and their effects. As critics like W. J. T. Mitchell and Mark B. N. Hansen have pointed out, in historical materialist thinking, mediation is a dynamic rapprochement between conflicting elements—like the relations of production and the political power structures—in a capitalist society.[18] This definition draws on the more general dictionary definition of "mediation" as "agency or action as a mediator; the action of mediating between parties in dispute; intercession on behalf of another."[19] Notably, historical materialists would also argue that capitalism functions not in spite of but rather through this logic of mediation. In this mode of reconciliation, driven by the commodity form and fungibility, antagonistic hierarchies are not eliminated but rather converted into asymmetrical values. (I will return to this meaning of mediation later in the introduction.)

Despite the best intentions of its curators, the Whitney could not evade this compromised logic of reconciliation. Even as the Biennial mediated to bridge the racial divide—by including Schutz's painting as well as work by several black artists—the museum did little to alter the well-established perception that it caters to a predominantly affluent and white public. As Bright noted in his Facebook video, he was also protesting because Schutz's painting—which was meant to be an empathetic representation of black trauma—was being exhibited at a museum that charges twenty-two dollars as its entrance fee and would, therefore, remain beyond the reach of the majority of African Americans.[20] Similarly, for Robyn Autry, it is the exhibition's aesthetic environment with primarily "white patrons strolling through the museum" that contributes to *Open Casket*'s complicity with a liberalism that laments antiblackness while keeping the institutional hegemony of whiteness intact.[21] My point, then, is that the mediation of blackness is, in this instance, also catalyzed by an acute awareness of an intermediary institutional "gaze" whose reconciliation of racial antagonism is structured by the conspicuous absence of black and brown bodies at the exhibition. As a corollary, the mediation of identity is also an intercorporeal affair, or a matter between bodies physically marked as "black" and "white."

In fact, this bodily (and second level of) mediation begins with Schutz's decision to intervene aesthetically as a mother—imagining herself in Mamie Till-Mobley's place—to transcend racial divides through her painting. But from the protestors' perspective, such a transracial feminine identification overlooks the capitalist imbrication of race and gender underlying Till's lynching. Till was murdered because he was perceived as a black man flirting with a white woman. The perpetrators were able to justify the lynching through a reified sexual and racial hierarchy between white and black bodies functioning as the underbelly of U.S. democracy. As soon as we accept that this fictional hierarchy continues to translate into physical violence against black bodies in our post–civil rights moment, we begin to see why Schutz's no doubt well-intentioned gesture has been read antagonistically. The artist's attempt to empathize with the black mother without a critical engagement with (her own) whiteness becomes, in the protestors' eyes, both an objectification and erasure of the history of Till's corpse, of the very material constraints of being identified as black in the U.S. capitalist economy.

Third, we cannot sidestep the implications of Bright protesting the painting and mediating his own blackness on social media. I would argue that Bright's decision to represent his identitarian wound through the digital economy of Facebook exemplifies precisely the potential that identity bears, as an aesthetically mediated fragment, to be absorbed into a neoliberal system of value production. For even as Bright protests Schutz's commodification of blackness, his own protest-as-video participates in what Jodi Dean calls "communicative capitalism." As Dean compellingly argues, capitalism in the digital era profits from acts of networked communication that pay lip service to the ideals of democracy and equality. Communicative capitalism substitutes meaningful social activism with the immediacy of social media performances where "expressions of dissent enrich the few and divert the many" and "private feelings become private property, belonging to the corporation who owns the platforms and traces of our social engagement."[22] Bright's decision to communicate his personal and political feelings via Facebook remains caught up within this larger capitalist logic where the "success" of the protest-as-video would be measured by the number of "likes," "dislikes," and "shares" it generates. The artist's reception of what Moten calls "mo'nin'"—albeit evocative of a resistive blackness—gives way to a racialized performance on Facebook that ultimately contributes to a private corporation's self-marketing as an especially "live" social platform and, less directly, to its advertisement-driven revenue system. Simultaneously, the video generates for both Bright and his object of protest what Dean, in "Faces as Commons," calls "circulation value," wherein value accrues in the form of media visibility achieved through accessibility and transportability. The video positions Bright as a dissident black artist in the global art market, securing him, for instance, enough cultural capital to raise money through a GoFundMe campaign that would allow him to fly to Paris to protest at another exhibition at the Palais de Tokyo gallery of contemporary art. In this campaign, however, Bright seeks to "reclaim his [own] image," one that was taken and circulated during his Whitney Facebook protest and subsequently used in an installation by the French Algerian artist Neïl Beloufa.[23] Bright's response to Beloufa's use of the Whitney image would appear to be contradictory, since his campaign protests the very circulation value on which it thrives. But such a contradiction makes sense in an economy where another protest-as-video to reclaim his own image will likely allow the artist to gain further circulation and visibility. Notably, as Bright's campaign draws on the power of crowdfunding, its success inadvertently gestures toward socioeconomic divides deepened if not created by communicative capitalism—between lives that have the technological and cultural resources to convert their identities into circulation value and those that do not.

Relatedly, Bright's ability to circulate digitally as a *black* artist and activist—criticisms of his art and politics notwithstanding—also highlights capitalism's ability to profit from the conversion of difference into circulatable value. According to Dean, one of the key features of communicative capitalism is that it makes difference and particularity less significant by encouraging netizens to reuse and recycle images and texts from others to express themselves. We live in a world where "images of others are images of me," since self-expression through emojis, GIFs, and memes demand constant borrowing and appropriation. In fact, in such an economy, the digital "selfie" is less a self-portrait of an individual and more a technological form that has a "collective subject, the many participating in the common practice, the many imitating each other" (Dean, "Faces as Commons"). Digital ephemera, in Dean's view, do not exist in isolation but as part of a mutating public montage and social practice that privileges commonality over particularity. It would appear that Bright's performance is strikingly in sync with this practice of commoning and substitution that Dean describes. The artist's Whitney Facebook protest, we might say, is a "selfie" that inserts itself in the place of (the face in) Schutz's painting, whose abstraction of Till's face also seems ready-made for digital repurposing. In this instance, however, the commoning and the regeneration of sameness is predicated on a splitting that engenders blackness as difference. The effort that Bright's Facebook video makes to communicate blackness as a collective experience is derived from the subjective fragmentation elicited before (but not just by) *Open Casket*. It is this split and differentiated ego that communicative capitalism beckons, to secure identity as racialized commonality, to labor to acquire racialized value through the circulation of the self-as-fragment. In other words, contra Dean, capitalism does not simply encourage the proliferation of sameness. It regenerates itself through a perpetual extrapolation and valorization of sameness or identity *from difference*.[24]

Thus, what the *Open Casket* controversy demonstrates is a geohistorically specific snapshot of the multiple, dynamic, and overlapping processes of mediation through which capitalism keeps identity politics alive. Attending to these processes, I would argue, is one way of reckoning with what Gayatri Chakravorty Spivak refers to as the "fragments of essences" in the first epigraph to this introduction. In the interview from which the epigraph is taken, Spivak approaches identity and its essentialist tendencies "not as an exposure of error, our own or others', but as an acknowledgement of the dangerousness of something one cannot not use."[25] Spivak cautions us that deconstructing essentialism as erroneous fiction does not make it go away; neither can deconstruction, as a reading practice, declare that identity is not meaningful for those who claim and use it. Rather, the more urgent critical task is to grasp how the production and persistence of the essence as an enduring identitarian fragment is bound up with the labor that the fragmented ego performs to find a foothold in a capitalist (communicative) economy. Neither a redemptive celebration nor an antiessentialist rejection of identity politics is sufficient for that analysis.

This leads me to the bigger contention of this book. *Identity* argues that the multiply mediated structure of the splitting of the minoritized subject revealed by the somewhat exceptional *Open Casket* controversy, in fact, informs more everyday experiences of identity politics under capitalism. It is the varied repetition of this structure and its production of identity as a fragmented and intermedial consciousness that I examine in the following chapters. Through a range of politically and formally distinct texts, I read identity politics as an oscillation between identification with and alienation from the appearance of the commodity form, or that which stands for idealized circulatable value.

Given that capitalism has always been transnational through economic and cultural strategies whose effects are felt rather locally, I make my argument through cultural texts from four national historical contexts: colonial France in the 1950s and 1960s; independent and socialist Algeria in the late 1970s; the multicultural United States in the 1980s; and neoliberal India in the twenty-first century. This global-local outlook of the project builds on the decolonial insistence that colonial matrices of power did not end with decolonization but rather mutated and took new forms in postcolonial and neoliberal contexts of governance in the Global North as well as the South. As Walter D. Mignolo reminds us, "coloniality" should not be conflated with the historical phenomenon of colonialism. Rather, coloniality should be understood as a tenacious logic through which racialized capitalism systematically "translated differences into values," a logic that continues to drive the intensively neoliberal current world order.[26] Similarly, Denise Ferreira da Silva describes the racialized body in particular as "value" accompanied by a sexed and gendered excess that is "always already defined in a given—economic and symbolic—productive regime: as object, other, or commodity."[27] The geographical and temporal shuttling from anticolonial identity in France to LGBTQ+ politics in present-day India is, therefore, central to the book's goal to examine historically contingent intermedial processes through which global-local identities materialize in hierarchical and transnational systems of value. One of my principal aims is to track, through these disparate and yet interanimating set of contexts, both the differences and similarities between aesthetic mediations governing identity production as capitalism moves and morphs across the spatial and temporal borders of one world, reinventing itself not just by inflicting a singular vision of global modernity but also through continual tensions between "cultural homogenization and cultural heterogenization."[28] In other words, my argument depends on acknowledging discontinuities between conjunctures—the vast differences, for instance, between the economic and political forces behind the production of blackness in colonial France in the 1950s and those regulating the discursive appearance of gay and lesbian identities in post-liberalization India in the 1990s. At the same time, across these various historical and political arrangements of minoritization, I show how identity—as the production and embodiment of racial, ethnic, or sexual difference—needs to be viewed as an egoic splitting brought on by aesthetic and quotidian mediations of value. To that end, each chapter in the book examines how, within a specific sociopolitical context of minoritization, global capitalism mediates identity so that the latter can be contained and regulated by the hierarchical split between use value and exchange (or circulation) value, shuttling between marginality and inclusion, resistance and conformity.

This split within value nurtures capitalism. But it also produces in identity an exceptional and yet normalized irreconcilability. On the one hand, identity functions as a necessary deprecation of the usefulness of the identified. The devaluation of the subject of identity is necessary to maintain the superiority of dominant ideologies functioning as a kind of "universal equivalent," whether it is the fetishized "inherent" value of whiteness in colonial Europe or of heteropatriarchal nationalism in neoliberal India. On the other hand, neoliberalism also lures the subject of identity with what Rey Chow calls "coercive mimeticism" or what Elizabeth A. Povinelli describes as "the cunning of recognition."[29] This is the zone of exchange or circulation where the subject of identity is encouraged to thrive and survive in a global-local economy by partaking in the logic of fetishism, by commoditizing identity's attributes—whether it is ethnoracial particularity or erotic preference—as "innately" valuable and egalitarian. In this zone, commodity fetishism promises identity that it can resist oppression and simultaneously make itself lucrative and agentic through an "intercalation of the politics of culture with the culture of capital" (Povinelli, *Cunning of Recognition*, 17). This inclusion of identity-as-culture into capitalism also makes it a potential source of surplus value. In each of its chapters, *Identity* shows why these twin operations of exclusion and ostensible inclusion need to be viewed as the effects of aesthetic mediations of race, ethnicity, gender, and sexuality fueling global capitalism.[30] Capitalist mediation produces a split and intermedial ego that exceeds representational capture. It is, however, precisely this unrepresentable excess or potentiality from which capitalism profits as the identitarian wound labors to become an essence by acquiescing to the fetishistic system of exchange, the promise of recognition and profit. As well, within each chapter, *Identity* attends carefully to class inequality and class divides as crucial economic and aesthetic supplements enabling identity's mythical transformation from an injury into a fetish. The book focuses on class relations and the global division of labor as socioeconomic processes that operate both through and independently of the identitarian categories of race, gender, and sexuality. The shifting classed dimensions of identity production, I suggest, can be glimpsed only through a context-specific intermedial analytic. Before elaborating further on the theoretical scope and intervention of the book, it will be useful to get a sense of the key texts and arguments of the individual chapters.

Chapter Outlines

Chapter 1 opens with the Martinican psychiatrist and revolutionary Frantz Fanon watching a Hollywood film at a theater in colonial France, a scene of reception at once comparable to and distinct from that of the black protestor before *Open Casket*. This moment in Fanon's polemical text *Black Skin, White Masks* is often read as a powerful illustration of the role that commercial Euro-American cinema played in the sedimentation of racial difference.[31] My reading, however, focuses on the egoic splitting that Hollywood's representation of blackness inflicts on Fanon, which I argue is not just an effect of the cinematic apparatus. Fanon himself alerts us that his fragmentation before the image is also mediated by his sociohistorical location in metropolitan France, his colonial relationship with the French language, and his acute awareness of the corporeal whiteness of the colonizer. This intermedial production of black identity in the movie theater is, therefore, inseparable from the routine linguistic and visual mediations of racial difference in colonial France. Drawing on the psychoanalytic theory of Françoise Dolto and Jacques Lacan, my reading of *Black Skin* focuses on the identitarian implications of the racialized wounding that the French language produces on an everyday basis. Fanon's critique of the Martinican desire to master the colonizer's medium, I suggest, allows us to rethink identity politics through a fundamental principle of commodity capitalism. Fanon shows us that it is not just colonial modernity but more specifically that modernity's intermediality that becomes the "laboratory" for the production of minoritized difference trapped between alienation and identification, use value and exchange value.

I develop this idea further in the final section of chapter 1 by turning to Fanon's *A Dying Colonialism*, and specifically his discussion of the role of radio in shaping Algerian anticolonialism.[32] Once again, the Fanonian analytic reveals that even as the radio catalyzes Algerian nationalism, the medium is not solely responsible for the message. Anticolonial splitting is also regulated by the popular perception of the radio as an ideological weapon of the colonizer, as a means for the French denigration of Arab culture. Consequently, the anticolonial appropriation of the radio remains bound to an "us versus them" binary sustaining colonial capitalism. In other words, I suggest that, in spite of its revolutionary optimism, Fanon's reading of radiophonic anticolonialism in Algeria is a prescient critique of identity's inability to break away from the tyranny of the colonial commodity economy. It is through the intermedial wounds of anticolonialism shaped by colonial racism that we must examine the engine of capitalism, as well as that of the ethnocentrism embraced by the postcolonial Algerian state (which is discussed further below and in chapter 3).

Chapter 2 returns to the U.S. context to examine ethnic identity production in the Asian American diaspora through Theresa Hak Kyung
Cha's experimental text *Dictée*. I argue that Cha's text not only scrutinizes Asian American fragmentation through racial divides characterizing
U.S. aesthetic politics but also situates that fragmentation within a
much larger geohistorical frame to unsettle binary oppositions between
the East and the West, ethnonationalism and liberal democracy.[33] Published in the shadow of mounting tensions in the Korean Peninsula
in the early 1980s, Cha's text both juxtaposes and weaves together
multiple political contexts of identity production: Japanese colonialism in Korea; the Korean War, which divided the country in two; and
the post–civil rights U.S. "melting pot." The literary-visual politics of
Dictée, I argue, foregrounds the aesthetic violence of the capitalist
abstraction and commodity fetishism mediating identity in all three
contexts. Cha's text reveals that the intermedial process of subjective
wounding that structures Korean anticolonialism—and through which
ethnic differences are converted into values—operates under different
guises in postcolonial Korean ethnonationalism and diasporic transnationalism. Crucially, chapter 2 claims that such an assessment of
the racial and gendered violence of the value form emerges only if
we attend to *Dictée*'s own aesthetic intermediality, its simultaneous
deployment of literary, cinematic, and photographic form in a transnational and decolonial frame.

Postcolonial feminism grappling with the gendered and classed contradictions of identity formation is the subject of chapter 3. My analysis
focuses on Assia Djebar's film *The Nouba of the Women of Mount Chenoua* (*La Nouba des femmes du Mont Chenoua*), controversial for its
subversion of the masculinist grand narrative of the Algerian struggle
for independence.[34] If Fanon cautions against the anticolonial fragment
mimicking the fetishistic logic of the colonial economy, Djebar's critique of official decolonization, I contend, rethinks Algerian feminine
identity as a further psychosocial splitting produced by that complicity
and repetition. The film demonstrates how the postcolonial feminine
fragment takes shape as Algerian women identify with the goals of anticolonialism while being alienated by its means. What Djebar's aesthetic
of fragmentation warns against is the ideology behind the means—a
state-controlled capitalism mediating itself over the next decade through
the aggressive Arabization of national culture and assaults on the civil
liberties of women and non-Arab citizens. Central to Djebar's aesthetic, I further argue, is an embodied politics of orality, listening,

and collective voicing. The feminine fragment in *The Nouba* remains split between a struggle against colonial patriarchal law and an ethical responsibility to hear the speech of rural Berber and Arab women excluded from the patriarchal history of anticolonialism. While such a mode of countercinematic—or what I call intermedial—listening is unable to halt identity production, it enables the feminine fragment to resist the lure of self-essentialization.

What would postcolonial queer politics look like if it began to reckon with its gendered and sexual essences as mediated fragments? How might we think of queerness as politics that does not evade but instead scrutinizes the means by which postcolonial neoliberalism regulates the terms of emergence of lesbian, gay, transgender, and other nonheteronormative identities? Chapter 4 addresses these questions by turning to South Asia's largest LGBTQ+ film festival, the KASHISH Mumbai International Queer Film Festival, held annually in Mumbai, India. I demonstrate that, on the one hand, the festival's ideology mirrors a cosmopolitan nationalism initiated by the economic liberalization of India in the 1990s. Viewed through this neoliberal and neoimperial ideoscape, LGBTQ+ identities appear to be a diverse and self-evident collectivity, at once "Indian" and transnational, with all its members being equally eligible for corporate and civic recognition. On the other hand, I contend that a number of contemporary Indian activist films—such as Nakshatra Bagwe's *Logging Out*, Karishma Dube's *Goddess* (*Devi*) and Debalina Majumder's *. . . and the unclaimed* (*. . . ebang bewarish*)—squarely challenge the festival's official and seemingly uncritical celebration of diversity and inclusion.[35] These films, most of which have been screened at KASHISH, aesthetically confront how queer identities are fragmented not just by the heterosexism of mainstream media commodities but also by normative and often state-sanctioned discourses of sexual and gender nonconformity. More fundamentally, a number of these texts deploy cinematic form to interrogate how queer identities are mediated by a regime of labor where colonial and postcolonial modes of exploitation coexist. To be "visible" as a queer Indian subject, I argue through these films, entails a differential and tactical negotiation of this overdetermined fragmentation in the postcolony. To follow the queer cinematic gaze in these scenes of cultural reception is to attend to the local political economy of queerness, one in which the queer(ed) subject may or may not be able to capitalize on difference and circulate as value. Thus, instead of idealizing "queer India" or "global queer cinema" as inherently transgressive sites, this final chapter calls for an urgent rethinking

of LGBTQ+ politics through class hierarchies, urban-rural divides, and
the contradictions of "progress" in postcolonial India. Decolonial queer
freedom, I finally suggest, must be envisaged as an unshackling of the
subject of identity from hetero- and homonormative mediations of difference and value, from the Sisyphean oscillation to which Fanon alerted us
on the eve of decolonization.

The analytical frameworks and methodologies driving *Identity* draw
from and contribute to several fields—in particular, film and media studies, philosophy, literary and cultural studies, and queer studies. Having
offered an overview of the individual chapters, I will now elaborate
on how the book engages with and distinguishes itself from the major
debates on identity politics in these fields. I begin with philosophical
interventions informing my approach to identity as a minoritizing constraint. Simultaneously, I indicate how I depart from these approaches
by reconceptualizing identity as a mediated egoic fragmentation that is
at once repressive and productive. I then discuss the central concept
of *mediation* at work in the book. Media studies and Marxist critique
shape my theoretical grid here. In the final section, I elaborate further
on what I mean by the *cunning of capital* and how subsequent chapters
uncover that aesthetic cunning by attending to identity's mediatedness.

Identity as a Schizophrenic Fragmentation

Concerned about the growing "identity disregard" both within and outside the academy, a number of scholars have argued for the need to
reexamine the causes and consequences of identitarian investments.[36]
Broadly speaking, this scholarship either views identity as a pernicious and violent imposition on individuals and groups or as a means of
collective resistance against socioeconomic discrimination and oppression. At once sympathetic to and complicating these claims, I contend
that identity is a malleable negotiation between resistive agency and
structural coercion regulated by capitalism. This regulation, as we shall
see, is as much a matter of aesthetics as it is of economics and politics.

Representative of critique that cautions against reifying socially
constructed notions of similarity and difference, Amartya Sen's view of
identity as a minoritizing constraint has had a formative impact on my
thinking. But my goals in this book are different from Sen's. In his book
Identity and Violence, Sen argues that if our identities are inescapably
diverse—an individual is simultaneously of a particular sexual orientation,

ethnicity, gender, and so on—identity politics is frequently manifested as a suppression of this plurality wherein "singular and belligerent identities" are imposed "on gullible people, championed by proficient artisans of terror" (2).

These political machinations, Sen insists, need to be countered not only by reaffirming the obfuscated plurality but also by reflecting on the roles that "choice" and "reasoning" play in an individual's or a group's privileging of one identity over others in a given social context (27). In contrast, I consistently interrogate the suggestion that to be drawn into identity politics is to be somehow politically "gullible." And to that end, I draw on Sen's own admission that the choice that one has to disregard the dominance of a certain identity (and, therefore, to value equally one's multiple affiliations) is often severely restricted. As Sen writes,

> The constraints may be especially strict in defining the extent to which we can persuade *others*, in particular, to take us to be different from (or more than) what they insist on taking us to be. A Jewish person in Nazi Germany, or an African-American when faced with a lynch mob in the American South, or a rebellious landless agricultural laborer threatened by a gunman hired by upper-caste landowners in North Bihar may not be able to alter his or her identity in the eyes of the aggressors. The freedom in choosing our identity in the eyes of others can sometimes be extraordinarily limited. (31, emphasis in the original)

Sen's redefinition of identity—as an ideologically manufactured alterity that exceptionally constrains and dominates the existence of the identified subject—will be crucial to my argument in this book. At the same time, I contend that, to comprehend the production of these constraints, we have to move beyond the assumption that identities are foisted upon the innocent or that they are concretized only through egregious acts like ethnic cleansing, hate crimes, and racial profiling. Instead, I argue for the need to examine identity as a constraint in more quotidian terms, through unexceptional and subjective encounters with the alterities—of race, gender, ethnicity, and so on—mediated by capitalism. These encounters, I suggest, reveal themselves to be unavoidable psychosocial negotiations with categories of difference that capitalism simultaneously produces as marginalizing and empowering. Through my readings of texts that make visible such routinized negotiations, I demonstrate that capitalism keeps identity politics alive by enabling a partial conversion of the fragmenting constraint into freedom and agency while keeping its structural violence and inequalities intact. My emphasis falls on a critical aesthetics that complements Marxist feminist and decolonial critiques of the false opposition between agency (or "choice" or "desire") and oppression within a commodity-driven economy.[37]

The agentic aspect of identitarian struggles is the focus of Linda Martín Alcoff and Satya P. Mohanty's introduction in the edited volume *Identity Politics Reconsidered*. Alcoff and Mohanty astutely point out that, contrary to what many of its critics on the left and the right suggest, identity politics cannot be dismissed as "ideological fictions, imposed from above."[38] Moving away from this notion of identity as illusion, they emphasize the need for "postpositivist" and "realist" accounts that will shed light on "the *complexity* that resides at the heart of identity-based political struggles and the subjective experiences on which these struggles draw" ("Reconsidering Identity Politics," 6, emphasis in the original). This emphasis on identity as a political collectivization—and, therefore, on identity's relevance as a historical frame of reference for mapping variegated social relations—informs my approach in this book, which begins with Fanon's phenomenology of colonial minoritization. In this context, I also follow Alcoff and Mohanty's lead in thinking of "minoritization" as a sociopolitical disenfranchisement stemming from "[relations of] power rather than numbers" (7). That is to say, the constraints of identity may be but are not necessarily accompanied by demographic marginality. Last but not least, my turn to Fanon is also guided by the postpositivist insight that a globally oriented analysis of identity politics cannot begin with the U.S. civil rights movement but must look for its antecedents in struggles against imperialism and slavery (Alcoff and Mohanty, "Reconsidering Identity Politics," 8).[39]

At the same time, what this book problematizes in the realist approach is the opposition between identity as the site of agency and identity as ideological fiction. This opposition comes to the fore when Alcoff and Mohanty claim that "social identities can be mired in distorted ideologies, but they can also be the lenses through which we learn to view our world accurately. . . . Often we create positive and meaningful identities that enable us to better understand and negotiate the social world. They enable us to engage with the social world and in the process discover how it really works" (6). Alcoff and Mohanty's language evinces a desire to weed out a misleading ("distorted") identity politics from a more useful and insightful ("positive and meaningful") variety. Consequently, the relationship between ideology and identity as a critical subjective lens remains untheorized. In contrast, I argue that, as a minoritizing constraint, identity becomes insightful only when it acknowledges its genesis in ideological distortion, when it sees its own positivity and meaningfulness not in opposition to but through the marginalizing effects of ideology as fiction. More specifically, I demonstrate that the effects and limits of identitarian agency cannot be understood without attending to the individual and collective fragmentation initiated by the ideology of the commodity form subtending capitalism. As I have suggested above in my discussion of the *Open Casket* protests, the assertion of black identity in contemporary U.S. culture and society becomes "meaningful" only in the wake of the splitting of the black ego before the fiction of whiteness as the universal equivalent. We might say that, as a contemporary instance of U.S. identity politics, the *Open Casket* protests pose questions that neither antiessentialism nor postpositivism is able to answer adequately: How does dominant ideology produce and maintain identity as a psychosocial experience of being minoritized and fragmented? In what ways does identity politics perpetuate a capitulation to capitalist ideology even as it generates the desire to resist dominant ideology? Finally, what is the role of mediation, the process that seems crucial to identity production under capitalism but remains unexamined in both postpositivist and antiessentialist accounts of resistance? To ask these questions is also to begin to tackle the implications of Stuart Hall's insistence that, as minoritized difference, identity must be seen as "the point of *suture*," a stitching or an intercession *between* the psychic and the discursive.[40]

This book addresses these questions by not dismissing but rather rethinking the antiessentialist critique of identity as a fictional experience of wholeness and plenitude. It has been well established that the critical insistence on identity's fictionality is heavily influenced by psychoanalytic thinking, specifically Lacan's account of the development of the neurotic human ego. I discuss multiple versions of this account (and not just Lacan's) at length in chapter 1. Here it will suffice to note that, in the dominant Lacanian narrative, the neurotic ego acquires its identitarian autonomy through a mistaken specular identification with an ideal image. Identification amounts to an illusory but nevertheless consequential and smooth assumption of this image. The moment of self-recognition—when the ego "realizes" its own identity—is, therefore,

also a misrecognition. For Lacan, this false plenitude of neurotic identity is the product of an "imaginary" narcissism that defines the "mirror
stage" of psychic development.[41] Louis Althusser's oft-cited thesis that
ideology represents "the imaginary relationship of individuals to their
real conditions of existence" draws directly on Lacan's neurotic account
of the mirror stage.[42] For Althusser, the "imaginary" is that psychosocial
domain without which ideology cannot function, and that makes subjects believe that, as individuals, they are coherent, autonomous, or
"centred" (On Ideology, 54). It is through this imaginary (mis)recogni-
tion of themselves as sovereign and independent agents in the "mirror"
of ideology that individuals are inserted into the normalized practices
of ideological state apparatuses like the church, the school, the family,
and so forth. By continually interpellating subjects or subjecting them
to ideology, these institutions reproduce the exploitative relations of
production necessary for capitalism. In other words, for Althusser, the
noncorrespondence between the material reality of exploitation and the
imaginary coherence and duplication facilitated by ideology structures
and maintains the class society in which we live.

As I argue in chapter 1, however, the historical experience of identity as a minoritizing constraint—under colonial capitalism, in this
instance—poses a significant challenge to the canonical narrative of
ideological or (neurotic) imaginary plenitude. As the latter defines
identity entirely through the intrapsychic labors of the presocial infantile ego, it also takes for granted the ego's ability to constitute itself
by disavowing the otherness of—and, therefore, (mis)recognizing itself
in—the ideal image. In contrast, through my reading of Fanon, I examine the production of a colonial black identity whose imaginary quality
is not based on a narcissistic experience of plenitude or sameness but
rather on a socially constructed and yet powerful wounded disposition
of being "different from" and "inferior to" the ideal image of Frenchness as whiteness. When Fanon qualifies Lacan's neurotic narrative
of the mirror stage by demonstrating how "for the black man . . . the
historical and economic realities must be taken into account," he subtly brings into view an entirely overlooked psychic structure of identity
formation.[43] In this radically minoritarian—but by no means minor—
reevaluation of the structure of the mirror stage, the nonwhite ego is
simultaneously held captive by and refused an identification with the
ideal image. Colonial capitalism demands that the colonized (mis)rec-
ognize and internalize the "intrinsic" value of whiteness—and, along with
it, the very notion of the universal equivalent propping up the racialized

system of exchange—while accepting and embodying their own hyper-visible nonwhiteness. In Fanonian terms, then, black identity can be an "accurate" sociopolitical lens only if it plots or graphs its fictional materiality through this psychic fragmentation and oscillation that serves as a matrix for colonialism's oppressive economic logic. Notably, as I have suggested above, my analysis does not pit Fanon against Lacan or psychoanalysis. In my reading, Fanon's attention to identity formation through egoic splitting parallels oft-ignored minoritarian accounts of the *schizophrenic imaginary* developed in the clinics of Dolto and Lacan. From this minoritarian clinical vantage point, too, identity is not a specular fiction of wholeness but a linguistic and visual wound that leads to the splitting of the corporeal ego. Viewed from within this composite decolonial and psychoanalytic framework, the subjective "realness" of identity politics—indeed, its unrepresentable psychic dimension—is an effect of the schizophrenic imaginary fragmentation instituted by French colonialism.[44]

A significant deviation from the ungeneralizable and yet influential notion of identity as neurotic plenitude, the schizophrenic colonial mode of identity production uncovered in chapter 1 serves as a crucial point of orientation and heuristic throughout the book. Part of what I develop in subsequent chapters is a critical aesthetics attuned to the schizophrenia of identitarianism in multicultural and postcolonial contexts of global capitalism. For instance, in chapter 2, I show how Cha's *Dictée* draws our attention to the paradoxical logic of U.S. multiculturalism, where ethnicity functions both as cultural capital and inassimilable difference. Analogously, Bagwe's short film *Logging Out*, I argue in chapter 4, lays bare the duplicity of a neoliberal structure of identification that promotes phallic masculinity as the emulable gay equivalent while keeping the heterosexual/homosexual hierarchy intact. In other words, I contend that whatever the "content" of identity politics, the schizophrenic attraction-repulsion structure frequently becomes the means by which capitalism capitalizes on identity. Thus, psychically speaking, the subject of identity is inveterately mired in a circumscribed state of flux and (neo)liberal potentiality.

Mediation through and beyond the Mass Medium

The controversy around Schutz's painting, I have proposed, also reveals the fragmentation constitutive of identity politics to be a multiply mediated, or *intermedial,* process. In this section, I will expand on this claim and further clarify how the book as a whole engages the concept of mediation. I will begin by outlining two distinct scholarly approaches— one that sees mass-mediated identity as asocial individualism, and another that considers it to be a fictive but powerful collectivization. Briefly noting the limits of these approaches, I will situate the book in a third strand of scholarship—especially Partha Chatterjee's reading of anticolonial splitting—that I see as being generative for the theorization of identity as a minoritizing fragmentation.

Media studies has long been concerned with the question of identity, albeit not always as a minoritizing constraint that feeds capitalism. If we take mediation to mean the operation and effects of mass media technologies,[45] we find that its most searing indictment comes from the Frankfurt school and specifically against the "culture industry" that promotes the myth of individualism. In his 1938 essay on the commodification of music, Theodor Adorno cautions his readers against the conformity that the culture industry packages as uniqueness and individual choice. For Adorno, while capitalism requires that "in broad areas the same thing is offered to everybody by the standardized production of consumption goods," it also masks this homogenization through "official culture's pretence of individualism which necessarily increases in proportion to the liquidation of the individual."[46] In stark contrast with his interlocutor Walter Benjamin's celebration of the democratizing potential of radio and cinema, Adorno reads the mechanical reproducibility of culture as a catalyst for a false individualism premised on commodity fetishism and its ersatz satisfactions.[47] For Marxist and psychoanalytic film theorists in France in the late 1960s and early 1970s, classical Hollywood cinema becomes the most significant mass medium in this regard, producing illusions of individual sovereignty in the darkened theater. Drawing heavily on Lacan's narrative of specular identification in the neurotic mirror stage, theorists like Jean-Louis Baudry and Christian Metz claim that one of the most pleasurable effects of the cinematic apparatus is also what needs a sustained ideological critique—the spectator's regression into a deceptive imaginary plenitude before the manufactured and yet entrancing visual spectacle.[48] While these theorists focus on cinema and their own cinephilia as their primary objects of study, they share with Adorno an underlying concern about mass culture's capacity to produce a phantasmal individualism.

As the status of cinema and the experience of watching films underwent irreversible transformations in the course of the twentieth century with the emergence of television, video, and digital media—or as prior technologies were "remediated" by newer ones—critical and cultural concerns around mediated individualism continued to be rearticulated through these technological shifts.[49] For instance, David Cronenberg's 1983 film *Videodrome* can be read as a dystopian and postmodern rendition of Adorno's critique of the culture industry, and specifically of television and video as relatively new media. The film's protagonist Max Renn has powerful hallucinations (induced by the eponymous and sensationally violent television show) in which his abdomen develops a slit that consumes VHS tapes. Max, therefore, literally consumes and is consumed by electronic media. We can think of the British children's television series *Teletubbies*—featuring colorful infantile creatures with televisions as abdomens—as an inverted celebration of the same phenomenon.

Subsequently, since the birth of the internet in the 1990s, several scholars have noted how a global economy increasingly reliant on large amounts of data and algorithmic simulation aggressively promotes the digital as the new medium enabling the consumer's individuation. For instance, Wendy Hui Kyong Chun examines how early U.S. television commercials for the internet exemplify the Lacanian (neurotic) logic of paranoid identification as they encourage viewers to envy and identify with the images of empowered and satisfied netizens. For Chun, these commercials at once reinforce and mask a technologically defined boundary between the "self" and the "other" that also becomes the basis of xenophobic distinctions between the West and the rest.[50] Examining social networking from an ethnographic and clinical perspective, Sherry Turkle argues that the lure of constant connectivity in the digital age is heavily geared toward the production of a "narcissistic self [that] gets on with others by dealing only with their made-to-measure representations."[51] In Turkle's view, this increasingly prevalent model of identity construction needs urgent critical attention not only because it is modeled on the simulacra of other people's lives on social media but also because the labors of identity construction leave traces of data, or an "electronic shadow" (*Alone Together*, 260) over which the consumer has little authority. John Cheney-Lippold has examined this electronic shadow as the raw material for an "algorithmic identity" that giant corporations like Google and Microsoft construct by gathering and analyzing information provided by the user.[52] This computational determination of who the user is *likely* to be (in terms of race, class, gender, or age) completely ignores the identity of the consumer as an embodied

subject, relying instead on predetermined categories, models, and mea-
surable types that make up the algorithms (*We Are Data*, 19). In this
new regime of identity as "datafication"—where contact between the
medium and consumers yields information about them that is beyond
their control—"essential truths do not and cannot exist" (11). In other
words, for Cheney-Lippold, there is little room for essentialism once
we begin to see identity as an effect of disembodied and ever-changing
dataveillance.

A second approach in media studies—theorizing identity not so much
in terms of consumerist individualism or datafication as a socially significant mediated collectivity—can be said to have been inaugurated by
Benedict Anderson's view of the nation as an "imagined community."
Anderson famously argues that, alongside the decline of a religious
worldview and sacral languages like Latin and classical Arabic toward
the end of the Middle Ages, print capitalism plays a defining role in giving rise to the secular and globally relevant concepts of the nation and
nationalism. In particular, with the emergence of the newspaper and the
novel in the eighteenth century, the notion of a "Messianic" or cycli-
cal time dominating religious texts and imagery is gradually replaced by
a "'homogeneous, empty time' . . . marked not by prefiguring and ful-
filment, but by temporal coincidence, and measured by clock and
calendar."[53] Anderson contends that the basic structure of both the
novel and the newspaper—involving social actors whose actions unfold
within a geopolitically bounded space at a given time—enables readers to imagine or conjure up the nation as a "solid community moving
steadily down (or up) history" (*Imagined Communities*, 26). Each reader's awareness of the existence of "thousands (or millions) of others"
performing the same ritual of consuming the newspaper at the same
time is also crucial to imagining the nation into existence (35). This
distinctive claim that print capitalism makes homogeneous or renders
equivalent the consumers' experience of time and history (which, in turn,
produces powerful collective sites of identification) has been frequently
adopted by scholars of visual and digital media. For instance, Ella Shohat and Robert Stam argue that in the twentieth century, cinema follows
print capitalism to become the medium catalyzing nationalist identifications. Euro-American narrative cinema's arrangement of events and
actions predominantly in a linear temporal frame, they suggest, serve
as "experiential grids or templates through which history can be written
and national identity figured."[54] Comparably, noting the intensification of temporal coincidence and connectivity in the digital era, other

scholars have drawn on Anderson to think of "imagined virtual communities" as sites of identification that are not always bounded by the nation form.[55]

Albeit offering distinct views of identity, the two approaches outlined above have at least two assumptions in common. Whether identity is viewed as an individual or a collective affair, its mediation is framed primarily as a seamless immersive encounter that easily blurs the boundaries between (the linguistic and/or visual) representations offered by the mass medium and the experiential grid and interpretive horizon of the consumer. The newspaper reader, the television viewer, or the netizen has no experiential difficulty "recognizing" the self as an ostensibly autonomous individual or part of a collective through the representational content offered by the mass medium. That is to say, the emphasis on an equivalence or a perfect correspondence between the consumer and the media commodity in both strands—especially in Anderson's theory of the homogeneity of imagined historical progress—is cognate with the psychoanalytic narrative of neurotic imaginary identification. The consumer's straightforward absorption of and into the media content (and, therefore, other consumers) seems to lead directly to identitarian sentiments of idealized membership, belonging, and inclusion. (Notably, in discussions of algorithmic identity, this relationship between the psychic and the discursive is less important, with the primary emphasis falling on the invisible gathering and interpretation of information.) Concomitantly, there is a tendency to privilege a single dominant mass medium as the principal catalyst for identity. If print, radio, and then cinema have shaped identities in the past, digital media, platforms, and their algorithms have not only altered but also taken over that crucial charge. The digital is now redefining the biotechnological nature of life itself—or so the narrative goes.

In contrast to these tendencies, to examine the mediation of identity as a minoritizing constraint, I develop a third approach drawing on global media and cultural studies broadly construed, one that demonstrates the need to move beyond the narrative of equivalence as well as the privileging of a singular technology or juncture of technological mediation. Here I would argue that Partha Chatterjee's analysis of anticolonial nationalism is an especially germane point of departure. In his study of anticolonialism in nineteenth-century Bengal (India), Chatterjee reminds us that the emergence of Asian and African nationalisms cannot be conflated with Anderson's notion of imagined communities gliding through homogeneous empty time. Developing during and in opposition to colonial rule, Asian and African nationalisms are, in fact, fabricated in a heterogeneous temporality, split between the inescapable political and economic reality that is Western imperialism on the one hand and a reactive valorization of a non-Western or "native" tradition on the other. As Chatterjee writes,

> Anticolonial nationalism creates its own domain of sovereignty within colonial society well before it begins its political battle with the imperial power. It does this by dividing the world of social institutions and practices into two domains—the material and the spiritual. The material is the domain of the "outside," of the economy and of statecraft, of science and technology, a domain where the West had proved its superiority and the East had succumbed. In this domain, then, Western superiority had to be acknowledged and its accomplishments carefully studied and replicated. The spiritual, on the other hand, is an "inner" domain bearing the "essential" marks of cultural identity. The greater one's success in imitating Western skills in the material domain, therefore, the greater the need to preserve the distinct-ness of one's spiritual culture.[56]

Three points are worth emphasizing. First, as a psychic split in the constrained colonized subject, the relationship between the inner and outer domains is not reducible to a public-private divide. As noted below, the cultural consumption and production maintaining the minoritized inner domain take very public forms. Second, the "essential" or "sovereign" nature of the inner domain is a paradoxical product of anticolonialism's opposition to—as well as entanglement in—the outer domain that is the colonial economy. If the inner domain of "essen-tial" Indian culture becomes a site for imagining anticolonial resistance long before organized political protests, this imagination also flourishes because of economic and technological resources made available by industrial capitalism. In other words, as colonial capitalism alters irrevo-cably precolonial economic and social arrangements—thereby undoing, to a certain extent, distinctions between the East and the West—anticolonialism turns to the politically constrained inner domain of culture to insist on that distinction as a reprieve from colonial rule. Third, the splitting of the colonized is heavily gendered. As Chatterjee observes later in his book, the inner domain is also inseparable from anticolonial patriarchy's vision of the "new" Indian woman. In this masculinist anticolonial discourse, the woman is both "modern" and the very embodiment of Indian "tradition" and, therefore, "essentially different from the 'Western' woman" (9).

Attending to anticolonial splitting in this manner allows us to see why print capitalism—as a vital motor of colonial culture—does not directly lead to the fiction of a homogeneous national identity in India. In fact, as Chatterjee further demonstrates, print capitalism plays multiple contradictory roles—furthering the colonial mission as well as the production of a vernacular culture that subsequently nurtures the inner domain of anticolonialism. On the one hand, "modern" Bengali language and culture begin to acquire the status of a commodity only after British traders and missionaries print the first books in that vernacular at the end of the eighteenth century. On the other hand, the same vernacular commodity is refused the status of the colonizer's language and culture as, by the first half of the nineteenth century, English becomes "the language of bureaucracy and emerges as the most powerful vehicle of intellectual influence on a new Bengali elite" (*The Nation and Its Fragments*, 7). Notably, while making governance easier, the imposition of English on the educated elite and middle classes also intensifies the latter's anticolonial desire to accord an equal if not higher value to the marginalized vernacular. This revalorization, as Chatterjee reminds us, is possible because the anticolonial intelligentsia have access to economic and technological capital:

> The crucial moment in the development of the modern Bengali language comes, however, in midcentury, when this bilingual elite makes it a cultural project to provide its mother tongue with the necessary linguistic equipment to enable it to become an adequate language for "modern" culture. An entire institutional network of printing presses, publishing houses, newspapers, magazines, and literary societies is created around this time, *outside* the purview of the state and the European missionaries, through which the new language, modern and standardized, is given shape. (7, emphasis in the original)

Forged through the reappropriation of Eurocolonial resources and know-how, anticolonial identity thus remains fundamentally reliant on commodity capitalism and its idealization of the equivalent or norm—in this case, the "modern" and "standardized" Bengali culture whose parameters are determined by the colonized elite. For Chatterjee, this also means that the mediation of the anticolonial dream of sovereignty is not only masculinist but also distinctly bourgeois, imagined at a remove from the lived realities of the masses constituted by the Indian peasantry (159–60). Anticolonial identity is politically and culturally significant not in spite of but rather because of this imbrication of race, class, and gender.[57]

We can, therefore, sum up Chatterjee's reassessment of the relationship between identity and mediation in the following manner: In contrast to theorizations of asocial individualism or social homogeneity experienced through mass media consumption, Chatterjee draws our attention to capitalism's ability to proliferate through the mediated production of identitarian experiences of difference, alienation, and heterogeneity. He shows us that, as a fiction of homogeneity, anticolonial essentialism originates not through an identification with the calendrical time staged by the print medium but rather through the racialized cultural derogation and differentiation accompanying the economic motives of colonialism. Print capitalism functions as a means of imposing as well as resisting that derogation. Thus, in a larger sense, what Chatterjee uncovers is the role that mediation plays in anticolonialism's extrapolation of identitarian value from difference. What the dominant colonial ideology misrecognizes as "inferior" culture is precisely what vernacular print capitalism seeks to reinvent as its identitarian ideal. As I have argued through my reading of the *Open Casket* protests, this extrapolation continues to be enabled by contemporary neoliberalism.

In this context, it is important to note that while Chatterjee examines the production of anticolonial culture through the conflicting uses of printing technology, language or the printed text is not the only site of psychic and discursive splitting in colonial India. The dialectical relationship between the inner and outer domains also takes shape through prevalent oral and visual forms of communication—from the colonial theater, to the jingle, to images produced by scroll painters in Bengal (*The Nation and Its Fragments*, 122). Scholars of visual culture have examined this point in more detail. For instance, when Shohat and Stam argue that early European cinematic endorsements of colonial exploits mobilize "a rewarding sense of national and imperial belonging" for the European spectator, they are also careful to note that the same films engender "a battle of national imaginaries within the fissured colonial spectator."[58] That is to say, alongside the domain of language and literature, cinematic spectatorship in the colony also becomes a form of consumption accompanied by a simultaneous internalization of and resentment toward racialized difference represented by European media.[59]

What I am emphasizing in Chatterjee's approach, then, is a method of reading identity politics through mediations of difference whose internal contradictions are ultimately regulated by the capitalist mode of production. The simultaneously economic, social, and technological *mediation of identity* is irreducible to the use of particular media. *Identity* not only builds on this approach but also suggests that Fanon's reading of anti-colonialism as a mediated schizophrenic wound anticipates this line of critique from within and across the Martinican and Algerian contexts. Simultaneously, I insist that the diverse manifestations of this wound in our contemporary moment call for an urgent reevaluation of identity as an effect of mediation by both considering and moving beyond the roles played by sociopolitically significant media technologies like language, film, or the digital. The Fanonian analytic is indispensable, since it demonstrates how the capitalist emphasis on value—a principal reason for minoritizing fragmentation—thrives not through a single aesthetic/communicational medium but rather several adjacent media or agents of mediation. It is in this sense that I view identity production to be a historically contingent intermedial process.[60] If chapter 1 examines this intermediality in the anticolonial context, the rest of the book investigates its operations in diasporic and postcolonial settings.

As I have noted, it is a reflexive intermediality of my aesthetic archive that allows me to broaden the scope of analysis and trace parallels between distinct geohistorical spaces. For example, Cha's text *Dictée*—examined in chapter 2—is explicitly intermedial in its form, incorporating not only multiple languages and competing literary modes but also uncaptioned images and theories of spectatorship. Departing from readings of *Dictée* that see its hybridity as the epitome of postidentitarian aesthetics, my analysis focuses on Cha's provocative representation of the adjacent actions of several media forms through which transnational capitalism manages identity production across colonial and postcolonial Korean as well as U.S. diasporic contexts. While chapters 3 and 4 focus on texts that are more easily classifiable as cinematic or visual, what I highlight through them is an implicit but once again historically self-aware aesthetic attention to the intermediations of difference and otherness. Chapter 3, for instance, turns to Djebar's *The Nouba* precisely because of how the film explores femininity as a visually, linguistically, and aurally mediated fragmentation in officially decolonized and "sovereign" Algeria. In chapter 4, I read Dube's short film

Goddess as a dissonant queer text that scrutinizes the splitting of lesbian identity between cinematic technology and class hierarchies in postcolonial India. In this way, throughout the book, I demonstrate the need to examine identity production not through singular technologies of mediation but through the fundamentally intermedial, aesthetic, and sensorial operations of capitalism.

This intermediality of capitalism, however, needs further elaboration, especially since I understand mediation to be a process that makes use of but also exceeds specific media technologies.[61] Without dismissing medium specificity, *Identity* consistently brings into play the Marxist view of mediation, which draws on the more general sense of the word as an intercession between contending entities. As Mitchell and Hansen point out, Karl Marx and Friedrich Engels undertake a radical rethinking of the Hegelian idealist approach to mediation. In the work of G. W. F. Hegel, mediation is an operation that enables the "sublation" or the suspension of the antagonism between the thesis and the antithesis constitutive of dialectical thinking. Mediation establishes the primacy of the Hegelian mind or "spirit" in that it allows "Absolute Knowledge to emerge triumphant as the culminating product both of philosophical logic and world history."[62] Marx and Engels, in contrast, shift the emphasis away from the operations of the idealized spirit and toward historical events and movement that shape human consciousness. As Mitchell and Hansen note, "Mediation designates the primary form of relation and reconciliation between contradictory forces in a society, between the material domain and culture, base and superstructure" (introduction, xx). That is, from the Marxist point of view—whose influence on Chatterjee's theory of anticolonialism will be discernible to the reader—examining mediation becomes necessary to gauge the nature and degree of agency that social actors have in a capitalist society.

Furthermore, dialectical materialism does not simply celebrate individual or collective agency, being keenly aware that what is striking about capitalism—and what makes capitalism so resilient—is its ability to mediate conflicting social actions and struggles to its advantage. Drawing on Hegel and Marx, Richard Gunn compellingly argues that when capitalism intervenes between two or more antagonistic entities, it also creates a new relation between them, a peculiar tense proximity that also defines the entities, bestowing on them attributes or characteristics that did not exist prior to the act of intervention. For Gunn, capitalist mediation leads to "an internal relation [that] is constitutive of the terms which it relates. . . . The mediation is *the mode of existence*

of the related term(s). This can also be expressed . . . by saying that
in such cases the mediation is the *form* or *appearance* of the term(s)
which it internally relates."[63] This vital relationship that dictates the
terms' appearance is particularly relevant to the colonial context. For
we can say that when capitalism mediates the antagonistic relationship between the colonizer and colonized, it also plays a crucial role in
determining how the very concepts of "colonizer" and "colonized" are
discursively and experientially understood in the colony and the metropole. In fact, this is an instance in which the two entities appear "as the
mode of existence of one another" (Gunn, "Marxism and Mediation,"
58) in a manner not entirely dissimilar from the Hegelian master-slave
dialectic. Capitalism mediates itself so that the colonizer and the colonized (mis)recognize and constitute each other at the same time. It
follows, then, that by controlling the appearance of the opposed parties
in terms of their mutual antagonism, capitalism protects its own interests, most directly by "incorporating, as its own mediations, that which
is or was non-capitalist" (61). This dynamism of capitalist valorization—
which proceeds through mediation as an open-ended struggle, conflict,
and identitarian resistance—is once again epitomized by the colonial
scene. As I have noted above, capitalism in colonial India does not simply
contribute to the antagonism between the aggressor and the aggrieved;
it also furnishes the major technologies for anticolonial agency and
resistance.[64]

    If dialectical materialism helps us understand how identitarian frag-
mentation proceeds through economic and cultural mediations that
involve but are not defined by mass media technologies, it also compels
us to broaden our notion of what counts as a medium or a mediating
agent. For even as vernacular print capitalism flourishes in colonial
Bengal "outside" the purview of the British government (see above)
and directly reflects the agency of the colonized, it is possible to argue
that the colonial capitalist state nevertheless continues to function as
a crucial mediating agent. Together with—or with help from—print
capitalism, it is more fundamentally the colonial state apparatus as an
institution that solidifies the entirely new hierarchical relation between
the British subject and the "native" Indian and, therefore, the ensuing anticolonial splitting. It is also the imperial state that institutes the
language policies and censorship laws that, in turn, lead to the anticolonial self-assertion through vernacular capitalism. Thus, from a
dialectical materialist standpoint, capitalism uses the colonial state
as a "medium" that then deploys colonial media—language- as well as

image-based technologies—as a kind of "prosthesis," an administrative tool. Arguably, as the apparatus mediating anticolonial identity, the
colonial state is itself not reducible to that prosthesis.[65]

Identity, therefore, uses the term "mediation" not only to refer to
mass media (such as literature, photography, radio, or cinema) and their
medium-specific properties but also in this second extratechnological
sense that dwells on the marginalizing effects of institutions as apparatuses of misinterpellation—such as the French colonial state producing
the "inassimilable" Arab subject in Algeria or British colonial law
labeling gender-nonconforming subjects in India as "criminal" and
"sexually deviant." Arguably, it is also my archive that drives my extratechnological approach to mediation. For instance, I demonstrate that,
as mediating "technologies," the colonial and the neocolonial states feature prominently in Fanon's and Djebar's representations (in chapters 1
and 3, respectively) of racial and gendered minoritization. I propose
that Cha's *Dictée* (in chapter 2) takes us, as it were, to the "heart" of
the mattering of identity politics. Its aesthetics focalizes the mediating
function of the commodity fetishism underpinning the very concept
of the modern military state, thereby offering a critical glimpse of the
internal relation that capitalism forges between liberal democratic "inclusion" and postcolonial ethnonationalism. Finally, through the Indian film
festival and visual media cultures discussed in chapter 4, I draw attention to the transnational corporation and, more broadly, the neoliberal
regime of labor as powerful mediating agents of queer (in)visibility in the
postcolony.

My interest in linking identity with labor—both material and
immaterial—throughout the book also necessitates a theoretical attention to the laboring *body*. Given my reading of identity as a splitting of a
corporeal ego, I would like to conclude this section by briefly noting how
the book attends to mediation as a process whose identitarian effects
are felt by and in the body. After all, it is the psyche *of* a body that feels
minoritized, constrained, and resistive relative to other surrounding bodies. As noted above, several scholars have argued that the boundaries
between our bodies and the media/information/data we consume and
generate—regardless of our social locations—are increasingly becoming irrelevant for corporate giants. Troubling this "posthumanist" focus
on the disembodying effects of technology, N. Katherine Hayles proposes a distinction between the normative and discursive construct
called the "body" and the nondiscursive, localized, improvisational, and
lived corporeal practices that she calls "embodiment." Hayles writes,

"Fissuring along lines of class, gender, race, and privilege, embodied practices create heterogeneous spaces even when the discursive formations describing those practices seem uniformly dispersed throughout the society."[66] While the body might easily disappear into technology, embodiment cannot, "for it is tied to the circumstances of the occasion and the person. . . . Along with these particularities come concomitant strategies for resistances and subversions, excesses and deviations" (*How We Became Posthuman*, 197–98). Thus, for Hayles, embodiment is the means by which the socially situated subject defies the normative body and its technocapitalist simulations.

While appreciative of Hayles's attention to the gap between established norms and lived experience, I argue for the need to see identity politics—the "fissuring" along capitalist categories of difference—as *embodiment* that is also mediated by capitalism. That is, as an embodied awareness or assertion of one's minoritized status, identity remains antagonistically bound to the normative body/bodies touted by capitalism. Part of what I attend to in the subsequent chapters—and discuss at some length in chapter 1—is how the psychocorporeal production of identity remains inseparable from the capitalist mediations of value. Spivak alerts us to the materiality of this discursive classification of the lived body when she notes that "as a text, the inside of the body (imbricated with the outside) is mysterious and unreadable except by way of thinking of the systematicity of the body, value coding of the body. It is through the *significance* of my body and others' bodies that cultures become gendered, economicopolitic, selved, substantive."[67] We can, therefore, say that the "significance" of identity is *embodied* in that identity is a testament to the socially produced hierarchical distinctions between bodies. Embodiment, in this instance, is the effect as well as the bodily medium of value production.

Moreover, if the origins of identity are discursive and its experience as a constraint often accompanied by technological and aesthetic mediation, it follows that the embodiment of identity both involves and exceeds the singular lived body. In other words, embodiment itself gets pluralized and caught up in identity's schizophrenic intermediality. To return one more time to the example that opened this introduction, the embodied production of black identity proceeds not just through the mere presence of the protestors' individual bodies at the Whitney Museum but also through their ambivalent "incorporation" of Schutz's painting, the performative video through which Bright acquires circulation value, and perhaps even the videos of antiblack violence of which Autry is reminded as a spectator of *Open Casket* (Autry, "Another Look"). Indeed, the embodied production of blackness can be seen as a variation on what Bishnupriya Ghosh calls "fractal personhood" in the second epigraph to this introduction.[68] The protestors' embodied identitarianism is neither fully subsumed by nor free of the painting and Bright's video as media commodities. Rather, it is dispersed among these commodities external to the individual body. Notably, this dispersal of identitarian embodiment through a "networked materiality" does not make the body disappear. Instead, the dispersion and fragmentation become the grounds for an embodied collectivization, the formation of a black "us" differentiated from a white/nonblack "them."[69] In other words, it is, in part, through identity politics that capitalism controls embodiment as potentiality.

The Aesthetic Cunning of Capital

I began this introduction by noting how both the protestors of *Open Casket* and their critics have turned to the domain of art and culture— commonly associated with the domain of the "aesthetic"—to articulate opposing stances of resistance. For Bright and his followers, reclaiming identity through art (and performative protest as art) is the necessary defense against capitalist exploitation. For antiessentialists like Fusco, the power of the aesthetic lies in its ability to unite us across our identitarian differences. As outlined above, the following chapters interrogate both these positions by examining how capitalism produces identity through aesthetic means that enmesh mass media, culture, economy, politics, and the body. Effectively, what *Identity* calls out is capitalism's cunning ability to promote the aesthetic *as both identitarian and non-identitarian "solutions"* to its own oppressive effects. In other words, the book contends that, to resist the pernicious effects of capitalism, it is crucial to attend to these aesthetic maneuvers. Neoliberalism's intermedial schemes hide in plain sight as we seek identitarian and non-identitarian redress in the aesthetic.

To begin to unravel and disassemble that camouflage, each chapter of the book performs a double movement, scrutinizing the capitalist origins of aesthetic identitarianism on the one hand, and interrogating the fetishism of a corresponding aesthetic antiessentialism on the other. For instance, in chapter 1, while examining the negritude movement's entanglement with the colonial racialization of the French language, I critique a strand of psychoanalytic literary scholarship that reifies the "Otherness" of language as a convenient aesthetic escape from the trap of imaginary identity. Specifically, chapter 1 reads Fanon against Tracy McNulty's argument that we need to move past identity politics through the instability of language as a signifying medium.[70] In chapter 2, I demonstrate that the avant-gardism of Cha's *Dictée* helps us uncover both an antagonism and an interdependence between language-bound identitarianism and nonidentitarianism. In fact, I suggest that Cha's textualization of this literary antagonistic intimacy can be read as an astute mirroring of the workings of neoliberal capital, which maintains its "Möbius" topology by mediating between seemingly opposed "anticapitalist" politics of subversion.

In the last two chapters of the book, this double movement within the argument is concerned with cinema-bound assertions of identity and its nonidentitarian alternatives. Djebar's *The Nouba*, I demonstrate in chapter 3, not only departs from the androcentrism of Algerian nationalist cinema but also enables an urgent rethinking of the antiessentialist claims of experimental film theory. I suggest that the film's intermediality—especially its politics of orality—problematizes Laura U. Marks's claim that avant-garde cinematic aesthetics can "touch" and move spectators beyond their identitarian commitments.[71] Similarly, the KASHISH festival and films discussed in chapter 4 allow me to examine critically the assumptions shaping both queer neoliberalism and cinephilic queer antiessentialism. In particular, this chapter is in dialogue with Karl Schoonover and Rosalind Galt's call for an antineoliberal queer "worlding" and their argument that such a worlding can be derived from cinema's medium-specific capacity to destabilize meaning and identity.[72]

In this way, *Identity, Mediation, and the Cunning of Capital* examines and counters a pattern of disciplinary formalism across the humanities. Both identitarian and nonidentitarian cultural critique—through the affordances of institutionalization and the symbolic capital that comes with it—frequently idealize the "liberatory" potential of a privileged medium of aesthetic expression. Whether drawn to literary, cinematic, or digital mediation as the basis of radical politics, these medium-bound alternatives to the injustices of misrecognition and maldistribution have, as their condition of possibility, the disavowal of the intermediality of the identitarian fragment. Therefore, in the pages that follow, the challenge is to resist the cunning of capital by attending to these deep fissures within the political economy of the aesthetic as well as the aesthetics of political economy.

The Aesthetic Wounds of Identity, or What Frantz Fanon Can Tell Us about Its Mediation

I begin this discussion of identification with two claims: first, that identification has a history—a colonial history; and second, that this colonial history poses serious challenges for contemporary recuperations of a politics of identification.
  —Diana Fuss, "Interior Colonies"

Inasmuch as anyone would be "for" the symbolic and "against" the imaginary, he would be operating in the imaginary. Ironically, the ethical imperative to accede to the symbolic and vigilantly to resist the imaginary is itself mired in the imaginary.
  —Jane Gallop, *Reading Lacan*

The entrance of art into the aesthetic dimension . . . is not as innocent and natural a phenomenon as we commonly think.
  —Giorgio Agamben, *The Man without Content*

Frantz Fanon's *Black Skin, White Masks* contains a memorable passage in which he describes his experience of going to the movie theater as a colonial black subject in metropolitan France. In the same passage, Fanon notes his response to *Home of the Brave*, a 1949 Hollywood film directed by Mark Robson and released in France with the title *Je suis un nègre* (*I Am a Negro*).[1] The plot revolves around the trauma of Private Peter Moss, scarred by World War II and his experiences of being African American among his white compatriots. The film opens with the

39

army doctor trying to cure Moss of his psychosomatic paralysis, the exact cause of which is unknown. It appears to be a combination of racism from Moss's peers, including his white best friend, Finch; the death of Finch in the war; and the protagonist's overall guilt and trauma as a survivor. Moss is cured by the end of the film, but only after the doctor yells a racial slur at him. Fanon's agitated response to the film in *Black Skin* focuses specifically on the final moment of reconciliation. In this scene, Moss and his white compatriot and fellow soldier Mingo (who has lost an arm in a special mission) find points of commonality in postwar America as a black man and a disabled veteran. Fanon writes:

> I can't go to the movies without encountering myself. I wait for myself. Just before the film starts, I wait for myself. Those in front of me look at me, spy on me, wait for me. A black bellhop is going to appear. My aching heart makes my head spin.
>
> The crippled soldier from the Pacific war tells my brother: "Get used to your color the way I got used to my stump. We are both casualties."
>
> Yet, with all my being, I refuse to accept this amputation.[2]

In this oft-cited scene of reading and being read through the sensory cinematic image, critics usually focus on the traumatic effect of the image on Fanon, or on cinema's ability to evoke resistant readings that exceed the ideological limits of a fictional narrative.[3] What has not been commented on is the fact that the nature of this aesthetic encounter, as Fanon describes it, is not determined by the sensory effects of a *single* medium or agent of mediation. Indeed, Fanon describes his experience of blackness in terms of interrelated frictional encounters involving *multiple* media and bodies: between the cinematic medium and Fanon's physiological and socially constructed body ("I can't go to the movies without encountering myself. I wait for myself"); between Fanon's body and the bodies of the other spectators ("Those in front of me look at me, spy on me, wait for me"); and last but not least, between the materiality or "body" of the racially objectifying medium of language ("a black bellhop," or *un nègre-groom* in the French original) and the screen image that Fanon reads through that linguistic objectification even as he refuses to be reduced to it. Simply put, for Fanon, the experience of blackness as a minoritized identity is informed by and split between several representational media in colonial France—in this case between language, image, and the body. And colonial capitalist race relations intervene in the affectively charged semiotic processes involving all three instances of mediation.

This scene of reception from *Black Skin* offers a striking illustration of my argument in this chapter—that the production and experience of anticolonial identity needs to be seen as a multiply mediated psychic splitting. I delineate this intermedial aspect of identity formation through Fanon's anticolonial responses to several mass media—such as film, literature, advertising, and the radio. At the same time, I argue that such scenes of mass-mediated identity production need to be viewed through a more systemic intermedial psychic fragmentation under colonial capitalism. That is to say, the materiality of anticolonial identity—mass-mediated as it may be—at once includes and far exceeds the specificities of particular media technologies. Identity begins to matter, more vitally, because colonial capitalism mediates the unequal relationship between the colonizer and the colonized simultaneously by linguistic, visual, corporeal, and technological means. In particular, while examining this context-specific intermediality, I pay close attention to Fanon's assessment of the French language as a racialized commodity and a colonial instrument of minoritization. *Black Skin* allows me to interrogate the disciplinary limits of literary anti-identitarianism premised on the "absolute" alterity of language. Finally, I suggest that colonial mediation sustains the wound of identity not only by denigrating the colonized but also by thoroughly enmeshing the latter's quest for freedom within a fundamentally oppressive capitalist logic of value production.

Here is a road map to help the reader navigate the major turns in my argument. I devote roughly the first half of the chapter to examine how *Black Skin* represents the formation of racial identity as a psychic splitting orchestrated by French colonialism. Departing from the common tendency in film and media studies to examine racialization in terms of visuality, I first turn to Fanon's text to uncover an "image-like" or imaginary quality that the French language acquires as a prosthesis for the imperialist state. I examine how language operates in tandem with the hierarchization of physiognomic difference, simultaneously constituting and fragmenting black identity in colonial France. Bringing Fanon into dialogue with psychoanalytic theory in these sections accomplishes two things: I show that Fanon's approach to blackness serves as an indispensable critique of the language-bound Lacanian antiessentialism that dismisses identity as a specular fiction, and I simultaneously argue for the need to see identity not through the ahistorical *neurotic* narrative of visual plenitude but rather as a *schizophrenic* and intermedial fragmentation instituted by the very logic of equivalence structuring colonial capitalist exchange. My reading of colonial schizophrenia serves as a guiding framework for the second half of the chapter. Here I return to analyze Fanon's anticolonial (dis)identifications with and reflections on colonial mass media in *Black Skin* and *A Dying Colonialism*. These scenes of schizophrenic dissonance and fragmentation serve as a broader critique of medium-bound aesthetic antiessentialism. I demonstrate how the properties of several aesthetic media—specifically literary form, cinematic indexicality, and radiophonic noise—are inescapably remediated by anticolonial introjections of the fetish of the commodity.

Identity as a Splitting under Colonial Capital

While antiessentialist critics often turn to radical French philosophy from the 1970s to scrutinize identity as a discursive construction—such as Michel Foucault's analysis of the invention of the homosexual as a "species" in nineteenth-century Europe,[4] and Louis Althusser's account of ideology as institutionalized misrecognition[5]—the contributions of thinkers like W. E. B. Du Bois and Fanon simultaneously preceding and revitalizing poststructuralist debates on the topic are less frequently recognized. Fanon captures the reality and the violence of identity politics with remarkable pithiness in the introduction to *Black Skin*: "We are aiming at nothing less than to liberate the black man from himself" (xii). Fanon's desire to be liberated from black identity, as the rest of his text demonstrates, is inseparable from *the manner in which* blackness comes to be constituted under the "civilizing mission" of French colonialism.

    Written while Fanon was training to be a psychiatrist in Lyon, *Black Skin* investigates how racial hierarchies in colonial France determine the development of an aberrant black identity among the colonized. Through a discomfiting analysis of race relations in the French Antilles, his native island of Martinique, and in metropolitan France, Fanon argues that black identity develops as a traumatizing racialized self-awareness as soon as the colonized Antillean subject comes in close proximity to the colonizer: "A normal black child, having grown up with a normal family, will become abnormal at the slightest contact with the white world" (122). As Fanon clarifies a few pages later, the "norm" in French overseas departments like Martinique (whose inhabitants enjoy a special political status as French citizens) is to encourage identification with a hegemonic French whiteness, to the extent that the black Martinican schoolboy might make the mistake of seeing himself as the colonizer and come to believe that the "Negro lives in Africa" (126). It is in this sense that identification, as Diana Fuss notes in the first epigraph to this chapter, is a fundamentally colonial process.[6] Yet the black schoolboy realizes the limits of this identification, as soon as he—much like Fanon himself—arrives at the metropole as a young man. His citizenship ceases to be a political privilege and his identity unfolds as another aberrant (but normalized) form of self-alienation: "Once he gets to Europe, and when he hears Europeans mention 'Negroes' he'll know they're talking about him as well as the Senegalese" (126–27). Here we have the beginnings of a theory of the split, *linguistically named*, and *identified* subject that, as we shall see, is quite distinct from the split "subject of language" frequently invoked in radical psychoanalytic rejections of identity politics.

Arguably, an earlier account of identity formation as a minoritizing fragmentation of one's consciousness is to be found in Du Bois's 1903 *The Souls of Black Folk*. For Du Bois, the legacy of slavery ensures that the African American "double consciousness" is a split entity, "looking at one's self through the eyes of [white] others, of measuring one's soul by the tape of a [white] world that looks on in amused contempt and pity."[7] The colonial splitting that Fanon observes is, therefore, a special case of Du Bois's double consciousness, one where the Antillean subject is encouraged to be alienated from his own blackness through a precarious political capital, and only until he sees himself as an object of the contempt of the racializing gaze.

Yet if Du Bois sees a "dogged strength" in the African American body that "keeps it from being torn asunder" (3), Fanon emphasizes the psychic as well as somatic fragmentation that everyday racialized interpellations produce in the French metropole:

> "Look! A Negro!" It was a passing sting. I attempted a smile.
>
> "Look! A Negro!" Absolutely. I was beginning to enjoy myself.
>
> "Look! A Negro!" The circle was gradually getting smaller. I was really enjoying myself. "*Maman*, look, a Negro; I'm scared!" Scared! Scared! Now they were beginning to be scared of me. I wanted to kill myself laughing, but laughter had

become out of the question. . . . The body schema, attacked
in several places, collapsed, giving way to an epidermal racial
schema. In the train, it was a question of being aware of my
body, no longer in the third person but in triple. . . . Instead of
one seat, they left me two or three. (*Black Skin*, 91–92)

In this well-known passage, the experience of being named, identified,
or hailed exposes what Fanon calls the "epidermal racial schema" of his
own body. This schema may be thought of as an "image" that the subject has of itself, on the fringes of conscious experience. Fanon makes an
important distinction between the epidermal schema and the more common biological notion of the "body schema" that the French neurologist
Jean Lhermitte developed in the 1930s. The body schema, according to
Lhermitte, denotes the nonconscious anatomical body image produced
by perceptive elements like vision and the vestibular sense.[8] In contrast,
Fanon insists on viewing the epidermal racial schema *sociogenically*,
through the coconstitution of biological and social experiences. Unlike
the body schema, the epidermal racial schema is a "historical-racial
schema" that is at once physiological and discursive. It is derived from the
body's experiences but also produced by "the white man, who had woven
me out of a thousand details, anecdotes, and stories" (*Black Skin*, 91).
In other words, for Fanon, the linguistic and discursive mediation of a
double consciousness accompanies a palpably physical experience of the
epidermal schema.

If being called "a Negro" at first seems innocuous—and, initially, even
amusing—to Fanon, the repetition of these calls soon becomes intolerable,
with their phobic import brazenly baring the antiblackness subtending
the colonial imaginary. The normalized linguistic act of naming also
functions as a perverse abstraction and anonymization that enables "the
Negro," the black, to stand in for *all* blacks. As Lewis R. Gordon notes
in his reading of Fanon, "Each black is, thus, ironically nameless by
virtue of being *named* 'black.'"[9] For Fanon, the "live" violence of this
linguistic abstraction has a rupturing effect on the ego, exposing the
historical-racial schema that is itself a product of anonymizing stereo-
types. Fanon's fragmented identity is thus triply split between his body
schema, the epidermal image, and a cognitive self that refuses but cannot prevent the "affective tetanization" produced by the naming (*Black
Skin*, 92).

In his essay "Figures of Interpellation," Pierre Macherey makes
a useful distinction between Althusser's and Fanon's accounts of

subjectivation.[10] Macherey argues that in Althusser's scene of inter-pellation, the call of ideology represented by the linguistic utterance "Hey you!" is ultimately not fully responsible for creating the subjects responding to the call, insofar as "[quoting Althusser] 'in every case, they are already subjects'" (13). In contrast, in Fanon's description, the simultaneously quotidian and exceptional hailing of the black sub-ject "underscores the cumulative nature of the process by which is installed—in the mind of someone, who, here says 'I'—the feeling of not being a subject like the others" (14). For Macherey, the Fanonian scene of interpellation is instructive because it shows how identity is installed through a relational encounter specific to colonialism, as "a sub-jective experience in the strongest sense of the term—that a man of colour may come to have of his 'being black' (or 'yellow,' or 'red,' it matters little, except for the fact that he is not 'white,' which, for its part, is supposed not to be a colour, and, therefore, to be the mark of colourlessness)" (16). In other words, the hailing produces identity as visual and physiognomic difference that matters to colonial racism insofar as that difference is created to be distinguished from whiteness. This demarcation of non-whiteness as difference simultaneously allows for its subordination to the "colorless" norm of whiteness—the invisible colonial commodity par excellence. As part of a broader and ongoing system of differen-tiation, then, the black epidermal image is beneficial to the French colonial enterprise. As long as the image persists as difference that does not dismantle the system that creates it, colonialism perseveres, turning colonies into a marketplace of difference for French metropolitan con-sumption while preserving whiteness (and "Frenchness") as the supreme commodity forever beyond the reach of the colonized.

Macherey also emphasizes the subjective fragmentation that is con-stitutive of identity in Fanon, where the subject is "divided between the necessity of saying yes ('it was true') and the desire to say no ('that had become impossible'), a sort of *double bind* that should be made the object of a specific analysis, as a potential bearer of pathological effects" (14, emphasis in the original). Even as he notes the linguistic man-ifestations of racial difference in the French colony, Macherey sees the Fanonian split subject to be primarily a product of *visual media-tion*, "constituted as such in the order of the visible" (15). This visually mediated subject, in his view, should be distinguished from the Althus-serian psychoanalytic subject "defined by the place that it occupies in the space of language" (15). Macherey is specifically referring to Althuss-er's Marxist use of Jacques Lacan's theory of the subject constituted by "the symbolic order." In prevalent accounts of this theory, language—as opposed to visuality—is the primary medium of subjectivation.

I would argue that the established opposition between the Lacanian subject of linguistic mediation (or the symbolic) and the Fanonian subject of visual mediation (bound to the image or the imaginary) fails to register a far more complex and intermedial account of identity politics that emerges in Fanon's analysis of colonial capitalism. This intermedial approach, in my reading, is also quite consistent with oft-ignored strands of psychoanalytic thinking. I have already started to indicate how, for Fanon, the production of blackness is not merely a visual matter. The French language plays a major role here as well. But before going further into Fanon's analysis of this language-image nexus, it will be useful to briefly review the dominant Lacanian account of the subject of language. In the following section (and again in chapter 2), I show how this canonical theoretical orientation continues to wield a certain disciplinary influence in the U.S. humanities, promoting "language" and/or "the literary" as the quintessential medium of non-identitarian politics. I invite the reader to be patient while reading the following section, since a discussion of the legacy of Lacan's theory of the subject of language and the imaginary ego might appear to be tangential to Fanon's concerns about colonial racism and oppression. It will become clearer in subsequent sections that Fanon's critical deployment of these psychoanalytic concepts are crucial to his understanding of identity as a multiply mediated wound inflicted by racialized capitalism.

The Identitarian Ego and the Nonidentitarian Subject of Language

Since the late 1970s, Lacanian scholars have routinely prescribed the radical alterity of the subject of language, "the unconscious," and unconscious "desire" as necessary alternatives to normative cultural politics predicated on notions of identity, meaning, and ideology. The binary opposition maintained here is between the symbolic alterity of language and the imaginary alterity of the ego.

Let me make this opposition clearer. In his 1949 essay on "the mirror stage," Lacan argues that somewhere between six and eighteen months after its birth, the human child projectively identifies with a specular image that resembles its human form. For Lacan, this primary narcissism constituting the imaginary ego is a moment of profound *misrecognition*, since the child represses the difference between its body fragmented by the drives and the idealized image that it is yet to become. This fictive ego, established through a "jubilant assumption" of the "ideal-I," cannot fully quell the subject's unconscious.[11] As the obverse of the ideal image, the fragmented body returns in dreams when clinical analysis "reaches a certain level of aggressive disintegration of the individual" (78). In spite of its illusory quality, however, the intrapsychic alienation in the mirror stage is highly significant because it produces "the finally donned armor of an alienating identity that will mark his [the child's] entire mental development with its rigid structure" (78), thereby becoming the basis of subsequent social identifications. The mirror stage is, therefore, not just a single event but a psychic "structure" that we repeatedly relive as social subjects.

In his lectures from the early 1950s, Lacan describes the clinical analysis of the typically neurotic analysand as a move beyond the imaginary and identitarian defenses of the ego and as an encounter with the nonnegotiable Otherness of language in the symbolic order. Notably, the symbolic is a structure of signifiers that "speaks" the subject but also resists particular signifieds and the fixity of meaning. In *Seminar I*, Lacan notes that the analyst's task is to create the conditions to dismantle the imaginary so that the neurotic analysand repressing his unconscious can move from imaginary "empty speech" to symbolic "full speech." If the neurotic ego of empty speech "loses himself . . . in the labyrinth of referential systems made available to him by the state of cultural affairs," it is full speech that "realises the truth of the subject" and constructs his unconscious desire.[12] Imaginary empty speech is concerned with identity, empirical realities, and sociocultural efforts to produce meaning. In contrast, language in the form of symbolic full speech—as the goal of analysis and the site of self-discovery in the unconscious and the locus of the Other—cannot be found in social and cultural experiences of meaning. In this version of the Lacanian clinic, analysis proceeds from imaginary otherness (with a small "o") to the symbolic or "big" Other that is language.

Arguably, neither the 1949 essay on the mirror stage nor *Seminar I* can be taken to be Lacan's final views on imaginary narcissism and the goals of analysis. And yet, this notion of the disintegration of the specular and neurotic ego—the movement from the identitarian imaginary to the anti-identitarian symbolic—has been adopted routinely by several deconstructionist-psychoanalytic critics ever since Lacanian thinking arrived in the United States in the 1960s.[13] In this strand of critique, imaginary meaning and identity can be transcended by turning to language, or the linguistic unconscious, as the primary medium of subjectivation. The mediation of the subject, here, is synonymous with the recursiveness of the sliding signifier and semiotic slippage.

A number of renowned literary scholars—from Shoshana Felman, to Christopher Lane, to Tracy McNulty—have pitted the egocentric subject of identity against the subject of psychoanalysis.[14] For the purposes of this chapter, I will discuss its iteration in McNulty's book *Wrestling with the Angel*. Arguing against readings of Lacan that reduce the symbolic to normative laws and regulations, McNulty proposes that we see the medium of language as a productive constraint—or an enabling impediment—to which the subject is invited to submit in psychoanalysis in order "to declare its freedom from the norms and ideals that prop up the ego, and to assume responsibility for its unconscious desire."[15] Locating analogies with the analytic experience of the symbolic in a variety of social and aesthetic spheres—such as the life of a sixteenth-century nun, philosopher Jacques Rancière's politics of dissensus, the art of Sophie Calle, experimental poetics of the Oulipo collective, and the Mosaic religion—McNulty invites us to think beyond the "predicate-driven understanding of the subject (*in terms of gender, class, or ethnicity, for example*) that forecloses any real understanding of *the [split] subject (of language, of the unconscious, of desire)* as distinct from the ego or social actor" (8, emphasis added).

McNulty's formalist position—which equates the "innate" properties of a privileged medium with the mediation of subjectivity—becomes clear in her view of the relationship between language and sociality. The "minimal social link," in her reading of Lacan, is not between people, or between one consciousness and another. Instead, it is an "intersubjective relation between the [unconscious] subject and the [symbolic] Other, or the locus of speech as such" (54). The Other, she argues, must be conceived of in metaphysical and nonhistorical terms, as an "empty locus supposed by every act of speech," and therefore "cannot be located in an environment" (68). Echoing the dominant Lacanian view, McNulty defines language as an "incomplete" or "lacking" signifying structure (of signifiers without signifieds) that is behind every (always already failed) human effort to communicate through language. To surrender to the enabling constraints of the medium of language, then, is to forget the specular ego and identity, to encounter

the unrepresentable dimension of "the real" or *jouissance* that the signifier cannot inscribe (61).

Notably, for McNulty, upholding the symbolic is not just an academic
enterprise; it is a concrete way to act to effect social change by moving beyond identity politics. As she points out, one of her major goals
is to examine "the relationship between desire and social change" (87).
Instead of confining herself to "the imaginary character of most social
and political projects," she wishes to "consider the social and political
spheres as sites where the [unconscious] subject (and not merely the
ego) intervenes, sites that may be transformed by subjective desire"
(86). She wants to foreground "the experience of the [individual] willing subject, rather than broad social and historical dynamics" (87).
Concrete social change is inconceivable as long as the subject of language and desire is trapped in the imaginary.

Perhaps unsurprisingly, to define the imaginary—the register that
must be dismantled to realize the promise of the symbolic—McNulty
cites and briefly summarizes Lacan's 1949 account of the mirror
stage:

> His analysis implies that such a mechanism [of identification
> with an ideal image] potentially subtends every interpersonal
> relationship, from the familial to the social to the religious or
> political. If the function of the interpersonal relation or group
> psychology is to support the ego by sustaining the strategies
> of seduction, psychoanalysis takes aim at seduction and the ego
> it sustains in order to gain access to the subject of the uncon-
> scious, the subject of desire. (94)

Earlier in the book, she notes, "What Lacan calls the imaginary is really
the response of the subject to this hole [the lack in the Other] in the perceived environment, which compels him to hear or to see something
in the place of this absence" (69). In both these definitions, imaginary identities appear to be the (neurotic) subject's cover-up for the
lack in language that, ultimately, must be exposed through political and
aesthetic immersions in the medium. Relatedly, in this view of symbolic mediation, identity politics is associated primarily with a pernicious
form of visuality, since the imaginary is grounded in an illusory image.[16]
This association becomes clear when McNulty refers to the imaginary
as "subjugating forms of representation that limit reason . . . to the

ontotheology of the image" (6). The radical Lacanian subject, then, is the subject who resists the image by discovering its subjectivity in and through the nonrepresentational potential of language and desire.

As tantalizing as the rewards might be for forgetting the bête noire of the identitarian ego and choosing the split subject of the symbolic instead, what remains unclear in this critically influential language-bound program is how and with what socioeconomic resources and motivations ethnicized, gendered, and/or classed subjects would ignore their imaginary egos—or overcome the daily interpellative processes of being identified and collectivized—outside the Lacanian clinic. McNulty's theory of symbolic mediation is neither able to explain the persistence of identity politics on a global scale nor account for its minoritizing aspects through the censure of specular plenitude. Furthermore, while this theory frequently associates visuality with limiting identitarian representations of race, class, and gender, it appears to be oblivious to the role that language—in spite of its nonidentitarian potential—plays in the representation and proliferation of these imbricated categories of difference under unequal globalization. Thus, its subversive intentions notwithstanding, McNulty's antiessentialism risks becoming what Rosemary Hennessy has called "class knowledge"[17]—a form of knowledge that seems to have nothing to do with classed or other forms of social oppression but indirectly serves the interests of late capital through its emphasis on "individual" freedom and acts of "transgression" complicit with neoliberal mandates of self-emancipation and self-care.

Indeed, this epistemic reification of language as *the* aesthetic medium that will solve the problem of identity politics is part of what the present volume is calling out as the cunning of capital. Even as global capitalism directly employs language to produce and sustain racial difference, radical scholarship in the North American humanities promotes an "unmediated" aesthetic immersion in the same medium as a political alternative to that difference. And this alternative thrives as an unfulfilled promised only by virtue of its status as "symbolic capital," tied to the privileged medium and the beneficiaries of that capital that include a rather select network of scholars, artists, departments, programs, universities, and publishers located primarily in the Global North.[18] In other words, it is through an elite disciplinary isolation and theoretical commodification of its singular properties (and the author-functions of proper names like Lacan certainly play a role here) that language can be "sold" as a nonidentitarian medium, ostensibly outside the system of value production. I should make clear that I see McNulty's

antiessentialism as being merely symptomatic of a much larger institutionalized trend of (often medium-bound) aesthetic politics.[19] I will
turn to several other manifestations of this trend in literary and moving
image studies in the later chapters of the book. While I will scrutinize
the work of individual scholars representing disciplinary and interdisciplinary trends, my larger goal will be to think with and against the
North American humanities as a neoliberal formation within which my
own scholarship remains implicated.

We now have at our disposal the critical framework necessary to examine how Fanon's anticolonial account of blackness destabilizes precisely
the hierarchy between language and image underpinning the psychoanalytic dismissal of identity. My argument, however, is not directed
against Lacan or even psychoanalysis. To the contrary, I show how differential clinical theory and Fanon's anticolonial polemics—when read
together but as cultural diagnostics that remain irreducible to each
other—allow us to grasp identity's unrepresentable "realness." Identity,
I argue, becomes real when the minoritized subject of colonial capitalism remains trapped within the symbolic-as-the-imaginary, with no easy
recourse to "nonhistorical" semiotic slippage as an exit strategy.

Black Identity in the Mirror Stage

Fanon's fraught relationship with psychoanalytic theory has received
substantial scholarly attention. We know that Fanon trained as a psychiatrist and not as a psychoanalyst. As is evident in the several passing
references he makes to the work of Anna Freud, Sigmund Freud, and
Jacques Lacan (*Black Skin*, 33, 41, 43, 139, 143), Fanon often draws
on psychoanalysis as a critical tool, but from a nonclinical perspective.
At the same time, he denounces the racially charged and procolonial
observations of analysts like Dominique-Octave Mannoni (64–88), as
well as clinical approaches that privilege "universal" psychoanalytic concepts over the specificities of political and cultural environments of the
analysands (130). Furthermore, as his biographer David Macey points
out, Fanon is not always theoretically consistent. For instance, his frequent evocation of "the unconscious" as a kind of "alienated false
consciousness" cannot be reconciled with the Freudian or the Lacanian
unconscious.[20] Macey rightly concludes that Fanon does not follow any
particular clinician or school systematically but cites psychoanalytic
theory rather eclectically, "anxious to assimilate the modernism of the

immediate postwar period," having moved from "the book-poor culture of . . . Martinique . . . to the book-rich culture of a university town in metropolitan France" ("Recall of the Real," 97). Nevertheless, in spite of his unsystematic use of psychoanalytic terminology, I propose that we revisit Fanon's deliberate and inadvertent expositions of imaginary identification as a multiply mediated process.

Fanon elaborates on the relationship between black identity and narcissistic identification in that long and much-discussed footnote in *Black Skin* in which he draws on Lacan's account of ego formation:

> On the basis of Lacan's concept of the *mirror stage* it would be certainly worthwhile investigating to what extent the imago that the young white boy constructs of his fellow man undergoes an imaginary aggression with the appearance of the black man. Once we have understood the process described by Lacan, there is no longer any doubt that the true "Other" for the white man is and remains the black man, and vice versa. For the white man, however, "the Other" is perceived as a bodily image, absolutely as the non ego, i.e., the unidentifiable, the unassimilable. For the black man we have demonstrated that the historical and economic realities must be taken into account. (139, emphasis in the original)

The key differences between Lacan's 1949 account of the mirror stage and Fanon's redeployment of it are worth noting. In Fanon, the subject's apprehension of its identity occurs not just through its own infantile specular image but also through the complexity of symbolic encounters saturated with racial difference in the colony. The experiences of a racialized Otherness producing identity, Fanon further insists, are not identical, being contingent on socioeconomic factors that are irreducible to the specular encounter with one's image or with the human form. That is to say, in Fanon's passage, there is, alongside the visual, a *nonspecular* social dimension to identitarian aggression.

There have been two kinds of responses to Fanon's passage. Literary critics like Homi K. Bhabha and Christopher Lane have argued that Fanon simply misreads Lacan, confining the radical Lacanian subject of language to the imaginary, thereby conflating imaginary identity with the nonidentitarian Otherness of language.[21] The other, diametrically opposed, response has been to defend Fanon's anticolonial vantage point. For instance, Kaja Silverman notes that, in Fanon, the mirror stage does not yield a coherent (Lacanian) body image for the black subject in the colonial Antilles.[22] Ranjana Khanna argues that the Other in *Black Skin* is not just a product of Fanon's reading of Lacan but also his reinterpretation of Sartrean phenomenology alongside his own experiences of the "pathology" that is colonialism.[23] Similarly, Fuss argues that Otherness does not have the same subjectivizing and mediating role in Fanon that it has in Lacan, since colonialism "blocks the migration [of the colonized] through the [Lacanian] Other necessary for subjectivity to take place. . . . The black man (contra Lacan) begins and ends violently fragmented."[24] The second group of critics is thus more willing than the first to dwell on the specificity of Fanon's account of the mirror stage, not least because Lacan had not fully formulated his own theory of language and its symbolic function in the early 1950s when *Black Skin* was written.

I will, however, advance a different reading of the same footnote by questioning the opposition sustained by both groups of critics—the opposition between the Fanonian subject and the Lacanian subject. As I demonstrate below, Lacan himself ultimately cautions against monolithic theories of subjectivation in which all subjects, regardless of their positions in the symbolic, liberate themselves from their imaginary identifications through an encounter with language.[25] Second, none of the critics seems to note that, in his footnote, Fanon does not cite from the 1949 essay but from an earlier essay by Lacan called "Les complexes familiaux dans la formation de l'individu" ("Family Complexes in the Formation of the Individual") that appeared in a volume of the *Encyclopédie française* in 1938.[26] Consequently, both groups also fail to notice that Fanon's attempt to theorize a form of racial identification—*that is both specular and nonspecular*—is quite consistent with this older version of the mirror stage.[27] Here is the passage in Fanon's text that explicitly notes the source:

> "The subject's recognition of his image in the mirror," Lacan says, "is a phenomenon that is doubly significant for the analysis of this stage: the phenomenon appears after six months and the study of it at that time shows in convincing fashion the tendencies *that currently constitute reality for the subject*; the mirror image precisely because of these affinities, *affords a good symbol of that reality*: of its *affective value*, illusory like the image, and of its structure as it reflects the human form" (*Encyclopédie française*, 8.40, 9, and 10). We shall see that this discovery

is fundamental: every time the subject sees his image and
recognizes it, it is always *"the inherent mental unity"* that is recognized. (*Black Skin*, 139, emphasis added)

Let us note briefly the particularities of this version of Lacan's mirror
stage. Unlike the 1949 version, the 1938 essay discusses the mirror
stage in the context of "the intrusion complex"—coinciding with the
experience of sibling recognition and rivalry—and is inseparable from
the familial and social environment of the subject. In the passage that
Fanon cites, Lacan mentions a nonspecular "affective reality" of the
subject that typically corresponds with but precedes the encounter
with the specular image. And indeed, turning to Lacan's 1938 essay, we
notice that, developmentally, the image in the mirror is somewhat secondary and is preceded by "imagos" *that are not really images*: they are
the subject's prespecular impressions of being nourished at the maternal breast, being a sibling, being part of a family, and so on. These
prespecular sentiments and conditions leading up to the intrusion complex, Lacan points out, "will therefore be extremely variable, on the
one hand, according to the cultures and the extension they offer to the
domestic group, [and] on the other hand, according to individual contingencies, and first of all the place that the subject occupies by chance
in the birth order, its place according to the dynastic position . . . that it
occupies in this way before any conflict, that of the privileged or of the
usurper."[28] While Fanon makes no direct reference to the prespecular reality of the subject, he does use the term "inherent mental unity,"
alluding to another significant moment in the 1938 essay, where Lacan
explicitly notes the typical conjunction between prespecular affect and
the mirror encounter: "If the search for his *affective unity* promotes in the
subject the forms in which he represents his identity, the most intuitive form is given, at this stage, by the specular image. What the subject
welcomes in the image is its *inherent mental unity*. What he recognizes
in it is *the ideal of the imago of the double*" ("Les complexes familiaux,"
42, my translation, emphasis added). Striking, here, is the subject's pre-
existent desire for "affective unity" that finds its "intuitive" response in
the mirror image. Instead of arguing that the image is, axiomatically, an
ideal, Lacan seems to suggest that the subject is *affectively predisposed
or socialized* to see it as the image of the double and an ideal image.[29]

Thus, instead of anachronistically choosing between Fanon's
"image-obsessed" identitarianism and Lacan's nonidentitarian subject

of language, it is more productive to examine how Fanon's anticolonial account further develops the interaction between specular and nonspecular (affective) identification found in Lacan's 1938 essay. When Fanon mentions "the imago that the young white boy constructs of his fellow man," he also alludes to a prespecular affective perception of whiteness as the norm in the metropole and the colony. This prespecular apprehension of whiteness then leads the subject—who is socially coded as white (and male) prior to any specular encounter—to identify with a racialized body image that already possesses an established social value. Racial hierarchies governing the colonial enterprise fuel the subject's "inherent mental unity" with the norm of whiteness, of which the mirror image becomes an objective correlative. Simultaneously, the affirmation of whiteness is also accompanied by the production of "blackness" (or the not white) as an unassimilable Otherness, as the "anti-image." Conversely, the same prespecular conditions make the white colonizer the Other from the perspective of the colonized (*Black Skin*, 139). This interchangeability suggests that the Other, in Fanon, refers less to a particular group or person and more to an historically, socially, and economically determined perceptual matrix through which racial difference is recognized, embodied, and experienced.

At the same time, Fanon makes clear that the colonizer and the colonized do not occupy the same position in this matrix, or that their experiences of the matrix are vastly different. For the Antillean subject, historical and economic realities intervene rather distinctly to shape the ego's responses to its body image and its relative social value. If, earlier, Fanon had claimed that Antilleans (unlike black subjects in Senegal) are encouraged to identify with the colonizer, the mirror stage footnote reveals a more complex matrix where such an identification is not a smooth process even when the Antillean is at home:

> It might be argued that if the white man elaborates an imago of his fellow man, the same should be the case for the Antillean. . . . *But we would be forgetting that in the Antilles perception always occurs at the level of the imagination.* One's fellow man is perceived in white terms. . . . It is not surprising to hear the mother of a family remark: "X . . . *is the darkest of my children." In other words, the least white.* . . . It is in reference to the essence of the white man that every Antillean is destined to be perceived by his fellows. (*Black Skin*, 141, emphasis added)

Once again, Fanon departs significantly from Lacan's 1949 narrative of the subject's jubilant assumption of the mirror image. He describes a situation in which identity is socially imposed and experienced as a manifest disjunction or scission between the self and the ideal image. The de-idealization of the black ego begins within the apparently harmless setting of the family, where maternal speech—or familial and social speech more broadly—is an initial and powerful medium of subjectivation with enduring effects. Through this speech, the subject learns to admire the ideal image, but without being permitted an easy identification with it. In other words, the nature of *linguistic mediation is such that the Antillean's perception always occurs or is perpetually stuck in this peculiarly fragmented version of the imaginary register*. For the proponents of symbolic mediation (like Bhabha, Lane, McNulty, and others), such a reading of the linguistic mediation of the subject would be outright unpsychoanalytic. And yet, this is precisely where Fanon offers a remarkable theory of identity production that, most likely unbeknownst to him, was simultaneously unfolding at a different register in the clinical intervention of the French psychoanalyst Françoise Dolto. The same theory of identity production would also find its approximation in Lacan's later theorization of schizophrenia as a clinical structure.

"Aberrant" Narcissisms in Dolto, Fanon, and Lacan

Psychoanalytic scholars critiquing identity as an imaginary illusion have rarely considered the theoretical contributions of Dolto, who was, in fact, Lacan's colleague and contemporary and extremely prominent in France for her work with children with schizophrenia.[30] Complicating Lacan's 1949 account of the mirror stage through her clinical experiences, Dolto argued that ego formation must be seen as a traumatic and differential encounter not with *one* image but rather *between two different images*: the scopic mirror image and a much older and more fundamental *linguistic* body image.[31] Dolto calls this prior image, whose formation precedes the specular encounter, an "unconscious body image." Not to be confused with either the Lacanian specular "I" or the Lacanian unconscious, this body image is a pre–mirror stage reticular structure created by the child's sensory experiences that are, from the very beginning, linguistic and social. The unconscious image, which Dolto (like Fanon) is careful to distinguish from (Lhermitte's notion of) the body schema, develops in response to the caregiver's verbal

and body language. This language is a combination of feeding, touching, talking to, and making noises around the child. As Dolto writes in
her book *L'image inconsciente du corps* (*The Unconscious Image of the
Body*):

> *The body image, therefore, developed itself as a network of lin-
> guistic security with the mother.* This network personalizes the
> experiences of the child, with regard to the sense of smell,
> sight, hearing, the modalities of touch, according to the specific
> rhythms of the maternal habitus. *But it does not individualize the
> child with regard to its own body*; for the spatial limits of its lin-
> guistic perceptions are blurred."[32]

The unconscious body image is the impression or history of a linguistic, affective, and somatic network between the habitus of the caregiver
and the child. This network predates the ocular individualization of the
mirror stage. At the same time, the formation of the image is a psychological individualization and the beginning of socialization insofar as it
produces an "unconscious" arising from the child's sensory and environ-
mental experiences. The image, crucially, is *not just premised on vision*
but is also structured by the *linguistic and affectively charged signifiers
that, in fact, begin to construct the child as a subject*. While the child
does not fully comprehend these signifiers, its body image is founded
through its active responses to them. Thus, Dolto calls this image "an
unconscious that is already relational" and "a pre–ego" that makes possible interhuman communications and miscommunications (*L'image
inconsciente*, 38, my translation).

While Dolto maintains that the unconscious body image is usually
cohesive and continuous (157), she is clinically most concerned
about the atypical, disturbed, and "wounded" body images that she finds
in her patients with autism, schizophrenia, and unusual phobias: "If the
fundamental narcissism is malattached to the body, that is to say, if
the base [unconscious] image by which the subject attaches itself to its
ego remains fragile, then emerges the threat particular to the phobic
state."[33] Crucially, through her case studies, Dolto notices that these
disruptions are fundamentally linguistic, while being overdetermined
by familial and social environments. For instance, in the course of the
analysis of a thirteen-year-old boy with schizophrenia, Dolto concludes
that the origins of the boy's wounded body image lay in familial arguments he had heard as an infant and whose negative affective force he

had internalized without fully comprehending their meaning. A partial reconstruction of that conversation in analysis tells the clinician "how the spoken word could have etched itself into the child—words with no meaning for him other than the *jouissance* of the death wish on his being."[34] A transferential dialogue thus reveals how the subject's wounded unconscious self-image has been structured through traumatizing social speech.

There is a striking point of convergence, here, between Dolto's clinical notion of the wounded unconscious body image and Fanon's sociogenic notion of the epidermal racial schema, one of the determinants of the experience of black identity. Both concepts rethink the complex relationship between the psyche, soma, image, and language by critically responding to limiting biological concepts of touch, sensation, and vision. Much like the wounded unconscious body image in Dolto, the epidermal racial schema is discovered as a diagram or an etching underneath the corporeal schema. The fact that Fanon refers to it as a historical-racial schema should not lead us to conclude that this diagram is fixed, or that it is engendered solely through the hypervisibility of the (skin tone of the) black body. It is important to remember that the "crumbling" of Fanon's corporeal schema and his awareness of a deeper body schema are both catalyzed by *linguistic assaults*: "*Maman*, look, a Negro! I'm scared!" (*Black Skin*, 91). Furthermore, these assaults and their tonal imports, repeated multiple times in *Black Skin*, alert Fanon to the existence of a deeply sedimented self-image that is also a linguistic-visual complex: "a thousand details, anecdotes, and stories" (91) about the objectified black body. We can, therefore, argue that the deceptively simple concept of the epidermal racial schema is the anticolonial cousin of Dolto's wounded unconscious linguistic body image. Unwittingly extending the Doltonian image into the colonial matrix, Fanon's nonclinical exposition of this racial schema forcefully demonstrates how the identity of the colonized is fundamentally traumatized by the ideological structure of the colonial apparatus.

What, then, is the relationship between the Doltonian unconscious body image—which, I am suggesting, is a significant precursor to Fanon's sociogenic principle—and the mirror stage? If Lacan's 1949 neurotic account presents the subject's isolated encounter with his specular image to be a seemingly gratifying experience, Dolto contends that the specular encounter is, in fact, a confusing and painful acknowledgment of the gap between the unconscious body image and the mirror image, which appears as an intrusion that is entirely removed from the child's somatic and sensorial experiences. That is why the child should not be alone or in an unfamiliar milieu at this stage: the nurturing presence of the speech, voice, and gestures of the caregiver familiar to the child is necessary and typically performs the important function of smoothing over the fragmentation created by this otherwise disorienting scopic image and the ensuing repression of the unconscious body image (*L'image inconsciente*, 151).[35] For the same reason, in atypical scenarios where social speech fails to perform this supportive symbolic function, the subject's unconscious image is wounded and the ego fragmented by the specular image. Schizophrenia is the extreme form that this fragmentation takes.[36] This idea—that the specular encounter could, potentially, fragment the ego's identity—is closer to Fanon's cultural and critical rethinking of identification/alienation in the colonial scene than it is to the dominant Lacanian account of the child's jubilant assumption of the image.

The differences between Dolto's and Lacan's accounts, however, do not remain watertight if we turn to Lacan's revisions of the imaginary after 1949. In 1960, Lacan also emphasizes the mediating role of the person carrying the child in front of the mirror, drawing our attention to "the gesture by which the child at the mirror turns toward the person who is carrying him and appeals with a look to this witness."[37] In this typical mirror encounter, Lacan suggests, the person carrying the child primarily "represents" the symbolic Other; and symbolic mediation furnishes the embodied and socially meaningful signifier that plays an important authenticating function in the constitution of the imaginary. In his 1963 *Seminar X*, the nature of the mirror encounter morphs yet again. This time, Lacan adds a further twist to the "jubilation" seemingly experienced by the child in front of the mirror. He argues that, lurking at the edge of the ego and its fascination with the image is, in fact, *an anxiety produced by the image*, by its falsity, experienced by the subject in terms of a "remainder" that does not have a specular dimension.[38] Anxiety, in the mirror stage, is both evoked and suppressed by a seemingly full image or spectacle in which "lack happens to be lacking" ("From the Cosmos," 42).

More important, from the 1950s, Lacan joins Dolto in underscoring the fact that schizophrenia involves a rather different apprehension of the mirror stage, an experience that is neither the false jubilation of misrecognition nor the moment of authentication witnessed by the symbolic Other. In *Seminar III*, Lacan had already made an important distinction "between alienation as the general form of the imaginary and alienation in psychosis."[39] If imaginary alienation is witnessed by the symbolic

Other in the typical neurotic scenario, schizophrenia or psychosis is the marked deviation from that norm: "We have been able to recognize that in psychosis the Other, where being is realized through the avowal of speech, is excluded."[40] *Seminar X* further elaborates on the psychotic's experience of the structure of the mirror stage, where

> depersonalization begins with the non-recognition of the specular image. . . . The subject starts to be gripped by a depersonalizing vacillation whenever he cannot find himself in the mirror. . . . Should the relationship that is struck up with the specular image be such that the subject is too captive to the image for this movement [toward the Other as witness] to be possible, it's because the purely dyadic relationship dispossesses him of his relation to the big Other.[41]

What stands out in this rarely discussed version of the Lacanian mirror stage is the possibility of the subject's *nonrecognition* of the specular image. The subject sees the image, is "captivated" by it, and yet cannot see himself *in* it and is actively impeded from becoming a full member of the symbolic law that language-bound critics idealize. Even though language "speaks" the subject, symbolic mediation has failed, become unsupportive, or gone awry, and a fragmented imaginary has taken over.

My reasons for delineating this alternative mirror stage scenario within clinical thought should now be clearer to the reader. As analysis moves from the clinic to cultural criticism, what gets repeatedly cited, normalized, and vilified is the neurotic account in which (imaginary) identity is the product of an inevitably successful misrecognition of the ideal image ratified by language. Such a view of identity formation ignores the complexities of the language-image relationship recorded in differential clinical theory, as well as the sociocultural formations of marginalized identities that fall between the neurotic and schizophrenic structures, between misrecognition and nonrecognition.

Prioritizing this discursively marginalized (but by no means insignificant) account of the fragmented ego, we can now return to the nonclinical colonial scene of fragmentation in Fanon with which I ended the last section. We will now be able to see the parallel between Lacan's scene of depersonalization and Fanon's description of the splitting of black identity through a dyadic relationship with whiteness. In Fanon, unsupportive linguistic mediation ("X . . . is the darkest of my children") and the consequent splitting of the black (or nonwhite) ego are both unexceptional and unavoidable, thereby revealing that which is deemed normal or typical in the metropolitan clinic to be an exceptional privilege. Thus, without medicalizing the predicament of being colonized, and probing instead the effects of what Khanna calls the "historical and material pathology" of colonialism,[42] it becomes imperative to think of not just the imaginary but rather the symbolic-imaginary (or language-image) nexus through which the "darkest" ego is denied recognition or de-idealized in the white speculum. As well, instead of beginning with the narrative of imaginary mastery or false plenitude, it becomes crucial to think of anticolonial identity in terms of the varying degrees of schizophrenic *(dis)identification* that the racially marginalized subject experiences as colonialism produces different positions—from "darkest" to "least dark"—at varying distances from the ideal image.[43] Notably, my use of "schizophrenia" here—and in the rest of this book—is neither strictly clinical nor simply metaphorical. What I am proposing be read as a Fanonian account of colonial schizophrenia is not derived from and, in fact, breaks from stigmatizing approaches to mental illness and disease.[44] In my argument, schizophrenia represents not a "black disease" characterized by aggression and hostility but rather the socioeconomic scaffolding behind the differential experience of an identitarian anguish that challenges, to a certain extent, hegemonic distinctions between the normal and the abnormal, the pathological and the nonpathological.[45] In this context, the "neutral" or colorless "autoscopic hallucination" (*Black Skin*, 140) that Fanon notes in some of his Antillean patients conspicuously demonstrates how the colonized can psychically neither inhabit nor sever themselves completely from their corporeal blackness *under certain schizophrenic symbolic conditions.*[46] Thus, Fanon's matrix of Otherness emerges in this colonial and schizophrenic scene because language (as the symbolic Other) has failed, or is repeatedly failing the racialized ego.

Racial Visibility and the Spectacular "Call" of Language

What exactly is the nature of the socioeconomic scaffolding achieved through language in colonial France? What are the circumstances under which language gets pulled as an agent of mediation into the French colonial state's capitalist enterprise that, in a sense, also "authenticates" the ocular production of black identity? And how is this "languaging" sanctioned by the colonial state different from the view of language (as full speech) adopted and prescribed by the advocates of anti-identitarian symbolic mediation?[47]

For Fanon, the colonized subject's quotidian experience of language is caught between racialized interpellation on the street and the colonial state's injunction to embrace the same language. He writes, "To speak means being able to use a certain syntax and possessing the morphology of such and such a language, but it means above all assuming a culture and bearing the weight of a civilization. . . . The more the black Antillean assimilates the French language, the whiter he gets—i.e., the closer he comes to becoming a true human being" (*Black Skin*, 1–2). In the colonial Antilles, fluency in received French is tantamount to the acquisition of a certain amount of racial capital, an acquisition that is accompanied by the political (and psychic) repression of every dialectal variation that deviates from the standard version. While the acquisition of this racial capital is not the same as being visually and socially recognized as a white subject, it offers some Antilleans a class mobility that would not otherwise be possible.

In a particularly memorable passage, Fanon emphasizes the violence of this "voluntary" effort to assimilate linguistically:

> The black man entering France reacts against the myth of the Martinican who swallows his r's. He'll go to work on it and enter into open conflict with it. He will make every effort not only to roll his r's, but also to make them stand out. On the lookout for the slightest reactions of others, listening to himself speak and not trusting his own tongue . . . he will lock himself in his room and read for hours—desperately working on his *diction*. (*Black Skin*, 5, emphasis in the original)

This colonial diasporic example demonstrates how the acquisition of linguistic capital involves a form of cultural complicity that is neither a passive submission to a linguistic norm nor a free adherence to ideologically neutral values. The literate and elite Martinican's desperate physical attempts to pronounce "correctly" the letter *r* testify to a class-driven disciplinary mechanism fueling colonial capitalism under which a particular set of linguistic practices becomes dominant and encourages the relentless conversion of linguistic capital into economic capital, and vice versa. If McNulty and others urge us to choose the subject of language over the politics of identification, Fanon's example reminds us of how unequal, asymmetrical, and dominative the politics of linguistic assimilation can be in the colonial scene. If racialized interpellation seeks to produce and limit the identity of the colonized subject, linguistic mimicry holds out the promise of but never guarantees a complete transcendence of that limitation.[48]

This scene of mimicry also makes visible the systemic absorption of language and the languaged subject into what Guy Debord calls "the society of the spectacle."[49] While Debord diagnoses the preponderance of spectacular *images* under capitalism as "a negation of life that has *invented a visual form for itself*" (*Society of the Spectacle*, 14, emphasis in the original), he also proposes that we think of the "image" both more metaphorically and transmedially. The visual image does not alone constitute the spectacular image mediating social relations. The spectacle is a much broader and more diffuse "language . . . composed of *signs* of the dominant organization of production—signs which are at the same time the ultimate end-products of that organization" (13, emphasis in the original). Exemplified by spectacular billboards and mass media images, this spectacular language of domination is, therefore, necessarily a combination of linguistic and visual signs.

The colonial "spectacularization" of the linguistic sign becomes clearer if we read Fanon's account of mimicry with and against Jean-Joseph Goux's use of the mirror stage as a metaphor for the production of exchange value. In his attempt to bring together Karl Marx's theory of the commodity and (the normalized neurotic account of) ego formation, Goux writes,

> We are familiar with this identification with the image of the *like*—the basis for ego formation. We know that [quoting Lacan] "the subject, in its sense of self, identifies with the image of the other" and further that "it is first of all in the other that the subject identifies and experiences itself." Just as [quoting Marx] "no commodity can function as equivalent for itself, can make of its own bodily shape an expression of its own value," but every commodity must, to express its value, "enter into relation with some other commodity considered equivalent, converting the bodily shape of that other commodity into the form of its own value," likewise the form and the formation of the ego must always occur through "an erotic relationship in which the (human) individual fixes upon an image that alienates himself." The ego has no existence, as such, apart from this specular relation of identification.

> This homology . . . did not escape Marx: "*It is with the human being as with the commodity.*"[50]

While Lacan and Marx may not agree on what it means to be "human," what Goux identifies in this isomorphism is the *visual substitution* common to the dominant neurotic narrative of the ego and the generation of the commodity form. The human subject acquires identity just as the commodity acquires value by being identified with a specular ideal, that which Lacan calls the "ideal-I" and Goux (following Marx) calls the "universal equivalent" or "general equivalent" (Goux, *Symbolic Economies*, 16).

Let us now note how Fanon's scene of linguistic mimicry both resembles and departs from Goux's account of value production. As in Goux's homology, the Antillean attempts to acquire exchange value by taking on the attributes of the universal equivalent: that which is recognized as an idealized standard against which value is measured. But there are also important differences. First, what Fanon emphasizes *is not just the visual but also the linguistic/acoustic commodity*, the commodity that "sounds" (and therefore "looks" or "acts" somewhat) like the spectacular equivalent. The commodity is "humanized" in that the black man attempts to transcend the limits imposed on blackness by approximating the linguistic ideal of the " properly French" subject. Furthermore, Fanon's example—where the nonnative speaker cannot trust and is always haunted by his own tongue—reveals a fissure in the apparently smooth process of attaining equivalence. Fanon's paradigm reaffirms the Marxist emphasis on the *unevenness* of exchange and, therefore, reveals the falsity of the narrative of perfect equivalence underlying Goux's account as well as identification in the neurotic mirror stage.[51] As Fanon points out, the success of mimicry—realized presumably with the Antillean's assimilation into French society—cannot be guaranteed. The languaged black subject is frequently called down for failing to embody "proper" diction, his split ego continually haunted by the possibility of failing to live up to language-as-spectacle: "The black man is *comparaison*. That is the first truth. He is *comparaison* in the sense that he is constantly pre-occupied with self-assertion and the ego-ideal" (*Black Skin*, 185–86). In this case, the cultural laborer's identity (as exchange value) expresses itself not through the easy appropriation of the equivalent but as a differential with an anxiety of inadequacy and an irrepressible remainder of his linguistic "black self" as use value. Even the most radical anti-identitarian critique has to grapple with this linguistic splitting of racialized identity between the subject's exchange value and use value, with the structure of equivalence that keeps the latter at the mercy of the former.[52]

If Fanon's example reveals a prejudicial character in linguistic capital that sustains identity as an internally split entity whose use value is never fully convertible into exchange value, a psychoanalytic parallel can be found, once again, in Lacan's reflections on schizophrenia. It is not that the schizophrenic—Lacan notes while commenting on the British psychoanalyst Melanie Klein's patient, Dick—is "without" language. His world and his speech are, however, restricted to a particular register or plane—that of "the call"—that deprives his imaginary of the remolding or rewriting typically undertaken by the symbolic:

> In any imperative, there's another plane, that of the call. It is a question of the tone in which the imperative is uttered. The same text can have completely different imports depending on the tone. The simple statement *stop* can have, depending on the circumstances, completely different imports as a call. . . .
>
> With Dick we are at the level of the call. The call acquires its weight within the already acquired system of language.[53]

Later in *Seminar I*, Lacan explicitly classes the call under the imaginary plane of "the *communiqué*" in which "one should include the accumulated prejudices which make up a cultural community . . . the psychological prejudices even."[54] The call, then, is neither empty speech nor full speech heard in the Lacanian clinic. Rather, it comprises the incontestably social, embodied, and formal aspects of speech—the tone, the stress, the visible gesture—that can, in their socially damaging forms, block the subject's full access to the symbolic order.

Again, without conflating clinical diagnosis and nonclinical critique, it is possible to argue that the labor that the colonized expends to learn "proper French"—focused on the commodified stress, accent, tone, and therefore the raciocultural prejudices attached to them—can well limit his experience of language to the plane of the communiqué or the call, which is also the dimension of the spectacle. While mimicking the spectacular r certainly does not produce the debilitating effects of clinically diagnosed psychosis, the psychic impact of this colonial call is not inconsequential. The subject's efforts to identify with and embody the call/spectacle under the mandate of colonial capital at once splits and forms his identity, while taking him further away from idealized notions of symbolic lack. The racialized consequences of the emergence of French as the spectacular call, then, is another explanation for the impossibility of a "pure" symbolic mediation in the colonial scene.

Language and/as the Image in the Maternal Mirror

By examining the role that language plays in Dolto's, Fanon's, and Lacan's accounts of schizophrenic narcissism, we have begun to trace the outlines of an intermedial account of identity production under colonial capitalism. To be clearer, the subject of identity is intermedial because its minoritizing constraints unfold somewhere between or simultaneously through language, image, and the body, *insofar as the materialities of none of these agents of mediation can be privileged in isolation over the others.* Writing in 1953, Lacan himself notes the intermedial production of imaginary identity in the following way: "Language is not immaterial. It is a subtle body, but body it is. Words are caught up in all the body images that captivate the subject. . . . Furthermore, words themselves can suffer *symbolic lesions and accomplish imaginary acts whose victim is the subject.*"[55] The linguistic signifier can create identitarian lesions that, in turn, limit future symbolic mediations. And what Fanon shows us is precisely how racially lesioned speech and visual perception simultaneously produce embodied and fragmented identities in a damaged colonial symbolic.

At the same time, certain similarities between the psychoanalytic and anticolonial approaches to identity do not make them identical. In fact, a clear difference emerges between the analyst's "typical" accounts of linguistic-specular identification and Fanon's descriptions of everyday black (dis)identification. We noted how, for Dolto, soothing maternal speech usually aids the child to manage the difference between the specular image and the unconscious image. And for Lacan, the person intervening in the typical mirror encounter is important only insofar as that person represents the symbolic Other that overwrites the imaginary. In contrast, Fanon presents us with two ordinary scenarios—one literary and the other personal/anecdotal—where maternal speech actively disciplines and splits the child's self-image. In a poem by Léon-Gontran Damas (from which Fanon quotes in *Black Skin*), it is the black Antillean mother who goads her son to avoid Creolisms and to speak "the French from France / The Frenchman's French / French French" (4).

And later, Fanon reminisces with regard to his own mother: "I am a black man—but naturally I don't know it, because I am one. At home my mother sings me [sic], in French, French love songs where there is never a mention of black people. Whenever I am naughty or when I make too much noise, I am told to 'stop acting like a nigger'" (*Black Skin*, 168). Moving beyond Fanon's individual psyche for the moment—and reserving the critique of his gender politics for the final section of this chapter—I would like to focus on the commonality between the literary representation and the anecdotal memory of the mother as an agent of a symbolic failure or of the successful mediation of capitalism.

In both of these examples, the Antillean mother strongly disapproves of her child's linguistic habits and social behavior with reference to a certain idealized notion of the French language and culture. The vocal command prohibiting speaking in Creole or "acting like a nigger" is a violent negation of the child's self-image and a coercive reconfiguration of his habitus. The same command potentially marks the beginning of the mimicry continued by the self-disciplining adult practicing the French *r*. Fanon's examples, therefore, point toward the unavoidable disruption—or even the impossibility—of linguistic security for the colonized continually bombarded with racially charged signifiers. The figure of the speaking mother, in these scenes, becomes a *split or cracked mirror* for the child, a mirror in which her visible corporeal nonwhiteness is at odds with the antiblack Frenchness idealized by her speech.

I turn to this scene of linguistic-specular fragmentation in particular because it points, once again, to the limits of language-bound critique that wishes to fight identity politics through the asymmetry, misfire, or constant slippage of meaning in the symbolic order. It is possible to argue that the injunction to "stop acting like a nigger," heard or seen in the maternal acoustic-specular mirror, does not "mean" anything substantive and is a symptom of the depersonalization before the ideal image of whiteness. But to disregard the imaginary significance of the phrase to celebrate semiotic indeterminacy is to disavow violently its epidermalization, the traumatic transfer of the epidermal schema from the mother to the child, and the profoundly ambivalent use of the signifiers *nègre* and *noir* throughout Fanon's text.

In these scenes with the mother's voice disciplining the child, we also return to a specifically colonial manifestation of the Lacanian call—the imaginary import of the tones, bodily movements, and volume of the mother's voice—that generates meanings as lesions in the child's imaginary. While discussing the experience of meaning in psychosis in *Seminar III*, Lacan reminds us that the subject experiences meaning in the course of a delusion without, paradoxically, fully knowing what that meaning is: "What is the subject ultimately saying, specially at a certain period of his delusion? That there is meaning. What meaning he doesn't know, but it comes to the foreground, it asserts itself, and for him it's perfectly understandable."[56] Lacan goes on to note that in "passional psychosis, which seems so much closer to what is called normal," the subject's experience of meaning is governed by the fact that he "can't come to terms with a certain loss or injury and because his entire life appears to be centred around compensation for the injury suffered and the claim it entails" ("Meaning of Delusion," 22). Later in *Seminar III*, Lacan identifies two poles along which meaning is experienced during delusions:

> The delusional intuition is a full phenomenon that has an overflowing, inundating character for the subject. It reveals a new perspective to him, one whose stamp of originality, whose characteristic savor, he emphasizes. . . . There, the word—with its full emphasis, as when one says *the word for, the solution to, an enigma*—is the soul of the situation.
>
> At the opposite pole there is the form that meaning takes when it no longer refers to anything at all. This is the formula that is repeated, reiterated, drummed in with a stereotyped insistence. It's what we call, in contrast to the word, the refrain. ("The Other and Psychosis," 33, emphasis in the original)

Lacan points to moments where the subject's experience of imaginary meaning and identity can become inexpressibly *real* under certain symbolic conditions. Simultaneously insisting on the intersection and difference between clinical and cultural approaches to the experience of meaning, we can see how racially objectifying terms like *nègre* or *noir* can be experienced from near-normal "passional" perspectives, as meaning that asserts itself without having a unique referent, as injuries experienced by marginalized individuals and populations. Within this cultural context, the signifier *nègre*, I want to suggest, also produces imaginary meanings for the racialized subject along the two poles that Lacan identifies: at one end is the colonial slur *nègre* as a reiterated, meaningless linguistic-visual stereotype or empty refrain that the colonized subject, nevertheless, experiences as a "meaningful" injury without a specific referent. At the other end is the anticolonial notion of negritude—a linguistic and more broadly cultural attempt to redefine blackness against that stereotype and resist the antiblackness embedded in everyday speech. Fanon repeatedly cites lines from a poem by Aimé Césaire to emphasize this oppositional origin of the meaning of negritude, even though he is aware that blackness is not reducible to a self-contained essence:

> My negritude is not a stone, its deafness hurled against
>   the clamor of day
> My negritude is not an opaque spot of dead water over
>   the dead eye of the earth
> . . . .
> It reaches deep down into the red flesh of the soil
> It reaches deep into the blazing flesh of the sky (*Black Skin*, 103)

Césaire's poem, we might say, rejects but cannot fully forget blackness as the stereotyped object of denigration, even as it attempts to move toward blackness as the "word," as self-affirmation. For Fanon, this experience is necessarily tied to a lived blackness and cannot be universalized: "Only the black man is capable of conveying it, of deciphering its meaning and impact" (*Black Skin*, 103).

I should reiterate that by seeing the black stereotype and (for some, a problematically masculinist) black identitarianism as the two poles of a "delusional" black experience, I am neither dismissing nor celebrating the politics of (dis)identification but insisting on its realness for the imaginary subject of race.[57]

When anti-identitarianism disregards this real fragmentation by seeking refuge in the medium of language, it also overlooks a certain *aesthetic dimension* of the experience of identity that is regulated by capitalism but exceeds the control of particular aesthetic objects, media, or individuals. We have already started to navigate this aesthetic dimension through Fanon's attention to the linguistic, somatic, and visual mediation of black identity. But to be more precise, what I have called (dis)identification may also be called an *aesthetic dissonance* that the black subject experiences while encountering the ideal image of whiteness or de-idealized representations of blackness. In language-bound antiessentialism, the ego's encounter with symbolic indeterminacy—uncovered frequently through the consumption of high cultural artifacts—is the truly radical aesthetic experience. In this zone of aesthetic purity and autonomy, the subject of language bypasses all imaginary constraints. Such a view of aesthetics, for instance, is conveyed not just by the title of McNulty's coda ("Toward an Aesthetics of Symbolic Life") in *Wrestling with the Angel* (237) but also the archive through which she retrieves the lack in the Other: avant-garde French performance pieces, Kantian aesthetics, and French experimental poetics (40–47, 228–33, 257–66). The problem here is that by approaching aesthetics entirely through the perceived autonomy of a privileged medium in primarily white European spaces of cultural production—and, therefore, evading entirely the complex intermediality of racialized capitalism—the antiessentialist critic risks espousing an exclusive "identity politics" of her own. Such an aesthetic politics, as Jane Gallop notes in the second epigraph to this chapter, betrays its profoundly imaginary privileges in the very attempt to escape it.[58]

In contrast to this binary opposition between the aesthetic and the identitarian, I will insist on their coconstitution in the final section of this chapter, wherein I examine Fanon's dissonant responses to mass media, including the film with which I began my discussion of *Black Skin*. Here I am drawing on scholars who have demonstrated how the categories of class, race, and gender are implicitly always at work in purportedly universalist formulations of the aesthetic, thereby making it impossible to think of a "pure" aesthetics or an aesthetic "sublime."[59] Simultaneously, I am following a robust body of scholarship that has argued for the urgent need to expand the concept of the aesthetic itself without exceptionalizing or dismissing it, by moving away from its restricted and purist definition as a discipline-bound "artistics." Following the work of scholars like Pamela R. Matthews and David McWhirter, Wolfgang Welsch, and Monique Roelofs, my analysis of the aesthetics of identity politics moves toward its etymological roots in *aisthesis* (Greek, meaning "perception" and/or "sensation"), which governs everyday life experiences and varying social identifications,[60] the distribution of the sensible,[61] and, indeed, the political problem of democratic individualism under capitalism.[62] As Giorgio Agamben notes in the third epigraph to this chapter, there is an aesthetics that is the condition of possibility for the valorization of art *as* art.[63] It is in this not-so-innocent aesthetic domain that we need to situate identity's schizophrenic dissonance.

Identity, Aesthetics, and Colonial Hypermediation

It is from within such a heterogeneous and plural framework—where aesthetics and politics are mutually implicated[64]—that Monique Roelofs examines Fanon's view of "coloniality as a form of aesthetic relationality" (*Cultural Promise*, 44). Roelofs identifies two related processes that bring race and aesthetics together, during and beyond colonialism: first, "aesthetic racialization" as a set of "aesthetic stratagems [that] support racial registers"; and second, "racialized aestheticization" as "aesthetic modalities" drawn from "racial templates" (29). In light of my discussion so far, the simultaneous insertion of visuality (primarily of skin color) and linguistic embodiment into the production of exchange value would be one of the most powerful instances of aesthetic racialization in the French colony. These aesthetic processes that are fundamental to how commodity capitalism works, I have also noted, unfold through intra- and interracial encounters in the colony, which in turn inform and are informed by aesthetic modalities reflected by colonial media technologies. Emphasizing the role that French literary texts, advertisements, cinema, and radio play in the colony as instruments of racialized aestheticization, Roelofs writes,

> Cultural productions advance whiteness . . . by shaping white worldviews and providing anecdotes and stories that endorse white myths about blacks. Mainstream artifacts and media . . . succeed at getting both white and black people to identify with white attitudes and perceptions. . . . This situation gives rise to a twofold aesthetic agenda: that of countering the effects to which white popular forms expose blacks, and of promoting alternative black voices. (44)

The negritude movement, then, would be an example of (the second process of) racialized aestheticization produced by the initial aesthetic racialization. It is worth noting, however, that while colonial media encourage (some) blacks to identify with whites, racialized aestheticization arises precisely because a certain kind of dissonance is built into the system. As noted earlier, in the Antillean context, identification is accompanied by a physical sense of not being identical with the colonizer. This dissonance could take the form of simultaneously feeling interpellated by and refusing the colonial regime of representation, as in the case of Fanon himself. Alternatively, it could take the form of wanting to be—and simultaneously feeling the anxiety of not matching up to—the ideal image, as in the case of the Martinican rolling his r's. In either case, between aesthetic racialization and racialized aestheticization, there seems to be an important intermediary stage: (dis)identification as an *aesthetic dissonance* that generates identity as an intermedial wound and gives birth to something like the politics of negritude.

In *Black Skin*, Fanon presents the act of reading colonial literature as one such paradigmatic site of aesthetic dissonance. For instance, fulminating against the Martinican writer Mayotte Capécia's autobiographical novel *I Am a Martinican Woman* (1948)—in which the female protagonist longs to be white and is in love with a white man—Fanon writes,

> Mayotte loves a white man unconditionally. . . . And when she asks herself whether he is handsome or ugly, she writes: *"All I know is that he had blue eyes, blond hair, a pale complexion and I loved him."* If we reword these same terms it is not difficult to come up with: *"I loved him because he had blue eyes, blond hair, and a pale complexion."* And we Antilleans, we know only too well that as they say in the islands *the black man has a fear of blue eyes.* (*Black Skin*, 25, emphasis added)

A few pages later, he continues: "Mayotte is striving for lactification. In a word, the race must be whitened; every woman in Martinique knows this, says this, and reiterates it. . . . The crux of the problem is not to slip back among the 'nigger' rabble" (29–30). Several scholars have critiqued Fanon's misogyny and his violent treatment of women in *Black Skin*.[65] Indeed, there can be no evasion of or apologies for his deeply disturbing remarks on the rape fantasies of women (156–57), especially since Fanon was well aware of the role of interracial sexual violence within colonial hierarchies (29). And, arguably, in the passages quoted above, Fanon also emerges as a "bad" literary critic. He not only conflates the author with the fictional character—denying any irony or complexity in Capécia's literary representation of her "own voice"—but then proceeds to accuse "every" woman of color in the Antilles of desiring whiteness.[66]

What interests me, however, is how Fanon's identity as a black male intellectual materializes through his *failure* to treat Capécia's text in its aesthetic particularities and complexities. This failure, I would argue, must be seen through the raciosexual constraints shaping the aesthetics of colonial relationality. From Fanon's perspective, the *meaning* of Mayotte's desire is not in any way "ambiguous" or "lacking"; instead, her erotic longing for blue eyes and blond hair unavoidably evokes the "anti-image" of blackness against which those attributes of whiteness are valorized. Simultaneously, this aesthetically dissonant experience of black identity takes on a particularly hostile form as Fanon's encounter with the text coincides with everyday experiences of being denigrated as a black man by a number of Antillean women in France: "We were talking with one of them [a Martinican woman in France] who as a last resort hurled: 'Besides, if Césaire claims his blackness loud and clear, it's because he senses full well there is a curse on it. Do the whites make such a fuss about their color? . . . Me, I would never accept to marry a nigger for anything in the world'" (*Black Skin*, 30). This aesthetic unfolding of black identity between the literary (or the "properly" aesthetic) medium and "nonliterary" social experiences—between printed words on a page and linguistic-specular insults (or "calls") assaulting the corporeal ego on the street—must also be understood through a related but distinct *institutionalized* force of capitalist mediation. And that larger institutional force is the official, state-sanctioned, and metropolitan reception of Capécia's novel. As T. Denean Sharpley-Whiting notes, while negritude critics largely ignored *I Am a Martinican Woman*, the novel was enthusiastically received by a Parisian jury comprising thirteen Frenchmen who awarded the author the prestigious Grand Prix Littéraire des Antilles in 1949, making Capécia the first woman of color to receive that prize.[67] For many black male thinkers (including Fanon) and writers associated with the negritude movement, this paternalistic endorsement itself would overdetermine or remediate the "meaning" of *I Am a Martinican Woman*, even though, as some have argued, the novel could, in fact, be seen as a *critique* of the Martinican desire for whiteness, thereby complementing Fanon's arguments in *Black Skin*.[68] From the anticolonial perspective, the radical potential of that critique is severely compromised by the tokenistic inclusion of a female Martinican author by the imperialist awarding body. For instance, Fanon himself reacts not just to the novel but also to "the enthusiastic reception" it has received in "certain circles" in metropolitan France (*Black Skin*, 25). It is this reception that also determines his conclusions about the novel and its author's assimilationist intentions.

In this way, Fanon's response to Capécia—problematic as it is—allows us to examine how the literary text can (re)materialize identity as an aesthetic dissonance, one whose origins and operations extend well beyond the aesthetic qualities (however defined) of the literary medium. To take this dissonance and its repercussions seriously (instead of dismissing Fanon as a bad reader) would mean examining the climate and repercussions of the structural violence of *aesthesis* in the colony. In other words, aesthetic dissonance could, potentially, make it impossible for the anticolonial subject to consider the aesthetic object as an "autonomous" entity outside colonial power relations.[69] It is, after all, an ineluctable blurring of the distinction between the artwork and lifeworld that splits Fanon's identity between his extreme identification with Capécia's protagonist—her acute awareness of her de-idealized nonwhite body—and his own alienation from (and reactive response to) a systemic eroticized rejection of black masculinity.[70] In this scene of plural mediation, we might say, the *imaginary* phrases (or content) like "blue eyes, blond hair" in the literary text take on a frighteningly *real form*, evoking a particularly discomposing affect in Fanon the reader: "the black man has a fear of blue eyes." Representation, irrationally, becomes a bodily felt reference, turning into a real delusion through the relentless societal infliction of misrecognition as recognition.[71]

We will now be able to see Fanon's reaction to the film *Home of the Brave* as another instance of a schizophrenic intermedial dissonance that is particular to the racialized commodity economy of colonial France. For the benefit of the reader, I will re-cite a few sentences from Fanon's response to the film:

> I can't go to the movies without encountering myself. I wait for myself. Just before the film starts, I wait for myself. Those in front of me look at me, spy on me, wait for me. A black bellhop is going to appear. My aching heart makes my head spin.
>
> The crippled soldier from the Pacific war tells my brother: "Get used to your color the way I got used to my stump. We are both casualties."
>
> Yet, with all my being, I refuse to accept this amputation. . . . When I opened my eyes yesterday I saw the sky in total revulsion. . . . Not responsible for my acts, at the crossroads between Nothingness and Infinity, I began to weep. (*Black Skin*, 119)

Film scholars like Mary Ann Doane and E. Ann Kaplan have turned to this passage to show how Fanon's identificatory anxiety in the colonial cinema squarely challenges theories of spectatorship offered by several psychoanalytic-Marxist film theorists in the 1970s and 1980s.[72] Often referred to as the Apparatus group, these film theorists like Jean-Louis Baudry, Christian Metz, and Laura Mulvey—much like the language-bound theorists of symbolic mediation—rely on Lacan's (1949) theory of the mirror stage to critique the illusion of mastery and transcendence promoted by the image. In their view, commercial Hollywood narrative cinema encourages spectators to regress to an imaginary space of illusory identification comparable to the mirror stage. As a reactivation of that primary narcissistic encounter, they argue, cinematic narcissism is also premised on a profound misrecognition of the self through the ideal image.[73]

Yet Fanon's encounter with *Home of the Brave* and its African American protagonist Peter Moss offers no such narcissistic refuge. For Fanon, the screen turns into a sky that engulfs him, severely curtailing his desires for self-expansion. In stark contrast with the hallucinatory experience of what Baudry calls "the transcendental subject" of the cinematic imaginary ("Ideological Effects," 43–44), Fanon is stuck at a differently delusional "crossroads between Nothingness and Infinity."[74] He is split between feeling objectified by the cinematic image and refusing that imaginary-real objectification, between seeing himself and refusing to see himself in the image. The crossroads that Fanon mentions thus becomes a temporal and historical impasse where the anticolonial ego is simultaneously fragmented and sustained, where the dynamics of (dis) identification cannot be explained through dominant Lacanian assessments of cinematic narcissism or its critiques.[75]

Thus, Fanon's anticolonial (dis)identification—his "unscholarly" response to a particular moment in *Home of the Brave*—cannot be understood through Apparatus theory.[76] If the latter assumes an uninterrupted and privatized cinephilic immersion of the spectator in the mass medium, Fanon describes his own aesthetic dissonance (as was noted at the beginning of the chapter) in terms of antagonistic contact between linguistic-visual content on the screen, his own body, and those of other spectators. Fanon's intermedial experience of blackness includes but also extends well beyond his particular encounter with the film as an aesthetic object. His response reveals the schizophrenic scaffolding and aesthetic production of black masculinity integral to French colonialism. The wounded association that Fanon makes between "a black bellhop" and the screen image of Moss, for instance, is inseparable from his acute awareness of his own linguistic-visual corporeal schema—a direct fallout of the everyday prejudicial "calls" discussed earlier in this chapter.

Of particular significance in this moment of dissonance in the cinema is what Doane calls a "confusion of the concept of spectacle"—or the blurring of the boundaries between representation and reference that I also noted in Fanon's response to Capécia's novel.[77] Fanon is fully aware that he is watching a fictional film. Yet, while he is watching *Home of the Brave*, it is as if Fanon's "I" hovers or is torn between his own body and the image of Moss. I want to approach this crack in the ipseity of the speaking "I" through the notion of cinematic "indexicality." This confusion, I will suggest, also prompts us to rethink the *materiality* of cinematic mediation.

In a discussion of indexicality as that which constitutes the specificity of cinema as an aesthetic medium, Doane reminds us of the two distinct and almost contradictory definitions of the concept of the "index" in the writings of the semiotician Charles Sanders Peirce:

> First, when the index is exemplified by the footprint or the photograph, it is a sign that can be described as a trace or imprint of its object. Something of the object leaves a legible residue through the medium of touch. The index as trace implies a material connection between sign and object as well as an insistent temporality—the reproducibility of a past moment. . . . The second definition of the index, on the other hand, often seems to harbor a resistance to the first. The index as deixis—the pointing finger, the "this" of language—does exhaust itself in the moment of its implementation and is ineluctably linked to presence. There is always a gap between sign and object, and touch here is only figurative.[78]

If the index as "trace" suggests a visual imprint that *physically* connects the represented object with its concrete and irreplaceable referent, the index as "deixis" is that property of language that allows us to refer to objects, people, and situations through indeterminate or "empty" signifiers—such as "I," "you," "this," "that," and so on—that point to something or someone with a sense of immediacy and directness but without guaranteeing semiotic fixity. As Doane further notes, a deictic signifier such as "this" is "evacuated of all content and simply designates a specific and singular object or situation, comprehensible only within

the given discourse" ("The Indexical," 134). This emptiness of the deictic index makes it seemingly opposed to the visual abundance of the
index as trace, which is most often seen as the fundamental property of
cinema.

As Doane goes on to show later in the same essay, however, the index
as deixis can be found in U.S. avant-garde cinema that constantly tests
the limits of the medium, disregards dominant cinema's privileging of
the certainty of visual "knowledge," and finds ways of reminding the
audience of the instability of signification. One of the most striking
examples that she offers is from Michael Snow's *So Is This* (1982), a
film that "consists entirely of words, with an emphasis upon various
forms of the shifter—'I,' 'you,' 'here,' 'now,' and especially 'this.' Mim-
ing interactivity, the film directly addresses its audience as the 'you' of a
present tense, that of the film's screening, in an ever new, ever unique
moment that repudiates the idea of film as recording or representation,
the trace of an object placed before the lens" ("The Indexical," 137).
Thus, in Doane's estimation, even as dominant narrative cinema heavily invests in the index as trace, more radical experimental cinema can
autonomously activate the index as deixis to challenge the illusion of
semiotic certainty offered by its rival. Linguistic-cinematic deixis, in the
avant-garde film, can demonstrate its power to refer to something that
cannot be visually confirmed but can, nevertheless, continue to haunt
the viewer.

Rather remarkably, what we observe in Fanon's response to *Home
of the Brave* is a certain kind of (mis)interpellative deictic function that
is produced by the index as trace but is beyond the control of this
particular film or the cinematic medium.[79] On the one hand, Moss's
image indexes or functions as a physical trace of the body of the African American actor James Edwards, who plays Moss in front of the
camera. On the other hand, the same image also functions as a kind
of haunting deixis or pointer that is not directly implied by the image
but takes shape within colonial discourse. Comparable to and complementing the abstraction operative in the linguistic naming of the black
subject, Moss's cinematic trace acquires a deictic quality pointing to
"all" other black male bodies beyond the screen. More specifically, for
Fanon, the image of Moss's body takes on the deictic or force of "You!"
directly pointing at or even "touching" him in the audience. In other
words, Fanon is unable to make a clear distinction between the indexical image as a trace (of the body of Edwards) and what he perceives to
be the object of the deictic index (his own body as the referent of the

"You!" represented by Moss's image). We see the effect of this indexical confusion and this "tactile" quality of the Hollywood image in Fanon's writing,[80] as "my brother" (Moss, played by Edwards) turns into the "I" that finally refuses "the amputation." This confusion also demonstrates the specificity of Fanon's bodily ego as a perceptive and expressive medium, operating through "conventions out of which . . . develop a form of expressiveness that can be both projective and mnemonic."[81] Cinema becomes a vital technological convention that makes Fanon a medium, articulating blackness through projection and recollection.

At the same time, several other *extracinematic* aesthetic aspects of the colonial relation also impinge upon Fanon's splitting as a medium in the cinema. For instance, if we detect in Fanon's rejection of "the amputation"—a reference to the friendship between Moss and Mingo in the final scene of the film—a repressed phobia of (interracial) same-sex intimacy, such a reading would have to take into account simultaneously the pervasive anticolonial anxiety around being feminized or "castrated" by the colonizer, Freudian readings of the homosexual as the "primitive" subject, and the feminization of Moss's character in the film.[82] Similarly, the splitting of Fanon's "I" through his (dis)identification with an African American male character cannot be explained without considering the embodied transnational connection he is compelled to make between two distinct institutions producing blackness—those of slavery and colonialism. As well, in Fanon's description, the confusion between the spectacle and himself as a spectator is contingent on the immediate context of reception—the presence of other presumably white bodies in the French metropolitan theater. Elsewhere in *Black Skin,* Fanon describes a similar confusion experienced by a black spectator watching a documentary on colonial Africa: "In France the black man who watches this documentary is literally petrified. Here there is no escape: he is at once Antillean, Bushman, and Zulu" (131). This manifestly oppressive experience of "vernacular modernism" demonstrates how the colonized—or his real experience of identity under colonialism—is split between his own body as a medium and other media, including the bodies of other spectators.[83]

Relatedly, if we pay attention to Fanon's pained and angry references in *Black Skin* to his dissonant encounters with the French slogan "Y'a bon Banania," we realize that the deictic immediacy of the cinematic black body may also come from linguistic-visual images that are, strictly speaking, not cinematic (17, 35, 92). The chocolate cereal called Banania entered the French market in 1917 with the image of

the Bonhomme Banania ("Good Man Banania"), a smiling Senegalese soldier who expresses his contentment with the cereal through
his slogan "Y'a bon Banania," which is pidgin for the French "C'est
bon Banania" ("It's good, Banania"). This image-text—suggesting an
equivalence between the color of the commodity and black skin, and
simultaneously infantilizing the smiling Senegalese soldier through his
pidgin speech—also exerts a coercive holding power on Fanon, forcing
a physical identification that he vehemently repels. Indeed, the poster
initiates what Gordon calls an "existential struggle against sedimented,
dehumanized constructions" led by Fanon, Léopold Senghor, and other
black intellectuals in the 1950s.[84] As Fanon writes, "Making him speak
pidgin is tying him to an image, snaring him, imprisoning him as the
eternal victim of his own essence, of a *visible appearance* for which he
is not responsible" (*Black Skin*, 18, emphasis in the original). Arguably,
this language-image relay—symptomatic, again, of the failure of symbolic mediation in the colonial scene—has a powerful effect on Fanon.
And it seems extremely likely that this image of the Senegalese soldier
deployed and exploited by Banania—even though it is not an indexical
trace—cast its own deictic shadow on Fanon's reading of the black soldier in *Home of the Brave*.

It is worth highlighting that Fanon's account of blackness as an
aesthetic dissonance can also be read in terms of a larger form of intermedial meaning-making that shapes mass media reception in Europe
from the mid-nineteenth century onward. As Jonathan Crary reminds
us, "The circulation and reception of *all* visual imagery is so closely
interrelated by the middle of the [nineteenth] century that any single
medium or form of visual representation no longer has a significant
autonomous identity. The meanings and effects of any single image are
always adjacent to this overloaded and plural sensory environment and
to the observer who inhabited it."[85] This communicational hybridization—or *hypermediation*, in today's parlance—that follows in the wake
of industrialization and mechanical reproduction creates, in Crary's
argument, an antiaesthetic distraction that constitutes the "central
feature of modernity" (*Techniques of the Observer*, 23). Offering a
historical and theoretical framework through which we can also read
Fanon's antiaesthetic aesthetic experiences in the movie theater, Crary
emphasizes the "adjacency" and a consequent amalgamation between
the body of the observer and surrounding images that determines the
meaning of a particular image: "Vision is always an irreducible complex of elements belonging to the observer's body and of data from an

exterior world" (70–71). For the author of *Black Skin*, however, the body—its epidermal schema—is itself, in part, a product of surrounding forms of mediation.

Furthermore, as Fanon demonstrates in *A Dying Colonialism*—offering another uncannily proleptic warning against aesthetic antiessentialism's celebration of semiotic failure—this body wounded by colonial capital does not necessarily require linguistic or visual "meaning" to be propelled toward identity. As my final example of aesthetic dissonance from Fanon will show, identity can materialize through the bodily remediation of even *the meaningless crackle of radiophonic sound*, split this time between the bodies of the colonized and the colonial radio apparatus in French-occupied Algeria.

As Macey notes, after spending three years working as a psychiatrist at the colonial hospital of Blida-Joinville in Algeria, Fanon resigned from his post to protest French imperialism and openly show his support for the Algerian anticolonial movement. He left his position in Blida-Joinville in 1956 and went into exile in Tunisia to join the National Liberation Front, headquartered in Tunis. *A Dying Colonialism* was published in 1959 as *L'an V de la révolution algérienne (Year Five of the Algerian Revolution)* and offers Fanon's firsthand experiences of the Algerian struggle as he worked with the National Liberation Front as a psychiatrist and a journalist.[86] In the second essay of this volume, titled "This is the Voice of Algeria," Fanon reflects on the impact that radio had as a mass medium on the Algerian Revolution and the emergence of a national consciousness.[87]

Fanon's focus on the complex politics of listening to the radio in colonial Algeria reveals how and why reception becomes intermedial not just in the context of visual imagery but also when nonvisual acoustic media are involved. Fanon points out that while "as an instrumental technique . . . the radio receiving set develops the sensorial, intellectual, and muscular powers of man in a given society" (*A Dying Colonialism*, 72), the colonizer and the colonized have contrasting relationships with the medium until the Algerian Revolution begins in 1954. As a technology invented in Europe, neither the French nor the Algerians can consider the radio "in calm objectivity" (73) or just in terms of its medium specificity.

From the French settler farmers' perspective, the act of listening to the radio—and specifically Radio-Alger broadcasts from Paris for French Algeria—is necessarily charged with an identification with Western

progress and the French civilizing mission. Radio becomes a prophy-
lactic against the culture of the colonized. As Fanon writes, "The Paris
music, extracts from the metropolitan press, the French government
crises, constitute a coherent background from which colonial society
draws its density and its justification. . . . Among European farmers,
the radio was broadly regarded as a link with the civilized world, as an
effective instrument of resistance to the corrosive influence of an
inert native society, of a society without a future, backward and devoid
of value" (71–72). Listening to the radio is firmly embedded in the
prejudicial dimension of the imaginary "call" of language and the colonizers' attachment to a "superior" French culture carried through the
airwaves. The Lacanian concept of the call is, in these instances, inseparable from radio as a delivery technology, insofar as the colonizers see
the technology also as a Western industrial achievement that can defy
geographical and linguistic barriers and carry mainland voices to the
colonial outpost.

In his inspiring philosophical and historical study of radio, John Mowitt identifies two significant properties of the medium that are highly
relevant in this context. First, in contrast to the indexical image of
cinema that typically attempts to immerse the viewer in a visual chro-
notope, the radiophonic voice creates an "interplanetary delocalization"
such that listeners are especially aware of their distance from the site
of transmission.[88] Mowitt makes clear that delocalization should not
be confused with "disembodiment," arguably because actual bodies are
always involved in both the transmission and reception of radio sound.
Second—and *because* of its delocalization of sound without the image—
the radio encourages a certain recontextualization or reprivatization of
its sonic transmissions (*Radio*, 83–84). For some cultural critics like
Walter Benjamin, this distance between the broadcaster and the listener, created by the particularity of radio technology, can lead to a more
active and critical form of listening. In Benjamin's view, as Mowitt also
notes, this potential is "wired into the radiophonic medium" and can
even undo the hierarchy between the "expert" broadcaster and the lay
listener, producing listeners with their own expertise and critical powers (76). The logic behind Benjamin's argument should sound familiar:
the properties of the radio as a medium can also become the site of its
transgressive uses.[89]

Mowitt, however, offers a compelling critique of Benjamin's celebration of radiophonic resistance by reminding us that "what needs to
be thought through in terms of delineating and practicing resistance are

the material conditions of its exercise" (82). Mediated instances of resistance need to be reassessed through "the structural character of the mass media" without confining critique to "the ethnographies of the agents of resistance, or at least not in some pretheoretical notion of agency devoid of structure" (82). These structural forms of mediation lie not just in the technologies shaping production and transmission but also in the institutional practices within which the technologies themselves remain grounded. Specifically, practices like the state regulating the nature of programming and bandwidth frequencies should prompt cultural critics to interrogate the privacy and critical agency purportedly accorded by radio technology (85–86).

Returning to Fanon's discussion of the French Algerian radio broadcasts, we note that the delocalization of the radiophonic voice, instead of distancing the French settler from the metropolitan site of transmission, exerts a magnetic pull through which the settler reaffirms his cultural difference from the colonized. The structural aspect of mediation is, in part, constituted by the French government's deployment of Radio-Alger as an aesthetically racializing and reassuring acoustic mirror in which the settler can hear his "own" voice. As Fanon notes, Radio-Alger functions as "a daily invitation" from the mainland to the settler, asking him "not to 'go native,' not to forget the rightfulness of his culture" (*A Dying Colonialism*, 71).

If, since its inception, French radio in Algeria transmits soothing voices that are supposed to ratify the white settler's self-worth as the general equivalent driving colonialism,[90] the same voices evoke a schizophrenic dissonance among the colonized. Referencing prewar monographs on hallucinations of Algerian subjects who repeatedly complain about highly aggressive "radio voices," Fanon writes,

> These metallic, cutting, insulting, disagreeable voices all have for the Algerian an accusing, inquisitorial character. The radio . . . already apprehended as an instrument of the occupation . . . assumes highly alienating meanings in the field of the pathological. . . . We have seen that the voice heard is not indifferent, is not neutral; it is the voice of the oppressor, the voice of the enemy. *The speech delivered is not received, deciphered, understood, but rejected.* . . . Before 1954, in the psychopathological realm, the radio was an evil object, anxiogenic and accursed. (88–89, emphasis added)[91]

What is striking in Fanon's account is the Algerians' *failure* to refuse or reject the radio. The voices cannot be kept out and their *jouissance* erupts through hallucinations of the colonized in spite of the refusal. In this context, Fanon's assertion at several moments in the chapter that Algerians in prerevolutionary Algeria hesitate to own radio sets and are indifferent to the medium (72–73, 92–93) needs to be qualified. Not owning a radio set did not mean the Algerians were, at any point, unaffected by the French radio apparatus or were unaware of its anti-colonial uses.[92] In fact, as Rebecca Scales points out, as early as 1934 the French government was concerned that the "natives" were tuning into anti-French Arab broadcasts from an unspecified location in Italy. By the mid-1930s, Algerian musicians and performers were using the microphones of Radio-Alger to challenge colonial authority and demand a greater role in governance.[93]

These early instances of the anticolonial use of the radio should not, however, lead us to ignore the psychosocial effects of the anxiety produced by the French deployment of the medium. Rather, we should see the early radiophonic anticolonialism as an effect, in part, of the aesthetic dissonance produced by the Parisian transmissions. That is to say, resistance to the Frenchness of Radio-Alger, paradoxically, follows from an incorporation of, or a certain "captivation" by, the "evil" object that represents colonial aggression, authority, and ethnocentrism. The radiophonic performance of an anticolonial national identity, we can say, is always already split (and not in any radical sense) between a wounded epidermal image of Arab Algerian "tradition" and the radio as a colonial technology of ethnocentric capitalism. As Mowitt aptly notes in his discussion of radiophonic anticolonialism in Fanon's essay, "Resistance, apart from indicating the stance of the colonizer, is here structurally conservative."[94] And as Fanon himself points out, by the late 1940s, European firms begin to profit from this ethnocentric history of the medium in Algeria by marketing sets through Algerian dealers, a move that ultimately contributes to a collective reinvention of radiophonic sound as the imagined ethnos in ways that perhaps the French government did not anticipate (*A Dying Colonialism*, 74).

Notably, according to Fanon, Algerians shift their stance decisively— from refusing the radio as an oppressive force to harnessing it as a technology for liberation—after Algeria joins the anticolonial front in the Maghreb in 1954. This shift becomes very clear with the launch of the radio broadcast called *Voice of Fighting Algeria* in 1956 (75, 84).

We can say that this is a shift from aesthetic dissonance to what Roelofs calls racialized aestheticization. Correspondingly, in psychoanalytic terms this is a move from experiencing the "meaning" of the radio as a fixed and oppressively colonial "refrain" to seizing it as the anticolonial "solution." Fanon describes the momentous shift in the following manner: "After 1954, the radio assumed totally new meanings. The phenomena of the wireless and the receiver set lost their coefficient of hostility, were stripped of their character of extraneousness, and became part of the coherent order of the nation in battle. In hallucinatory psychoses, after 1956, the radio voices became protective, friendly" (89). At the same time, Fanon makes it very clear that he sees this communal alteration of the meaning of the radio as a fallout of the systemic psychopathology and depersonalization created by colonialism. As he writes in a footnote, elaborating further on the parallel between the clinical and colonial contexts, "Plagued by his accusing 'voices,' the victim of hallucinations *has no other recourse but to create friendly voices*. This mechanism of transformation into its antithesis that we here point out *has its counterpart in the disintegrating colonial situation*" (89n7, emphasis added). Building on my Fanonian critique of Goux's theory of value, we can say that the dissonance inflicted by the colonial radiophonic voice as a general equivalent at once produces and is warded off by the fantasy of a *new* equivalent of the "friendly" Algerian national voice through which the colonized can assert their own identity as a competing exchange value. In this context, we should note that both the accusations and the assurances represented by the medium are also the result of widespread illiteracy in colonial Algeria, which made the radio more accessible than print media to the vast majority of the colonized population (82).[95]

The complexly intermedial production of a new Algerian identity comes to the fore in a noteworthy scene of radio reception in which Fanon describes the Algerians' efforts to listen to their own broadcasts in the face of French efforts to jam the transmission:

> The programs were then systematically jammed, and the *Voice of Fighting Algeria* soon became inaudible. A new form of struggle had come into being. . . . In the course of a single broadcast a second station, broadcasting over a different wave-length, would relay the first jammed station. The listener, *enrolled in the battle of the waves,* had to figure out the tactics of the enemy, and *in an almost physical way circumvent the strategy of the adversary.*

> Very often only the operator, *his ear glued to the receiver*, had the
> unhoped-for opportunity of hearing the *Voice*. The other Alge-
> rians present in the room would receive the echo of this voice
> through the privileged interpreter who, at the end of the broad-
> cast, was literally besieged. (85, emphasis added)

The struggle for and collectivization of anticolonial identity unfolds literally as well as metaphorically through an embodied relationship with
the radio. The literal or physical struggle of the Algerian operator to listen to the *Voice* by checking different wavelengths and "gluing" himself
to the radio set—a fusion that, I would argue, begins with his earlier
"refusal"—determines whether he can listen to the voice and, therefore,
what information he can glean about the revolution. Simultaneously,
in the "battle of the waves," the act of jamming and the circumven-
tion of that jamming become a metaphor for armed physical struggles
between the French military and the revolutionaries. From the Algerian perspective, owning a radio and "fighting" to listen to the broadcast
constitute a "virtual" means of participating in the war of independence:
"Having a radio meant paying one's taxes to the nation, buying the right
of entry into the struggle of an assembled people" (84).

It is hard to ignore Fanon's revolutionary optimism in these passages.
Writing in the fifth year of the revolution, which would continue for
three more years and thus beyond his death in 1961, Fanon is extremely
hopeful that the radio will play an exceptional role in the victory and
the future of the Algerian people. For instance, hearing the use of
French alongside the vernaculars of Arabic and Berber in the *Voice of
Fighting Algeria* leads him to observe that these multilingual broadcasts
are "an expression of a non-racial conception" of the emerging national
consciousness, which would be crucial to bridging ethnic and social differences *within* the Algerian population, to the task of "developing and
of strengthening the unity of the people" (84). Because of (the mediation by) the anticolonial broadcast, French is seemingly no longer the
oppressive cultural capital it was in *Black Skin*. It has instead become
"an instrument of liberation" (90).

Fanon's enthusiasm for these potentially liberatory broadcasts has led
political theorist James R. Martel to read the revolution as a paradigmatic
instance of anarchic "misinterpellation." For Martel, misinterpellation
is constituted by unexpected responses to liberal acts of interpellation,
wherein the unexpected or marginalized subject who is not supposed to
answer does so with an anarchic promise to change the system.[96] While

misinterpellation, he argues, is "built into the very system that would oppose and obfuscate it," it can also expose and productively expand the failure of liberal acts of interpellation (*Misinterpellated Subject*, 5). Examining the Algerian Revolution through Fanon's writings, Martel contends that the colonized perform a subversive misinterpellation by hijacking French radio and the French language, both being interpellative media initially meant for the colonizers and imperialist domination (123–25).

Two critical moves guide Martel's reading of Fanon. First, he is inspired by Benjamin's faith in radio's intrinsic capacity to empower the critical faculties of listeners (126). Second, he makes a firm distinction between (colonial) interpellation and "counterinterpellation meant to expose and ruin the workings of colonial subjectivity" (125). That is to say, for Martel, there is necessarily a gap between institutionally fostered moments of identification and "individual" radical acts of disidentification and resistance. Even as it arises out of (the failure of) the structure of interpellation, misinterpellation can break away from this structure and allow for "a plethora of identities and agencies, a cacophony of calls to emerge, formed out of resistance and struggle" (127).

I find Martel's call to action to look for alternatives to liberal capitalism to be infectious and uplifting in many ways. And, yet, such an anarchic celebration of identity-as-misinterpellation struggles to account for— and, therefore, has to distance itself from—the violence of nationalist identity politics that erupted in Algeria and many other newly decolonized countries in Africa and Asia.[97] My main reservation, here, is that Martel's theory of misinterpellation seems to posit "resistance" without paying enough attention to the racialized structure of misinterpellation or misrecognition that is constitutive of minoritizing interpellation and identity production under French colonialism. As I have argued above, for Fanon, being identified as the nonwhite colonized subject is always already coupled with disidentification. Every state-sanctioned act of social interpellation of the colonized begins as a misinterpellation. And this "structure of feeling" of being misinterpellated as black or Arab is actively fostered by the imperialist state and is, therefore, not a "byproduct" of interpellation that colonial capitalism cannot handle.[98] In fact, colonial capitalism purposefully mediates itself through practices of misinterpellation that split identity between the exchange value of the ideal image of Frenchness and the denigrated use value of the colonized. I have also suggested that the Algerian "refusal" of radio is, in reality, a coercive incorporation of the medium determined by

colonial misinterpellation. Martel's Benjaminian celebration of anticolonial radio relies on a disavowal of this coercive incorporation as well as
its long-term effects.

My point, here, is that it is only through an analysis of the systemic
forms of misinterpellation through which capitalism mediates itself that
we can track the *continuities* between colonial and postcolonial identity
politics. These continuities, in other words, need to be seen in terms
of structures of misinterpellation that are carried over by a commodity
economy, which is introduced on a global scale by colonialism and does
not end with decolonization. As several scholars have pointed out, the
endurance of this fundamentally inegalitarian commodity economy in
Algeria—indeed its "rebranding" through the rhetoric of national identity and state capitalism—was exemplified by an "economic nationalism"
that went hand in hand with calls for the "Arabization" of politics and
culture since the country's first constitution of 1963.[99] While nationalist demands for the adoption of classical Arabic as the official language
could be seen as a form of redress for decades of French cultural
imperialism, the state-sanctioned Arabization campaign has also led
to the violent marginalization and suppression of other dialects, languages, and freedom of speech in postcolonial Algeria. Commenting on
the rise of a new symbolic capital, the fundamental concept of which
bleeds into the postcolonial through the colonial, Khanna writes, "Arabic is also achieving the status that French once had in the region; it is
becoming the language of power designed to obliterate local cultures,
often for corrupt political ends" (*Algeria Cuts*, 76). There is no secure
distinction, then, between identity politics in this oppressive form—
still acting on its wounds rooted in the colonial past—and the "new"
identities about which Martel is optimistic. The worry, then, is that an
anarchic celebration of the "plethora of identities" produced through
misinterpellation risks ignoring the historical forms of political and aesthetic oppression that condition, endure, and, in that sense, ultimately
defeat the Algerian Revolution.[100]

I will conclude this discussion by noting how Fanon himself, in spite
of his optimism, cannot avoid voicing his own reservations. Although
stirred by the revolutionaries' use of French in their broadcasts, Fanon
briefly strikes a more vigilant tone, anticipating the linguistic antagonism that would persist in the postcolonial period: "Using the French
language was at the same time domesticating an attribute of the occupier and proving oneself open to the signs, the symbols, in short to *a
certain influence of the occupier*" (*A Dying Colonialism*, 91, emphasis

added). This anxiety of influence would, in fact, shape Algeria's decision to choose English as its second language, thereby further demoting French influence.[101]

Furthermore, Fanon's enthusiasm for the radiophonic construction of anticolonial identity is tinged with a reflexive awareness of the dangers of misinterpellation. Fanon tells us that, even as the French authorities' jamming of the radio signal often made the Algerian broadcasts choppy and broken, if not entirely inaudible, listeners would nevertheless fill in the gaps through a collective "autonomous creation of information" (*A Dying Colonialism*, 86). He goes on to describe the scene of collaborative reconstruction:

> Under these conditions, claiming to have heard the *Voice of [Fighting] Algeria* was, in a certain sense, distorting the truth. . . . It meant making a deliberate choice, though it was not explicit during the first months, *between the enemy's congenital lie and the people's own lie*, which suddenly acquired *a dimension of truth*.
>
> This voice, often absent, physically inaudible, which each one felt welling up within himself, founded on an inner perception of the Fatherland, became materialized in an irrefutable way. Every Algerian, for his part, broadcast and transmitted the new language. . . . The radio receiver guaranteed this true lie. (87, emphasis added)

In this account of radio listening, Fanon narrativizes the Algerian project of racialized aestheticization, its movement toward a climax in which, out of the radiophonic crackle, arises a new imaginary "mirror." This mirror reflects a postcolonial nation-to-be. As I noted earlier, in relation to the spectrum of meaning production that Lacan identifies in psychosis, with the launch of the Algerian broadcast, radio is no longer the insulting "refrain" for the colonized but rather the "word," or the enigmatic solution, to colonialism. Fanon draws our attention to the real, bodily, and unrepresentable materiality of the "truth" produced by this solution: the listeners cannot refuse what they claim to hear in the acoustic mirror, which they incorporate and then broadcast, transforming themselves into media. At the same time, Fanon reminds us of the *delusional quality* of this new narcissism, of its origins in the aesthetic dissonance produced by the "enemy's congenital lie." That is to say, albeit emerging in defiance of the fantasy that is the colonial project, the ideal image of the postcolonial nation—temporarily smoothing over differences among "the people"—becomes "true" as a reactive and severely wounded mechanical reproduction of that same project.[102] Because of this relationality, we can also call this new reactive lie an intermedial fantasy, constructed simultaneously by radio technology, revolutionary militancy, embodied and illiterate listening, and the limits of colonial power. Perhaps unintentionally, Fanon's gendered personification of this fantasy as "the Fatherland" becomes an eerie presentiment of the paternalizing form that Arabization would take in Algeria in the decades to come.[103]

To return one more time to the relationship between medium specificity and (failed) symbolic mediation in the colony, let us linger briefly in that static noise, that "active crackling" that precipitates the birth of the nation (A Dying Colonialism, 88). In radio and sound scholarship, the "static" is frequently described as the material substrate of radio listening, as meaningless noise upon which meaningful listening is experienced. As Derek P. McCormack writes, "Radio's atmospheric associations did not necessarily depend upon the broadcast of clearly audible speech or music. Rather, before the presence of a voice that makes meaningful sense, the crackle and buzz of radio noise already provided a field of background vibratory potential from which a sense of other worldly presences could be felt."[104] Described in these terms, meaningless radio noise is a nonlinguistic "presence" that precedes and shapes meaning without itself being reducible to meaning. As noted earlier, in theories of symbolic mediation, language—because of the structuring "lack" or "defect" in the signifier—becomes the privileged medium of experiencing the uncertainty of meaning and, therefore, avoiding the problem of identity. Fanon's emphasis on the identitarian and alienating consequences of the signifying crackle, however, forces us to rethink meaninglessness as a technologized experience that is not reducible to language and its formal properties. Relatedly, Fanon's account of the Algerian reception of the crackling signifier demands that theorists of subjectivation be attuned to the conditions under which the very lack of meaning materialized by the signifier becomes the grounds for differential experiences of identification, for affective transfers between "on air" bodies and listening bodies that are neither visible nor audible to each other. In this case, then, the material effects of radiophonic meaninglessness—or of "bad reception"—cannot be understood or ignored by insisting on the primacy of language, the subject of the symbolic order, or the latter's inability to secure meaning. Instead, these effects must be examined through a much broader understanding of the materiality of mediation and aesthetic reception. For N. Katherine Hayles, the "materiality" of an aesthetic medium or an object is not merely its medium-specific physical characteristics but rather "an emergent property created through dynamic interactions between physical characteristics and signifying strategies."[105] Fanon's representation of radiophonic noise certainly points in that direction, prompting us to note how identity emerges out of the welter of mediated meaninglessness of colonial violence and fragmentation, through "meaning-making practices in which communities of users/readers/interactors participate."[106]

Codetta

As a minoritizing constraint, identity is typically celebrated as resistive agency or dismissed as ideological fiction. In contrast, through Frantz Fanon's reflexive anticolonialism, this chapter has examined identity production as a hypermediated egoic fragmentation under French imperialism. The material realness of the identitarian fragment, I have suggested, lies in its origins and entrapment in the fiction of the racialized general equivalent driving the colonial mode of production. The psychoanalytic concept of the imaginary, I have also argued through Fanon, is especially useful to theorize the intermedial nature of identitarian fragmentation. The prevailing critical tendency is to view imaginary narcissism (and, therefore, identity) primarily in terms of neurotic identification and specular equivalence. This chapter has, instead, emphasized a multiply mediated schizophrenic structure of (dis)identification and dissonance that keeps the minoritized ego both bound to and alienated from the socially dominant ideal image. Finally, the chapter has offered a critique of the nonidentitarian "subject of language" by paying close attention to the role that French plays as the proverbial lingua franca, catalyzing identitarian fragmentation in the colonial scene. Yet as the rest of the book will argue, this intermedial dissonance is by no means confined to French colonialism; neither are its identitarian effects limited to colonialism as a historical event. As we shall see in chapter 2, Theresa Hak Kyung Cha's *Dictée* further develops the Fanonian analytic of the aesthetic wound to attend to the entanglements between colonial, postcolonial, and liberal democratic contexts of identity production.

Aesthetic Divides and Complicities in Theresa Hak Kyung Cha's *Dictée*

To be ethnic is to protest—but perhaps less for actual emancipation of any kind than for the benefits of worldwide visibility, currency, and circulation. Ethnic struggles have become, in this manner, an indisputable symptom of the thoroughly and irrevocably mediatized relations of capitalism and its biopolitics.
    —Rey Chow, *The Protestant Ethnic and the Spirit of Capitalism*

Artistic critique becomes the new defining critique of capitalist society. . . . Artistic critique, based on the antagonistic complementarity of bourgeois and bohemian, avant-garde art and the market, is transformed into the affirmative creativity of the new economy.
    —David Roberts, "From the Cultural Contradictions of Capitalism to the Creative Economy"

The domain of the aesthetic, as I have noted in the introduction and chapter 1, can simultaneously bolster conflicting approaches to identity politics. If Parker Bright and his followers wish to retrieve identity from the clutches of commodification through art and protest as art, antiessentialist artists and scholars see the aesthetic—or a particular aesthetic medium—as precisely that which has the potential to undo the imperialist egoism behind identity politics. In this chapter, I read Theresa Hak Kyung Cha's *Dictée* as a text that, in fact, reveals the complicities between these two apparently opposed modes of resistance to capitalist norms. In particular, I argue that *Dictée*'s formal intermediality offers provocative critiques of both Asian American and avant-garde aesthetic alternatives to identitarian essentialism.

My reasons for choosing Cha's text are, however, not only artistic but also historical. *Dictée* was published in 1982 against the backdrop of political conservatism and escalating military tensions between the United States and North Korea. As several commentators have argued, contemporary U.S. politics, marked by aggressive military fetishism and economic nationalism, is a product of as well as an eerie throwback to the nuclear and foreign policy during the years of President Ronald Reagan's administration. This comparison rings disturbingly apt as I draft this chapter in October 2017, as the USS *Ronald Reagan* patrols menacingly in waters east of the Korean Peninsula hoping to curb the "rogue" North Korea's nuclear ambitions, and as U.S. news networks (both liberal and conservative) continue to construe an absolute opposition between Western/U.S. democracy and North Korean ethnonationalism.[1] The relevance of Cha's text in this moment, I argue, also lies in its inconvenient but necessary historical reminder of the aesthetic production of ethnic identitarianism regulated by both colonialism and democratic capitalism.

Before going into the details of my argument, it will help to introduce the reader to the manifest aesthetic plurality of *Dictée*. Drawing on multiple genres (such as lyric and experimental poetry) and several media (literary, cinematic, and photographic), Cha's text defies description and classification. Fragmented by several languages and voices, it consistently refuses a single authorial position. *Dictée* is divided into nine sections, eight of them named after a Greek muse and her field of expertise, seemingly invoking a European/Western orientation or an epic tradition. But the heterogeneity of the content and stylistic choices in each section compels readers to continually adjust their cultural and geopolitical expectations. While *Dictée* is notoriously difficult to synopsize, I will point out three aesthetic-political modes for the purposes of my analysis. The first (literary) mode is constituted by reflections on Japanese colonialism in Korea and the Korean War from several, often anonymous, points of view. One of the prominent voices within this mode is that of a diasporic U.S.-based narrator writing to a Korean parent decades after the war. Of interest here are the narrator's meditations on the continuities as well as discontinuities between anticolonial nationalism, postcolonial ethnocentrism, and diasporic multiculturalism. I will provisionally refer to these reflections as corresponding to an ethnic-diasporic mode. The second (literary) mode in *Dictée* is that of experimental poetry that resembles Beckettian inner speech, often refusing to stabilize into a coherent speaking subject. Notable here are Cha's other narrators' meditations on the themes of writing, speaking, cinematic spectatorship, and patriarchal oppression. Last but not least, Cha's use of a visual mode—through uncaptioned photographs, photocopies, and Korean and Chinese inscriptions—repeatedly reminds the reader that *Dictée* is invested in representational practices that exceed the domain of the literary and may even be described as counterliterary.

A number of critics have noted how these multiple aesthetic modes and media in Cha's text at once relate to and undermine each other. Lisa Lowe, for instance, observes that, through its experimental style, *Dictée* foregrounds its formal preoccupation with "confluences and disjunctions . . . conflict and interdependency" between media.[2] And yet, these critics have largely ignored the ideological problematic implicit in Cha's emphasis on interdependency and intermediality. They have instead asserted the text's aesthetic—specifically literary—antiessentialism as its politicocultural value. This antiessentialist literary reading of Cha's text has taken two distinct but related forms. Some critics have read *Dictée*'s formalism as that which enables its author to produce a resistive and emancipatory literary voice that is ethnically specific but resists essentialist identity politics. This stance becomes most conspicuous in *Writing Self, Writing Nation*, an anthology that was published in 1994 (with essays by Lowe and other Asian Americanist scholars) and sought to claim Cha as a poststructurally inclined Korean American or Asian American feminist writer. Moving away from this recuperation of a nonessentialist "difference," other scholars like Juliana Spahr and Timothy Yu have argued that the literary avant-gardism of *Dictée* lies its ability to de-emphasize or even transcend altogether the political limits imposed by ethnic identifications.[3] My own argument in this chapter complicates both the Asian American and avant-gardist readings. I contend that through its enactment of the complicities and disjunctions between aesthetic modes and media, *Dictée* refuses to seek refuge in the literary and, instead, offers a multilayered narrative of identity production under colonial and neocolonial capitalism. In particular, I focus on the text's exposition of identitarian violence mediated at once through literary, cinematic, and photographic form.

Departing from the rhetoric of literary subversion dominating the reception of *Dictée*, I begin the chapter by examining how the text represents language as an agent of capital's coercive mediations. I suggest that what *Dictée* tracks is, in fact, the mobilization of linguistic form and content by the aesthetics of capitalist reification and identity production in ethnonational as well as liberal democratic contexts. Here I also show how, through its strategic deployment of experimental Language poetry, *Dictée* exposes an instance of what I have called *the cunning of capital*—the latter's ability to posit antirepresentational aesthetics as the "solution" to identity politics while masking its own aesthetic operations to sustain identitarian divides. The last two sections of the chapter turn to the visual mode in Cha's text. I first examine how *Dictée*'s reflections on cinematic form and spectatorship further reveal the limits of literary anti-identitarianism. I suggest that the text prompts the reader to read sexual difference as an identitarian dissonance inexorably regulated by a capitalist-cinematic "apparatus." And, in the final section, I argue that Cha's photographic formalism—even as it resists semiotic fixity—is haunted by a referentiality that demands to be read through the violence of colonial abstraction.

Institutionalized (Literary) Protest as Coercive Mimeticism

Arguably, language itself is a major character in *Dictée*. Yet contrary to what literary critics (both in the Asian American and avant-garde camps) have argued, it is difficult to see language as an emancipatory medium in the text. In the first half of *Dictée*, Cha's writing seems especially aware of language as a medium through which the subject is interpellated by the voice of dominant ideology and language as cultural capital. *Dictée* opens with a scene of language instruction—the verbatim transcription of a dictation exercise, including the utterances of compositional directions and punctuation marks. An approximate English translation of the French passage follows the transcription:

> Aller à la ligne C'était le premier jour point
> Elle venait de loin point ce soir au dîner virgule
> les familles demanderaient virgule ouvre les guil-
> lemets Ça c'est bien passé le premier jour point
> d'interrogation ferme les guillemets au moins
> virgule dire le moins possible virgule la réponse
> serait virgule ouvre les guillemets Il n'y a q'une

chose point ferme les guillemets ouvre les guille-
ments Il y a quelqu'une point loin point ferme
les guillemets

Open paragraph It was the first day period
She had come from a far period tonight at dinner
comma the families would ask comma open
quotation marks How was the first day interrogation mark close quotation marks at least to say
the least of it possible comma the answer would be
open quotation marks there is but one thing period
There is someone period From a far period
close quotation marks[4]

These transcriptions defamiliarize the familiar exercise of dictation
by overfollowing or misinterpreting the mandates of the exercise, spell-
ing out instructions and punctuation, and even visually replicating on
the printed page the different lengths of pauses taken or to be taken
by the speaker(s). Lowe notes succinctly that *Dictée* "proposes 'dictation' as its emblematic *topos*," where the formalized act of following
linguistic instruction is also the scene of ideology's self-reproduction:
"Dictation is at once a sign for the authority of language in the formation of the student, a model for the conversion of the individual into a
subject of discourse through the repetition of form, genre, and example,
and a metaphor for the many regulating reproductions to which the narrator is subject in spheres other than educational" ("Unfaithful to the
Original," 38, 39). The dictator demands an impeccable written reproduction or translation of what is dictated, just as institutions demand
perfect conformity to acts of interpellation. Yet in Lowe's view, Cha's
literary defamiliarization not only exposes the workings of the authoritarian structure of dictation but also becomes the means of revolting
against that interpellative structure: "The subject of *Dictée* recites poorly,
stutters, stops. . . . She fails to imitate the example, is unfaithful to the
original" (39). This linguistic defiance of the interpellating voice, Lowe
contends, is evidence of Cha's (and, by extension, Asian American)
"female difference" (42) resisting the ideology of "faithful reproduction"
(41) and "the ideal of equivalence" (42) often guiding literary debates
on translation and authenticity.[5]
    Such a reading of resistance, however, overlooks the fact that, while
the writing subject in Cha's preface deviates from the norms of dictation,

there is nothing in the deviations themselves that indicate consequences beyond their textualization. Simply put, there is no way to confirm if these performances constitute a student's rebellious responses (i.e., if the student is aware of them as such) or if they are syntactically "incorrect" responses demonstrating the "incompetent" student's extreme internalization of the dictational norms and, therefore, their sheer ideological power. Moreover, as several critics have noted, *Dictée* is prominently attuned to the historical role of language as an instrument of colonial and neocolonial domination. Lowe herself acknowledges the presence of this Fanonian insight in the prefatory passages:

> The translation of the French example into English not only breaks with the formal rules of dictation, but as English is itself an adopted "foreign" language for the Korean subject, the representation of the dictation is from the outset already a fictionalized amalgam that allegorizes the historical influences of both American imperialism and an earlier French missionary colonialism. . . . The choice of English as the translating language . . . registers the increased suppression of the Korean language with the imposition of each western colonial language. (40–41)

Here Lowe contravenes her own argument about aesthetic infidelity by (rightly) pointing out that both English and French have long been capitalist instruments of cultural oppression. (This, obviously, is true not just for Korea but for several Asian and African countries.) Therefore, even if we assume that the consecutive passages in *Dictée*'s preface signal an act of transcription undertaken by a single subject, it remains unclear what kind of "break" from cultural imperialism—or the underlying commodification of a particular language—is achieved by the purposive or inadvertent (mis)translation from one colonizing language into another.[6] As well, Lowe's own reference to cultural imperialism suggests that the tactic of aesthetic infidelity may be the privilege of only those bi- or multilingual subjects who have access to English and French as cultural capital.[7]

Notably, Lowe's celebration of *Dictée* as a subversive "Asian American text . . . a woman's text" (35) represents a larger desire within Asian American studies in the 1990s to isolate a diasporic-feminist literary politics of difference that is critical of identity-as-essence while still holding on to ethnic and gendered particularities. Indeed, essays by several other contributors in *Writing Self* also repeat, to different degrees, this critical move to see language as *the* medium that allows *Dictée* to claim a (paradoxically) nonidentitarian identity politics. For instance, commenting on Cha's use of nonnormative speech, Shelley Sunn Wong writes, "To utter in this way is to undermine identity and to make difference visible again."[8] In a similar vein, L. Hyun Yi Kang notes that the "language of *Dictée* is multiple and ever-shifting—words and voices are decentered, recalled from the margins, exclusive, unclaimed, indecipherable, and then again viscerally clear."[9] For all these critics, it is Cha's turn to the "inherent ambiguity and instability of . . . language" (Kang, "'Liberatory Voice,'" 88) that makes *Dictée* a nonessentialist and yet Asian American text. While *Writing Self* does not explicitly invoke Derridean or Lacanian literary criticism, it would not be far-fetched to claim that what is at work here is, in fact, an Asian American version of a language-bound theory of subjectivation. Rephrasing the collective claim of the authors of *Writing Self* in terms of the deconstructionist-psychoanalytic theory of linguistic mediation discussed in chapter 1 of the present volume, we can say that even as Cha's text disrupts the field of U.S. literatures through its Asian or Korean American difference, it adopts a literary formalism that can displace essentialist identityspeak through the medium specificity of language as a system of differences, of signifiers without fixed signifieds.[10]

In *The Cultural Capital of Asian American Studies*, Mark Chiang provocatively argues that, in the 1990s, Asian American studies turned to this well-established "brand" of Euro-American literary formalism to secure institutional legitimacy in the U.S. academy.[11] More specifically, the language-bound politics of difference that Asian Americanists found in *Dictée* served as a much-needed academic capital at a time when political capital in the form of ethnic specificity had reached an impasse and, in fact, conflicted with the neoliberal university's domestication of insurgent difference.[12] As Chiang writes, "*Dictée* facilitated a critique of identity politics and its aesthetics of realist representation and authentic (or positive) depictions. What 'difference' made possible in this context was the elaboration of a politics of form rather than content, which meant that Asian American literary studies could recalibrate its scale of value so that it would correlate with the structures of value in the dominant cultural field" (133). Thus, in Chiang's view, *Dictée* gave Asian American studies the cultural capital it needed through an ideological and stylistic kinship with a canonical and esteemed Euro-American politics of form. This kinship allowed not just Cha's text but also Asian American literary studies to be recognized within the academy.

Chiang's attention to literary form-as-value in the U.S. humanities resonates deeply with my critique of disciplinary fetishism and the aesthetic cunning of capital throughout this book. But it does not quite follow from Chiang's discussion (since he does not actually offer a reading of *Dictée*) that Cha's formalism is congruent with mainstream literary antiessentialism, or that her text encourages an easy separation of form from content, or even that its formalism is solely *literary*.

To begin to move beyond this dominant reception of Cha's experimentalism as unadulterated literary formalism, let us return to *Dictee*'s prefatory passages. As noted above, the use of French and English in the scene(s) of dictation serve to foreground not so much a decontextualized performance of aesthetic infidelity as the persistence of these languages as agents of cultural imperialism. Cha's stuttering speaker, then, does not so much deviate from as draw our attention to the norms that *all* speakers of these languages have to internalize and master to be recognized as "competent" users. Put differently, Cha's representation of certain formalized rules of writing and speech alert us to their cultural force and political persistence well beyond the scene(s) of dictation with which the text opens. This formalism—where the medium of language confesses to its ideological uses through a performative denaturalization—is also an early indicator of what I would describe as the self-consciously open structure of *Dictée*. If the intermediality of *Dictée* tries to resist anything from the very beginning, it is the critical attempt to read the text as a self-contained aesthetic totality in which an idealized "hybrid" Asian American voice performs individualized acts of linguistic defiance. My goal in this chapter, then, is also to rescue *Dictée* from this well-trodden narrative of literary resistance.

Relatedly, I would argue that if Francophone and/or Anglophone readers find Cha's ungrammatical passages to be momentarily alienating, that alienation also functions as a subtle reminder of the *differential and disparate labors* of everyday acts of linguistic transcription and translation. While Cha does not tell us if the two passages are written by "native" speakers of English or French, both passages thematically introduce a female figure who has "come from afar," a female migrant navigating an unfamiliar language in a new country. (This gendered figure will become a recurring presence, further troubling Lowe's theory of literary resistance, especially in Cha's more experimental sections.) Thus, the appearance of this figure in these prefatory passages— mimicking the terse and fragmented form of telegraphic messages that also come from afar—signals to readers *Dictée*'s interest in representing the splitting of the subject and subjective identities under various technological and institutional systems of mediation.

Such a reading of the opening dictation passages is in keeping with my larger focus in this book on the structural inequality of capitalist equivalence that shapes the intermediations of difference-as-identity. But more important, such a reading also fits with the passage in *Dictée* that immediately follows the dictation scene(s). In this passage, Cha presents a female figure who appears to be "at the moment of entering a system of signification."[13] This figure is ironically called a *diseuse* (French for "a chatty person"), since she struggles to repeat the utterances of others, to mimic "accurate" speech:

> She mimicks [*sic*] the speaking. That might resemble speech. (Anything at all.) Bared noise, groan, bits torn from words. Since she hesitates to measure the accuracy, she resorts to mimicking gestures with the mouth. The entire lower lip would lift upwards then sink back to its original place. She would then gather both lips and protrude them in a pout taking in the breath that might utter some thing. (One thing. Just one.) But the breath falls away. With a slight tilting of her head backwards, she would gather the strength in her shoulders and remain in this position. (3)

In this passage, Cha draws the reader's attention to the expressive body of failing or aborted linguistic utterance, to the physical dimension of the speaker's failure to produce "accurate" speech. The speaker's "groans" evoke and are yet distinct from what Stephen Best and Saidiya Hartman have called "black noise"—marginalized extralinguistic utterances defined primarily in terms of their negative relation to capitalism.[14] Unlike the captive black slave, Cha's speaker actually attempts to conform to linguistic norms and to mimic the speech of others. Her anxieties around accuracy produce moments between silence and speech in which her body is both ready to and prevented from inserting itself into language. While Cha does not offer us any empirical or sociocultural information about the speaker in this passage, her description recalls, nevertheless, Frantz Fanon's critique of failing symbolic mediation in the colonial imaginary. Much like the Martinican in *Black Skin* who physically struggles to "roll his *r*'s," to imitate and embody the ideal image of the universal linguistic-racial equivalent,[15] Cha's speaker attempts to insert herself into a language through bodily gestures and noises that ultimately take the place of meaningful speech. Cha's meticulous description of the movement of the speaker's lips, shoulders, head, and breath foreground the labor behind every act of signification. But once again, Cha alerts readers to *the relativity of the experience of this labor*—the speaker, at this point, is unable to fully emulate the norms of accuracy internalized and performed by the others: "She allows herself [to be] caught in their threading, anonymously in their thick motion in the weight of their utterance" (4). She cannot be "heard" on the page, except through silent parenthetical inner speech that signifies her desperation to speak, to say "Anything at all."

In an italicized passage that follows this description and moves the text into that space of inner speech, Cha focuses on the conflicted state of the speaker who is wounded by the failed attempt at speech and the ensuing silence: "*It murmurs inside. It murmurs. Inside is the pain of speech the pain to say. Larger still. Greater than is the pain not to say. To not say. Says nothing against the pain to speak. It festers inside. The wound, liquid, dust. Must break. Must void*" (3, emphasis in the original). What are the origins of this painful wound? If the wound is produced by the inability to speak, that inability originates in the linguistic norms represented by the speech of other speakers, "in the weight of their utterance." In other words, the speaker's psychic and somatic wound is governed by the speech of (imaginary) others.

This linguistic pain—which flows imperceptibly into and within the speaker like a "liquid" but also feels like solid "dust" blocking her organs of speech—is reminiscent of Fanon's description of the epidermal schema and Françoise Dolto's account of the wounded unconscious body image (see chapter 1). Both these wounded self-images constituting the subject's physical and social awareness of herself, we will recall, are created through the aesthetic dissonance of linguistic mediation. Similarly, it is language from and as imaginary otherness that constitutes and materializes the speaker's body in Cha's preface: "She allows others. In place of her. Admits others to make full. Make swarm. All barren cavities to make swollen. The others each occupying her. Tumorous layers, expel all excesses until in all cavities she is flesh" (3–4). There is a marked ambiguity in this process of (the speech of) others turning into tumorous or pathological flesh of the speaker. Initially, Cha suggests there is some form of agency involved, where the speaker "allows" entry to the others. At the same time, Cha seems to acknowledge that the speaker is constituted by otherness that is also beyond her control, making the "occupation"—which the speaker is observing and ostensibly allowing—to be a fait accompli.[16] As Fanon's example with the

Martinican also reminds us, this indeterminacy between agency and conformity, freedom and subjection, is characteristic of the process of acquiring cultural competence, of becoming a (competent) "subject" with exchange value. In Cha's example, however, the speaker seems to be paralyzed in a reflexive moment in the margins of the transactional economy of language. She is figured as a witness to the force of otherness that occupies and swarms within her while she is unable to occupy or swarm in a reciprocal manner. In that sense, Cha's *diseuse* has even less agency than Fanon's elite Martinican.

The institutional nature of this otherness that at once grants agency to and oppresses the narrator becomes clearer in a later passage in Cha's preface, where dictation gives way to a catechetic dialogue. This exchange—structured in a question-and-answer format—is also represented as a scene of (mis)interpellation where a (Christian) subject is hailed as being identical with God's "mirror image":

> *Q. WHO MADE THEE?*
> *A. God made me.*
> *To conspire in God's Tongue.*
> *Q. WHERE IS GOD?*
> *A. God is everywhere.*
> *Accomplice in His Texts, the fabrication in His Own Image, the pleasure the desire of giving Image to the word in the mind of the confessor.*
> *Q. GOD WHO HAS MADE YOU IN HIS OWN LIKENESS*
> *A. God who has made me in His own likeness. In his Own Image in His Own Resemblance, in His Own Copy, In His Own Counterfeit Presentment, in His Duplicate, in His Own Reproduction, in His Cast, in His Carbon, His Image and His Mirror. Pleasure in the image pleasure in the copy pleasure in the projection of likeness pleasure in the repetition. Acquiesce, to the correspondence. Acquiesce, to the messenger. Acquiesce, to and for the complot in the Hieratic tongue. Theirs. Into Their tongue, the counterscript, my confession in Theirs. Into Theirs.* (17–18, emphasis in the original)

Cha's representation of religious ideology in this scene is markedly Althusserian. Religion becomes a specular relation of moral accountability between two subjects, the first being subjected to the second—the (masculine) figure of "God."[17] Significantly, in Cha's rewriting of the catechetic exchange, the response recasts religious devotion as unrelenting acts of "confession" and "acquiescence," highlighting the relations of power and implicit coercion governing Christian instruction. In this rescripting of catechism-as-confession, Cha's writing once again restages the indeterminacy between conformity and individual agency, alienation and identification. At one level, the capitalization of the questions directs the reader's attention to the hierarchy between the two voices. The hierarchy is also made visible through the final question offered as a statement of fact—"*GOD WHO HAS MADE YOU IN HIS OWN LIKENESS*"—as an already-learned lesson that the response repeats and further explicates. The mirror of religious rhetoric has already taught the subject(ed) ego to take the divine male image as its own, to take pleasure in the projective identification with "His" image in language. At another level, however, Cha's use of words like "conspire" and "complot" in the responses—as well as her emphasis on the masculinist nature of religious instruction—make this catechetic dialogue explicitly ironic.

Early on in the exchange, it becomes clear that Cha is not merely repeating standard catechetic responses but inserting an "active" respondent into the exchange, one who wishes to use God's language to plot against divine authority. While the respondent's own gender remains elusive, Cha's writing foregrounds the gap between the question's insistence on ideological conformity and the respondent's alienation accompanied by a recognition of the gendered hierarchy reinforced by religious authority. In fact, Cha's respondent subtly recalls Luce Irigaray's observation that the dominant account of subjectivation "has always been appropriated by the 'masculine.'"[18] The speaker's identity, then, stems from this skeptical awareness of a nonmasculine subordinate position, a dissonance between the speaker's self-perception and the divine ideal image of masculine authority.

Thus, we can say that Cha's passage deviates from Louis Althusser's scene of reduplication in two ways. First, the respondent does not want to be merely "accountable" to God. The respondent also wants to protest or conspire against God, perhaps even take God's place. But there is a second movement in or twist to the respondent's confession. The respondent's desire for protest is also distinguished by an awareness or an *anxiety that the individual act of plotting will turn into a collective counterconfession or counterinterpellation*: "Acquiesce, to and for the complot in the Hieratic tongue. Theirs. Into their tongue, the counterscript, my confession in Theirs. Into Theirs." What I am underscoring is the respondent's final ambivalence around the *collectivization* of the protest and minoritarian counterscript. The respondent is aware that this complot or conspiracy in and against the "Hieratic tongue" can demand a new form of acquiescence to a collective "God," thereby *turning into a new form of interpellation that promises "freedom" through subjection.* Thus, instead of simply celebrating the "unfaithful" counterscript,[19] *Dictée*'s preface provocatively calls on the reader to reflect further on this predicament of identification-as-alienation, to think of the circumstances under which the alienated voice might find its individual counterscript to be coopted by a collective, still "Hieratic," and, therefore, institutionalized "tongue."

In this way, the respondent's suspicion of the collective domestication of dissent emerges as a prefiguration of more contemporary diagnoses of capital's absorption of minority difference. Here *Dictée* anticipates Chiang's diagnosis of the institutionalization of Asian American studies as well as a highly influential critique of *the confessional form* acquired by minority protests under late capital. In her widely cited book *The Protestant Ethnic and the Spirit of Capitalism,* Rey Chow uses the term "coercive mimeticism" to mean a confessional mode of self-representation, of continual self-disclosure through which the marginalized subject rebels against dominant ideology.[20] Ultimately, the terms of this confession, Chow argues, remain coercively bound to dominant understandings of difference regulated by racialized labor and capital. Drawing on Michel Foucault's critique of the confessional turn in Western society—where self-referentiality has come to stand for an apparently unmediated nonrepresentational "truth"—Chow writes,

> In Foucault's analysis, self-referential speaking is not only *not* the individual or unique way out of the errors of representation that it is often imagined to be; it is also the symptom of a collective subjection. To represent, to examine, to confess about oneself incessantly are compulsive acts that imagine the self as a refuge beyond the reach of power—an alibi from speaking (of anything), so to speak—when the self is simply a relaying vehicle for institutional forces of rational systematization at the individual level. (*Protestant Ethnic,* 114–15)

In Chow's reading of Foucault, the confession as a form of protest binds the subject to structures of power that can accommodate seemingly resistant forms of mimeticism. The confessional turn, in fact, is a sign of the subjection of entire groups to those same structures.

Notably, this confessional and coercive mimeticism—the paradigmatic instance of which is to be found in the field of cultural labor like "Asian American literature"—is also the process that can explain the production and containment of the protestations of "ethnic" difference and identity (Chow, *Protestant Ethnic*, 125). As Chow notes in the first epigraph to this chapter, "to be ethnic" under contemporary capitalism is "to protest," to labor to disclose continually one's ethnic specificity (48). Drawing on the work of Max Weber, Chow further argues that this assertion of ethnic difference is to be understood through a certain "spiritual" dimension of capitalism, a secularization of the Christian notion of labor as the means to salvation (43). Yet what is obtained through these labors of confession is not actual "salvation" from the categories of ethnic difference but a certain amount of social visibility and recognition as ethnocultural capital.[21] In other words, the rewards of being able to commoditize confessions of difference also keep the laboring protestant ethnic trapped within racial hierarchies subtending capitalism (24).

Additionally, Chow's theory of coercive mimeticism emphasizes an ineluctably *collective* dimension of ethnicity that originates in a "thwarted narcissism" of the ethnicized subject under U.S. democratic liberalism (249). In Freudian psychoanalysis, narcissism is often seen as an asocial stage of self-absorption that all subjects pass through but must eventually give up to become social subjects.[22] But for subjects who belong to minoritized ethnic groups, the opportunity for narcissistic solipsism is quite limited, since the conventional distinction between the individual and the collective cannot be maintained in these instances. As Chow writes,

> In the case of the Asian American . . . the narcissism that is thwarted is not necessarily individualistic in nature. Indeed, precisely because the label "Asian American" (and its equivalents in American society, such as "African American" and "Native American") is construed as relating to a minority culture or minority community that mediates between the single individual and society at large, its status is that of an extra category—one that is neither strictly a private, personal self nor strictly a public society that includes everybody. (*Protestant Ethnic*, 141)

The ethnic quest for a narcissism that has been denied to an entire group—or the protestation of ethnic difference—is, by definition, a collective affair that exceeds the individual ethnic subject. Ethnicized self-assertion is, therefore, not self-referential or autobiographical in any simple sense. Yet the transindividual protestation of ethnic difference from the mainstream is "freedom" with subjection precisely because the naming of that difference is also determined and controlled by the mainstream. In other words, unlike the authors of *Writing Self*, Chow does not see the celebration of ethnic difference—however internally heterogeneous that difference might claim to be—as separable from the capitalist logic that creates racial and ethnic differences. The uncomfortable question to pose, then, is not how minority difference has resisted capitalism, but rather how these differences have been managed by capitalist forces that have endured through their flexibility and mutability: "How does the 'inner' human force—including especially the soulful force of resistance and protest—come about *in* capitalism and further enhance the progress of capitalism?" (*Protestant Ethnic*, 46, emphasis in the original). The "spirit" of capitalism, in Chow's estimation, has played a fundamental role in producing the performative structures of ethnicized identity and difference.

Dictée offers us subtle intimations of this confessional spirit from its early passages. As we noted above, through its allusion to Althusser, the catechetic exchange in Cha's preface points to a certain continuity between religious and capitalist modes of mystification. The religious confession misinterpellating the minoritized respondent mirrors and is mirrored by the capitalist mode of production. Simultaneously, like Chow, the respondent in *Dictée*'s preface confronts both the actualization and the co-optation of the minoritarian counterscript, one that the respondent cannot prevent, after all, from becoming "theirs." This, I would argue, is *Dictée*'s reflexive prefatory voice, which remains suspicious of the power of minoritarian cultural protests to dismantle capitalism and its oppressive production of identity-as-alienation. Cha's preface does not tell us anything more about the substance and form of these counterconfessions. But it does foreshadow, as I demonstrate below, *Dictée*'s representation of both ethnic identitarianism and nonidentitarian experimentalism as competing protest aesthetics regulated by the capitalist mode of production. That is to say, instead of privileging form or aesthetics over identity politics, *Dictée* reveals how ethnonationalism and avant-gardism are both aesthetic and yet incommensurable acts of coercive mimeticism. In the following section, I turn to Cha's exploration of the formal operations behind ethnonationalism, of ethnic identity as an aesthetic wound of colonial-capitalist abstraction.

Identity as an Aesthetic Wound of Colonialism
and Liberal Democracy

Cha's commentary on the origins of ethnonationalism in colonial capitalism is most conspicuous in the first half of *Dictée*. Again, echoing
Fanon on language as a vital mediator of colonial capitalism, the first
two sections of the text delve into the linguistic aspect of modern Korean
nationalism, which emerges in the wake of Japanese occupation in the
early twentieth century.[23] After paying tribute to the forgotten Korean
revolutionary Yu Guan Soon and acknowledging the difficulty of retriev-
ing her story from official historical records, the narrator in the section
titled "Clio History" observes,

> Japan has become the sign. The alphabet. The vocabulary. To
> *this* enemy people. The meaning is the instrument, memory that
> pricks the skin, stabs the flesh . . . that rests as record, as docu-
> ment. Of *this* enemy people.
>
> To the other nations who are not witnesses, who are not sub-
> ject to the same oppressions, they cannot know. Unfathomable
> the words, the terminology: enemy, atrocities, conquest, betrayal,
> invasion, destruction. They exist only in the larger perception of
> History's recording, that affirmed, admittedly and unmistakably,
> one enemy nation has disregarded the humanity of another. . . .
>
> To the others, these accounts are about (one more) distant
> land, like (any other) distant land, without any discernible fea-
> tures in the narrative, (all the same) distant like any other.
> (32–33, emphasis in the original)

Language, the narrator reminds us, is central to the colonial wounding through which Korea is compelled to view itself under Japanese
rule. The overwhelming racialized presence of the Japanese state and
its prosthetic use of the Japanese alphabet together function as the
determinant "meaning" that "pricks" and "stabs" the Korean body. This
wounding mediated by the state and its linguistic imperialism leads to
an anticolonial dissonance or (dis)identification that is somatic as well
as aesthetic, derived from but not reducible to representation, at once
imaginary and real. As in Fanon, the narrator's emphasis is not on aesthetics per se but on what Monique Roelofs has called the "coloniality
as a form of aesthetic relationality," on anticolonialism as a physical, perceptual, and intermedial process shaped by colonial capitalism.[24]

It is worth noting that the narrator also emphasizes the impossibility of "knowing" or feeling that dissonance without being a "witness" to or living through such a political and aesthetic oppression. Instead of dismissing the narrator's position as "cultural essentialism,"[25] I would argue that this emphasis on the geopolitically specific resonance of the capital-bound sign "Japan" sounds particularly contrapuntal when read alongside poststructuralist literary criticism, and specifically Roland Barthes's 1970 *Empire of Signs*. I am thinking here of Barthes's touristic celebration of the mobility of the linguistic signifier. Let us recall that Barthes's insistence in *Empire*, on the "meaninglessness" of the fictive "text" called "Japan"—and his desire to transcend the fixity of meaning—is predicated on his ability to separate himself from the country, its people, and its (colonial) history *as a distant tourist*. As Barthes observes upon his arrival in Japan in the 1960s,

> The murmuring mass of an unknown language constitutes a delicious protection, envelops the foreigner (provided the country is not hostile to him) in an auditory film which halts at his ears all the alienations of the mother tongue: the regional and social origins of whoever is speaking, his degree of culture, of intelligence, of taste, the image by which he constitutes himself as a person and which he asks you to recognize. Hence, in foreign countries, what a respite! *Here I am protected against stupidity, vulgarity, vanity, worldliness, nationality, normality. . . . I live in the interstice, delivered from any fulfilled meaning.*[26]

Barthes's status as a French tourist who does not speak or comprehend Japanese becomes the cornerstone for his representation of Japan as a mysterious empty sign. In contrast, the narrator of "Clio History" reminds us that colonized Koreans do not have the privilege of that protective envelope of ignorance and cannot, therefore, luxuriate in what Barthes calls the "opacity" of the Japanese language (*Empire*, 10).[27] In other words, Cha's narrator suggestively points out that it is only through a privileged indifference to colonial capitalism—and to the stark difference between Japan's political treatment of France and Korea—that the French critic can theorize a fictive Japan as a collection of fluid signs and erotic bodies "without hysteria, without narcissism" (Barthes, *Empire*, 10). It is that indifference that Cha's narrator wants to put aside to evaluate Korean ethnonationalism in relation to the racialized logic of Japanese colonialism. The section titled "Calliope Epic Poetry" continues reflecting on Korean anticolonialism, this time through a reenactment of the narrator's mother's experiences of linguistic repression under Japanese rule:

> You speak the tongue the mandatory language like the others. It is not your own. . . . The tongue that is forbidden is your own mother tongue. . . . The one that is yours. Your own. You speak very softly, you speak in a whisper. In the dark, in secret. Mother tongue is your refuge. It is being home. Being who you are. . . . To utter each word is a privilege you risk by death. Not only for you but for all. All of you who are one, who by law tongue tied forbidden of tongue. You carry at center the mark of the red above and the mark of blue below, heaven and earth, tai-geuk; t'ai-chi. It is the mark. The mark of belonging. Mark of cause. Mark of retrieval. (Cha, *Dictée*, 45–46)

The concept of being at home in one's mother tongue or of belonging produced by linguistic unification would be anathematic to prevalent deconstructionist-psychoanalytic approaches to language, where one is never at home in one's language and, as a subject of language, one is always already a stranger to oneself. Again, Cha's narrator deftly shows how such antihumanist and language-bound alternatives to essentialism need to contend with the multiply mediated processes through which the Japanese repression of the Korean language fuels an embodied nationalism. Much like the Algerian scenario that Fanon recounts in *A Dying Colonialism* (see chapter 1), the decolonizing investment in "the nation"—exemplified here by the *tai-geuk*, or yin-yang symbol, on the nineteenth-century Korean flag—cannot but be a wounded repetition of the logic set in motion by Japanese colonial capitalism. The linguistic suppression introduced by the latter informs and morphs into an affective attachment to the Korean flag, a visual and aesthetic proxy for the postcolonial nation-to-be.

Such reflections on identity production in *Dictée* thus demand a rethinking of the dominant critical opinion that Cha's text "refuses" or "rejects" identity politics. In fact, my position is that Cha takes on the challenging task of historicizing ethnonationalism even as some of her narrators and readers remain somewhat removed from that ethnonationalism for historical reasons. In a later section called "Melpomene Tragedy," the narrator admits to not having access to Korean as a "mother tongue" (unlike the mother in the previous passage) by virtue of being interpellated differently as an immigrant in another country: "I speak in another tongue now, a second tongue a foreign tongue" (80). The narrator's use of the word "foreign," however, suggests that the colonial ethnonational wounds sustaining the identitarian native/foreign distinction persist in that historical moment of articulation.

Moreover, even from the narrator's own sociohistorical position, being a transnational diasporic subject does not mean a reprieve from identity politics or its capitalist logic. The narrator of "Calliope Epic Poetry" describes identity production as a form of alienation caused by the bureaucratic process of *belonging* to a nation, of becoming a U.S. citizen. This is a process that triggers a psychic splitting:

> I have the documents. Documents, proof, evidence, photograph, signature. One day you raise the right hand and you are American. *They give you an American Pass port.* The United States of America. *Somewhere someone has taken my identity and replaced it with their photograph. The other one. Their signature their seals. Their own image.* And you learn the executive branch the legislative branch and the third. Justice. Judicial branch. *It makes the difference.* The rest is past. (56, emphasis added)

Recalling the scene of coercive mimeticism from the preface—where individual identity is subsumed under institutionalized collectivization—the narrator of *Dictée* offers a pithy and yet strikingly materialist account of the production of U.S. identity. This identity is produced, according to the narrator, through a certain erasure of an existing or prior identity. Citizenship, we might say, is represented as a formal process where the prior identity is replaced with the reconstructed and abstract image of "the U.S. citizen." This image is symbolically ratified by the U.S. state, but it also produces an aesthetic dissonance in the narrator who no longer recognizes the self in that form. While this expropriation applies to all citizens, it is felt as a palpable loss by the immigrant narrator being reconstructed into a citizen. This new identity, for which the passport serves as material proof, is coconstituted by and, therefore, perceptually split between the narrator's own body, a government-approved photograph that bears that body's imprint, official seals and signatures, and linguistic-cultural labors that the narrator performs to pass a citizenship test administered by the state. Here *Dictée* foregrounds the various kinds of governmental mediation through which the narrator's new identity as a citizen is produced as being "different" from the prior identity of being a foreign national and noncitizen. Additionally, I would suggest that in this passage, Cha's text invites us to see the passport—which is perhaps the most sought after and surveilled identity document because it legitimizes the citizen in the eyes of the U.S. government—as a "media text" or mediating agent whose affective significance is frequently ignored by both aesthetic celebrations and dismissals of identity politics.

Dictée, however, does not treat the prior foreign identity of the narrator as an essence to be idealized. While the narrator does not tell us how this non-U.S. identity came to be produced, its romantic nationalist character surfaces briefly in the narrator's emotional response to coethnics—immigration and security officials at the airport—during a visit to the former homeland: "I know you I know you, I have waited to see you for long this long" (58). But this knowledge is decisively undermined through an antianagnoristic scene where the same coethnics refuse to recognize the narrator as one of their own:

> You return and you are not one of them, they treat you with indifference. All the time you understand what they are saying. But the papers give you away. Every ten feet. They ask you identity. They comment upon your inability or ability to speak. Whether you are telling the truth or not about your nationality. They say you look other than you say. As if you didn't know who you were. You say who you are but you begin to doubt. They search you. . . . Their authority sewn into the stitches of their costume. (56–57)

If, as Chandan Reddy argues, "to occupy the place and logic of the U.S. citizen is to situate oneself structurally, and willy-nilly, within an imperial neoliberal state and social formation," then that structural position created by liberal democracy—represented by U.S. identity documents and "foreign" speech in the passage above—fragments the narrator anew in the presence of coethnic government agents in the former home country.[28] The narrator's sense of belonging to a people and a nation is eroded irreversibly by the lack of correspondence that the officers notice between a "native" appearance and "nonnative" speech and documents. Crucially, from the narrator's point of view, this ethnocentrism is not solely located in or reflected by the questions posed by individual officials. Rather, its origins are more insidious, systemic, and formal, "stitched" to the officials' uniforms and, therefore, to a coercive authority and mimeticism orchestrated by the state apparatus. By the end of the narrator's reconstruction of this encounter, the nostalgic mirage of "knowing" one's coethnics or ethnic identity is shattered by a hostile nationalism that is, in fact, the obverse of that mirage: "They check each article, question you on foreign articles, then dismiss you" (Cha, *Dictée*, 58). At this point, all that remains of the narrator's identity and self-knowledge is the lesion created by ethnonationalism, itself a lesion produced by colonialism.

Even as the authors of *Writing Self* extol *Dictée*'s discovery of difference as an alternative to ethnic essentialism, Elaine H. Kim's contribution to the volume contains a moment that reproduces the romantic nationalism of Cha's narrator. This is the moment at which Kim dwells on her emotional response as a Korean American to Cha's use of the Korean folk song "Bong Sun Hwa."[29] This song appears in "Calliope Epic Poetry" immediately after the narrator's reflections on Korean linguistic nationalism. The narrator recollects (in translation) the following lines from the folk song:

> *Standing in a shadow. Bong Sun flower*
> *Your form is destitute*
> *Long and long inside the summer day*
> *When beautifully flowers bloom*
> *The lovely young virgins will*
> *Have played in your honor.*
> In truth this would be the anthem. The national song forbidden to be
>   sung. (46, emphasis in the original)

In this song, which was censored by the Japanese, the flower symbolizes Korea under colonial rule, a Korea whose form is now impoverished but had once been flourishing and in full bloom. Kim's response to the song is worth quoting at some length:

> Reading in *Dictée* the words of the Korean folk song *Bong Sun Hwa* was profoundly unsettling to me because I had never expected to see lines from that song on a printed page in English. . . . It was not just that the words were Korean. It was what the song meant—history, memories, and feelings of people so remote even from me, although in a vastly different way from their remoteness to most other Americans, that they might have been from another planet. . . . In a sense *Bong Sun Hwa* and much else besides became part of *a secret life we lived, always in America but never of it.* It was important to me

to think of what was "ours," though ignored and refused in the dominant culture, as deliberately kept secrets. . . . Belonging to that secret world somehow made more bearable the relationships outside it. That may be why *Dictée*'s display of *Bong Sun Hwa* and other Korean cultural icons, which were to me *fragments of endangered identity, made me so uneasy.*

What had been imposed as a secret was justified as a void, as invisibility, lack, and absence in the dominant culture. Yet the secret's vitality was maintained through memory passed on in my childhood world, *a world that was to me no more or less "real" than what went on beyond the walls of our household.*[30]

This scene of reception of a remediated oral media text stands out for its insistence on the inseparability of form and content. For it is not merely the words of the song but its appearance in the hegemonic English language that unsettles the Korean American critic. What Kim responds to is the linguistic-visual form in which Korea now appears on the printed page. Paradoxically, the inclusion of Korea and Korean culture in translation does not elicit an unequivocal celebration of U.S. multiculturalism. To the contrary, the English translation reminds Kim of the exclusion or marginal status of Korean Americans in dominant representations of U.S. culture. In other words, literary or aesthetic *form* functions, in this instance, less as a sign of a major disruption of the U.S. literary market and more as a reminder of the liminal status of Korean and Asian American literary cultures within that market.

In fact, we can say that the form and content of the Korean song (as perceived by Kim through *Dictée*) activate in her literary criticism the quest for what Chow has described as a lost, collective, ethnicized narcissism. Kim seems somewhat aware that the "secret life" of this thwarted narcissism—including the feeling of being unsettled by the English letters—is produced by (the failure of) liberal democratic U.S. society that makes ethnic minorities like herself feel as if they are "in America but never of it." At the same time, Kim's own critique of multiculturalism is overridden by the culturalist valorization of "what was ours," the need to make the "Korean" in "Korean American" measure up to the universal equivalent of "American." Kim's recognition of the coercive logic of capitalist multiculturalism, then, is finally domesticated by the unrepresentable real dimension that her Korean identity acquires as an imaginary wound. Through Kim's response, we can begin to track a transnational continuity between the aesthetic materialization of anticolonial nationalism (see chapter 1) and that of ethnic identitarian-ism in diaspora.

Cha's narrator in *Dictée*, however, moves beyond this romantic national-ism to underscore the dialectical relationship between ethnic difference and capitalist imperialism in less uncertain terms. Returning to Seoul in 1980, decades after the division of Korea into a capitalist South and a communist North in 1945, the narrator writes (in a letter addressed to the Korean mother) in "Melpomene Tragedy,"

> Our destination is fixed on the perpetual motion of search. Fixed
> in its perpetual exile. Here at my return in eighteen years, the
> war is not ended. We fight the same war. We are inside the same
> struggle seeking the same destination. We are severed in Two by
> an abstract enemy an invisible enemy under the title of libera-
> tors who have conveniently named the severance, Civil War.
> Cold War. Stalemate. (81)

In her reading of this passage, Kim points out that Cha is alluding to a particular period of turmoil in South Korea from the late 1970s to the early 1980s. Following the assassination of the South Korean dic-tator Park Chung-hee, violent demonstrations and uprisings marked this period that culminated in a military coup d'état and the Gwangju Uprising against military rule in 1980.[31] While Cha's narrator situates these conflicts in the postcolonial present, they are also seen as a his-torical repetition, a continuation of "the same war." This war is figured through the interconnection between two historical events. As the narrator's allusion to (the mother's) exile makes clear, the first event is the Japanese colonial occupation, a catalyst for the rise of Korean nationalism. And the second historical event—which the narrator sees as a continuation of the initial act of colonial aggression—is the Korean "Civil War."

Significantly, the narrator sees this war and the subsequent develop-ment of competing postdivision northern and southern nationalisms in the Korean Peninsula as the work of "an abstract enemy an invis-ible enemy" responsible for the "severance." Historically, the Korean War has been analyzed as a complex encounter between U.S. capital-ist forces on the one hand and Chinese and Soviet communist forces on the other. This was an encounter that began with the entry of Soviet and U.S. troops into Korea to dismantle Japanese colonialism in 1945, and consolidating in the process their own national and economic interests in the region. While the narrator does not name names, U.S. imperialism is implicitly held culpable for this stalemate and the intensification of hostilities between the south and the north. The term "Cold War" was coined and used by the Western bloc, and capitalist powers frequently described U.S. forces as "liberators" of South Korea.[32] But why, then, does Cha's narrator describe the enemy as "abstract" and "invisible"? And how would this enemy be responsible for a longer war that began with the Japanese occupation?

The narrator offers us a clue in an earlier passage in "Clio History," reflecting on the Japanese perception of (anticolonial) Koreans as the "enemy":

> The "enemy." One's enemy. Enemy nation. Entire nation against the other entire nation. One people exulting the suffering institutionalized on another. The enemy becomes abstract. The relationship becomes abstract. The nation the enemy the name becomes larger than its own identity. Larger than its own measure. Larger than its own properties. Larger than its own signification. For *this* people. For the people who is their enemy. (32)

On both sides, the "enemy" is produced through an "institutionalized" and violent process of reciprocal abstraction. The abstraction that colonial capital initiates through its repression of the colonized is repeated in the anticolonial response. Crucially, this abstraction also has *perceptual* and *aesthetic* consequences, making each side appear larger than it is in terms of its own "measure," "properties," and "signification." The bigger enemy controlling both sides, then, is the abstraction itself.

It is useful to read this image of abstraction offered by Cha's narrator alongside Anne Harrington de Santana's analysis of the militaristic dimension of capitalism, and especially the fetishistic logic of militarism in which both capitalist and so-called communist nations remain implicated. For Harrington de Santana, a state's abstract and reflexive determination of "the enemy" can be understood in terms of a threat-value constituted by the enemy state's *perceived* destructive effect as opposed to its actual efficiency.[33] The production of this abstract threat-value on either side of the Cold War, Harrington de Santana further argues, follows the logic of commodity fetishism, in which the relative value of the nation-as-commodity masquerades as its intrinsic value: "The value of commodity A is only expressed through its equivalence to commodity B, and vice versa. The fetishistic misrecognition occurs when the value of A no longer appears to be determined reflexively through its relationship to B, but rather that the physical substance of A always already had the property of being the equivalent of B" ("Nuclear Weapons," 338). The work of commodity fetishism, then, is to make a relationship of interdependence between two commodities appear as a contest between two inherently valuable commodities. The perceptual production of a nation's threat-value (or its status as the enemy) follows this process of reification or abstraction as well. Competing claims of threat-value made by two nation-states appear to stem from each state's "physical" essence or innate nationalist-militarist ethos, masking the history of their relationships and transactions with each other as well as with other states. Or, as Cha's narrator puts it, each nation appears to be independently "larger than its own signification."

Thus, in the context of the division of Korea in its moment of freedom from Japanese occupation, "the invisible enemy" identified by Cha's narrator is not just the United States but also the *formal and abstracting violence of capitalism*, the fetishism of the commodity form that both transcends and shapes the capitalist/communist divide and persists in the movement from colonialism to postpartition ethnonationalisms. The stalemate of ethnonational and identitarian warfare in the Korean Peninsula is determined by the aesthetics of capitalist reification that begins with Japanese colonialism and continues with Soviet and U.S. exceptionalisms.

I would, therefore, argue that *Dictée*'s nuanced reflections on the formal production of identitarian difference—moving between the individual and the collective experiences of capitalist abstraction—cannot be reduced to the liberatory Asian American politics of literary difference promoted by *Writing Self*. Lowe acknowledges that *Dictée* is not a "univocal" text. And yet, she theorizes Asian American difference by reducing the text's polyphony to the performative actions of a single "subject of *Dictée*."[34] As I have demonstrated, Cha self-consciously deploys a range of voices—some more "audible" than others—that are differently positioned under colonial, neocolonial, and liberal democratic contexts of domination. Cha's use of a semifictional narrator—whose life narrative draws on several details from Cha's biography but remains irreducible to it[35]—suggests that the text refuses any easy conflation between this narrator and the author. And while readers have a privileged access to this particular narrator's voice, they are simultaneously made aware that there are several other noncongruent voices and ideological

positions structuring the heterogeneous text, such as that of the narrator's mother, the anonymous woman in the preface struggling to acquire
a new language, the Korean revolutionary Yu Guan Soon, Koreans in
Hawaii seeking U.S. intervention, and the ethnocentric officials wounding the narrator's nationalism. Even in the passage on the division of
Korea quoted above, the narrator's nostalgic use of the collective "we" is
immediately qualified by the reference to the partition and the enduring
divisiveness that the partition has produced. Thus, while the polyvo-
cal structure of Cha's text exhibits an aesthetic of fragmentation that
Fredric Jameson associates with the postmodern cultural logic of late
capital, it is not an aesthetic that makes difference random and, instead,
constantly reminds us of the relational and hierarchical production of
these differences.[36]

Identity politics in *Dictée*, I have so far argued, is not undone through
the medium of language. Rather, the text repeatedly demonstrates how
language remains caught up in coercive mediations through which ethnoracial divides are sustained. This claim, however, is yet to confront the
argument—made, once again, from a formalist literary standpoint—that
there are several passages and sections in *Dictée* in which a nonidentitarian avant-garde mode of writing replaces the text's emphases on
race, imperialism, and diaspora. It is the relationship between these two
modes—the ethnoracial and the avant-garde or experimental—that I
take up in the following section.

An "Antagonistic Complementarity" between
the Ethnic and the Avant-Garde

In his reading of *Dictée*, Timothy Yu notes that Asian Americanist interpretations of Cha's text (exemplified by, for instance, the *Writing Self*
anthology) focus primarily on the "narrative elements at the expense of
its more abstract sections."[37] By "abstract," Yu means a style of writing
that refuses the first-person lyrical "I" associated with mainstream as
well as dominant Asian American poetic conventions. And in this refusal,
Yu further points out, Cha draws on the avant-garde style of "Language"
writing that developed in the United States in the 1970s (Yu, *Race
and the Avant-Garde*, 17).[38] Before offering my own reading of *Dictée's*
avant-gardism, a brief account of Language poetry and its historical
context will be necessary.

In his book *Crisis and the US Avant-Garde*, Ben Hickman shows how Language poetry grew out of a disintegration of the left and its anticapitalist agenda during and after the U.S. economic recession of 1974–75.[39] This period saw the collapse of various mass labor organizations, the dissipation of antiwar movements, increasing privatization, rising unemployment, and the capitulation of formerly pro-worker unions and organizations to the demands of the political and business elite: "As Language poetry was establishing its group identity from about 1975, the use of economic crises to assault working conditions and democratic freedoms—what would become known as neoliberalism—had just begun" (Hickman, *Crisis*, 141). In response to this crisis, experimental poets like Bruce Andrews, Charles Bernstein, Steve McCaffery, Bob Perelman, and Ron Silliman argued that the counterassault against capitalism needed to be waged linguistically, since capitalist ideologies are primarily propagated through language. Andrews and Bernstein's magazine *L=A=N=G=U=A=G=E* became the venue for a radical experimental assertion of poetics *as* politics inspired by a heady mix of French poststructuralism, Russian formalism, and Marxism. Language poets maintained that the conventional uses of language, grammar, and syntax "can be likened to profit in capitalism."[40] And the dominant linguistic tendency to produce meaning, to represent or describe objects "external" to language is the result of capitalist reification: "The repression of the product (labour) nature of things is called the commodity fetish. In language it is a fetish of description."[41] The naturalized predilection for linguistic referentiality is, therefore, not just the malaise of the dominant poetic mode but the structural basis of the capitalist economy.[42]

Language poetry's attack on capitalism, however, did not entail challenging U.S. imperialism abroad or racioeconomic inequalities at home, presumably because such efforts would entail a certain reliance on the "fetish of description." Instead, the Language poets hoped to decommodify language and the avant-garde by emphasizing the impersonal materiality of language, "the taking of the language out of the person,"[43] the poetic and political quest for the "signifier when devoid of its signified."[44] (This rhetoric, its "Marxism" notwithstanding, is strikingly similar to the language-bound antiessentialism discussed in chapter 1.) In terms of poetic practice, this meant rejecting the representational lure and exploring, instead, the "inner" reality or the "wordness" of language, often through formal devices like alliteration, assonance, wordplay, and phonemic shifts.[45] Crucially, for the most vocal Language poets, the "conception of oppositional language was not posed as one political activity among others, but as *the* political action of its time."[46] That is to say, for these practitioners, poetic labor was in a unique position to stand in for *all* other forms of labor, and poetic writing was *the* avant-garde form of anticapitalist struggle.[47]

In this connection, it is important to note the sociopolitical fissure between the Language project and the identitarian struggles of racially marginalized groups in the United States in the 1960s and 1970s. For a number of Language poets, the representational demands of minority groups like African Americans and Asian Americans ran counter to the avant-garde aim to dismantle capitalism through a politics of nonrepresentation. In fact, Silliman explicitly voiced his concern about rising black nationalism, which he thought was dividing the left in the United States.[48] Similarly, Bernstein made the controversial claim that, given its origins in identity politics, African American poetry could not be included in the antibourgeois struggles of Language poetry.[49] Paradoxically, this anxiety of having to compete with other identitarian political and aesthetic struggles led the nonidentitarian Language poets to demarcate purposefully their own social and aesthetic identity. As Yu writes of this self-definition, "The Language poets had to acknowledge themselves as a socially as well as aesthetically delimited group, characterized by their own racial, gender, and class positions in a manner comparable to that of writers grouped together as Asian Americans, African Americans, or Latinos" (*Race and the Avant-Garde*, 3). Thus, in spite of its opposition to referentiality and identity politics, Language poetry's turn to the "wordness" of language needs to be seen through the inescapably identitarian nature of the fragmentation of aesthetic politics in the neoliberal United States. Yu compellingly argues that the Language group should not be seen only in terms of its self-perception as "the avant-garde" but also as a (white) "ethnic" community or "a minority culture" (5) that was in competition with other ethnic (and equally avant-garde) groups driven by different social identifications.[50] I would go further and suggest that the self-demarcation of Language poetry as a recognizable form of aesthetic praxis may also be seen as a form of *coercive mimeticism*, one in which culturally marginalized white poets felt compelled to confess their ostensibly nonidentitarian aesthetic-political identity not just against capitalism but also in opposition to the dissenting groups of color.[51] This obsessive confession of a poetics of nonrepresentation and a difference from the mainstream, however, did not necessitate an examination of how or why minority politics in the United States would find it impossible to give up on issues of representation and referentiality. Instead, as the welfare state collapsed under neoliberalism, the privileges of race, class, and gender bolstered by the same neoliberalism produced an ideological enclosure from within which the Language poets could assert the radically democratic nature of nonrepresentational form. In other words, the self-positioning of Language poetry against identity politics was, from its inception, regulated by the racializing aesthetic cunning of neoliberalism.

How does *Dictée* engage with the Language poets' ideology of poetic form? There are several passages in Cha's text that bear a strong resemblance to the avant-garde valorization of language for itself and the disruption of the reader's narrative and referential expectations. For instance, the section "Erato Love Poetry" ends with a poem whose first four lines run as follows: "It had been snowing. During the while. / Interval. Recess. Pause. / It snowed. The name. The term. The noun. / It had snowed. The verb. The predicate. The act of" (118). Snowing is not represented as an extralinguistic natural phenomenon that language describes. Rather, it is presented as a phenomenon whose experience is dependent on language and writing. Cha's use of three different tenses—the past perfect continuous, the simple past, and the past perfect—demonstrates how the experience of the same phenomenon can be varied through linguistic manipulation. Relatedly, the desire to seek refuge in language and writing as the basis of a resistive subjectivity—echoing, again, the claims of the Language poets—recurs in the second half of *Dictée*. For instance, toward the middle of "Thalia Comedy," the following lines appear in the middle of Cha's indirect representation of an anonymous woman's inner thoughts: "*She says to herself if she were able to write she could continue to live. Says to herself if she would write without ceasing. To herself if by writing she could abolish real time. She would live*" (141, emphasis in the original). The same section ends with "She returns to word. She returns to word, its silence. If only once. Once inside. Moving" (151). In these moments, Cha's text comes close to Language poetry's declaration of writing—its preference for the mute, nonreferential, and mobile signifier—as a form of a countercultural "living" that disregards normative representational practices and ideologies. These avant-gardist declarations in *Dictée* have led Yu to suggest that, for Cha, writing becomes the desirable alternative to the historical repetition and identitarian stalemate represented in the first half of the text: "It is also, finally, an embrace of writing itself as the master discourse that moves out into agency from the stasis of history" (*Race and the Avant-Garde*, 107). Echoing the Language poets' position, Yu claims that, for Cha, "politics must be first and foremost a question of language, and thus it is [nonrepresentational] writing that must provide the basis for any attempt to resist domination" (132).[52]

I would, however, argue that *Dictée* declares no such triumphant victory for avant-garde writing. Even as Cha's character wishes that "she were able to" abolish time and history through writing, it is impossible to sustain the claim that the text is fully or finally interpellated by such an aesthetic politics. Instead, readers are confronted with a gap between the ethnic-diasporic and the Language currents in *Dictée*, textualizing the divide between Asian American and avant-garde communities and their political concerns throughout the 1970s and 1980s.[53] Yu himself acknowledges this tension in Cha's text: "What *Dictée* provides is neither a means of choosing between experimental and Asian American methods of reading and writing nor a synthesis of the two. . . . *Dictée* shows us a way of keeping these two paradigms in productive tension, always visible but never resolved" (122). Paying attention to this "productive tension," then, necessitates that we, as readers, do not privilege the avant-garde over the ethnic, or writing over history, but rather that we note how *Dictée* includes and reveals the limits of that utopian avant-garde desire through its divided aesthetic terrain. For instance, the section titled "Elitere Lyric Poetry" could be considered to be predominantly experimental. Yet Cha opens this section with a photograph of an anticolonial rally against Japanese martial law in Korea in 1919. What Yu calls antihistorical writing is prefaced and haunted by an image of colonialism as a very different kind of writing, closer to perhaps what Jacques Derrida describes as a *via rupta*—a broken path or territory "written, discerned, and inscribed violently as difference."[54] (I discuss this photograph in more detail below.) Concomitantly, Cha's previous allusion to the aesthetic abstraction through which capitalist reification maintains the Korean stalemate also poses a challenge to an uncritical valorization of abstract writing.

This productive tension between the ethnic and the avant-garde paradigms, I would further argue, suggests that *Dictée* is, at some level, aware of Language writing as one historical and ideological formation among others. This awareness is also reflected by the text's recurrent interruptions of its avant-garde meditations on language with passages on broken and inaudible speech, strongly reminiscent of the wounded female speaker in Cha's preface. Here, too, the speaker is struggling to find a voice:

> At times, starts again. Noise. Semblance of noise. Speech per-
> haps. Broken. One by one. At a time. Broken tongue. Pidgeon [sic]
> Tongue. Semblance of Speech. (158)
>   Maimed. Accident. Stutters. Almost a name. Half a name.
> Almost a place. Starts. About to. Then stops. Exhale swallowed to a
> sudden arrest. Pauses. (159)
>   Being broken. Speaking broken. Saying broken. Talk broken. Say
> broken. Broken speech. Pidgon [sic] tongue. Broken word. (161)

In these passages, the wounded subaltern in the margins of discourse may be seen as a figuration of the ideological limits of an avant-garde practice that believes it can resist capitalist domination by using language as its key weapon. At the same time, Cha's orthographic play on "pidgin" also attests to the fact that such an ideological formation is also part of *Dictée*'s own history. In these moments, *Dictée* reveals its cognizance of itself as a text whose "various aesthetic elements may be the product of distinct ideological formations, may belong to disparate 'histories,' so that it is not necessarily identical, ideologically speaking, with itself."[55] Furthermore, the insertion of linguistic play *within* these scenes of subaltern exclusion could be read as a caustic critique of the institutionalization of the avant-garde's poetic protest, its capitulation to neoliberalism's cunning, and the domestication of dissent through the aesthetic. Given that Language poetry was fully integrated into the U.S. academy by the 1990s—with leading poets like Bernstein acquiring tenure and even appearing on prime-time television—*Dictée*'s avant-garde foresight, we can say, lies in its foreshadowing of this neoliberal containment of a radical aesthetic ideology.[56] Cha's ambivalent deployment of experimental writing can, therefore, be read alongside Peter Bürger's appraisal of the avant-garde: "The failure of the avant-garde's aspirations to alter social reality and its internal aesthetic success (the artistic legitimation of avant-garde practices) are two sides of the same coin."[57]

How might we reinterpret the intimate and yet tense relationship between the avant-garde and the ethnic-diasporic modes in *Dictée*, then, if that relationship cannot be reduced to an opposition between writing and history, or abstract form and content? Terry Eagleton reminds us that contradictions in aesthetic ideology need to be understood in terms of relations of dominance and subordination that are ultimately controlled by the general (capitalist) mode of production.[58] Going further, David Roberts argues that these seemingly conflicting formations (such as writing versus history, form versus content) are, in fact, "symbiotic" or "complementary" in that it is by staging them as incommensurable oppositions that capitalism masks its formal or aesthetic operations. Describing the relationship between bourgeois culture and the bohemian artist in the nineteenth century, Roberts writes:

> The relation of the bohemian artistic subculture to the host society in this period is best described as one of "antagonistic complementarity" in the sense that the bourgeoisie and bohemia implied, required, and attracted each other. This complementarity was subject, however, to a fundamental misreading by the bohemians. Instead of recognizing the structural nature of this complementary division of labor, bohemians tended to grasp this relationship dynamically as an irreconcilable opposition, in which the bohemian form of life constituted a living testimony to the incompatibility of art and commerce, aestheticism and utilitarianism.[59]

Roberts suggests that the bohemian artist could idealize the opposition between bourgeois life and bohemian life—and deny their structural codependency—only by disavowing the aesthetics of commerce, of the market relations that simultaneously allowed and negated the status of art as anticapitalist, subsequently absorbing that art into the capitalist system. Turning to *Dictée*, we can see how, by juxtaposing and intertwining two distinct forms of aesthetic abstraction that capitalist oppression makes possible—ethnonational identitarianism on the one hand and nonreferential aesthetic resistance on the other—Cha, in fact, unmasks and highlights the complementarity between the two modes. In other words, *Dictée* refuses to yield to this cunning of capital; it refuses to offer aesthetic anti-identitarianism as a respite from identity politics. Identity and nonidentity coconstitute Cha's textualization of capitalism's crafty aesthetic loop, its Möbius strip–like topology, where opposite sides become one while also remaining distinct.[60]

Yet as we have already noted, *Dictée*'s aesthetics are not exclusively literary. Cha's metacritical reflections on the aesthetic topology of capitalism recurrently include *visual* media or allusions to visual media texts. How exactly does this turn to the visual both expand on and move beyond the antagonistically complementary literary approaches to identity politics within the text? In the following section, I begin to address this question by examining the role that cinematic writing—or the cinematic "cut"—plays in *Dictée*'s representation of the gendered dimension of the aesthetics of racialized capitalism. Cha's subtle exposition of the imbrications between race, nationalism, and sexual difference in and through the capitalist-cinematic apparatus, I suggest, works to displace its own opposition between the ethnic and the avant-garde literary modes. Bringing into view a "cinematic mode of production," Cha's text further complicates its own critique of competing modes of literary resistance against capitalist oppression.

Identity in the Cinematic Cut

Cha's turn to the cinematic imaginary from within the print medium is by no means an aesthetic whim. In 1980, two years prior to the completion of *Dictée*, Cha had published a volume of essays with contributions from psychoanalytic film and cultural theorists—like Jean-Louis Baudry, Roland Barthes, and Christian Metz—as well as a number of experimental artist-theorists like Maya Deren, Thierry Kuntzel, and Dziga Vertov. Speaking to the wide range of contributions to the volume, Cha notes in the preface that her goal is to present a "'plural text' making active the participating viewer/reader, making visible *his/her position in the apparatus.*"[61] Philip Rosen reminds us that, in the context of 1970s film theory, "the apparatus" may be understood as "the cultural determinations and effectivities of the cinematic machinery and of the disposition of production and exhibition technologies and techniques."[62] The apparatus is where culture and cinematic machinery are welded together. As I have already suggested in chapter 1, for Apparatus theorists like Baudry and Metz, this "machinery" is not merely the technology used in the film industry. It has a psychic and social dimension as well, constituted, in part, by the narcissism of the spectator transfixed by the cinematic image. Cha both draws on and problematizes this approach to the cinematic image as an ideological lure in *Dictée*, in the section called "Melpomene Tragedy," which opens with a description of an anonymous female spectator:

> She could be seen sitting in the first few rows. . . . Closer the
> better. . . . Better to eliminate presences of others surrounding

> better view away from that which is left behind far away back
> behind more for closer view more and more face to face until
> nothing else sees only this view singular. All dim, gently, slowly
> until in the dark, the absolute darkness the shadows fade. . . .
>   The submission is complete. Relinquishes even the vision
> to immobility. Abandons all protests to that which will appear
> to the sight. . . . Break. Break, by all means. The illusion that the
> act of viewing is to make alteration of the visible. The expulsion
> is immediate. Not one second is lost to the replication of the
> totality. Total severance of the seen. Incision. (79)

What begins as a description of a cinephile ends as a critical diagnosis
of the machinations of the cinematic apparatus. In the first paragraph,
the spectator's desire to be as close to the image as possible is strongly
reminiscent of Barthes's description of spectatorial immersion in the
darkness of the movie theater: "I press my nose against the screen's mirror, against that 'other' image-repertoire with which I narcissistically
identify myself . . . the image captivates me, captures me: I am *glued* to
the representation."[63] Cha's description of this cinematic enclosure in
the first paragraph—through a long sentence devoid of punctuation—
evokes a "pre-hypnotic" state that Barthes associates with the weaving of
a "veritable cinematographic cocoon" ("Leaving the Movie," 345, 346).
At this point, Cha's and Barthes's spectators seem indistinguishable.

In the second paragraph, however, the two spectators part ways. The
model spectator in Barthes, let us note, is one who simultaneously
maintains the imaginary illusion and achieves a Brechtian distance
from it. The "image-repertoire," Barthes claims, "vanishes" as soon as
the spectator attacks it with "ideological vigilance," a scrutiny of the ideological underpinnings of the cinematic image (349). The more desirable
and appropriately cinephilic strategy, he goes on to note, is to maintain
the fantasy space and luxuriate in an internal split, "as if I had two
bodies at the same time: a narcissistic body which gazes, lost, into the
engulfing mirror, and a perverse body, ready to fetishize not the image
but precisely what exceeds it: the texture of the sound, the hall, the darkness, the obscure mass of the other bodies" (349). In other words, for
Barthes, spectatorship should ideally be a doubly hypnotic experience, at
once taking pleasure in the plenitude of the image and cultivating a distance from it.

Albeit beginning with the spectator's amorous attachment to the cinematic image, *Dictée* offers a suggestive rebuttal to Barthes's position.

The narrator describes the spectator's submission to the image but then urges the viewer, and even the film itself, to dispel "the [Barthesian] illusion" that the act of spectatorship alone can "alter" (let alone dissolve) the imaginary. The illusion, then, is not the image to which the spectator submits, but rather that the effect of its visibility is "merely" illusory or ideological. Moreover, for Cha's spectator, the cinematic imaginary is not associated with a plenitude that activates a pleasurable fetishism. The use of surgical vocabulary ("severance," "incision," and "expulsion") suggests an invasive and alienating experience of the image—or what I have called aesthetic dissonance—to which Barthes (as well as other French male critics like Baudry and Metz) seem oblivious.

In this context, the significance of sexual difference cannot be overlooked in Cha's representation of the female viewer, given that *Dictée* was published a few years after the appearance of Laura Mulvey's two influential essays on the gendered construction of the spectator in classical Hollywood cinema. Indeed, cinematic incision plays an important role in Mulvey's critique of the male gaze in her essay "Visual Pleasure": "Conventional closeups of [the female protagonist's] legs . . . or a face . . . integrate into the narrative a different mode of eroticism. One part of a fragmented [female] body destroys the Renaissance space, the illusion of depth demanded by narrative; it gives flatness, the quality of a cut-out or icon rather than verisimilitude to the screen."[64] For Mulvey, patriarchal Hollywood severs or dismembers the female body as a fetish and, simultaneously, expels the woman from the masculine position of spectatorial mastery and diegetic control. Implicit here is an argument about the use of the elemental cinematic cut—the means to move from shot one to another—to fragment, cut up, and re-present the female body to sustain the patriarchal and capitalist gaze. Put differently, in addition to its heteromasculine narrative themes and structures, it is classical Hollywood's phallic logic of incision that prompts Mulvey to challenge the masculinist fantasy of imaginary plenitude. Thus, Cha's incisive critique of cinephilia could be read as a subtle homage to Mulvey's feminist call to destroy the stock of the imaginary—not merely through spectatorship but also by attempting to "free the look of the camera" ("Visual Pleasure," 209). In her follow-up essay Mulvey argues that, confronted with Hollywood's logic of severance, the *identity* of the female spectator also undergoes an incision or a splitting, as she is compelled to oscillate between being a desiring subject and a fetish object.[65] In other words, *as* sexual difference, the identity of the woman is compelled to confront the incision or wound inflicted by the commoditized image of herself. Notably, in Cha's passage, the object of the incision is ambiguous. In the phrase "the severance of the seen," that which is "seen" could be the woman-as-image. But it could also be the female spectator who "could be seen sitting in the first few rows."

This ambiguity—or uneven interchangeability—between female subject and object is confirmed in the section "Erato Love Poetry," in which the anonymous woman at the theater is represented both as a spectator and a character in her own filmic reality. Crucially, Cha's description of the female spectator mimics a genre of writing that is integral to the cinematic apparatus—the shooting script with cinematographic directions:

> Extreme Close Up shot of her face. Medium Long shot of two out of the five white columns from the street. She enters from the left side, and camera begins to pan on movement as she enters between the two columns, the camera stop [sic] at the door and she enters. . . . She selects a row near the front, fourth seat from the left and sits. Medium Close Up, directly from behind her head. (96)

Cha's cinematization of the spectator's "reality"—where her representation is determined by "invisible" cuts between shots—exemplifies what Michael Stone-Richards has called Dictée's experimental "parallelism of screen and page."[66] At the same time, this experimentalism—similar to Cha's turn to avant-garde writing—does not privilege form over content, and in fact, can be read as a productive hindrance to purely formalist celebrations of medium specificity, what Stone-Richards calls the "mediumicity" of the film apparatus ("Commentary," 166).[67] The cinematically spliced representation of the female spectator-as-image is followed by the narrator's reflections on the audience's assumptions about the female protagonist, and possibly of the film that the spectator herself has also gone to watch: "One expects her to be beautiful. The title which carries her name is not one that would make her anonymous or plain. 'The portrait of . . .' One seems to be able to see her. One imagines her, already. Already before the title" (Cha, Dictée, 98). This juxtaposition—of the technologically fragmented female body and the patriarchal imaginary—makes apparent the simultaneously cinematic and extracinematic abstractions that at once absorb and alienate the female spectator. That is to say, while the woman-as-spectacle is anticipated on the screen, it also becomes clear that the cinematic techniques of severance that produce "the woman" (as simultaneously subject and object, consumer and commodity) have become a mode of social and visual perception that includes but is no longer confined to the screen or to film technology. Thus, in this account of spectatorship, *Dictée* seems to suggest that it is not just film theory but the larger discursive debate around the very identity category of the "woman"—its assertion as well as its deconstruction—that has to contend with the visual constitution and fragmentation of femininity as a commodity.

The "cinematicity" of *Dictée* thus introduces another level of complexity to its approach to identity politics. If literary critics often privilege Cha's turn to language to recuperate her as the ethnic or avant-garde rebel artist, they do so by overlooking *Dictée*'s representation of capitalist visual perception as a gendering and sexing "machine." The aesthetic dissonance between the woman as a social subject and her cinematically mediated representation is captured pithily in the middle of "Melpomene Tragedy": "SHE opposes Her. SHE against her."[68]

We should note that while Cha's references to cinema can certainly be interpreted without reflecting on the aesthetics of capitalist alienation,[69] such a reading would ignore how these references, in fact, offer a prescient glimpse of what Jonathan Beller would later describe as the "cinematic mode of production."[70] Beller uses this term to mean the intensification of social alienation under capitalism by visual means, beginning with the invention of photography and cinema in the late nineteenth century. Notably, he reminds us that the cinematic mode of production does "not only . . . refer to the set of institutions traditionally configured as 'the cinema,' in popular usage, but . . . to the manner in which production generally becomes organized in such a way that one of its moments *necessarily* passes through the visual, that is, that it creates an image that . . . is essential to the general management, organization, and movement of the [capitalist] economy" (*Cinematic Mode*, 10). In Beller's argument, cinema does not simply reflect (as Mulvey suggests) the patriarchal imaginary and its phallic desire. Rather, techniques of vision and abstraction in the cinematic mode of production become crucial for the reproduction and consolidation of that desire. Like Cha, Beller also draws on the image of the incision, the severance, or the cut to describe cinematic alienation, tracing its origins in an earlier moment in industrial capitalism: "'The cut,' already implicit in the piecemeal production of assembly-line work, became a technique for the organization and production of the fetish character of the commodity and then part of a qualitatively new production regime long misnamed consumerism" (9–10). The cinematic incision segments "reality" in frames to produce new relations between the consumer and the image-as-commodity. Yet as Cha's critique of cinematic reception tells us, the commercial narrative cut also engenders a new way of commoditizing, regulating, and fragmenting the identity of the female or feminized consumer.[71]

Furthermore, in one of its most opaque yet evocative moments, *Dictée* also uses the image of severance to suggest a correspondence or complementarity between the formal operations of the cinematic apparatus and the state apparatus of (U.S.) "democracy." Critics commenting on Cha's avant-garde use of cinema have rarely noted that a map of the Korean Peninsula precedes her description of the female spectator and her experience of severance in "Melpomene Tragedy" (Cha, *Dictée*, 78). Conspicuous in the map is the Demilitarized Zone (DMZ), the official line of division separating North and South Korea. Initially, this representation of Korea's partition—a severance determined in part by capitalist interests—seems to have little to do with cinema's splitting of the female spectator. But the map's significance becomes clearer once we note that the moment of cinematic reception is followed by the narrator's letter to the mother, a letter that reflects on the stalemate in the peninsula and its "imaginary borders" (87). This juxtaposition of the two imaginaries is followed by two final paragraphs in which the severances inflicted by cinema and the state apparatus become indistinguishable:

> Arrest the screen en-trance flickering hue from behind cast shadow silhouette from back not visible. Like ice. Metal. Glass. Mirror. Receives none admits none. Arrest the machine that purports to employ democracy but rather causes the successive refraction of her none other than her own. Suffice Melpomene, to exorcize from this mouth the name the words the memory of severance. (88–89)

How might we interpret this catachrestic comparison between (or fusion of) the cinematic screen and the DMZ? Here Cha's narrator appeals to the reader to arrest the coercive mediations of a screen, as well as those of a political machine, that have taken on each other's traits. The cinema screen and its projection now resemble the impermeable DMZ; and the democratic U.S. state purporting to liberate Korea through the DMZ mimics the cinematic apparatus, severing the Korean subject, forcefully "refracting" or deflecting her identity through its incision. This similarity between the cinema screen and U.S. liberal democracy can be seen as an impossible image of the cinematic mode of production, in which the abstraction inflicted by the cut—both informing and informed by the apparatus of capitalism—is responsible for enduring identitarian dissonances. That is to say that, for Cha's narrator, cinema is not just that which causes gendered aesthetic dissonance in and beyond the movie theater. Reflections on cinematic alienation also allow for an assessment of the psychosocial consequences of territorial divisions grounding claims of liberation, democracy, and ethnic difference. Thus, alongside the unresolved tension between its ethnic and experimental literary modes, Cha's cinematic mode presents itself as another significant obstacle to the recuperation of *Dictée* as a liberatory nonidentitarian text. It is in this sense that the text's diagnosis of identity politics is forcefully intermedial.

The Referent in and beyond the Photographed Event

The photograph, Barthes writes in his now-classic *Camera Lucida*, is a unique visual medium because it bears an indexical trace of the referent.[72] Adding a third level of complexity to *Dictée*'s intermedial view of identity is, in fact, its turn to photographic referentiality. In the final section of this chapter, I will demonstrate that even as *Dictée* draws our attention to photography's complicity with capitalism in the production of referential and identitarian violence, it does not jettison the referent in favor of nonreferential formal abstraction. On the contrary, Cha's photographic formalism calls on the spectator to reconstitute the referent in relation to the identitarian violence of capital both from within and beyond the photographed event. Here, too, Cha's text at once draws on and departs from Barthes's reflections on the essence of photography.

As was noted earlier, one of the narrators in *Dictée* associates the passport photograph with the liberal democratic abstraction that produces a U.S. identity through citizenship. It is worth pointing out that this photographic abstraction—the process by which the referent of the image is ratified by (the state's) linguistic authority—is not an exceptional political phenomenon but rather an extension of dominant and naturalized cultural practices. W. J. T. Mitchell reminds us that the "normal structure" of visual representation involves a "discursive or narrative suturing of the verbal and the visual: texts explain, narrate, describe, label, speak for (or to) the photographs; photographs illustrate, exemplify, clarify, ground, and document the text."[73] Language typically makes use of and circulates the image by making it "speak" in specific ways, repressing its referential excesses. Furthermore, as critics like Jonathan Crary and Allan Sekula have pointed out, this regulated traffic in photographs as a discursive currency has been inseparable—since the invention of photography—from its homologous relationship with money and capital.[74] The passport photograph that Cha's narrator mentions, therefore, falls squarely within this economy that is powered by the rhetorically valued (or devalued) image.

Scholars examining *Dictée*'s use of actual photographs have argued that, by withholding contexts and captions, Cha subverts dominant visual practices, thereby liberating the photograph from semiotic fixity and the journalistic imperative to document and name particular events. Yet it certainly does not follow that this semiotic plurality liberates the text or the reader from identity politics. The much-discussed frontispiece with a Korean inscription, appearing on the verso of *Dictée*'s title page, serves as a powerful introduction to the visuality-identity problematic elicited by photographs throughout the text. The frontispiece is the reproduction of an inscription that, when translated, reads, "Mother, I miss you, I'm hungry, I want to go home to my native place."[75]

While Cha does not label or explain this image, several critics have noted that the author and location of this inscription remain contested. According to some historians, the inscription was carved on a wall of a Japanese mine by a Korean hand, and serves as evidence of the forced migration of Korean laborers in the colonial era. From this perspective, the inscription originates in its author's position as a colonized subject. Contradicting this claim, other historians argue that the inscription appears not in a mine, but in a tunnel also built by Korean laborers during the Second World War as an escape route for the Japanese emperor. The language of the inscription, these historians point out, marks it as after Korea's independence. The suggestion, then, is that the writing cannot be read as proof of colonial oppression and may, in fact, be a later nationalist fabrication.[76]

A number of critics have claimed that, by refusing to take sides, Cha's frontispiece alerts the reader to the instability of photographic evidence and, therefore, distances itself from an ethnonational politics of visibility and lost origins.[77] I would, however, suggest that the frontispiece gestures toward evidence of a different kind, one that the inscription (and its mechanical reproduction) reveal without having to confirm or deny the identity of its author. By refusing to take sides, *Dictée*

Frontispiece of *Dictée*.

does not merely posit both readings as possibilities. It also creates a critical vantage point that allows us to see how the second reading (that the inscription is a postcolonial nationalist "concoction") becomes possible only because of an undeniable historicity and historical memory of the first (colonized Koreans being forced to work in Japanese mines). That is to say, through its silent insertion of this inscription, *Dictée* compels antiessentialist critics of cultural nationalism to confront the lingering effects of colonial violence.[78] Arguably, the faded and grainy photocopy used in the text announces its remediation of and historical distance from the original inscription and its photographic reproduction(s). At the same time, the same grainy fragment stands out as a form of haunting, a reminder of the possible eruption of the historical memory of colonial exploitation in (or its continuation into) the postcolonial present.[79] Thus, although it is an image of an inscription etched by a human hand (and not the photograph of an actual person), the frontispiece alerts readers to the ability of the photographic image to index something that is, strictly speaking, not in its visual frame. The haunting, we can say, is possible because of the simultaneous operation of the two meanings of indexicality outlined by Peircean semiotics—the index as a visible mark or impression, and the index as the possibility of a referent, but one that marks the referent's absence from the scene.[80]

This destabilization and expansion of the concepts of referentiality and the referent ("who or what are we looking at?") is continued by Cha's use of newspaper photographs throughout the text. For instance, "Clio History" opens with a portrait of a woman, who is identified as Yu Guan Soon on the facing page (29). But the text's final uncaptioned photograph reveals how the earlier photo and its caption establish the referent Yu Guan Soon (and contribute to the mythologization of her identity as a revolutionary) by manipulating a larger photographic event. The Korean revolutionary's identity, we realize, is established photographically by obscuring her position among and relationship with other referents— other women dressed in the traditional Korean *hanbok*. Who are these other women who remain unnamed in Cha's text? When, where, and under what circumstances was this second photograph taken?[81]

Such questions remain unanswered in *Dictée*, creating gaps between its literary or linguistic content and our spectatorial encounters with

Uncaptioned photograph of Yu Guan Soon in *Dictée*.

Uncaptioned group photograph with Yu Guan Soon in *Dictée*.

these photographs. But these encounters—because of the lack of contextual information—also draw us *into* these images, prompting us to reflect on the relations between visible, partially visible, or invisible referents that produce the photograph. For even the second photograph, we notice, is cropped, half-obscuring the faces of two women to the (spectator's) left, referents who are at once inside and outside the frame.

In her analysis of the visual politics of *Dictée*, Thy Phu rightly points out that by excluding the captions and the contexts for these images, Cha both highlights and attempts to eschew the institutionalization and commodification of meaning.[82] Yet Phu's attendant claim that, by removing these photographs from their contexts, Cha posits a minority politics of an invisible "not-I who evades intelligibility" ("Decapitated Forms," 35) requires further scrutiny. First, such a celebration of invisibility assumes that *Dictée* espouses a single ideology of nonidentity, and in that assumption, ignores Cha's intermedial account of identity production. Second, Phu implicitly suggests that the referents of these photographs—the historicity of the locations, actions, and gestures captured in these images—can be somehow cast aside through the formalist mandate of "unintelligibility" in Cha's text.[83] Put differently, while celebrating Cha's politics of invisibility, Phu forgets to ask whether *Dictée*'s photographic aesthetics imposes such a politics of invisibility and

Uncaptioned photo of mass gathering in *Dictée*.

unintelligibility on its referents. Does Cha's plural text suggest that the plurality of the referentiality of these photographs can be reduced to the individual artist's purported desire to be invisible and unintelligible?[84]

To argue otherwise, and to suggest that *Dictée*, in fact, asks spectators to think of *the terms of the visibility* of its referents, I will pause briefly on two photographs. The first, with which Cha opens "Elitere Lyric Poetry," is an uncaptioned newspaper photo of a mass gathering.

In spite of (or rather because of) the absence of a caption directing our reading of the photograph, it is impossible to ignore that this is a mass of people—the vox populi—that has made itself visible as a collective.[85] On the one hand, the photographer dictates the terms of the visibility of this collective through the photograph. The photographer instrumentalizes members of the crowd to capture them *as* a mass, rendering them indistinct from each other. Crucially, however, for those spectators of the image who recognize the photograph (or choose to investigate its provenance), the referents do not float in an image devoid of context. They are necessarily tied to the 1919 March 1 Movement against the Japanese occupation—specifically, demonstrations in Seoul in front of Deoksugung Palace.[86] It is just as crucial to note that this persistently identitarian reading of the photograph—as an instance of anticolonial Korean nationalism—would not be possible without the photographer's instrumentalization of the protestors, the decision to represent ethnicity as abstraction through the medium of photography.

On the other hand, by suspending its context, *Dictée* also urges readers to read the image in terms of a structural colonial violence beyond the photographer's gaze, by examining (however speculatively) what the photograph reveals about its referents in excess of the photographer's and Cha's intentions.[87] We note that the camera has caught the crowd as its members have turned to look at something or someone beyond the frame. We spot a participant's open mouth, an expressive face turned toward the event we cannot visualize. (Is it a rallying cry, a penetrating prophetic voice? Can the participants see the camera?) The solemn faces of some of the other participants in the front also reflect the gravity of the event. And the sheer density of the crowd—the proximity between bodies—suggests that these participants have gathered not only to stand together but also against or in opposition to the perceived event. Whatever detail we choose (or whatever detail chooses us) during our encounter with the photograph, we are invariably drawn to this ominous other event that lies both within and beyond the photographer's encounter with the crowd. This partially visible event that has left multiple traces in the image, we are led to recognize, is the condition of possibility of the photograph before us. Given the location and historical moment—and in the absence of further contextual information—we can intuit that this threatening event is Japanese colonialism itself. Thus, if the rally and, therefore, the photograph are ultimately conditioned by the violence and atrocities characterizing colonialism, that violence is not directly or immediately visible in the image.

Ariella Azoulay's redefinition of the atrocity photograph is apropos in this regard. Arguing against the dominant critical tendency to locate violence or horror *within* the atrocity image, Azoulay writes,

> A photograph pictures atrocity when it is created under disaster circumstances *regardless of what it captures*, even when no visible trace of the atrocity is actually left in it. In other words, photographs picture atrocity by their mere coming into

being in disaster conditions, but the atrocity that they picture
is not reducible to that which has been established as its visual
attributes.[88]

For Azoulay, the presence or absence of overt signs of violence or bodily
harm in the photograph does not alter the ontological fact that when
a photograph is produced under an atrocity, it is inescapably a representation of that atrocity. Cha's use of the rally photograph, I will suggest,
similarly prompts us to see identitarianism not simply in terms of
"visible" anticolonial nationalism but as the effect of the atrocity of colonialism that is both present and absent in the image. In other words,
far from prescribing invisibility or dismissing referentiality, Dictée asks
us to grapple with the difficult and yet ethically necessary task of inter-
preting the identitarian violence producing the image by going beyond
the image's given caption or description. Cha's text demands that we
reconstruct the referentiality of the photograph both from within and
beyond what it claims to depict.[89]

Another undated and uncaptioned photograph that appears in "Clio
History"—frequently described as a scene of crucifixion of Korean mar-
tyrs by Japanese soldiers[90]—calls for a similar examination of the
multiply mediated relationship between referentiality and identitarian
violence. At one level, the photographer becomes directly implicated in
"producing" the referents on the cross through the violence of capital,
not only because of the colonial atrocity that the photographer allows
to unfold before the camera but also because the performative element
of the crucifixion serves as visual capital for the photograph to circulate as a commodity. While we do not know if this is a clandestinely
taken photo, the distance between the camera and the photographed
event is also significant. The spectacle of capital punishment is captured
without inculpating or revealing the identities of the Japanese military
officers. At the same time, ethnonational divides between the tortured
and torturing referents are clearly delineated for the spectator.

Simultaneously, Dictée's intriguingly contradictory references to this
photo lead the reader to examine the relationship between the referents more closely, separating the photographer's intentions from what
the camera captures. Right before the photo appears in "Clio History,"
the narrator reflects on "The decapitated forms. Worn. Marred, recording a past, of previous forms" (38). The very next paragraph, however,
moves from this image of an exhausting, wounded, and slow depletion

Uncaptioned photo of prisoners tied to crosses in *Dictée*.

to sudden death or cessation: "All else age, in time. Except. Some are without" (38). These two possibilities—quick extermination and slow death—seem to align with the referential contingencies that surface in the photograph. At first glance, it would appear that to be the referent of this photograph would be to either kill or be killed instantaneously in the name of ethnic difference. But on closer inspection, we note that none of the soldiers is visibly carrying a weapon, raising the possibility that the torturers initiated and the tortured experienced a slow death before or after the photographed event. Notably, the proximity of one of the officers to the crosses suggests a form of communication or exchange in progress between the torturer and the tortured. Is this a moment of negotiation at which the tortured referents have some hope of survival by acquiescing to be "marred" repetitions of an iconic image for the torturers' pleasure? Or is this a moment at which the tortured are asserting their wounded identity and referentiality by defying the torturer, choosing death in the name of martyrdom, unaware that their martyrdom is, at that very moment, also being converted into visual capital? I raise these questions not to suggest that the answers can be definitively found inside or outside Cha's text. Rather, my point is that to engage with the indeterminacies of photographic mediation in *Dictée* cannot mean an elision of the question of the referent, the latter's relationship with identitarian wounds—"the decapitated forms"—inflicted by the mediations of capital.

Codetta

If Theresa Hak Kyung Cha's *Dictée* has so far been read as an ethnic or experimental text that resists identity politics through its literary or visual formalism, I have argued that what the text thwarts is, in fact, such a medium-bound emancipatory conclusion. I have demonstrated how *Dictée* foregrounds individual and collective identity production as an intermedial process of fragmentation that is inseparable from capitalist abstraction and alienation. Anne Anlin Cheng begins her reading of Cha's text by arguing that "although, and perhaps precisely because, *Dictée* is not interested in identities, it is profoundly interested in [deconstructing] the processes of *identification*."[91] Yet by the end of her analysis, Cheng remains unconvinced by her own distinction between "identity" and "identification": "It is insufficient to say that Cha deconstructs social identities such as race and nationhood, for she is painfully aware of *the inseparability of construction from deconstruction*" (*Melancholy of Race*, 166, emphasis added). In that sense, my reading of *Dictée* begins where Cheng ends. I have investigated the sociopolitical implications of this complicity between construction and deconstruction, identification and alienation, in Cha's text. I have argued that even as Cha draws on avant-garde and nonrepresentational aesthetics, the latter remain implicated in the text as coercive mimeticisms regulated by colonial and neocolonial capital. In other words, *Dictée* does not posit nonidentitarian aesthetics as an alternative to identity politics. The aesthetics of identity and nonidentity remain bound to capital's cunning Möbius strip logic of antagonistic complementarity. Finally, Cha's defamiliarizing turn to visuality, I have claimed, also challenges utopian hopes of a literary-aesthetic emancipation from referentiality. *Dictée* reminds us that a critical account of identity politics cannot seek refuge in "the instability of language." Neither can it privilege visual abstraction or unintelligibility over the historicity of the referent. A more radical nonidentitarian project can begin only by taking stock of the modalities of linguistic and visual mediations of identitarian violence under particular contexts of capitalist freedom-as-subjugation.

CHAPTER 3

The "Haptic" Feminism of Assia Djebar's *The Nouba of the Women of Mount Chenoua*

It is important to consider the changes that colonization brought to understand the scope of the organization of sex and gender under colonialism and in Eurocentred global capitalism. If the latter did only recognize sexual dimorphism for white bourgeois males and females, it certainly does not follow that the sexual division is based on biology.

—Maria Lugones, "The Coloniality of Gender"

From my initial efforts to search the memory of peasant women in the mountains of Dahra, in Arabic or sometimes in Berber, rising with the memories of their searing pains—I received an irrevocable shock. A call to my roots, I would even say an ethical and aesthetic lesson, from the women of all ages of my maternal tribe.

—Assia Djebar, "Discours de réception"

In the last chapter, I demonstrated how the aesthetics of Theresa Hak Kyung Cha's *Dictée* alerts us to a cinematic (and more broadly visual dimension of) identity production in a commodity economy. Cha's poetics, I argued, draws attention to cinema's complex entanglement with a larger multimodal apparatus that is capitalism, mediating identitarian dissonance that is at once racialized and gendered. In this chapter, I turn to Algerian writer and filmmaker Assia Djebar's *The Nouba of the Women of Mount Chenoua* (*La Nouba des femmes du Mont Chenoua*) to examine how the medium of cinema itself can be used to reflect on this dissonance.[1] I choose Djebar's film for two reasons. First, *The*

141

Nouba explicitly foregrounds the intermedial gendering of postcolonial identity as its central concern. Second, I am also interested in Djebar's experimental style—defined by the fusion of fiction and documentary, the refusal of a transitive and apparently seamless narrative structure, disjunctions between sound and image, and so on—because it raises important questions about the representability of feminist politics and identity politics more generally.

I begin this chapter by situating *The Nouba* within the dominant masculinist discourse of Algerian nationalism and nationalist cinema. I then examine the film's depiction of feminine identity as a psychic splitting brought on by the patriarchal and capitalist underpinnings of colonialism as well as the Arabization of decolonized Algeria. The second half of the chapter focuses on Djebar's turn to the cinematic avant-garde. There I continue the book's larger interrogation of the critical opposition between identity politics and anticapitalist aesthetic innovation, specifically by bringing *The Nouba* in conversation with Laura U. Marks's theorization of a nonidentitarian "haptic" or "tactile" cinema. I demonstrate that Djebar's film draws on haptic aesthetics not to transcend identity but rather to draw attention to the intermedial nature of ethnic-feminine fragmentation within a (neo)colonial matrix of governance and state power. The final section of the chapter explores this haptic dimension further through the film's attraction to gendered subaltern speech as well as its awareness of the differential experience of feminine marginalization in postcolonial Algeria.

The Nouba in the Time of National Chauvinism

Several scholars have noted that, from the early 1960s onward, the Algerian anticolonial movement turned to film production and distribution with an explicitly nationalist agenda. Cinema followed in the footsteps of anticolonial radio, with both mass media being far more popular than print because of Algeria's low literacy rates for the better part of the twentieth century. Filmmaking by and for Algerians coincided with the formation of the provisional Algerian government in 1961. Technological and financial resources that this government made available, in fact, led to the production of the first Algerian shorts. The nationalization of the film industry in 1964—two years after Algeria's independence from France—further solidified the founding ties between cinema and the state.[2]

As a prosthesis for state-sanctioned nationalism, filmmaking in post-colonial Algeria came to be dominated by what has been called *cinéma moudjahid*, or "freedom fighter cinema." This was a cinema that very quickly took on a majoritarian agenda, firmly in line with the ideologies of the National Liberation Front (Front de libération nationale, FLN)—the organization that led the anticolonial movement and then became the ruling political party after independence. As Guy Austin writes, "Since *cinéma moudjahid* was an official history of the liberation struggle, it centred on the FLN and tended to marginalize . . . the contribution of the *moudjahidat* [female freedom fighters], and was always filmed in Arabic."[3] I discuss this gendered and ethnicized aspect of anticolonial and postcolonial nationalism—that includes but is not reducible to cinematic production and consumption—in more detail in the following section. It would be useful to recall here, however, how radio served as an acoustic "mirror" for the Algerian nation-to-be during the struggle for independence. Much like that reactive radio-phonic fiction of the homogeneous "Fatherland"—which Frantz Fanon describes as the "people's own lie" concocted to counter the "congenital lie" of the colonizer—cinematic depictions of Algeria as a patriarchal Arab nation served to disavow the psychosocial fragmentation that had endured well after decolonization.[4]

Although made with funds from the state-owned Algerian Radio and Television Broadcasting (RTA), Djebar's *The Nouba* offers a trenchant critique of this narrative of a monoethnic and male-dominated nation. Through testimonies and stories that Djebar's own relatives—peasant women in the mountains of Chenoua in northern Algeria—recount to a fictional character Lila, the film creates a powerful alternative *herstory* of the revolution. These women, who come from Arab and Berber ethnic groups, reflect on their active participation in the anti-colonial movement and, more implicitly, on their marginalization in Algerian history and society. Weaving these interviews together is Lila's voice-over, which also contemplates her failing marriage and her own lingering trauma of the revolution. Andalusian chants and extracts from Algeria-inspired compositions by the Hungarian musician Béla Bartók punctuate Lila's ruminations and her interviews with the peasant women. Music, song, and voice are deeply intertwined elements of the oral tradition on which *The Nouba* draws to retrieve this alternative narrative of the nation. As the film's prologue informs us in Arabic, the word *nouba* means "the daily history of women" as well as "a sort of symphony, in the classical music known as Andalusian, with certain rhythmical movements."[5] Yet even as it constructs what Austin calls a "hetero-biography" (*Algerian National Cinema*, 65) that centers not an individual but a multigenerational and collective feminine subject, *The Nouba* also grapples with the difficulties of reclaiming and representing the feminine across socioeconomic divides.[6] Most conspicuously, the peasant women's testimonies throw into sharp relief the mobility and social freedom—limited as they may be—to which the protagonist-interviewer Lila has access as an educated architect returning from abroad to her natal village.

Sexual Difference as (Neo)Colonial Alienation

To examine these complexities of the feminine and feminism in *The Nouba*, I will begin with the film's representation of Lila's subjectivity, and in particular her dissonance with the mainstream nationalist nostalgia for the Algerian Revolution. *The Nouba* opens with what appears to be a scene of marital failure and alienation of affections. In this expository scene that establishes Lila and Ali as a couple, the young woman walks toward a doorframe with her back to the spectator, while her voice-over declares a desire to be heard while avoiding an ocular gaze: "I speak, I speak, I speak. I don't want anyone to see me." As the camera briefly cuts to a medium shot of Ali staring despondently from a wheelchair, it becomes clear that, in this moment, the gaze that the protagonist wishes to avoid is both wounded and male. Specifically addressing Ali and his condition, the voice-over sets up a paradoxical relationship of alienation marked by proximity and intimate knowledge: "I don't want you to see me as I really am. Prisoner, fate made you a prisoner in silence . . . time and space." Lila sounds concerned and deeply affected by her husband's immobility while simultaneously seeking a reprieve from his gaze. The actions of the characters also mirror this intimate alienation. Throughout the scene, they remain in close proximity—Lila even touches Ali's shoulder as she walks around his wheelchair toward a window—but without exchanging a word with each other. The voice-over that primarily gives us access to Lila's thoughts, together with Ali's silence, further heightens the emotional distance between the two characters. What the scene establishes, then, is Lila's subjective oscillation between a rejection of the male gaze and a desire to communicate with the bearer of that gaze. This contradiction surfaces poignantly in her voice-over later in the same scene: "You won't touch me, not now . . . not any time soon. . . . If only you would speak but you don't want to." The scene of marital discord and the failure of communication between the sexes, then, is also a scene of feminine psychic splitting in front of—or (dis)identification with—a silent, damaged, and postwar masculinity.

The implications of this splitting, however, do not remain confined to the couple on-screen as soon as we turn to the political economy of sexual difference in colonial and postcolonial Algeria. Feminist philosopher Maria Lugones argues that coloniality required for its operation not just the naturalization of racial hierarchies but also that of sexual difference: "Biological dimorphism, heterosexual patriarchy are all characteristic of what I call the 'light' side of the colonial/modern organization of gender. Hegemonically these are written large over the meaning of gender."[7] For Lugones, the ideological and perforce gendered construction of the dimorphic male/female binary in modern Europe at once constituted and was constituted by "the coloniality of power" that introduced race as a fundamental human classificatory category. Sexual dimorphism, as she notes in the first epigraph to this chapter, is not just a product of biology ("The Coloniality of Gender," 7). In short, coloniality may be seen as the field of power in which racialization and the dimorphic sex-gender system—together privileging the "male" anatomy and white heteromasculinity—coconstruct and reinforce each other.

Yet as Lugones also points out, the "light" side of this system taking shape in enlightened Europe had a "dark" counterpart—colonialism as a Western masculinist undertaking, an economic enterprise that also articulated itself through the violent disruption of precolonial and "non-Western" cultural norms and values (16). Writing in the context of French colonialism in Algeria in the mid-nineteenth century, Pierre Bourdieu emphasizes the gendered aspect of this economic assault. He reminds us that the French colonial policy of land grabbing—which necessarily meant large-scale displacement and resettlement of the indigenous populations—was also an attack on precolonial familial structures, to the extent that "the patriarchal family is dispersed and often torn apart."[8] Cultural imperialism complemented this physical violence against and the deracination of the colonized. As Mohamed Benrabah demonstrates in his study of the politics of language in Algeria, the colonial administrative policy that made French the official state language also disregarded preceding patronymic systems. Under the French system, a common (and often derogatory) surname imposed on members of the same family supplanted the importance attributed in precolonial Algeria to the name of the father appearing before a first name.[9] The "Frenchification" of Algeria was designed to target Islam and the majority Arab population in particular. But the colonial state subsequently used the same policy to denigrate the language and culture of the Berber minority—agricultural tribes living in the mountains since late antiquity and weathering invasions by Phoenicians, Romans, Arabs, Turks, and, finally, the French (Benrabah, *Language Conflict in Algeria*, 22, 28). Crucially, the French attack on precolonial cultures did not end patriarchy in colonized Algeria and instead gave it a counterhegemonic Arab nationalist form. In fact, anticolonial organizations like the FLN actively drew on the gendered colonial ideology and saw themselves as the means "to restore a threatened [Arab] masculinity."[10]

With the reinstatement of Arab masculinity as an implicit goal, anticolonialism had a direct impact on the daily lives of Algerian women. We might even say that the politicoeconomic *value* of the Algerian woman began to be recoded in patriarchal-religious terms soon after the French invasion in the nineteenth century. As Marnia Lazreg argues, the precolonial Muslim practice of Algerian women wearing the hijab took on an entirely new anticolonial meaning: "The veil became women's refuge from the French denuding gaze. However, its form changed, becoming longer, and it acquired a new significance as a symbol of not only cultural difference but also . . . of virtue among many Algerian girls growing up during the colonial era. Thus, *hijab* (protection) became the antidote to *kefsh* (exposure)."[11] Veiling posited native femininity as resistance against sexual exposure to and potential seduction by the colonizer. At the same time, as a measure of the value of native femininity, the virtue represented by the veil was derived from a colonial capitalist ideology of race that was itself welded to the gender binary. As Austin writes, anticolonialism's "need for legitimation (which, in the absence of democracy, it sought in Islam as well as elsewhere)," combined with "nationalist ideology, and paranoia about 'Western' or 'French' models of modern identity, including feminism, ensured the maintenance of the status quo. Patriarchy was . . . sacralized by . . . religion" (*Algerian National Cinema*, 68).[12] Effectively, Algerian nationalism asserted its own non-Western value and Islamic identity both in opposition to and in complicity with the androcentrism and dimorphism of the colonial project.

In her essay "Forbidden Gaze, Severed Sound," Djebar argues that the anticolonial desire to save the Algerian nation-as-woman from the phallic French gaze not only led to a heightened sexual segregation in colonial society but also the suspension of any reciprocal dialogue between the opposed sexes: "In Algeria, it was precisely when the foreign intrusion began in 1830 . . . that a gradual freezing up of indoor communication accompanied the parallel progressive French conquest of exterior space, an indoor communication becoming more and more deeply submerged: between the generations, and even more, between the sexes."[13] The obverse of the normalization of this heteroerotic alienation was a double standard wherein Algerian women were expected to cover and sequester themselves to avoid exposure at all costs while anticolonial masculinity defined itself precisely in opposition to these restrictions on the female body. As Djebar asks, "Is a woman—who moves around and therefore is 'naked'—who looks, not also a new threat to their exclusive right to stare, to that male prerogative?" (139). Thus we can say that the nationalist production of Algerian femininity kept intact the phallocentrism of the colonial mode of production. At once refusing and emulating the colonizing phallus as the universal equivalent, the masculinist anticolonial ego became the site where, as Gayatri Chakravorty Spivak argues, "the case of the money-form, and that of the ego-form in the dialectic of the phallus, support each other and lend the subject the attributes of class- and gender identity."[14] I would add that the anticolonial view of the (Algerian) phallus as the equivalent—through the money form promoted by colonial capitalism—is not only gendered but also racialized. But precisely because Algeria sought to redress wounds inflicted by colonial phallocentrism with anticolonial phallocentrism, the identity of the Algerian *woman* was reconstructed through yet another fragmentation and alienation in the mirror of nationalism. The woman's experience of her (by definition patriotic) identity could not but be split between the masculinist vision of the sovereign Algerian nation and a phallocentric view of her anatomy that regulated the terms of her visibility and participation in the nation-building project. To make metadiscursively visible the identity of the woman in colonial Algeria is, therefore, to account for this experience of feminine splitting, which, as Djebar points out, is accompanied by a repressive domestic-political blockage.

Before returning to *The Nouba*'s aesthetic engagement with this fragmentation, it will be useful to turn briefly to the regulation of sexual difference in postcolonial Algeria, especially in the years leading up to and immediately following the film. Significantly, following Algeria's independence in 1962 and until the late 1970s, the Algerian state remained staunchly socialist, taking specific measures to counter the effects of colonial capitalism. The influence of the military and Soviet-inspired socialism increased substantially after the coup of 1965, which removed the first president, Ahmed Ben Bella, from his office and brought Colonel Houari Boumédiène to power. The Boumédiène era saw several efforts to reverse the dire economic repercussions of the French appropriation of agricultural land. The newly minted socialist state confiscated lands held by the French *pied-noirs* to redistribute them among the formerly colonized, established state farms and even attempted an agrarian revolution in the early 1970s.[15] Simultaneously, some politicians felt compelled to acknowledge that the sociocultural marginalization of women could no longer be encouraged or ignored. The Boumédiène-led 1976 National Charter included an entire section on "the promotion of the Algerian woman," which argued that the recognition of the Algerian woman as a "citizen of free, revolutionary, and socialist Algeria" could not be contingent on "the patriotic and social roles she played alongside her male companions."[16] The government seemed poised to overhaul completely the economic and cultural baggage from its colonial past.

The realities of the postcolonial state, however, were starkly different. The socialist principles espoused by the politicians in power were shot through with the Arabo-Islamism that had shaped the anticolonial movement. From the 1960s onward, the Algerian government undertook an especially aggressive and orthodox program of Arabization that aimed to undo but also mimic the colonial logic of "Frenchification" and the minoritization of other languages and cultures. Proponents of Arabization not only demanded "the replacement of French by Arabic in all walks of life . . . but its use as an instrument of linguistic and cultural assimilation for national unity and the affirmation of an identity that is exclusively Arab and Muslim."[17] Giving Arabic the status of French, therefore, also meant identifying Algeria's non-Arab inhabitants— especially the Berbers—as "outsiders." At the same time, Arabization was, from its inception, a contradictory exercise. Even as the Algerian state wished to rid the nation of colonial influence, French continued to be the language of the political elite, who now began to educate their children in France and other European countries.[18] This neocolonialism underpinning Arabization created a growing schism between what Ahmed Moatassime calls "a French speaking culture of social well-being and an Arabo-Berber culture of poverty."[19] Unsurprisingly, those calling for Arabization also encouraged tightening patriarchy's grip over the postcolonial nation that, on paper, advocated for women's rights as equal citizens. While the Boumédiène presidency led to a sharp increase in women's literacy, the state's increasingly orthodox interpretations of Koranic law further intensified the colonial isolation of women as a separate class. This isolation culminated in the draconian 1984 Family Code that severely curtailed women's rights and legalized patriarchal control over divorce, reproduction, and the right to adopt.[20]

It is perhaps not accidental that the escalation of Arabo-Islamic disciplining of sexual difference coincided with the dismantling of the socialist state and Algeria's entry into the global free market in the late 1980s.[21] Within a decade after independence, the government realized that its version of state capitalism had only increased national unemployment, intensified the divide between the urban and the rural, and failed to address an acute housing crisis in the cities. The masculinist nation that had just begun to pride itself on its economic autonomy was compelled to give in yet again to the exigencies of foreign capital. Like many other young postcolonial economies in Africa and Asia in that decade, Algeria was "swept up by the tsunami of globalization which, in a debtor's world, translated into huge expectations of compliance with demands set by global capitalists."[22] Thus we can say that as Algeria "willingly" yielded to neocolonial domination, Arabization asserted itself as a postcolonial variation on anticolonial phallocentrism, as a general equivalent that ultranationalists hoped to wield as a cultural buffer against the aggressive infiltration of transnational capital. Consequently, Arabization needed to fabricate the Algerian woman as the "supplement" against which it could define itself and declare its own value in the domestic national context.

Femininity as Political Liminality

We are now well placed to return to the opening scene of Djebar's film. If the androcentric Algerian state and state-approved cinema produced discursive speech to silence those it identified as women, then this scene can be read as a provocative repudiation of that male braggadocio. If Algerian masculinity established its symbolic capital by claiming to "protect" the nation's women, Ali's vulnerability and Lila's alienated attachment in the opening scene gesture toward a far less sanguine predicament. The figure of the injured patriarch with a dispirited mien evokes neither an image of postcolonial independence nor one of socialist progress. The couple's inability to dialogue with each other in the postcolonial present also signals a persistence of the communicational paralysis initiated by the dimorphic colonial gaze. Notably, in this scene, there is an inversion of the dominant nationalist paradigm. The film begins to break the discursive silence imposed on Algerian women through Lila's voice-over. And it is the male figure, Ali, who is barely articulate throughout the film, as if to underscore the emptiness of the claims of nationalist rhetoric as well as its historical elisions. Predictably, Djebar's representation of Algerian masculinity did not please the RTA. The broadcasting company showed *The Nouba* only once on national television, with critics complaining that the film offered "a disrespectful and limited view of the male war veterans."[23]

At the same time, even as its opening scene inaugurates what may be called the historiographic "female gaze," *The Nouba* does not represent femininity as some inherently radical "multiplicity" outside of the historical-dialectical forces of capitalist patriarchy, which is a common reading of the film and to which I will return later. Rather, the film deploys *multiple* gazes that refuse to separate Algerian femininity from the trauma of (anti)colonialism. Initially, it seems as though feminine remembering could be the much-needed reprieve from Ali's defeated masculinity, what Djebar herself describes as "the gaze of the paralyzed man" and "the dance of impotent desire."[24] As Lila stands by her window turning her gaze outward and away from the domestic stasis inside, her voice-over declares her hopes for such a refuge: "I wander in the past . . . in my memories . . . and then I leap again." But the "past" reveals itself as still-unfolding trauma as soon as Lila starts to remember the war. Irreparable loss, the voice-over is forced to acknowledge, has accompanied decolonization: "Independence, the dawn . . . that was yesterday. I have lost everyone, my mother, my father, my uncle . . . my brother disappeared. So, why return? To speak about death and fire?" In this moment, the film offers us an audiovisual correlative to Lila's memory of the revolution in the form of a montage that combines fictional reenactment with documentary footage. Themes of incarceration, brutality, and devastation come to the fore as we move from a shot of a female prisoner behind bars, to military trucks entering a village, to a fortress in the mountains, to fires blazing in a forest. Cries of women, children, and men, as well as the sounds of airplanes and explosions, remind the spectator of the human cost of the revolution, whose representation strains the documentary impulse. In other words, in stark contrast to freedom fighter cinema's glorification of martyrdom, these images foreground a traumatic memory of revolutionary violence and its consequences. The montage, we might say, represents a historical consciousness attuned to the involuntary, repetitious, and hallucinatory nature of traumatic memory. At the same time, as a traumatic hallucination of which Lila herself is also a "spectator," the montage gestures toward "a psychical or 'historical truth' whose meaning has to be interpreted, reconstructed, and deciphered."[25]

It is significant that there is no male figure visible in the entire montage and that the first shot is that of an unidentified female prisoner. Here, too, the film explicitly departs from the dominant anticolonial tendency to monumentalize the male martyr. At the same time, the position of the female prisoner parallels that of the postcolonial subject Lila standing behind a window earlier in the scene. As the camera returns to frame Lila in a close-up in the final shot of the scene, the voice-over reinforces this commonality between the nameless colonial prisoner and the film's protagonist: "I was fifteen. With a hundred years of suffering." This is a remarkable moment when the "I" of Lila's voice-over announces itself as both individual and collective, staging an indeterminacy that will be also be complicated later in the film. But as the voice-over pithily observes—and as the analogous images of feminine

Lila remembers a female prisoner from the war in *The Nouba*.

In *The Nouba*, Lila's position behind the window parallels
that of the prisoner she remembers.

internment foreground for the spectator—this identitarian collectivization is predicated on a suffering that is unequivocally experienced in
gendered terms. That is to say, through its opening scene, *The Nouba*
seems to suggest that Lila does not share her identity with other Algerian
women in any ontological sense. Rather, her identity is split between her
own experience of gendered oppression and her perception of the marginalization of other Algerian women across sociohistorical divides. This
"critical identification,"[26] therefore, begins to lay bare a certain dissonance between "woman" and the grand narrative of anticolonialism, her
liminal position at once inside and outside the masculinized sphere of
political and cultural activity.

Visually, *The Nouba* emphasizes this liminality of the feminine by
placing Lila recurrently in front of the window and in the doorway—
threshold spaces between the domestic space and the outdoors. As
Ranjana Khanna notes in her reading of the film, "In these junctures of
subjectivity—of interiority and exteriority, of memory and the present—
doorways frame a fragmented subject whose form appears almost

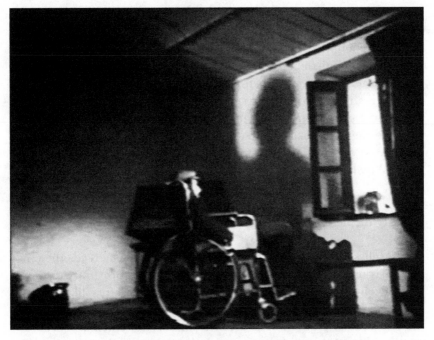

The wounded patriarch Ali gazes outside while his wife Lila
(in shadow) observes him in *The Nouba*.

indistinguishable from her shadow" (*Algeria Cuts*, 127). In other words,
through images of Lila in these in-between spaces, the film external-
izes the unrepresentable psychic splitting and containment constitutive
of postcolonial femininity. Arguably, this confinement cannot be interpreted too literally, since Lila frequently moves between the inside and
the outside. Lila's confinement is, therefore, also discursive, arising from
the gendered political economy of the postcolony.

In this connection, we should note that while the film excises male
martyrdom from its (or Lila's) memories of the war, it also offers a few
striking images of androcentrism-as-incarceration. A brief scene toward
the beginning of the film begins with a medium shot of Ali deject-
edly looking at a young woman through the bars of a window, as Lila
watches him from the doorway. The same scene deconstructs the male
gaze through a long shot of Ali facing Lila's towering shadow. Here
the androcentric gaze is not only not "sovereign" but is also compelled
to confront the "supplement" that is central to its constitution. As
feminine recollection in *The Nouba* critically reevaluates nationalist

nostalgia, postcolonial phallocentrism is, perhaps, in such moments in the film, given the opportunity to rethink its baseless separatism and sense of superiority. The feminine shadow or supplement reveals itself to be both the mirror image and the "anti-image" of the phallocentric ego. In other words, contrary to how some critics have read *The Nouba*, I am suggesting that the film does not simply reverse the capitalist binary such that a gynocentric gaze supplants or becomes the desirable alternative to the male gaze.[27] Instead, femininity and masculinity stand for imbricated and yet distinct metaphorical prisons shaping the postcolonial malaise.

Identity through a Haptic Optics

In his well-known essay on *The Nouba*, Réda Bensmaïa reads the film's emphasis on fragmentation as an indication of its proximity to experimental cinema—especially that of European directors like Chantal Akerman, Marguerite Duras, and Alain Resnais—and their rejection of the grammar of Hollywood and other commercial cinemas.[28] There is considerable merit to this argument. Indubitably, *The Nouba* rejects the commercial narrative emphasis on continuity editing, motivated action, and diegetic closure. As well, on several occasions, the film plunges the viewer into Godardian reenactments of mythical and historical events, thus deliberately thwarting spectatorial expectations of narrative transitivity and linear progress.

Yet I would also argue that to read *The Nouba*'s aesthetics primarily through the European avant-garde is to elide the complexity of its representation of Algerian nationalism and postcolonial femininity. Just as the avant-gardism of Cha's *Dictée* does not bypass but confronts the aesthetics of identitarian splitting (see chapter 2), so, too, do the experimental attributes of *The Nouba* ultimately move us toward a nonessentialist account of the production of the essence—the simultaneously econopolitical and embodied experience of feminine fragmentation. In other words, I am suggesting that the film's aesthetics neither celebrates nor ignores the capitalist production of the woman-as-fragment.

To examine the identitarian implications of Djebar's avant-gardism, it will be useful to recall that what makes *The Nouba* distinct from contemporary films on the revolution is its refusal to glorify the male martyr. Going further, we can say that Djebar's film deviates from not just a narrative focus on men but a certain masculinist visual ideology that determines the manner in which the Arab Algerian male is placed at the center of the narrative space and action. As Austin points out through his readings of a number of anticolonial Algerian films preceding *The Nouba*, this is an aesthetics that typically represents the nation as (an oft-feminized) land or territory over which the colonized must, as a masculinized or patriarchal collective, regain control and ownership.[29]

Paradoxically, it is a *colonial* visual aesthetics that serves as the grist for these *anti*colonial images of spatial mastery. Anticolonial cinema at once resists and vernacularizes a mode of vision that also shaped European colonialism as a gendered and racialized project of territorialization. A number of scholars have demonstrated how with the invention of artificial perspective during the European Renaissance came the privileging of an idealized spectatorial position defined by its purported visual prowess. This mode of looking especially benefited the colonial subject literally seeking to control spaces and populations that had just become the objects of his vision. As Austin notes, drawing on the work of John Zarobell, "The European colonial project is one of spatial mastery, disciplining space. This project has been served by visual media such as painting, photography, and cinema, creating . . . 'a form of image production in which the force of technology sustains the illusion that progress is a definitive result of colonial development'" (*Algerian Cinema*, 51).[30] We cannot, of course, forget that its "illusory" nature notwithstanding, this visual disposition to control the colonized subject was accompanied by very concrete and physical acts of violence and displacement in Algeria as well as other colonial contexts.

Film theorist Laura U. Marks has examined this capitalist desire to control and claim the object of vision in more general terms, calling it the predominant attribute of an "optical visuality." For Marks, optical visuality designates commodity culture's tendency to reduce the image to a consumable sign.[31] As the mode of vision fostered by commercial narrative cinema but originating much earlier in Enlightenment idealism, optical visuality "depends on a separation between the viewing subject and the object" (Marks, *Skin of the Film*, 162). It is a visuality that consolidates the viewer's position as a consumer by representing the image as an object of "identification" as well as something to be possessed (166). We might say that it is, in fact, the optical imagery of dominant capitalist cinema that produces what Jean-Louis Baudry calls the "transcendental" spectator (see chapter 1).

Returning to the Algerian context, we find that masculinist freedom fighter cinema *appropriates optical visuality as anticolonial resistance* when it substitutes the implicitly white male European transcendental spectator with the colonized male viewer. Austin makes this appropriation clear in his discussion of freedom fighter cinema. For instance, he demonstrates how Tewfik Fares's *The Outlaws* (1969) draws on generic conventions associated with the Hollywood Western with the express purpose of transferring spatiotemporal mastery from the white Western hero to the Arab Algerian male protagonist and spectator.[32] In this way, optical visuality becomes a reason as well as a "remedy" for the fragmentation of the colonized within the colonial mode of production.

The avant-gardism of *The Nouba*, then, lies in its refusal to repeat the gendered anticolonial bid for optical mastery. What Djebar's film rejects is not just the conventions of Hollywood cinema but also their anticolonial vernacularization, in which the colonized spectator is encouraged to emulate the territorializing visual impulse of the colonizer. A noteworthy example of this shift away from anticolonial spatial mastery can be found early on in Djebar's film, immediately after a doctor visits Ali to assess his recovery. As Lila steps outside with the doctor at the end of the visit, the camera shifts its focus to the landscape, first panning to the right and then slowly back to the left. The high-angle mobile frame simultaneously captures the sky, the sea, the seashore, and the movement of villagers whose particulars remain indistinguishable because of the camera's distance from them. The image departs from optical control and certitude in that there is a certain confusion between figure and ground, a certain lack of depth in that the light blue sky blends with the deep blue sea, and the latter with the rocky beach. And, while discernible, human action is not the privileged object of vision but absorbed into the tapestry of an awe-inspiring topography that the camera is unable to frame fully. Additionally, we hear lilting diegetic music as soon as the scene begins, but its source remains off-screen at this point. If dominant colonial and anticolonial cinemas typically produce the spectator as an "all-perceiving" subject by maintaining the figure/ground, subject/object, and viewer/viewed dichotomies, this is a paradigmatic moment in Djebar's film that *involves* the viewer in a vast and internally complex natural-cultural assemblage. That is, we move away from a spectatorial mastery to a sensorial *interaction* with the image of the landscape that we are made aware is not fully available to the protagonist or to us.

Indeed, it is possible to argue that this scene in the film employs and elicits what Marks calls "haptic" vision. Distinguishing this vision from optical visuality, Marks writes, "Haptic looking tends to move over the

The camera refuses spatial mastery while observing the
landscape in *The Nouba*.

surface of its object rather than to plunge into illusionistic depth, not
to distinguish form so much as to discern texture. It is more inclined to
move than to focus, more inclined to graze than to gaze" (*Skin of the
Film*, 162). Unlike optical visuality that reduces the image to a commodity, haptic visuality produces a "tactile" intimacy with the image, a
destabilization of the hierarchy between the spectator and the image.

If *The Nouba* reproduces the massive landscape as a surface that the
viewer can "touch," but only from a distance and with a humbling awareness of the partiality of spectatorial vision, the next few shots in the same
scene further develop the haptic mode, albeit in a contrasting manner.
The spectator involved in the scenery is plunged into tightly framed
close-ups of village women in the midst of their daily chores. This rapid
shift in scale is disorienting, compelling the viewer to readjust their
relationship with the image and, once again, become aware of the
manipulated nature and the limits of cinematic vision. At the same time,
the camera—unsteadily grazing the women's faces, the fabric of their
clothing, and a pair of hands feeding a crackling open fire—invites
a spectatorial engagement that approaches the object of vision with a

A woman throws hay into a crackling fire in *The Nouba*.

certain intimacy, "with only the desire to caress it, not to lay it bare" (Marks, *Skin of the Film*, 191).[33] Thus we can say that, in this scene, Djebar's film seeks to distinguish its haptic representation of Algeria and the *nouba* of Algerian women from centuries of optical visuality.

What, then, is the political work done by avant-garde haptic visuality? Crucially, for Marks, haptic visuality is cinema's solution or a more radical alternative to the limits of identity politics. In her book *The Skin of the Film*, in which she theorizes the optical/haptic distinction, Marks initially approaches identity "as a process rather than a position" that has been "productive for many [minority] artists" (4). As an agentic quest performed by filmmakers and spectators, identities are "never static but always relational, capable of creating links among different groups that transform those groups" (19). But while cinema is the necessary "pre-text" around which artists and viewers form coalitions within and across identities, the haptic mode—often adopted by experimental minoritarian filmmakers—makes clear that its appeal "to a politics of identity is limited" (21).[34] This is because, according to Marks, the experience

of the haptic "appeals to the limits of naming and the limits of understanding, and this is where it is most transformative" (21).

Before arguing that Djebar's *The Nouba* can, in fact, be read as a powerful critique of this cinema-bound anti- or postidentitarianism—even as
the film clearly demonstrates haptic tendencies—I would like to isolate
a few assumptions guiding Marks's argument. First, it is clear that Marks
refers to identity in minoritarian terms, as a matter of racial or gendered
marginalization. Yet her theoretical understanding of identity production
remains tied to the dominant psychoanalytic account of a false disembodied equivalence promoted by the mirror stage and its reactivations
in the cinema. She writes, "Theories of embodied [haptic] spectatorship
counter at their root theories of representation grounded in the alienation of visuality from the body, in particular Lacan's theory of the mirror
phase, which has been so influential in cinema studies. The mirror-phase
theory of subjectivity is based on a fundamentally alienated selfhood
that is constructed visually, when the infant comes into awareness of
being seen from the outside" (150). And then later, "Haptic cinema does
not invite identification with a figure . . . so much as it encourages a bodily
relationship between the viewer and the image. Consequently . . . it is not
proper to speak of the *object* of a haptic look as to speak of a dynamic
subjectivity between looker and image" (164, emphasis in the original).

A few points require scrutiny here. First, it is *in opposition to* identity as
an effect of specular plenitude and illusory identification—popularized
by the neurotic version of Jacques Lacan's theory of the mirror stage (see
this volume's introduction and chapter 1)—that Marks theorizes haptic
cinema's anti-identitarian potential. In other words, if haptic cinema,
for Marks, goes beyond the limits of identitarian naming, it is because
this process of naming (or identity production) is to be understood primarily as an optical experience of visual mastery and presence. Thus,
even as Marks blames psychoanalysis for conflating spectatorship with
illusory identitarian plenitude, she also relies on that hegemonic specular definition of identity to celebrate the nonidentitarian nature of haptic
visuality.

Relatedly, Marks sees both identity production as well as its dissolu-
tion to be primarily a cinematic or visual enterprise. If optical imagery
produces identity through a misleading identification that ultimately
keeps intact the hierarchy between the spectator and the image, the haptic aesthetic is offered as the handy solution where "the act of viewing
is one in which both I and the object of my vision constitute each other"

(183). The implicit suggestion, then, is that we can begin to resist capitalist identity production by producing and consuming cinema or visual
art with haptic tendencies and, in the process, give ourselves over to
the other-as-image, even if that "giving-over" can only be metaphorical
(191–92).

Finally, Marks's haptic/optic distinction also relies on a hierarchical
opposition between *touch* and *sight*. As her celebration of cinema as
an aesthetic medium amply demonstrates, Marks does not consider all
vision to be linked to commodification. But she does consider tactility
to be an inherently more democratic and superior form of epistemology
compared to that which is primarily visual. In fact, for Marks, cinema
can be radically anti-identitarian and egalitarian because it can convert vision and the visual into something tactile. Denoting an intimacy
between bodies that exceeds visual representation, cinematically cul-
tivated tactility is understood to be immanently nonantagonistic and
opposed to capitalist abstraction. To put it in Marks's own words, "Tactile values simply make life better" (165).

I would like to suggest that, in contrast to Marks's approach, *The
Nouba* deploys the haptic not to transcend identity politics but rather
to attend to the variegated context of the production of feminine (dis)
identification or dissonance in postcolonial Algeria. The film demonstrates that identity production in this sociopolitical milieu includes
but is by no means determined by—and, therefore, cannot be transcended through—the consumption and production of cinema. Put
differently, in my reading, *The Nouba* does not mobilize the haptic to give
spectators the convenient aesthetic satisfaction and solution of undoing (their own) identities by "touching" the image of the (feminine)
other. Instead, haptic visuality creates the conditions to reflect on the
gendered fragmentation of the other without instrumentalizing or elid-
ing her historical difference from the spectator. Furthermore, the haptic
also gives way to a certain destabilization of the haptic/optical dichot-
omy, gesturing toward a wounding or "tactile" capacity of the moving
image to evoke the unrepresentable trauma of identitarian violence.

As if to remind the spectator of the persistence—however
attenuated—of an optical gaze, a shot of Ali looking at the village
women through a window follows the haptic images of the landscape
in *The Nouba*. Ali's detached gaze is then contrasted with Lila's position
among the villagers. The haptic is invoked once more as tree branches
being carried by a peasant woman almost graze the lens as she walks
past the camera. But no sooner does the film suggest the "superiority" of

the haptic than it begins to alert us that what is being perceived haptically is, in fact, suffused with the violence of identitarianism.[35] Standing
next to Lila and viewing the same landscape, the doctor tells her in a
somewhat patronizing voice, "This is our country. On these mountains,
we were free." While the significance of the doctor's nostalgia remains
ambiguous—it is unclear if he is optimistic about reclaiming precolonial
freedom or laments its impossibility—his utterance initiates a dramatic
shift in the visual-aural mood of the haptically represented scene. The
film now interrupts its own immersive assemblage with images reminiscent of the montage representing Lila's fragmentation in the opening
scene. Shots of musicians performing by the sea are intercut with images
of the burning forests. The sounds of bombing and human cries from
the montage spill over into this scene and even supplant momentarily
the folk music wafting through the air. What begins as a haptic representation of rural Algeria is, therefore, utterly transformed by what we,
as viewers, recognize to be Lila's memories of the Algerian Revolution.
Feminine (dis)identification becomes the obverse of the haptic image.

Indeed, I would argue that the insertion of the montage at this point
introduces a certain confusion between the haptic and the optical
modes. On the one hand, as a collage of archival or "impersonal" images
of colonial violence, these images of the past could be said to represent optical visuality. On the other hand, as audiovisual signifiers that
have traumatic and historical significance (not just for Lila but, potentially, for spectators of the film who have been, in some way, affected
by the revolution), the same images could be seen to have a certain
wounding or "tactile" quality that is not immediately visible "in" them.
In other words, I am suggesting that by piercing the apparently salubri-
ous haptic mode with optical memories of the struggle for independence,
the montage also alerts viewers to a potentially injurious tactile effect
of optical representation. Arguably, the film does not want spectators to
"give themselves over" to the images and sounds of the montage. But
the images in the montage become unavoidable traces of traumatizing
identitarian violence, traces that also touch or bear on Lila's subjectivity and reflect her gendered alienation and aesthetic dissonance within
(a haptically represented but androcentric) Algeria. Thus, the unrepresentable psychocorporeal effects of the archival images to which the
disruptive montage subtly gestures are starkly different from the haptic
intimacy that Marks seeks to retrieve to bypass identity politics.[36]

According to Marks, the optical image is "cool and distant" and
the haptic image "warm" and inviting because of the latter's nonvisual

sensorial qualities (*Skin of the Film*, 176). This warmth of the medium is part of the nonidentitarian pleasure of the spectator-consumer who surrenders to the image. The scene under discussion ends by challenging (unwittingly) the ethicopolitical premises of this claim, reminding the viewer to move beyond the pleasures of spectatorial consumption toward an understanding of the historical location and the body of the imaged other. Right before she retreats indoors from the landscape whose haptic representation has been interrupted by tactile optical violence, Lila's final words to the doctor are "I feel cold." Here *The Nouba* seems to caution us that, even as the privileged spectator might feel the warmth of anti-identitarianism while brushing up against the other-as-image, that warmth might well be a privilege denied to the others (on-screen or in the theater) who continue to be subjected to chilling reminders of their identitarian fragmentation. Notably, *The Nouba* also introduces a sensorial indeterminacy here, as raging fires and searing explosions lead to Lila's sensation of coldness at the end of the scene.

"Listening" for Identity's Intermediality

My analysis thus far will have already signaled to the reader that the avant-gardism of *The Nouba* lies not only in its critique (and critical deployment) of the optical *visual* image but also in its unconventional use of the acoustic elements of music, sound, and the voice. In this section, I continue to rethink Marks's theory of haptic spectatorship but through *The Nouba*'s attachment to the *languaged voice*—specifically female Arabic and Berber voices. It is through its docufictional proximity to these voices and the gendered and classed experiences evoked by them that *The Nouba* moves from Lila's individual fragmentation to a collective feminine marginalization. These voices are also the reason why Algerian language politics enters the film's intermedial depiction of the feminine.

As I mentioned at the beginning of the chapter, the interviews that Lila conducts of the women in the villages of Chenoua give us a glimpse of their *nouba*, or the rhythms of their everyday life. Significantly, as the interviewer—and perhaps even as the "surrogate" of Djebar the filmmaker—Lila expresses a strong desire to involve herself in the *nouba* not just through visual observation but through an attentive *acoustic* labor. As Lila's voice-over notes several times in between these interviews, "I am not looking for anything. But I'm listening. How I love to listen!" The work of listening, I will suggest, becomes another experimental technique that the film adopts alongside the visual to reflect on the feminine. But what does listening entail and produce in *The Nouba*? Given that Lila—much like Djebar—remains separated from her relatives by her class position and education, what does it mean to listen to and *make audible* the "feminine" across intracultural divides while holding on to an awareness of gendering as one of the principal means of capitalist value coding?

Arguably, empirical subaltern speech is central to the film's feminist goals. There is a recognizable continuity between the experiences of the protagonist and the filmmaker. In a speech delivered after being elected member at the Académie française in 2006, Djebar describes her own momentous encounter with her relatives during her research for and the production of *The Nouba*:

> From my initial efforts to search the memory of peasant women in the mountains of Dahra, in Arabic or sometimes in Berber, rising with the memories of their searing pains—I received *an irrevocable shock. A call to my roots, I would even say an ethical and aesthetic lesson*, from the women of all ages of my maternal tribe: as they remembered their experience of the Algerian war, but also evoked their everyday life. Their speech flowed freely, with surprising images, little stories that were bitter or funny, always letting forth a sense of faith, harsh or serene, *like a spring that washes and removes grievances.*[37]

Djebar's remarks alert us to a *tactile* effect of vernacular speech that at once shocks and assuages her subjectivity. This tactility, however, is inseparable from the writer and filmmaker's individual history as a colonial Muslim Berber woman from a middle-class background. Unlike her rural relatives and, indeed, most Algerian women of her generation, Djebar had access to a French colonial education system and even attended the prestigious and highly selective École normale supérieur in Paris.[38] But this immersion in metropolitan language and culture also meant a severance from the languages of her childhood. Djebar learned to write primarily in French, while also realizing later that the "anti-colonial narrative becomes deformed and indeed compromised when created in the language of the coloniser" (Hiddleston, *Assia Djebar*, 2). Thus, mediating Djebar's experience of a "call to her roots" in the passage above—as she listens to the speech of her peasant relatives—is the "grievance" of an unavoidably imperialist immersion in

French accompanied by the loss of the vernacular. At the same time, for Djebar, the colonial class and race dynamics marginalizing vernacular languages and dialects are also bound up with the politics of postcolonial chauvinism. As she notes elsewhere, "'Arabization from above' . . . has become, for me, the linguistic equivalent of war. Official Arabic is an authoritarian language that is simultaneously a language of men."[39] Thus, Djebar's identitarian shock in the mountains of Dahra is also the effect of a sexed, gendered, and classed gap between elite masculinist Arabic and the everyday speech of her rural relatives. The patriarchal mode of value production against which Djebar situates the tactile "ethical and aesthetic lesson" from her maternal tribe is at once colonial and postcolonial.

Djebar's account of her own embodied reception of vernacular speech in a pro-filmic context offers us another opportunity to think with and against Marks's theory of haptic aesthetics. As noted above, in Marks's view, cinematic consumption and immersion decisively mediate and determine subjectivation: the optical image produces identitarian detachment while the haptic image elicits nonidentitarian proximity. The haptic, in particular, becomes another name for cinema's ability to activate the potentialities of the spectator's body. As Marks writes in *Hanan al-Cinema*, her book on experimental Arabophone film cultures,

> Recent world cinema is taking an embodied turn. It is shifting from classical cinema's techniques for narrative [optical] representation . . . to [haptic] techniques that immerse the spectator in the event and call out to her own body to respond. These techniques emphasize that the medium is itself a body that makes contact between bodies—not only human or living bodies, but anything in the pro-filmic world, can be brought into contact with the body of the viewer by the apparatus.[40]

Without suggesting for a moment that the films that Marks includes in her impressively varied archive are not aesthetically complex, I want to signal in her approach what I see as a problematic privileging of the properties of the "body" that is cinema over the historical bodies and lives of imaged referents and spectators. In fact, I would argue that here we find an anti-identitarian *cinematic* instance of what I have called *the cunning of capital*. For Marks, the so-called cinematic body and the sensory "contact" that it initiates is—much like the materiality of *language* in Lacanian cultural critique discussed in chapter 1—inexplicably outside or resistant to capitalist value coding. Experimental cinematic production and consumption are miraculously free of—and ostensibly free the spectator from—the identitarian differences of class, race, gender, and/or sexuality. As Marks insists in the same book, the experimental cinematic body "deals with energies that are not yet captured by the discourses of identity. . . . They operate a little below the radar of discourse and identity, because that's where they can be most creative" (*Hanan al-Cinema*, 313). To reiterate, in this utopian zone of "creative" or aesthetic indistinguishability between cinema and spectator, embodiment and identity are fundamentally opposed. For Marks, identity can and should be put aside through the liberating affective embodiment that is cinema.

In contrast, in Djebar's reflections as an experimental filmmaker, we notice a critical insistence on the mutual implication of embodiment and identitarian difference. Notably, alongside visual mediation, capitalist-statist deployments of language play a crucial prosthetic role in Djebar's reflections on identity as an embodied and aesthetic experience of minoritization. In other words, when read against Djebar, the postidentitarian claims made in the name of haptic visuality become tenable only because the methodology behind the claims actively ignores the differential and multiply mediated experiences of identity in colonial and neocolonial phallocracies.

It is also in this attention to linguistic mediation that I see a contiguity between Djebar's approach to identity politics and the Fanonian intermedial analytic driving the argument of this book. Both Djebar and Fanon are attuned to the role that language plays as a corporeal "image," catalyzing egoic splitting that sustains identity as a lingering aesthetic dissonance. Moreover, both thinkers attest to the draw as well as the limits of seeking political refuge in identitarian aesthetics. In chapter 1, I demonstrated how, in *Black Skin*, Fanon attempts to celebrate the "meaning" of blackness through the negritude movement while also seeking to liberate the black subject from blackness. In Djebar, we notice a comparably ambivalent attempt to reinvent the fragmented Algerian feminist self through the voices of the peasant women of Chenoua, to reinvent her Francophonie by "incorporating" a form of vocal utterance that "washes and removes grievances." As she goes on to note in the same speech to the Académie française,

> The young woman architect in *La Nouba des femmes du mont Chenoua* returns to the place of her childhood. Her eyes resting

on the female peasants seek an exchange of words: their conversations mingle. . . . My French had been set alight just so
twenty years ago, from the night of the women of Mount Chenoua. . . . They greet me, and protect me. I carry with me, over
the Atlantic, their smiles, their images of "shefa'," that is to say
"healing." Because my French, layered with velvet *but also the
thorns of languages once suppressed, will perhaps heal my memory's wounds.*[41]

Of significance is Djebar's assessment of her own identitarian wound
in intermedial terms. The historically grounded cinematic gaze of the
filmmaker—alongside that of her protagonist Lila—is unable to isolate
tactility and embodiment from the voices-as-images of the women of
Chenoua. The referential power of these acoustic images lies in their
ability to signify identity and culture grounded in colonial-patriarchal
repression. Thus, it is simultaneously language, image, the gendered-
ethnicized body, and the androcentric state that mediate Djebar's
identity as an Algerian feminist. We might say that Djebar's response
evinces what Lacan calls a "passional" perspective—oscillating between
a perception of the voices as signs of gendered injury and a desire to
"heal" her own injuries through those same voices. Put differently, this
is an oscillation between aesthetic dissonance and ethnofeminist aestheticization. As I also demonstrated in chapter 1, this schizophrenic
movement between two poles of meaning reveals an aesthetic dimension of identity that is particular to racialized capitalism. We should also
note that Djebar's oxymoronic association of the "thorns of languages
once repressed" with "healing" challenges any nostalgic reclamation
of the empirical feminine voice as "pure" presence or prediscursive
plenitude.[42]

   In fact, I would argue that, as the result of Djebar's return to her
"roots," *The Nouba* levels a feminist critique of the colonial and anticolonial abstraction of the Algerian "woman" that is unprecedented in
the nation's history. The voices that the film includes are among the
first to speak out against that homogenization and uncritical postcolonial patriotism. As Algerian feminist Marie-Aimée Hélie-Lucas wrote
in the 1980s,

   We [Algerian women] are made to identify with "the nation," "the
   people," conceptualized as an undifferentiated mass, without
   conflicting interests, without classes, and without history—in

> fact, we are made to identify with the State and the ruling
> class as legitimate representatives of "the people." . . . In Alge-
> ria, many of us, including myself, kept silent for ten years after
> Independence, not to give fuel to the enemies of the glorious
> Algerian revolution. . . . Our rightist forces exploit our silence.[43]

Hélie-Lucas alerts us to an identification-as-alienation that she and many other activists endured in silence and that structured their identities as feminists. Through Djebar's film, Lila's interviewees begin to shatter that silence without being urban or educated political activists, remembering the Algerian Revolution in ways that were certainly not part of the official discourse in the 1970s. Instead of celebrating the male war heroes, some women in the film speak proudly of farming the land and cooking for the guerillas; others describe their experiences of being imprisoned and tortured by the French for hiding the guerillas; and still others remember the revolution through the deaths of their husbands, sons, and daughters. Two anonymous and unseen voices give us a partial account of Zoulikha, a forgotten heroine of the resistance tortured and executed by the French. Zoulikha's body, we learn, disappeared mysteriously after her execution, and she remains a "martyr" without a tomb or even a memorial. What these voices testify to, then, is both the diversity and commonalities between feminine experiences of the same war. While some voices evince a desire to be recognized by the postcolonial nation, others subtly gesture toward the limits and violent effects of that (mis)recognition.

The Nouba is also careful to remind us that its representation of the feminine cannot be totalizing or absolutely transparent. The interviews are woven into the film as an intransitive collage in which the voice of the interviewee is often not subordinate to the image, and vice versa. Some voices remain—to invoke Michel Chion's term—"acousmatic," their sources remaining off-screen and invisible.[44] These acousmatic voices do not exert any central authority over the images or each other. Instead, they are heard as sporadic and often partial responses to Lila's questions. As Bensmaïa points out, the film proceeds by offering spectators "a world . . . in gestation . . . dispersed fragments" that are "not summed up by an overarching signifier" ("*La nouba des femmes*," 877).

Yet unlike Bensmaïa—who reads the film's refusal of totality and its representation of a "female body . . . inscribed in multiplicity" as a liberating political alternative to capitalist-patriarchal objectification (878)—I interpret Djebar's aesthetics of fragmentation as a diagnosis

of a representational crisis introduced by class and gender discontinuities within a neocolonial social structure. In other words, in my
reading, the cinematic fragment becomes the means of underscoring
the difficulties of re-presenting the voices of peasant women who have
very little control over the discursive process—the economic, political, and technological conditions shaping their cinematic visibility and
appearance on national television. The feminism of *The Nouba*'s postcolonial aesthetic lies in part in its ability to be attentive to fissures
within feminist discourse. As Spivak points out, in the discontinuous
ground of feminization that is postcolonial Algeria "the recovery of
a woman's voice is useless . . . . if it does not acknowledge that the
woman-in-culture may be the site of internalized phallocracy."[45] The
cinematic fragment in Djebar's film becomes essential to negotiate this
divided field and the oppressions normalized within that field.

In this context, the film's use of fictional reenactments to disrupt many
of the interviews plays a crucial role. These reenactments insist on the
gap between the women's voices—which are also often not explicitly or
transparently antipatriarchal—and the film as a feminist intervention.
One reenactment in particular, unfolding alongside the interview of a
woman Lila refers to as "Djamila's mother," exemplifies this approach.
We see Djamila's mother briefly as she begins to narrate a local story
of Abdel Rahman el Shami, a shepherd who eventually became a tribal
patriarch and saint with seven wives. The reenactment begins as soon
as the interviewee begins her story, adding another layer of performativity to the oral narrative already embedded in the semifictional
interview. The spatiotemporal continuity of the interview is interrupted
as the interviewee's voice is both supplemented by and removed from
these reenacted shots of the shepherd-turned-saint tending to his flock.
In other words, Djamila's mother's voice generates a fictional excess—
contributing to the film's plural "voice"—that she, as the storyteller,
cannot fully control.

This excess generated by and yet removed from the subaltern voice is
most conspicuous toward the end act of the reenactment that involves
the disobedient seventh wife of the patriarch. In the story that Djamila's mother narrates, the seventh wife is "a stranger" who enters and
depletes the patriarchal granary that was, before her transgression, "full
of honey, butter, and oil." From the oral account, the spectator does not
learn of any specifics of the wife's actions and only their consequence.
The patriarch simply informs his people that his wife "stripped you of

my blessings." In Djebar's visual retelling, however, the story of feminine theft and betrayal becomes a highly stylized dance of liberation in a granary that looks like a theatrical set. In this scene, the wife "depletes" the granary by setting free doves trapped in tall jars. In other words, in the reenactment, the wife reveals and refuses the incarceration on which patriarchal bounty depends. There is an ironic disjunction, here, between the patriarchal loss that Djamila's mother narrates—"that evening people came to find all the jars empty"—and the high-angle shot of the smiling female liberator seen from the point of view of the liberated doves. In this way, *The Nouba* employs the empirical voice of the interviewee not to suggest a singular meaning, a unique presence, or even an individual body in control of its utterance. Instead, the reenactment of the protofeminist transgression of the seventh bride simultaneously joins and displaces the voice of Djamila's mother. Accompanying and yet maintaining its distance from the oral narrative, the reenactment makes clear that there can be no "direct" communication of the subaltern female voice even or especially when the voice is testimonial. The (use of the) voice of the subaltern other—where otherness follows, in part, from socioeconomic differences within women as a minoritized group—will always be a certain kind of ventriloquism. Thus, even as it listens to the intermedial production of gender as a psychosocial fragmentation, the avant-gardism of *The Nouba* self-consciously resists claiming that fragment as an essence.

As well, a manifest vocal opacity operating alongside the film's rescripting of the Algerian Revolution serves as a corrective to the necessary ventriloquizing of the subaltern. In "Forbidden Gaze, Severed Sound," Djebar notes how, in the dominant nationalist context, "the sound of the mother . . . woman without a body and without an individual voice, finds once again the sound of the collective and obscure voice" (146–47). Androcentric nationalism requires the appropriation of the maternal voice, de-eroticized and tethered to expressions of cultural identity like "the land," "the village," "the clan," and "the family." In *The Nouba*, maternal voices are neither exclusively gynocentric (i.e., free from patriarchal control) nor fully available for nationalist appropriation. In another mythical moment of reenactment in the film, the camera hovers near several groups of women telling stories to children in a spacious courtyard. These are, as Lila's voice-over informs us, "old women whispering by night" whose "stories become wonders in the dreams of children. And history is revisited . . . by the fire in broken words and voices searching for one another." Intriguingly, these diegetic voices are literally whispers whose words and intentions remain inaudible to the spectator.

I read this scene of collective whispering as a cinematic instantiation of what Spivak calls the postcolonial feminist labor of *aphonie*. Spivak borrows this concept from Djebar's novel *Fantasia*, in which Algerian women—to whom the novel's narrator intently listens—do not speak aloud but whisper their stories in a voice that lies somewhere between speech and silence: "Words that are too explicit become such boastings as the braggard uses, and elected silence [*l'aphonie*] implies resistance still intact."[46] Spivak reminds us that, as a representation of women's resistive potential that Djebar can only articulate in French, *aphonie* becomes speech that is "midway between women's oral culture and patriarchal scripture," a formal device that demonstrates the feminist's ability to listen to the subaltern sister while simultaneously acknowledging the impossibility to echo, or respond *as* her ("Echo," 29). Similarly, the use of the aphonic voice in *The Nouba* is an indeterminate but necessary gesture, navigating the contradiction between the resources of the state-owned RTA that makes Djebar's film possible and the subaltern women's body and speech excluded from the Arabization implemented by the same state. As a strategically experimental gesture—which I would argue also has a nonvisual and haptic quality—*aphonie* is a necessary exposition of the intermedial production of female identity and femininity in postcolonial Algeria. Aphonic whispers in the film urge the spectator to listen for intra-identitarian differences and heterogeneities that strain representation but are, nevertheless, engendered by the politicoeconomic staging of feminine difference.

Codetta

I have argued in this chapter that Assia Djebar's film *The Nouba* critically diagnoses femininity as a liminal aesthetic supplementation of the patriarchal logics of Algeria's colonial and postcolonial economies. I have examined how feminine identity in the film remains split between a desire to belong to the postcolonial nation and its alienation from a patriarchal and capitalist nationalism whose origins lie in the colonial mode of production. The closing of the film powerfully restages this schizophrenic dissonance (which I began analyzing through my reading of the opening scene). *The Nouba* ends with another montage—this time of a series of shots of peasant women who appear earlier in the film—including some dancing in the caves of Dahra. Over these images, we hear a voice singing an upbeat Saharan song of feminine recognition in the postcolonial nation: "Women shall never return to the shadows. Let's ask the present you and I. She has kindled the spark of the past. . . . All that was difficult will become easy. . . . We'll live a dream of bounty and ease." On the one hand, the song is imbued with the optimism of the Boumédiène era and its pro-women National Charter. On the other hand, the spectator cannot but listen for the implications of a *possibly male* voice dreaming of "bounty and ease."[47] The patriarch in Djamila's mother's story—and, indeed, the film's own *aphonie*—haunt this melodic celebration of postcolonial plenitude.

Furthermore, the now celebratory image of women dancing in the caves at once covers up and re-elicits the uncertain status of this subterranean (or subdiscursive) site of feminine culture. In an earlier scene, *The Nouba* juxtaposes these performances of female folk dancing against Lila's somber reflections (in voice-over) on brutal colonial aggression and patriarchal control with which the caves are historically associated: "The cave of Dahra where you [the women of Chenoua] waited out the battles and where sometimes the enemy buried you alive." And again, later, in another scene: "The women were dancing and singing . . . but under the ground." The voice-over's allusions to the precolonial practice of making women retreat to the caves (so that men could defend their "honor" in combat), as well as the French colonial technique of trapping and suffocating Algerian civilians in caves in the mid-1800s, make it impossible for the spectator to see the subterranean dances as an uncritical glorification of Algerian culture.[48] In fact, I would argue that the triumphant masculine rescripting or domestication of the ambiguity of these subdiscursive performances at the end of the film anticipates uncannily the extreme postcolonial repression that would follow soon after the release of *The Nouba* in the form of the Family Code. The ending of *The Nouba*, then, does not make the film naively optimistic. Rather, nationalist euphoria, here, becomes deeply ironic, underscoring the feminine as aesthetic dissonance.

Finally, my analysis of aesthetic dissonance in *The Nouba* has moved through and between the film's critical uses of the cinematic image, subaltern speech, and embodied feminist listening. I have suggested that when viewed through this reflexive intermediality, the avant-gardism or countercinematic attribute of Djebar's film can also be said to lie in its resistance to the aesthetic maneuvers of capitalism. Ultimately, what the postcolonial, feminist, and tactile cinematic aesthetics of *The Nouba* rejects is not just patriarchy but also the seemingly egalitarian aestheticization and reification of its own medium. That is to say, this is cinema that refuses to take refuge in cinema as a solution or an alternative to the inequities arising from the capitalist production of gender and, more broadly, from identity as a plurally mediated constraint. Turning the wheel of the kaleidoscope that is global postcoloniality, I further develop this countercinematic approach to sexed and gendered identities in chapter 4, the final chapter of this book. But I do so through the queer dissonance of more contemporary and lesser-known films from contemporary India.

CHAPTER 4

Queer Aesthetic Dissonance in Neoliberal Times

I want to argue that gay men and lesbians have *not* always existed.
Instead, they are a product of history, and have come into existence
in a specific era. Their emergence is associated with the relations of
capitalism; it has been the historical development of capitalism—more
specifically, its free labor system—that has allowed large numbers of men
and women in the late twentieth century to call themselves gay, to see
themselves as part of a community of similar men and women, and to
organize politically on the basis of that identity.
  —John D'Emilio, "Capitalism and Gay Identity"

In Anglophone activist and academic discourses, the adjective "queer"
is often used as an action verb, suggesting acts of resistance against
heterosexist and capitalist norms. Deploying the term from various vantage points, the proponents of "queering," however, have not been able
to agree on the mode, goals, or even who the beneficiaries are of such
acts of transgression. On the one hand, *to queer* is often to reinterpret
heteronormativity through one or more nonheteronormative identities
represented by the abbreviation LGBTQ+. "Queer" is often a shorthand
for that entire (still-developing) abbreviation, representing a sexually
minoritized collective demanding recognition. Within the same semantic field, "queer" also stands among established and emerging identities,
declaring both its difference from and solidarity with them. On the other
hand, "to queer"—especially since its entry into U.S. academic discourse
as "queer theory" in the 1990s—has a markedly nonidentitarian con-
notation. In fact, according to a well-regarded strand of queer theory,
the indeterminacy of sex and desire is the very means to refuse not

just the apparent stability of sexual and gender identifications but also the larger capitalist politics of naming and fetishization of difference as identity. In short, "queer," here, is seemingly queerer than the queer that stands with and for identity politics.[1]

My main goal in this chapter will be to undo and displace this hierarchy between nonidentitarian and identitarian articulations of queer politics through an intermedial analytic. Sexual/queer identity politics in its current capitalist articulations, I will argue, can neither be uncritically embraced nor summarily dismissed. Instead, queerness needs to be examined as a differential experience of a fragmentation between several forms of mediation regulated by neoliberal capital. In keeping with my methodology throughout the book, this final chapter insists on *mediation* as a capitalist process that includes but is not determined by media technologies (see, in particular, the introduction). More specifically, I contend that in neoliberal and postcolonial India—the geohistorical focus of this chapter—the mediation of queer identities is inseparable from intercessions on the part of the postcolonial state, transnational corporations, and, perhaps most fundamentally, the neoliberal regime of labor.

To make this argument, I continue with my emphasis on cinema and spectatorship from chapters 2 and 3. I have two main reasons for the cinematic inflection of this chapter. First, visual culture plays an undeniably important role in the construction of queer politics and identities both locally and transnationally. As Karl Schoonover and Rosalind Galt write in *Queer Cinema in the World*, "Cinema is a critical means by which queerness *worlds* itself, a means by which queers negotiate local and global subjectivities. Therefore, to engage with the politics of global queerness, we must attend to its cinematicity."[2] Taking this claim seriously, this chapter takes as its objects the KASHISH Mumbai International Queer Film Festival (held annually in Mumbai) and a number of films from India, most of which have been screened at the festival. Yet even as I engage with Schoonover and Galt's insights on the "cinematicity" of global queerness, I also interrogate their desire to see cinema as an inherently anticapitalist and anti-identitarian queer medium. This leads me to my second reason for focusing on the cinematicity of postcolonial queerness. I contend that the KASHISH festival and the films I analyze collectively constitute a multiform site that brings into view the contradictions of queer identity production in contemporary India. On the one hand, I argue that KASHISH's identitarianism is explicitly neoliberal, necessarily drawing on the nationalist, globalist, and corporatized rhetoric of self-consolidation and consumerism for its survival in a heterosexist free market economy. On the other hand, I show how a number of films curated by the same festival gesture toward the intermedial fragmentation of queer identities that its neoliberal rhetoric disavows. In other words, through my analysis of these films and the contexts of their production, exhibition, and reception, I delineate a reflexive cinepolitics that acknowledges both its complicity in and its inability to regulate fully the capitalist staging of identitarian essences and their supplements.

I begin with an analysis of the neoliberal ideology and self-presentation of the KASHISH film festival. Here I situate the festival's simultaneously global and local approach to queer identity politics in the broader context of India's entry into the global free market economy in the 1990s. I examine how, as a beneficiary of transnational flows of capital in postliberalization India, the festival (through its official rhetoric, trailers, publicity, sidebar events, and so on) de-emphasizes the socioeconomic inequalities and multiple mediations subtending queer politics in the country. This first section also analyzes the role of emergent corporate sponsorship at the festival and in Indian queer politics more generally. In particular, I examine two queer sponsor videos screened at KASHISH that, I argue, reflect the festival's tactical allegiance to a corporatized logic of entrepreneurial queer citizenship. This allegiance posits not just cinema but a thoroughly corporatized cinematic mode of production as *the* privileged medium for queer identitarianism. The second section of the chapter engages in a productively frictional dialogue with a seemingly opposing ideological position: Schoonover and Galt's idealization of cinema as an immanently queer, antineoliberal, and nonidentitarian medium. I begin by interrogating their reading of KASHISH as a transgressive queer space and then move to a broader critique of their approach to identity, aesthetics, and cinema-bound resistance. Schoonover and Galt's formalist departure from identity politics, I demonstrate, largely ignores the multiply mediated production and internal splitting of queer identities in the neoliberal postcolony. The third and final section analyzes a number of films that draw the spectator's attention precisely to this intermedial queer fragmentation. Postcolonial queer dissonance, in these films, returns us to the book's opening gambit: to move beyond the culturalist celebration and aesthetic disavowal of identity politics.

The KASHISH Film Festival and Queer India Inc.

Since its debut in 2010,[3] the Mumbai International Queer Film Festival known as KASHISH (or "allurement," in Urdu) has prided itself on not just being "South Asia's biggest LGBTQ film festival" but also "the first and only LGBTQ . . . film festival in India to be held in a mainstream theater, and the first Indian LGBTQ film festival in India to receive clearance from the Ministry of Information and Broadcasting"[4]—no doubt a significant feat in a country where homosexuality was, until 2018, a criminal offense. During this period, KASHISH has lived through and survived a precarious sociolegal climate where sexual minorities in India have been decriminalized, recriminalized, and decriminalized a second time. The festival was launched just months after the Delhi High Court, responding to a decade of national activism, restricted the application of a British colonial statute long considered an antisodomy law.[5] In July 2009, the High Court declared that Section 377 of the Indian Penal Code (IPC) criminalizing "carnal intercourse against the order of nature" was unconstitutional and violated the fundamental rights of Indian citizens. This landmark judgment was heralded as India's own Stonewall Rebellion, and the decision to launch KASHISH the following summer in a posh Mumbai multiplex reflected the euphoria of this postverdict moment.[6] But this victory was short-lived, or at least abruptly halted in 2013 by a reversal of the 2009 High Court judgment. Responding to appeals from right-wing religious groups and dismissing the concerns of what it called a "minuscule fraction" of the Indian population, the Supreme Court of India—the highest judicial authority in the country—reinstated the British colonial statute, with convictions carrying up to ten years of imprisonment.[7] Finally, in September 2018, pressured by continuing activism and following its own ruling on Indian citizens' fundamental right to privacy, the Supreme Court reversed its earlier decision, decriminalizing, for the first time, same-sex practices in private between consenting adults.[8]

Within this atmosphere of uncertainty and instability—where the law can reassess at any time whether the queer subject is a good citizen or a criminal—KASHISH has no doubt emerged as an alternative public sphere, a heterotopic and ludic cinematic space from where some Indians can speak back to heterosexism and queerphobia.[9] KASHISH is distinctive, too, because it is organized by the LGBTQ+ production company Solaris Pictures, whose strong connections with queer activist and HIV/AIDS prevention groups enable the festival to reflect on the civil rights and social needs of the sexually marginalized.[10] The festival receives hundreds of entries annually from emerging Indian filmmakers, many of whom work on very small budgets and would otherwise find it impossible to reach national and international audiences. Additionally, through its collaborations with multinational corporations, national and international distributors, and Mumbai-based cultural institutes and film schools, the festival has drawn a wide range of attendees: queer activists and media makers from India and abroad, culture aficionados, scholars, diasporic Indians such as myself, cinephiles, producers, Bollywood stars, social workers, and even government apparatchiks.

Yet KASHISH's need for national and international recognition in a hostile juridicopolitical environment has also compelled it to rely heavily on a liberal rhetoric of coming out, on an "it gets getter" narrative in which to be queer is to assert a preformed erotic identity, at once unique, self-evident, and, intrinsically democratic. The festival trailer for the 2015 edition of KASHISH—themed "Reaching Out, Touching Hearts"—exemplifies this tendency. Unmistakably exhortatory in its tone, the on-screen text of the trailer (appearing against a montage of shots from several films selected by the festival) encourages queer Indians to emerge from the shadows of anonymity and isolation: "The closet is no place for one's true self. . . . It's dark, sad, and a place for tears. . . . Step out, the world is waiting. . . . Break free, for the seasons will change. . . . It gets better when you find someone. . . . To embrace and love. . . . And when you stand up, others will stand up as well."[11] The liberal overtones of the trailer cannot be missed. It calls upon queers to believe in what Eve Kosofsky Sedgwick calls the "promise of gay self-disclosure."[12] It demands that queer Indians find their "true" self through an identitarian assertion of same-sex love outside the closet. It reassures queers that these collectives formed by coming out of the closet are intrinsically egalitarian. Also implicit in the trailer's rhetoric is the assumption that "the closet" is a temporary hindrance that can be surmounted through a singular act of self-disclosure. In other words, there is little or no room in this exhortation to engage critically with the closet as a regulatory structure that keeps the hetero/homo binary intact and, in fact, makes "coming out" an interminable process (Sedgwick, *Epistemology*, 67–68).

This liberal view of the closet needs to be read alongside the trailer's urgent counsel to queer India to join "the [already uncloseted and free] world." Queer Indians, the trailer suggests, need to assert their queer selves without further ado—regardless of their socioeconomic

Still from KASHISH Film Festival trailer, 2015.

positions—to join the global queerscape of erotically liberated nations. The same sentiment is expressed by an image from the 2015 trailer where a heart-shaped Indian flag appears as part of a much larger arboreal global queer alliance of nation-states as hearts. This buoyant and optimistic image is seductive. But it also "demands" to be historicized. For the image not only promises a global queer democracy but also evokes an event and a process that is, in fact, KASHISH's condition of possibility—the liberalization of the Indian economy in the 1990s. Here it will be necessary to digress from the festival to give the reader a sense of the contradictory and, indeed, queer effects of this process by which India joined "the world" at that time.

The term "liberalization" is used in the Indian context specifically to refer to several economic reforms that the Indian government began in the 1980s in response to a major fiscal crisis, and then aggressively implemented from 1991 onward to make the state more permeable to global capital. Leaning heavily toward deregulation and corporate tax cuts, these reforms made export, import, and foreign direct investment much easier than before, with countries like the Netherlands, the United Kingdom, and the United States emerging as the major investors. The exposure to foreign capital and commodities, in turn, primarily benefited (in addition to the business and financial elites) emergent Indian middle classes poised to become conspicuous consumers. As Rupal Oza writes, "The expansion of the consumer goods market fulfilled aspirations of the middle class as televisions, scooters, and refrigerators became icons of mobility. . . . The reforms promised to fulfill long-held middle class aspirations of joining the ranks of global consumers. . . . The consumption lifestyle was bolstered by advertisements, newspapers, magazines, and television programs that filled the popular imagination with attitudes reflecting the new modern middle classes."[13] These reforms, in other words, led to the production of a consumer imaginary that was simultaneously Indian and transnational. Yet the same measures—encouraging privatization and the withdrawal of (already inadequate) state services—widened income inequalities and the urban-rural divide. As Abhijit Sen notes, "The massive increase in rural poverty, by over 60 million people, in the first 18 months of reform was to a very large extent a direct result of the stabilisation-cum-structural adjustment policies."[14] Rural poverty had long been an issue, a direct fallout of British colonialism that had officially ended in 1947 but had left behind a partitioned India and a deeply divided social fabric.[15] Unsurprisingly, the postcolonial rise in poverty exacerbated already existing class differences. As Stuart Corbridge and John Harriss write,

> The partiality of the reforms . . . is confirmed not so much by the controls which India's proprietary elites may or may not exercise over economic policy . . . but by the consistency with which the reforms have failed to promote the economic or political interests of those who are excluded from India's "new" regime of accumulation. In practice too . . . the reforms have eroded further those institutions of state which might once have been turned to by the less powerful as a possible source of redress for the "hidden injuries of class."[16]

The emergence of an upwardly mobile and transnational middle class as a result of liberalization was, therefore, accompanied by a decline in the living standards of a sizable section, if not the majority, of the Indian population.

Simultaneously, even as the elite and middle classes wished to see themselves as global consumers, the state's loss of economic control coincided with the rise of Hindu nationalism and postcolonial assertions of cultural authenticity. Cultural conservatism sought to translate liberalization in exclusively "Indian" terms. According to Corbridge and Harriss, the appeal of the Hindu nationalist Bharatiya Janata Party among Indian elites lay in its promise "that by being fully and truly themselves, rather than attempting to imitate or emulate western values and ways of being, Indians will be able to assert themselves and secure for the country the status and recognition which India should have in a globalizing world" (*Reinventing India*, 174). Furthermore, the Hindu Right's cultural nationalist resistance to the West was a revitalization of a highly gendered and heterosexist strand of anticolonial nationalism that "imagines the nation as feminine . . . and has aimed to create a modern masculine Hindu culture so that her 'sons' shall be capable of protecting her" (189). The Hindu fundamentalist intolerance toward religious and sexual minorities since the 1980s and 1990s is thus inseparable from this desire for "masculine" impermeability and self-fortification, itself a displacement of the anxieties stemming from the vulnerabilities of the economic permeability of the nation-state (93–118). (We should note strong parallels between this iteration of postcolonial pro-capital religious nationalism and the Arabization of Algeria discussed in chapter 3.)

Paradoxically, "complemented" as it was by right-wing homophobia, India's postcolonial entry into the global market also created the conditions for the emergence of an organized and urban queer politics and activism over the next two decades. Here I will draw on Naisargi N. Dave's incisive ethnography of queer activism in India to make a few key points. First, Dave draws our attention to the metropolitan and global-local nature of the Indian lesbian and gay movement in its early stages:

> Indian lesbian and gay politics has been shaped by transnational circulations of people and agendas, from peripatetic scholars like the founder of Indian lesbian activism, Giti Thadani, to the Swedish agency that funded Indian lawyers to fight for the decriminalization of same-sex sex in India. Furthermore, the emergence of collectivized gay and lesbian politics in India in the late 1980s and early 1990s coincided neatly (and not coincidentally) with the liberalization of India's economy in 1991 and the acceleration of the global fight against HIV/AIDS. The history of queer activism in India is, in other words, inseparable from the history of neoliberalism, nongovernmental organizations (NGOs), the politics and anti-politics of development, and the agendas of a modernizing state and a transnational public health apparatus.[17]

Dave emphasizes the cosmopolitan networks of activists and organizations—and, therefore, the movement of cultural and finance capital across borders—that were instrumental in making queer activism visible on the domestic and international stage. It is important to note that Dave's argument is *not* that "lesbian" and "gay"—as sites of identification and cultural resistance—were Western or foreign impositions. Rather, she demonstrates how these sites were *locally* produced through demographically limited but affectively and politically significant encounters with transnational capital. Dave's analysis both builds on and recontextualizes John D'Emilio's well-known argument that serves as the epigraph to this chapter: the transformation of same-sex *behavior* into subcultural gay and lesbian *identities* in the United States in the mid-twentieth century would not have been possible without modern capitalism. In particular, it was the emergence of a wage labor system that allowed some men and women to organize their personal and political lives around their erotic desires. Those who were "free" to sell their labor power in urban centers were able to construct their lesbian and gay identities outside the stranglehold of the heteronormative family that had earlier been capitalism's privileged unit of production.[18] This cultural and political mobilization around same-sex desire became possible a few decades later in India, but not without the transnational capital that liberalization made available.

Second, Dave contends that Indian and diasporic mass media played a significant role in furnishing these moments of queer identification. Same-sex-desiring Indians with access to English-language print media and newsletters became aware of and were interpellated by the descriptors "gay" and "homosexual" after these terms began circulating in articles and interviews by the mid-1980s. Coming-out interviews by prominent Indian and diasporic activists in newsletters and on the radio offered to many gay Indians "moments of cathartic recognition, along with first contact with *Bombay Dost* [India's first bilingual gay magazine]" (Dave, *Queer Activism in India*, 43).[19] Simultaneously, confessional letters written by women from all over the country to the Thadani-led lesbian Sakhi collective made it clear that by the 1990s "Indian women outside of elite, urban activist networks could and did consider themselves to *be* lesbian. Their concern was not with the genealogy of the identifier, or its nefarious links to global capitalism" (41, emphasis in the original). In other words, that the word "lesbian" did not come from a vernacular Indian language was not necessarily a problem for many same-sex-desiring women.

Indeed, to a certain extent, the signifier "lesbian" functioned as a linguistic and erotic mirror in which the women "recognized" themselves.

At the same time, this recognition was, for many, rather partial and
marked by exclusion. Many of the letters written to Sakhi, as Dave is
compelled to acknowledge, are shot through with "sensations of lack
and declarations of need" (51) that brought into view the cultural and
economic differences *within* the collectivity conjured by the signifier
"lesbian." Class divides surface in the gap between the nonmetropolitan
lesbian letter writers' aspirations "for travel and transnational connection . . . lesbian marriages in the north . . . traveling . . . to Sakhi's
promised land" (52) and the realities of their inability to be cosmopolitan
migrants as well as their need for anonymity in the face of homophobic violence (56). Thus, even as these women sought to legitimize their
same-sex desire through the signifier "lesbian," they lacked the wherewithal to join the kind of political activism that Sakhi represented as a
metropolitan lesbian organization.

In Dave's estimation, then, the economic liberalization and neoliberalism that followed have simultaneously mobilized and hindered queer
freedoms in postcolonial India. While cosmopolitan networks have produced new sites of identification, the same networks have also been
unavailable to a large number of metropolitan and nonmetropolitan
queer Indians. Indeed, this disparity poses a serious challenge to Dave's
research project: "Although lesbians exist across the class spectrum, their
activism is largely limited to people with means. . . . My research lacks
sustained attention to lesbianism in rural areas and urban slums in part
because these sites have been marginalized from the lesbian politics
I analyze here" (28). Econocultural divides in the postcolony generate
discontinuities or dissonances between nonheteronormative desire and
mass-mediated identity politics that calls itself "lesbian" or "queer." As
we shall see later in the chapter, Karishma Dube's film *Goddess (Devi)*
and Debalina Majumder's . . . *and the unclaimed (. . . ebang bewarish)*
grapple in different ways with precisely this scission.[20]

We can now see why, as a beneficiary of liberalization, KASHISH cannot explicitly vocalize the socioeconomic contradictions noted above.
Tasked with the mission to dialogue with the neoliberal mainstream,
the global vision of the KASHISH festival trailer, in a sense, has to disavow the poverty (queer or otherwise) that surrounds South Mumbai's
art deco Liberty Cinema, with its rich teak interiors and rococo plas-
terwork.[21] Indeed, the 2015 trailer image of "touching [nation-states
as queered] hearts"—also featured on the festival catalog cover that

year—is contiguous with what I have elsewhere called the representational regime of the "homoglobal." The homoglobal, I argue, is a regime where queerness, as a form of neoliberal transnationalism, *appears* to have overcome homonationalist racism, imperialism, and class divides.[22] We might perhaps even say that this discursive regime presents queer multiculturalism and globalism as the means to overcome geopolitical divisions and hierarchies. In the homoglobal village—the KASHISH tree made up of hearts fits in rather well here—queer love becomes a metaphor for a cosmopolitan commingling of diverse cultures that have seemingly suspended their heteropatriarchal nationalisms. As well, the homoglobal is a regime that foregrounds the globality of queerness through forms of media consumption, travel, and alliances that are frequently transnational. In other words, the homoglobal equates queerness not just with same-sex desire or gender nonconformity but (more implicitly) with a certain kind of mobility, global exposure, access to technology, and spending power. What homoglobal media overlook, therefore, is not just political conflict but also the mediation of queer (dis)identifications through the international division of labor.[23]

It should also not come as a surprise that KASHISH, which typically screens films from over forty countries each year, subscribes to this discourse of queer cosmopolitanism.[24] Since its inception, the festival has had a wide range of international partners, including developmental organizations like the United Nations Development Programme and the United Nations Joint Programme on HIV/AIDS (more commonly known as UNAIDS), the Canadian and U.S. governments, cultural organizations like the Alliance Française, U.S.-based companies like IBM, the LGBTQ+ media distributor Wolfe Video, and even the gay mobile app Scruff.[25] These partnerships have required the festival to mold its self-image quite consciously in accordance with the dominant international rhetoric of queer rights and visibility, with the attendant hope that queer Indians will learn to see themselves through the festival— and in sync with the project of liberalization—as citizen-consumers of the (queered) world. Advertisements placed in the festival's catalogs by Wolfe Video and the YouTube channel GayDirect (promising "LGBT" media "on demand" and "anytime anywhere") stand out as digital affirmations of the homoglobal imaginary that defies geopolitical borders and divisions.[26]

At the same time, it is important to note that KASHISH combines its homoglobal aspirations with a substantial dose of localism to ensure mainstream national endorsement. By localism, I do not only mean the festival's attention to films produced in several regional Indian languages but rather a careful insertion of local identities and globally recognized Indianness into its self-production and programing. For instance, the trailer for the 2017 festival (themed "Diverse One") opens with an animation sequence where a panoply of nonnormative identities (spelled in English) fly in from the edges of the screen toward the center. Each identity occupies and settles into its own space on the screen while remaining in intimate proximity to each other. This assemblage finally allows for the materialization of a rainbow-colored humanoid face against a black backdrop. The message is quite clear: all these identities are distinct but united in their efforts to make visible the queer face of humanity. The inclusion of the "metrosexual" in this assemblage perhaps signals the festival's desire to include the urban mainstream. But just as—if not more—significant here is the inclusion of the South Asian identities *hijra* and *kothi* that do not typically appear (or are not as visible) in the global/transnational abbreviation LGBTQ+. This multiply queer face of humanity, then, is one that is especially attuned to Indian and South Asian specificities.

Much like the globalism of the 2015 trailer, the regionalism of the 2017 trailer calls for a historical rereading that KASHISH also cannot explicitly allow into its rainbow vision. On one level—even as *gay* remains the most conspicuous identity in the image and closest to the "mouth" through which multiply queer India speaks as "one"—it can certainly be argued that the festival intends to create a level playing field for all identities.[27] That is, we can agree that the festival declares an intention to include the vernacular identities of *hijra* and *kothi* just as it includes the other more global identities. On another level, the very representation of these identities as "diverse [but] one" elides the systemic postreform inequalities within which the two vernacular identities emerged in India. Another brief digression will be necessary to elaborate on these disparities.

A number of scholars have demonstrated how the influx of HIV/AIDS funding after liberalization also engendered conflicting forms of queer identification in India from the 1990s onward. First, as Dave points out, there has been a blatantly sexed imbalance in international funding. "No-risk" lesbian women's groups have, since the very beginning, felt excluded from steady streams of money reserved for "at-risk" same-sex-desiring men (*Queer Activism in India*, 29–40).[28] Second, NGOs and activists reaching out to same-sex-desiring men have not always been able to agree on the language of interpellation. In his essay "The Kothi Wars," Lawrence

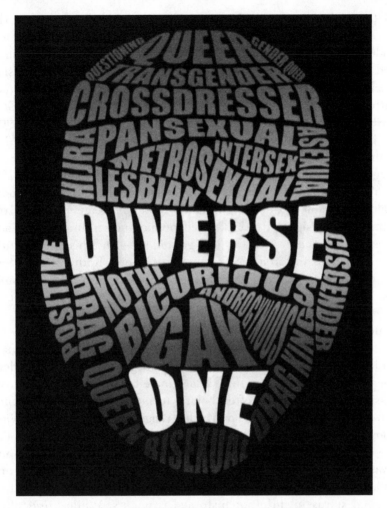

Still from KASHISH Film Festival trailer, 2017.

Cohen examines how the competition over HIV/AIDS funding in the 1990s saw a bitter linguistic and cultural divide between NGOs that saw *gay* as an appropriate identitarian category for same-sex-desiring men in India, and those that saw the same term as an elite and urban identity not applicable to the plurality of same-sex practices between South Asian men. In particular, NGOs supported by the Naz Foundation claimed that *kothi*—the Urdu and Hindi word designating a gender-nonconforming, nonelite man who desires to be penetrated by another man—was a culturally more "authentic" descriptor than *gay* in the South Asian context.[29]

Yet as Cohen convincingly argues in a Foucauldian vein, while the concept of the *kothi* was in circulation within certain indigenous transgender communities in Chennai in southern India, it became a widely used category *because* of the intervention of Naz-sponsored transnational NGOs. In other words, if *kothi* ultimately turned into a culturally "authentic" sexual identity, it did so because of the postcolonial NGOs' construction of non-Western "difference" in the early to mid-1990s. The purpose of this (self-)essentialization was to produce the *kothi* as a vulnerable subgroup that would fit into predetermined non-Western categories of global HIV/AIDS discourse, thereby becoming suitable for Western financial benevolence.[30] Consequently, for many non-Anglophone same-sex-desiring Indian men, *kothi* became the preferred identity that designated a lack of economic and cultural capital and access to healthcare—in a way that *gay* did not—and this lack, in turn, granted "access to foreign NGO funds" (Cohen, "Kothi Wars," 299). The constitution of *kothi* as a distinctly non-Western sexual identity was, therefore, intimately bound up with the developmental logic of HIV/AIDS funding.

Furthermore, the construction of the *kothi* subject in the 1990s unfolded alongside the simultaneous reconfiguration of another vernacular identity—the *hijra* as an indigenous transgender, or "third gender," subject. The *hijras* of South Asia are male-born (or intersex) cross-dressing individuals who often belong to hierarchical lineages called *gharanas* aligned with Hindu or Muslim religious practices. Some *hijras* choose to undergo ritual castration and/or penectomy to enter a lineage or acquire higher status within it. Yet as scholars like Cohen and Gayatri Reddy argue, viewing *hijras* solely in terms of their sexual and gender nonconformity obscures the sociocultural complexity of their marginal status in different historical moments. While *hijras* often enjoyed certain privileges and even political power as slaves in precolonial Muslim imperial courts in India, the origins of contemporary *hijra* communities can be traced back to their persecution as "eunuchs" under British colonialism. The Criminal Tribes Act of 1871 called for the regulation and surveillance of eunuchs as a separate and criminally prone tribe or caste. Through this act and the repealed antisodomy statute (IPC 377), colonial law constructed the *hijra* body as the site of deviance and criminality against which heteropatriarchal Victorian colonial morality defined and defended itself. Since then, the *hijras'* occupations have included ritual blessing after childbirth in middle-class families in return for money and gifts, begging, and/or sex work.[31]

In postliberalization India, *hijras* were initially not included in—and were, in fact, actively rejected by—the mainstream urban gay movements. As stigmatized figures on the fringes of society, they were seen as the antithesis of the urban respectability that gay activists were after. As Cohen writes, "'Hijra' in this sense occupied a larger semantic space than the associations of those formally received into the hijra community and referred to a generalized position of masculine abjection including impotent men and other men 'like that' presumed to desire being anally penetrated."[32] Simultaneously, on the HIV/AIDS front, sexual health activists started reaching out to established *hijra* lineages, interpellating them as vulnerable sexual subalterns and potential beneficiaries of developmental aid. Aniruddha Dutta argues that these efforts to include *hijras* in the national HIV/AIDS discourse have also led to new assertions of *hijra* "authenticity" predicated on membership in lineage households.[33] Through a complex network of support from NGOs, donors, and the state, *hijra* activism has, therefore, generated its own politics of identification that does not hesitate to exclude "lower-class networks of diverse gender/sexually marginalised people outside *gharana* [lineage] households, who evidence varying degrees of public visibility . . . such as people who sexually network (cruise) in public spaces, male sex workers and cross-dressed beggars in trains" (Dutta, "Epistemology of Collusion," 832). That is to say, claims of "authentic" *hijra* culture driven by neoliberal demands for self-consolidation have begun to obfuscate the inexorably economic and public dimension of *hijra* livelihoods.

Arguably, the Indian queer movement today—in which KASHISH signals its membership through a democratic theme like "Diverse One"—has progressed significantly since the 1990s. Both the 2015 and 2017 KASHISH editions that I attended had a sizable presence of *hijra* and non-*hijra* transgender activists, directors, actors, and volunteers. Documentaries, fictional features, and short films focusing on transgender communities in India and South Asia more generally have also become a staple at the festival. In other words, that KASHISH makes a sincere effort to include a broad range of global and local queer identities is not in dispute.

What requires interrogation, however, is the ideological impression that the polymorphous rainbow-colored face of KASHISH conveys, which is that all these identities constitutive of the multiplicity are distinct but *otherwise equivalent and autonomous* categories of being queer in postcolonial India. In other words, by suggesting that *kothi* and *hijra* identities are primarily representative of the "diversity" of Indic queerness—and, therefore, easily comparable to the cosmopolitan "metrosexual" or "pansexual"—the festival's official rhetoric subscribes to a solidly neoliberal model of inclusion that does not question the history of these identities or address the conditions that produced them in the first place. What this rhetoric covers over, then, is the fractious mediations shaping these queer attachments—the fragmented constitution of *kothiness*, for instance, between the postcolonial politics of language, the financialization of poverty and HIV/AIDS, and, of course, the bodies, desires, and precarious socioeconomic positions of the (partially) interpellated subjects. "Diverse" thus becomes a buzzword—a value in and of itself—that must ignore the queer inequalities inflicted by neoliberalism.

KASHISH's enthusiastic inclusion of local and regional identities should also be seen alongside its tactical celebration of what I would call a "brand India"—a legitimization of queerness through its Indianness both domestically and transnationally. This mode of self-presentation surfaced repeatedly through sidebar discussions and stage performances framing and punctuating the screenings at the festival. For instance, in 2015, on one panel, Indian lawyers and activists inspired by the just-passed Irish referendum on gay marriage urged a way forward by lobbying local and state-level politicians and civil society organizations, appealing to the "Indian traditions" of marriage and family cohesion. At a forum on transnational productions the same year, established directors and producers advised younger filmmakers working with queer issues to attract foreign funding by marketing their work specifically as "Indian content." Both these events—which included festival organizers and speakers from the public and private sectors—explicitly endorsed the strategic and flexible valorization of *queerness through Indianness* to navigate a range of political and economic forces that could be local and orthodox or global and cosmopolitan.

I would also argue that KASHISH's geographic, cultural, and ideological proximity to the Mumbai film industry plays a significant role in its definitive emphasis on making queer India marketable and commodifiable. On both occasions that I was in attendance, spectacular crowd-pleasing performances choreographed to hit film songs at once drew on and resignifed the nationally and globally popular idiom called Bollywood. Many of these performers (such as a group of energetic and strapping male dancers on stilettos who call themselves High Heel

Hotties) have become festival favorites, wowing KASHISH audiences each year with their gender-bending appropriations of raunchy song-and-dance routines. Yet in the presence of Bollywood glitterati—whom the festival frequently invites as chief guests and jury members—these queer resignifications also risk turning into politically dubious fawning. KASHISH's genuflection before Bollywood star power was especially apparent in 2017, when a live stage performance was stopped to ensure that the chief guest—a popular male Hindi film actor—could be given his red-carpet entrance.[34] The festival's desire to queer mainstream Hindi cinema, therefore, remains questionable, precisely because such queering primarily seems to entail temporarily rescripting but also revering the position that Bollywood occupies as a commodified spectacle of Indianness both in the country and on the global stage. In this context, the insertion of same-sex desire or gender-bending into Bollywood's still-dominant elite heteronormativity not only keeps intact but also ends up buttressing the fetishism behind the adulation for the "hot" Bollywood actor who deigned to grace the festival for a few minutes.[35]

My point, then, is that KASHISH's performance of localism alongside homoglobalism remains caught up in the neoliberal compulsion to perform India as an "alluring" commodity that can compete and be consumed in the global marketplace.[36] The commercial logic of this queer nationalism is pointedly captured by an advertisement that appeared in the 2011 festival catalog. The ad features a lineup of brown-skinned models wearing trendy T-shirts with proqueer slogans, and celebrating in seemingly unironic terms, the salability of a chic and sexy queer India out of the closet and in the free market, or *azaad bazaar* (in Hindi), the latter also being the name of the advertiser, which called itself "India's first LGBT Pride Store."

Finally, KASHISH's desire to make queer India both visible and marketable is closely tied to the fundamentally capitalist ideology of its corporate sponsors. In her trenchant analysis of the emergence of sexual identities under late capitalism, Rosemary Hennessy points out that, as the primary vehicle of capital transmission, the transnational corporation operates through a process of localization such that the "local" begins to function "as a self-defined space for the affirmation of cultural identity" while obscuring the regulation and management of that identity in the interests of global capital (*Profit and Pleasure*, 8). The darker side of the corporatized celebration of the local is, therefore, an abstraction whose main goal is to maximize the extraction

Azaad Bazaar ad in the 2011 KASHISH catalog.

of surplus value. A close reading of two sponsor videos screened at KASHISH 2017 will make clearer the regulation and abstraction shaping the localization of queerness in neoliberal India.

A promotional video made by Godrej—an Indian conglomerate and one of the major corporate sponsors of KASHISH—was released on You-Tube in September 2016 and played repeatedly between screenings at the festival the following year. Titled "LGBT Inclusion in Godrej," the video showcases the Mumbai-based global corporation as a queer-friendly employer.[37] The video opens with a shot of Godrej employee Apekshit Khare gliding up in an elevator with a sparkling glass wall behind him. As we catch a glimpse of the ritzy interiors of Godrej's headquarters through the glass wall, and then cut to an interview shot, Khare speaks to the camera in English, informing viewers that he is one of the first employees to be extended same-sex partner benefits by the corporation. The diversity policy at Godrej, he remarks, "helps us bring our whole selves to work. . . . And I am sure it helps in being productive because I am not diverting my energies pretending to be somebody I am not." The same video features Godrej's first transgender employee, Nyra D'Souza, who talks to the camera seated on a swing in a pristine white conference room with sleek white furniture. Like Khare, D'Souza describes the corporation as a queer space that has made her whole, alleviated her identitarian anxieties, and allowed her to reconcile her private and public selves: "I do have a gender dysphoria. And the first time when I stepped in[to] Godrej, I realized that [the] dysphoria was lost. . . . Here I am . . . working in [sic] Godrej . . . fulfilling my dream." For both interviewees, Godrej epitomizes the progressive private sector where they can be their true selves.

Unexceptional as it may seem aesthetically in its use of the "talking head" format (and a not-so-subtle emphasis on Godrej's corporate sheen), the political and cultural significance of this short video cannot be overstated. Bhaskar Sarkar and Janet Walker point out that the frequent use of talking heads in social documentaries must be seen as an effect of a larger "'testimonial apparatus'—which produces the detail and emotion of suffering in and through the constitution of the spectator subject."[38] The testimonial apparatus is an ideological structure that assumes that the invisible interlocutor will not only hear the suffering subject but also intervene to address their demands for social justice (Sarkar and Walker, introduction, 2). In the Godrej video, however, the individual testimonies are not so much declarations of suffering as they are, collectively, a testimonial *for* the corporation. While they do allude to suffering in the past, their main purpose is to announce the endurance and triumph of the talking subject and, crucially, to represent the corporation as the reason for that triumph. Thus, by including actual employees, the video solidifies the image of Godrej as a liberal Indian corporation, one that is implementing its mission to protect the rights of LGBTQ+ employees in accordance with a United Nations initiative.[39] The image of an *Indian* corporation as a queer refuge is significant, too, in the context of activists' ongoing struggles with the state to decriminalize homosexuality and the Indian government's refusal to vote in favor of a UN resolution banning the death penalty as a form of punishment for consensual same-sex relations.[40] Corporate responsibility, in this context, becomes the beacon of hope for many queer Indians who have felt actively ignored and, before the decriminalization in 2018, even hounded by the illiberal state apparatus.

At the same time, the video does not celebrate queerness per se but as an identitarian attribute applied to the educated, ambitious, and entrepreneurial citizen-subject. In other words, through these model employees, Godrej—whose own "brand India" originates in its strong connections with the anticolonial *swadeshi* movement in the mid-nineteenth century as a soap and lock manufacturer[41]—reinvents its image as a postcolonial corporation that values Indian queerness in the form of self-governance and responsible citizenship. And in light of this mode of queer inclusion, the shiny interiors of the Godrej head-quarters foregrounded in the video take on an ethicopolitical charge. Instead of being merely eye-catching, corporate space becomes a safe and democratic enclave that respects individual desires and protects *certain* queers from the discriminatory tendencies of the normative world outside.

Consequently, Godrej's narrative of incorporation is effective only if, along with the corporation, the KASHISH viewer ignores the sexed and classed distributive injustices shaping queer (in)visibility in India. For queer localization and abstraction are contingent on the exclusion of the nonelite, non-Anglophone, and noncorporate queers, such as *hijra* or *kothi* subjects, some of whom may be attending the festival but fall outside the purview of Godrej's protective embrace. Intriguingly, the corporation's executive chairperson, Nisaba Godrej, made this exclusion quite clear during her remarks at the festival's opening ceremony in 2017: "All of you know that corporates don't . . . do anything just from the good[ness] of our hearts. . . . We come out here hoping . . . maybe we will get a few résumés from . . . places that are not inclusive."[42] Even as festival organizers feted Godrej and its video's inclusivity, one of its scions made explicit that which the video leaves unsaid: membership in the corporate managerial and submanagerial class is the precondition for the self-consolidation and civic protection of the local Indian queer.

Within a few months of the launch of the Godrej video, the U.S. cor-poration Procter & Gamble (P&G) released its first video celebrating queer India. Released in March 2017, the commercial went viral—garnering nine million hits on YouTube within a few weeks—and even occasioned a special panel discussion on corporate responsibility at KASHISH that year.[43] Titled "#TouchofCare," the video was made by P&G's over-the-counter brand Vicks, a household name in India for cold and flu remedies. The commercial opens with a teenage girl sit-ting on a bus, ruminating on her life as she travels to boarding school. The girl's voice-over (recorded in Hindi with English subtitles) tells a moving story of how she was tragically orphaned ten years ago, and then adopted by a kind stranger whom she came to see and love as her mother. Through a series of flashback shots and the accompanying voice-over, the commercial foregrounds the maternal touch and care nurturing the adopted child. This maternal touch is represented primarily through shots of the mother's hand cooking for the child, caring for her when she is sick, and comforting her when she is frightened. The significance of this visual synecdoche becomes clear once the camera finally pans to reveal the mother (seated next to the daughter on the bus) to be the Indian transgender (*hijra*) activist and adoptive parent Gauri Sawant.[44] The commercial ends with a moving scene as mother and daughter say their goodbyes at the boarding school, and Sawant finally walks away, holding back her tears. That this is a Vicks commercial is revealed to the viewer at the very end, with the appearance of the Vicks logo right after the tagline "Everyone deserves the touch of care," and next to the final tagline, "Caring for Families for Generations." Thus, although ostensibly coded as noncorporate (when compared to the Godrej video), the commercial also invites consumers to see the corporate "family" as a refuge for the marginalized queer Indian.

Once again, however, the global corporation's inclusion of the local queer comes at a price: the domestication of queerness in accordance with the ideological demands of P&G's local market in India. For if P&G offers Sawant the platform to represent herself as the empirical Indian transgender subject, it does so by constructing the activist's marginalized identity primarily in terms of her "maternal" abilities. More specifically, to be visible as a transgender subject, Sawant has to fit into the trope of maternal compassion that has played a central role in shaping Vicks's brand image in India over several decades. Here the transgender parent is permitted to "queer" the heteronormative family, but only by upholding the patriarchal division of labor in the domestic space, by inserting herself in a series of Vicks commercials (with which P&G's Indian audiences would be quite familiar) featuring devoted Indian mothers and wives tending to their sick children and husbands with the Vicks cold remedy VapoRub.[45] As P&G executive Nitin Darbari notes in a statement linking Sawant's commercial to the brand image, "Vicks has always been about the gentle touch of a mother's care, as she caresses and gives relief to her child."[46] In the commercial, Sawant emerges as the iconic "Vicks mother" in a flashback in which she stays up all night attending to her coughing daughter. Vicks's fetishization of feminine and maternal care is subtly reasserted as the familiar green-capped blue bottle of VapoRub becomes briefly visible in the foreground, as the necessary supplement to Sawant's transgender maternal hand in the background.

The problem here is not just with the trope of maternal care but the subjugation of gender nonconformity to heteronormative demands made by the trope as a brand image. Following these demands of its market and customer base, Vicks attempts to reduce transgenderism—a complex interplay of erotic, economic, and cultural factors governing the life of the empirical trans- or *hijra*-identified subject in contemporary India—to responsible motherhood that can be seen as being worthy of social justice and recognition. By extension, the commercial suggests that *all* transgender subjects are welcome to claim their rights so long as they can similarly prove their heteronormatively measured mettle as worthy parents. Here, through the scripted and heartwarming voice-over associated with the actors playing Sawant's daughter (which is also the "voice" of the corporation interceding on Sawant's behalf),[47] the video performs a carefully orchestrated slippage between mythologized maternal care, transgender identity, and the Vicks brand.

In this context, it is productive to read both the Godrej and Vicks videos as instances of what Oishik Sircar calls "spectacles of emancipation" that are characteristic of the neoliberal era.[48] Sircar uses this term to mean abstract and inflated representations of social justice produced in India in the wake of economic liberalization. Drawing on Guy Debord's concept of "the spectacle"—the linguistic-visual image that serves as a key site of capital accumulation (see chapter 1)—Sircar demonstrates how the Indian state and the global free market economy operate in tandem to promote such buoyant representations of socio-economically marginalized subjects as rights-bearing citizens. Since the state, in this scenario, abdicates its own responsibilities to cede to the market, the latter not only determines the terms of the representation of the subjects in need of emancipation (as enterprising, capable, self-governing, and so forth) but also frames human rights and freedoms as concepts that will materialize *only* in a thoroughly privatized environment (Sircar, "Spectacles of Emancipation," 533).

As was noted regarding the Godrej video, the corporation positions itself as the state's surrogate in extending protections and benefits to the queer citizen and simultaneously frames that queerness in strictly neoliberal terms. Queer Indians can reap the benefits offered by Godrej's spectacle only if they have the means to access that corporate sanctuary. The Vicks video performs its surrogacy a little differently. It constructs its spectacle of freedom by recognizing the transgender subject from within a naturalized ideology of the "family" and the figure of "the child" that, in fact, constitute the state's principal instrument of governmentality.[49] Vicks capitalizes on Sawant's compassionate act of adopting an orphan and feeds on the moral force of its own "spectacle of childhood" [50]—where a normalized image of the mother-child bond becomes an accumulation strategy—to ensure that the commodification of transgender rights not only becomes palatable but *desirable*.

Yet as Sircar also reminds us, the preponderance of corporate spectacles of emancipation does not mean that the state loses its sovereign power over its citizens. In fact, the spectacle of emancipation often takes the form of the corporation ultimately passing the buck to the state and its "rule of law." In spite of the glaring gap between judicial populism and the violence perpetrated by the Indian state in the name of "human rights," it is through the corporate spectacle that the state advertises itself and the law as the cure to deeply ingrained social prejudices ("Spectacles of Emancipation," 552–60). The Vicks video also epitomizes this statist underside of spectacles of emancipation, in that it ends with the voice of the child promising redress through (and *as*) the law to come: "My Civics book says that everyone is entitled to basic rights. Then why is mom denied them? That's why I'm not going to be a doctor, I will be a lawyer . . . for my mom." In a closing sleight of hand, P&G punts Sawant back to the state at the same moment it promises her emancipation through nonstate intervention.

The Vicks video was the focal point of a panel discussion at KASH-ISH 2017 on corporate involvement in LGBTQ+ activism in India. The panel—which included Sawant, the director of the Vicks commercial, and representatives from Godrej and IBM—was by and large effusive about how "corporate India is taking the lead to promote diversity in society and at the work place."[51] Sawant's own responses, however, were more measured. While acknowledging that the commercial had won her some recognition and fame, the activist noted that she had agreed to shoot the video on condition that Vicks would not "use" or "instrumentalize" her own daughter as the voice of its brand.[52] If Sawant's decision to exclude her daughter reveals her own reservations against Vicks's strategies of accumulation, her awareness of the limits of her own commoditization come into view in a 2017 interview published soon after the video went viral. As Sawant notes in that interview, "I have become well known, but I still live in a slum. No one will want me as a tenant. When so-called respectable housing societies don't allow people from other religions or single women to rent apartments, who are we, mere *hijras*?"[53]

Sawant's forceful rejoinder to the liberal euphoria around Vicks's benevolence—and her lived experience of her own spectacle's failure to emancipate—prompt us to read her queer identity as a schizophrenic negotiation in the postcolony. Sawant's identity is buoyed by a commodified Vicks-sponsored image of transgender maternity, on the one hand, and chastened, on the other hand, by the econocultural mediations that continue to ostracize her *hijra* body and appearance. If this intermedial aspect of Sawant's experience of her queer identity is disavowed by the homoglobal and homonational aspirations defining KASHISH's self-image, it erupts periodically through the postcolonial dissonance of the films that I examine in the final section of this chapter. Yet my attention thus far to the cunning that neoliberalism exercises through a corporatized cinematic mode would be rather partial without a consideration of its disciplinary doppelgänger—the exaltation of an anti-identitarian and anticapitalist queerness in film studies. Thus, with Sawant's rejoinder in mind, I turn to Schoonover and Galt's queer cinephilia in the next section.

The Allure of Cinema as Nonidentitarian Queerness

In their reading of KASHISH in *Queer Cinema in the World*, Karl Schoonover and Rosalind Galt also acknowledge the festival's neoliberal tendencies. But they ultimately argue that the festival's resistance to capitalism, in fact, lies in its ability to make queerness occupy the mainstream, and, therefore, short-circuit straight/queer and other identitarian divides: "The festival's self-descriptions emphasize visibility, human rights, and acceptance in ways that do not immediately scream radical queerness. . . . But the mainstream location also insists on constructing queer space within and alongside 'non-queer' spaces. . . . Indeed, the festival expands that public sphere, promiscuously mixing audiences for queer and non-queer films, along with activist and entertainment films" (94–95). The authors then go on to note that "the KASHISH festival locates queer audiences in a counterpublic that seeps into the official public sphere. . . . Programming consciously addresses diverse Indian audiences by including films in Marathi, Bengali, and other national languages, and events engage minorities such as *hijras*, who are often excluded from mainstream cultural spaces" (96).

From Schoonover and Galt's perspective, then, KASHISH localizes and mixes in a queer counterculture that the mainstream is unable to fend off. The festival incorporates nonheteronormative differences in a way that makes it an internally plural "counterpublic." As well, this plural queerness becomes an asset that sponsoring corporations want to cultivate as part of their civic engagement: "Sponsorship has often come from corporate human relations departments that see their support as contributing to the betterment of employees. Thus, corporations have understood KASHISH's value in terms of public life, and not as an elite, prestigious, or exclusive cultural event" (97). That is to say, in Schoonover and Galt's reading, corporatized global queerness is something to which KASHISH submits as a tactic, not only for financial support but also to make the corporation more inclusive and egalitarian.

The difference between my own reading of KASHISH and that offered by the authors of *Queer Cinema* should be clear to the reader. As I have argued above, the festival's localization of queerness through corporations like Godrej and P&G makes it neither antineoliberal nor anti-identitarian. And even as this localization sincerely and valiantly battles homophobia and transphobia in India, its egalitarianism is delimited by the hierarchies that neoliberalism has historically produced and sustained in the country through an acutely uneven field of social mobility that disciplines and includes some queer subjects while excluding others. The question, then, is why and how Schoonover and Galt are able to celebrate the localization of queerness in this manner. What is it that shapes their decision to leave unexamined the heterogeneity of the mediations of queer identity in postliberalization India? As I shall argue, Schoonover and Galt's idealization of queer localism is ultimately bound to a disciplinary desire to valorize and retrieve cinema as an inherently queer, anti-identitarian, and anticapitalist medium. Put differently, in their argument, it is to (what they regard to be) the *medium specificity of cinema* that a festival like KASHISH ultimately owes its radically local anti-identitarian queerness.

The assumptions guiding this cinema-bound resistance to capitalism—which should remind the reader of Laura U. Marks's cinephilia in chapter 3—requires a closer examination. Written with an admirable intellectual scope, *Queer Cinema* takes seriously its mission to challenge Euro-American and neoliberal LGBTQ+ identity politics by examining a broad range of films, film cultures, and genres from a wide variety of locales. For instance, Schoonover and Galt's discussion of the political potentialities of queer film festivals and, indeed, of the queer potentiality of cinema moves nimbly from the United States to India

to Botswana in the space of a single chapter. Simultaneously, throughout the book, the authors trace connections between these diverse
cinemas and cinematic environments that they argue are incommensurable with the global commodification of queerness. In contrast to the
latter's "limiting identity politics," Schoonover and Galt posit the notion
of "'worlding' to describe queer cinema's ongoing process of constructing worlds, a process that is active, incomplete, and contestatory" and
that offers "alternatives to embedded capitalist, national, hetero- and
homonormative maps" (5). In particular, the authors believe that "non-
Western cinemas of sexual and gender dissidence may be one place
from which that world can be reimagined" (24). Thus, if the West has
historically imposed its neoliberal queer identity politics on the non-
West, then Schoonover and Galt seek to uncover "locally and regionally
specific politics, social practices, and sexual intimacies" (48) through
non-Western cinemas that are able to offer alternatives to (Western) capitalist formations. In short, uncovering nonhomonormative expressions
of gender and sexuality in non-Western films and film cultures reflects
the means of "finding resistant ways of living in the world" (29).

Queer Cinema's desire to upend neocolonial narratives of the West
"liberating" the erotically subjugated non-West is no doubt a welcome
critical move. The difficulty with that move, however, lies in the cinematic nature of queer worlding that the authors promote through a
partial reading of neoliberalism and the aesthetic regulation of identity
politics. From the outset, Schoonover and Galt's valorization of local
and global queerness relies on a view of globalization as a homogenizing process that ignores difference such that "everything carries the
same exchangeable value" (24). In their view, neoliberal identity politics is a Western commodity fetishism that demands "global citizenry"
(44) and promotes "liberal diversity, and bland interchangeability" (69).
Yet, as I have argued in this volume's introduction and chapter 1, this
reading of capitalism as only enforcing perfect (neurotic) equivalence
fails to take into account how the same system of equivalence has historically generated and continues to generate minoritized identities
and difference as (schizophrenic) *nonequivalence* both in the West and
non-West, and frequently in tension with what is deemed to be "Western." Postliberalization queer politics in India, I have suggested, also
demonstrates this split dynamic of simultaneous homogenization and
heterogenization. The KASHISH festival, as we have seen, mirrors
this tension as it oscillates between being global and including local
queer identities that also become sources of surplus value. In other

words, contra Schoonover and Galt, it is not at all clear how local queer cinematic practices and politics challenging Westernization as homogenization are necessarily outside or resisting neoliberalism.

By avoiding the messiness of globalization and its discontents, *Queer Cinema* is, therefore, able to corral local difference into a utopian enclosure of cinema and its properties. This enclosure is then given the name of anti-identitarian queerness. For Schoonover and Galt, cinematic resistances to neoliberal identitarianism are ultimately attributable to "what is unique about cinema and its ability to nourish spaces that are not reducible to capital" (5), to cinema as "a queerly inflected medium" (6). Cinematic worlding is possible ultimately because "the dynamism of the cinematic image pushes against the reification of meaning, as it keeps the signifier in motion, never fixing terms of relationality" (7). In this context, "queerness" is that cinematic potential to be radically anti-identitarian and resist semiotic fixity. Schoonover and Galt's claims about the mobile queerness of the cinematic signifier and its ostensibly anticapitalist potential is, therefore, comparable to Marks's celebration of haptic cinema. Albeit drawing on very distinct bodies of theoretical scholarship and films, both Schoonover and Galt's *Queer Cinema* and Marks's *Skin of the Film* represent an aesthetic politics in which the privileged medium—the moving image—offers through its medium-specific properties the promise of liberation from the clutches of capitalist reification and identity. But as I have noted in chapters 1 and 2, the same tendency can be found in a strand of literary studies in which the medium specificity of language and its similarly mobile signifier (as opposed to the visual image) is purportedly endowed with the same ability. I have also demonstrated that, as these medium-bound formulations of aesthetic resistance shore up symbolic capital (in the service of the "autonomy" of their disciplines, the neoliberal academy, and its containment of insurgent difference), they do so by sidestepping entirely the ongoing aesthetic production and extremely heterogeneous experiences of identitarian fragmentation. Seemingly sensitive to the varying contexts and differential labors of spectatorial participation in the cinematic apparatus, Schoonover and Galt's reification of the cinematic signifier and "queer stratum of the cinematic" (7)—seductively phrased but clamoring for further historicization and theorization—falls into the same trap.

Also at stake is how Schoonover and Galt define cinema and its purportedly anti-identitarian capabilities. The authors insist that the cinematic "apparatus" needs to be understood multimodally, at "the intersection of text, exhibition, *and audience*" (80, emphasis added). To view the apparatus in these terms, they contend, is also to refuse "accounts of the [cinematic] medium that pose it as a sinister commodifier of human life and equalizer of experience" (33). Schoonover and Galt are thus keen to move away from totalizing and homogenizing accounts of cinematic reception. In this ostensibly empowering version of the apparatus, spectatorial encounters with individual films and festivals engender alternatives to neoliberalism in various complementary ways: by replacing identity with a "cinematic space of affect and affection across cultures" (75), offering "expanded agency to the queer figure" (54), or infecting noncinematic aspects of the cinematic event with the medium's "plastic aesthetic experience" (90). In short, the cinematic apparatus becomes the context-specific encounter or event in which certain films are able to produce anti-identitarian queer affect, agency, and aesthetic experiences that dismantle the homogenizing neoliberal stockade within which spectators are otherwise trapped.

Yet, the dominant ingredient of what Schoonover and Galt celebrate as affect and agency is the familiar opposition between aesthetic form and ideology, or in this case, between *cinematic form* and *identity politics*. Even as Schoonover and Galt recognize the importance of context-bound spectatorship in the constitution of the cinematic apparatus, a rather decontextualized approach to form and affect takes precedence, much like the "body" of cinema does in Marks's theory of haptic visuality. More accurately, cinematic form *becomes* politics, offering the miraculous theriac that queer subjects need—regardless of their geohistorical positions—to be disembedded from their neoliberal entanglements. As the authors write, "We argue that every film constructs a world *formally* and that this worldliness has *the capacity to recalibrate its own parameters. Worldliness can shift the terms of agency and power and has the ability to create effects in the world* (25, emphasis added). A few pages later, they argue that the antineoliberal cinematicity of global queerness "is legible at the level of individual films articulating *the worldly in their form and style*. For example, *Wusheng feng ling / Soundless Wind Chime* (Kit Hung, 2009) figures transnational queer desire via elliptical montages and sound bridges, graphic matches that link different times and spaces, and synthetic edits that align bodies via analogy rather than synchrony. We are interested in these *spaces enabled by film form and the geopolitical questions they pose*" (29, emphasis added). From this cinephilic perspective, form-as-convention—which cinematic technology makes possible and individual film texts innovatively deploy—becomes quite readily the means of subverting capitalist ideology and normative queer identities.

There are at least two related assumptions about spectatorship at work here. First, it is implicitly assumed that the perception of film *form*—literally represented by montages, sound bridges, graphic matches, and other stylistic devices—will conjure some kind of liberatory space in the minds of *all* spectators, a space that will be a nonidentitarian utopia regardless of the grounds of spectatorship. Cinematic form, in other words, has the power to affect all spectators equally, leading them to forge connections between spaces and temporalities that capitalism usually keeps separate. What seems to have disappeared is Schoonover and Galt's acknowledgment of the diverse ways of reading and reacting to the apparatus and, therefore, film form. To reinvoke together N. Katherine Hayles (see chapter 1) and Mark Chiang (see chapter 2), what is evacuated from this critical desire to valorize and capitalize on film form is an understanding of the *materiality* of the medium thàt includes the diverse (and often conflicting) reading practices of the audience. In other words, Schoonover and Galt's insistence on the antiessentialist effects of film form ultimately privileges an abstraction of the film text from the context of viewing. (There is also the perhaps more pragmatic but no less important question of *access* here: Who does and who does not have the leisure time and resources in postcolonial India or elsewhere to watch films and transform their identity-bound lives? But I will save this question for my reading of the film *Goddess*, below.)

The second implicit assumption concerns the relationship between aesthetic form and identity as an essentialist ideology. For the authors of *Queer Cinema*, form is primarily a matter of "cinematicity," the artistry allowed by film as a queer medium. It is a cinema-specific aesthetic form that generates nonidentitarian affect and sensations in the spectator and that therefore demands the film theorist's disciplinary attention. Consequently, what is or must be elided by this cinema-centric embrace of the aesthetic is any consideration of aesthetic form as *aisthesis* in the intermedial production and experience of identitarian essentialism (see chapter 1). Schoonover and Galt's position seemingly aligns with that of literary critic Ellen Rooney, who argues that form is that which refuses to capitulate to dominant ideology. For Rooney, form is "the force that permits the text to emerge as ideology's or theory's interlocutor, rather than as its example."[54] For Schoonover and Galt, form is the queer force proper to cinema and is mobilized by certain films to resist the ideology that is neoliberal identity.

Rooney, however, is careful to remind us that form is not something that the text hands to the critic on a silver platter. Instead, form emerges as "both the enabling condition and the product of reading" ("Form and Contentment," 18). If form emerges, in part, as an effect of reading, it follows, then, that the nature and effects of the *embodied labor* of reading or spectatorship cannot be ignored to privilege either form's idealized social promise or its "pure exteriority" devoid of subjectivity.[55] This labor must also be seen as being contingent on the analytic tools at the disposal of the culturally and historically located reader-spectator. And because of its material, discursive, and mediated nature, there can be no guarantees that this labor—which yields (a certain perception of) form—will necessarily move the spectator from essentialism to antiessentialism. In fact, her desire to pit form against ideology notwithstanding, Rooney is compelled to note that the ideology of essentialism must itself be seen as a matter of form, in that "essentialism appears as a certain resistance to reading, an emphasis on the constraints of form, the limits at which a particular form so compels us as to 'stipulate' an analysis."[56] These constraints on form, I have argued in previous chapters, acquire racialized, gendered, and classed dimensions to produce identity as aesthetic dissonance. I have also argued that capitalism nurtures itself not only by disavowing its aesthetic fabrication of essentialism but also by cunningly staging a tug of war between identity politics and seemingly nonidentitarian aesthetics. Thus, in their quest for a cinema-bound aesthetic antiessentialism, Schoonover and Galt risk complicity with this cunning of capital. Despite its democratic agenda, queer worlding starts to resemble neoliberal homoglobalism.

In the third and final section of this chapter, I approach queer film form rather differently. Form *and content* in the following films, I argue through my no doubt sociopolitically delimited interpretive labor, does not whisk the queer subject away from identity. Rather, film aesthetics becomes a means to track the cinematic as well as extracinematic mediations shaping queer (dis)identification and dissonance with and within neoliberalism. Film form makes visible how the ego encounters identity through multiple sites of mediation. In some ways, these films return us to the process of capitalist mediation that seems to be missing entirely from *Queer Cinema*'s assessment of neoliberalism: the dialectical process of reconciling opposites while maintaining the primacy of exchange value (see the introduction to this volume). I would also say that my turn to aesthetics in and through these films does not fly from but attempts to fathom the historicopolitical depths of Sawant's dissonant question: "Who are we, mere *hijras*?"

The Labors of Queer (Dis)identification in
an Economy of Exclusion

Indian LGBTQ+ rights activist and filmmaker Nakshatra Bagwe's short film *Logging Out* (2012) offers a campy and yet serious reflection on the mediated nature of erotic identifications and intimacies in the digital age.[57] After a series of failed attempts to find love online, the film's protagonist, Aayush, meets a stranger, Ved, on a gay social networking website. The interaction between the two college students unfolds on a screen within the screen as a series of rapidly typed exchanges between two profile pictures—Aayush's headshot and Ved's lean muscled torso. This courtship, however, ends rather abruptly the second time the two men meet online. When Aayush refuses Ved's request for "hot" nude photographs, the latter goes offline, disappearing from the conversation. Aayush stares at his screen for hours waiting for Ved to return. And when his labors go unrequited, Aayush gives in to the demand of his erotic ideal, taking a series of seminude and nude photographs of himself. The protagonist's attempt to pursue his gay identification and approximate his ideal image, however, does not lead to a satisfactory romantic resolution. Aayush appears disappointed and dejected after seeing his own photographs. The film ends with him looking despairingly at the image and profile of his (still-offline) object of desire, and, finally, logging out of the network when a new stranger invites him to chat.

What interests me in *Logging Out* is not so much its critique of the blurring of the pornographic and the romantic in the digital age as the film's persistent foregrounding of the relationship between sexual identification and visual-performative labor. As a film that is structured around the protagonist looking at his screen and laboring to be looked at (and therefore desired), *Logging Out* can be seen as a historically specific—and "critically queer"[58]—cinematic annotation to media theorist Jonathan Beller's pithy and powerful dictum, "To look is to labor." As I noted in chapter 2, for Beller, visual attention has become the paradigmatic site of value production since the rise of the internet. This form of attention, he argues, is routinely mobilized to sustain the relations of production that define late capitalism. The labor of looking at the commodity image—and simultaneously being the "object" of the attention the image commands—also marks the beginning of the labor to have and to become the commodity that is supposed to guarantee pleasure, happiness, love, wealth, success, and so forth. While the commodity image

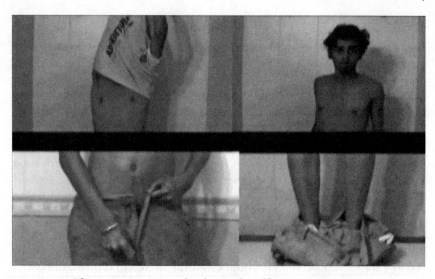

The protagonist Aayush takes nude selfies in *Logging Out*.

can function as money or social currency, its materiality lies not its tangibility but in its performativity. More simply, the image that one wishes to become cannot be spent (as money can be) but must be produced or performed.[59] Into its representation of this intermedial link between digital consumption and self-production, *Logging Out* inserts gay male identification as a normalizing labor that is activated by the image of idealized masculinity. For the gay Indian protagonist of the film, however, this labor does not result in a smooth conversion of use value into exchange value. The protagonist's self-image—presented to the viewer as a series of stills on the screen—occupies an equivocal position, somewhere between becoming a commodity and an anticommodity.[60]

On the one hand, in terms of the narrative, the images testify to the compulsion to conform to an established system of erotic value production. The inadequate lighting, amateurish framing, awkward poses, the protagonist's fragmented and visibly nonmuscular body, and his wary expression collectively foreground the difference between the contingencies of his situation and the erotically pleasurable image he labors to produce. On the other hand, the formal choices produce a certain spectatorial unpleasure by foregrounding the subject as a fragmented object, ironize the genre of the "hot" selfie, and simultaneously call attention to the entwinement of coercion and autonomy inscribed in that very mode of erotic self-production.[61] Thus, as products of the protagonist's labors of identification with the screen-as-mirror, these images—at once comical and grim—perform a queer dissonance with the commodity image without being able to break away fully from its tyranny. We can say that critical queerness, here, is the cinematization of queerness's aesthetic captivation by and alienation from the normativity of commodified gay masculinity.

Notably, this dissonance can also be seen as a critique of the liberal rhetoric of inclusion of KASHISH, where *Logging Out* had its first public screening in 2012 and won the Audience Choice Award that year. As we saw in the previous section, KASHISH advertises itself as the festival whose main goal is to "continue mainstreaming of queer issues and their lives" and "to rally public opinion towards equality and dignity for gay, lesbian, bisexual and transgender persons."[62] In this description, alongside the distinctness of the marginalized identities, the festival asserts its desire to "mainstream" and therefore accord "equality and dignity" to the same identities. To borrow the famous words of Michael Warner, KASHISH does not apparently see "the trouble with normal" or the dangers of assimilating with heteronormativity and the privatization of sex and gender.[63] And yet, as a film contributing to the festival's queer politics, *Logging Out* is a cutting appraisal of precisely the price of such an assimilationist mode of inclusion. Bagwe's short film—while not explicitly positioned as a critique of commodity capitalism—raises nonetheless the difficulty of a liberal celebration of gay identification in a (homo)normatively eroticized digital subculture. Instead of seeing this identification as being distinct and yet-to-be-mainstreamed, the film asks its spectators to consider the regulatory and hegemonic forms that queer erotic idealization and self-management have *already* taken (for some) through e-intimacies, following the demands and pleasures of the free market. In other words, unlike the festival's mission statement that desires the normalization of queer identifications, *Logging Out* seeks to disabuse its spectators by suggesting that the digitally mediated aesthetic violence of normalization is well underway, postcolonial homophobia notwithstanding. The only option—the film suggests both emphatically and enigmatically—is to "log out" of this system of value production. In this way, the experience of (gay) identity as an intermedial aesthetic dissonance—engendered by the hierarchy between use value and exchange value, between the body and the body image—resurfaces in a novel form in the film's postcolonial scene of immaterial and material erotic labor.

This dissonance is more implicit in Sharon Flynn's documentary *I'dentity*, which was shown at KASHISH 2014.[64] The film documents the struggles of two male-to-female transgender subjects living in Mumbai: Ghazal, a screenwriter who comes from a middle-class background in Patiala, in northern India; and Nadia, an HIV/AIDS outreach worker who grew up in rural Vijayawada in the south. Like many other activist and educational films screened at KASHISH, the talking head or testimonial format of this short draws our attention to what Sarkar and Walker describe as "tenacious expressions of a desire to overcome adversity, to keep on living, to secure the future of a community" (introduction, 4). Unlike the Godrej sponsor video discussed above—in which the primary role of the queer subject is to testify to corporate benevolence—the activist orientation of Flynn's film is clear in its emphasis on individual agency and self-invention. Here the act of narration itself—such as Ghazal's account of her trauma of being "trapped" in a male body, or Nadia remembering her abusive childhood—becomes central to the protagonists' labors of self-determination. Part of the reason for this work of remembering (the partial nature of the interviewees' stories and the filmmaker's editorial decisions notwithstanding) is to create a first-person record of the subjects' survival of the very odds they describe.[65] Thus, there is no doubt that, on one level, the film asks us to read Nadia's and Ghazal's transitions as individual agency triumphing in the face of pervasive transphobia. Their speech acts represent the celebration of identity as individual choice, as a "right" that should not be denied.

And yet, on another level, the film also calls into question its own narrative of agency and individuality through tensions and contrasts between its testimonies. Toward the beginning of the film, Ghazal's cisgender friend Doris tells us why she is convinced of one's right to choose one's appearance: "When a girl is not happy with her eyebrows she can just go to the salon and get her eyebrows done, nose jobs, everything is OK. Why not genitals? It's as simple as that. If one is not happy with the way one looks, they can change." Here Doris articulates a progressive postcolonial queer stance that makes sense of transition through a broader neoliberal mantra of choice and self-improvement. Yet the film, through its deliberate juxtaposition of Ghazal's and Nadia's narratives of transformation, also reminds us that this freedom is not equally available to all gender-nonconforming subjects in contemporary India. While Ghazal speaks of an exceptionally supportive environment at home in Patiala, as well as resources that allow her to go to Thailand for her surgery, Nadia's testimony reveals a far less privileged experience—which includes being rejected by her family, trafficked from her village into sex work in the city, and, eventually joining a *hijra* community. Nadia's encounter with the medical establishment, we learn, has also been an ordeal. Compelled to seek out unregulated medical procedures in Mumbai because of her limited means, she finds herself bleeding for days after the surgery. Thus, through a stark contrast between the two testimonies, Flynn's film does not simply idealize transgender agency but also reads that agency through the differentials of class position, education, financial resources, and access to health care. In other words, the contrast between the two narratives of transformation discursively constructs "agency" and "choice" as things that are not merely individual but also unavoidably social, economic, and relational.

Furthermore, I would argue that the film also points toward the multimodality of transgender identity formation—specifically, extra-cinematic mediating forces that shape the individual testimonies within the narrative while also operating institutionally far beyond the singular context of witnessing or filming. Sarkar and Walker draw our attention to such mediating forces through the concept of the "archive," an intermediary and nominative power that makes the documentary testimony available and audible: "The archive is the place where we return to trace the beginning of things; it is also the site where authority inheres, which confers legitimacy."[66] The archive can be seen as an econopolitical force constitutive of the testimonial apparatus, a mediating agent that determines the terms of comportment of the testifier. One such mediating agent—whose intercession is impossible to ignore in Flynn's film—is the medical establishment that alone wields the authority to name and authenticate the transgender subject. Immediately after Ghazal's account of her parents' acceptance of her transgender identity, we hear from Dr. Gurvinder Kalra, a neuropsychiatrist and a sex specialist. In what is perhaps meant to be an educational moment for the audience, the medical expert informs us that "there are only two genders that can exist. And transgenders are everything and anything that exists apart from this gender binary. And transsexuals are individuals who are ready to cross the gender binary. So if a male decides, 'Yes, I want to undergo a sex change operation to become a female,' that's a transsexual." While we cannot be certain if the inclusion of this sound bite is also meant to be ironic, the contradiction accompanying the clinical explanation is quite explicit. On the one hand, transgenderism is that which "exists apart from" or defies the gender binary. On the other hand, there are "only two genders that can exist" and from which the transsexual must necessarily choose. The sex-gender binary, or sexual dimorphism, is at once revealed to be a social construction and legitimized by the medical expert, the "archon" nominating trans identity.

As queer and media theorist Sandy Stone reminds us in her well-known essay "The *Empire* Strikes Back," it is this contradiction that enables the late capitalist clinic to profit from what it has itself labeled "gender dysphoria." The clinic that enables the transgender subject to "cross" the gender binary is, in fact, also in charge of policing the binary. That is to say, the clinic that "cures" gender identity crises is also an "apparatus of the production of gender."[67] Stone is, of course, referring to the twentieth-century clinic in the United States. But Flynn's film also calls on the spectator to read transgender agency in India through the postcolonial clinical apparatus that allows Ghazal and Nadia to be legally recognized as women. As Ghazal informs us toward the end of the film, "So, today my passport says I am female, my driving license, my pan [*sic*] card. And all of this could come about because I got a certificate from my doctor. . . . He was very particular about writing infertile female on the certificate. But it's still female." Ghazal's testimony confesses to identity's negotiations with and inability to escape the heteronormativity of the clinic and the law. As well, it is here that queer documentary cinema acknowledges its limited mediating function in the postcolonial testimonial apparatus.

The testimonial format of Flynn's film, then, does not simply claim transgender agency but subtly points toward the plural mediation of that agency—and indeed the splitting of trans identity—by "archival formations with established command structures and entrenched social interests" (Sarkar and Walker, introduction, 19). A brief but powerful moment in the middle of the film visually underscores this intermedial trans fragmentation. While listening to Nadia's testimony, the camera shifts to cutaway shots so that we can watch her learn to move in a "feminine" fashion by mimicking a woman on a computer screen dancing to a popular Hindi song. This is a remarkably dissonant view of identity production in the film, where "the image and the real [of gender identity]" mutually define each other "through the inscriptions and reading practices of late capitalism."[68] In this scene of mimicry and performativity, the transgression and the reinscription of identity as a commodity cannot be easily separated from one another. Self-possession and self-elision cannot be neatly isolated from each other, as perhaps suggested by the enigmatic apostrophe in *I'dentity*, the title of Flynn's film.

Another film that confronts head-on the economic complexities of transgender identity is Kiran Pawar's fictional short *Existence*
(*Astitva*).[69] The film opens in medias res at a *badhai*—a ritualized blessing that a *hijra* performs in return for money and gifts in households
with newborn children or during other festive occasions.[70] A close-up
of one of the performers—partially revealing her face to the camera—
establishes her as the protagonist. The film then cuts to a flashback in
which several brief scenes narrativize the protagonist's past. We see her
growing up, being taunted and abused for her gender nonconformity,
being denied employment, becoming homeless, and ultimately taking
up begging and sex work. Unlike Flynn's *I'dentity*, Pawar's film does
not claim to be a documentary. The quick cuts, dramatic music, and
use of amateur actors constantly alert us to its fictionality. At the same
time, I will suggest that the film advances an argument that echoes and
extends postcolonial queer critiques of liberal Western endorsements of
hijra erotic dissidence.

In her critically acclaimed book *With Respect to Sex*, Gayatri Reddy
urges transnational queer scholarship to move beyond "the speculariza-
tion" of *hijra* identity.[71] Countering the queer-critical tendency to see
the *hijra* "as one more actor in the global drama of subversive sexuality"
(31), Reddy emphasizes the complex interplay between "kinship, religion,
class, and hierarchies of respect" governing the lives of India's indigenous third gender (2). Through her ethnography in the southern city of
Hyderabad, Reddy observes that the norms, rituals, and hierarchies shaping *hijra* communities cannot be uncritically valorized as erotic "diversity"
since they remain firmly tied to everyday experiences of social stigmatization (96). As well, the "thirdness" of the performativity of gender is not
unambiguous, since many *hijra* individuals identify as women and with
the binary male/female framework (32). In other words, for Reddy, *hijra*
resignification—like transgenderism more broadly—at once unsettles
and reinforces gender norms (128–29).

Without suggesting that its protagonist is an empirical *hijra* subject,
Existence highlights this ineluctable indeterminacy between inclusion
and debasement—capitulation and resistance—as the film's flashback
scenes of assault and deprivation dissolve into the *badhai* with which
the film began. At this point, the film alternates between the frenzied
dancing of the defiant protagonist and a metanarrative dramatization
of her social predicament. In this dramatization, we see the protagonist literally hanging from one side of a scale, at first with a derisive
cisgender man, and then a woman, on the other side of the scale. The

The *hijra* protagonist hangs on a scale in *Existence*.

protagonist struggles but is unable to bring her side of the scale down—failing, therefore, to approximate either the male or female ideal. Her struggles to approximate every available specular equivalent lead to disparagement and disappointment. The very naming of the third gender, the film suggests through this moment of dissonance, arises in and preserves the archival and mediating function of the binary system.

This rhetorical image literalizing the very notion of equivalence as inequivalence acquires an unforeseen significance in light of debates in India on the issue of transgender rights. *Existence* was screened at KASHISH in 2010. Four years later, in April 2014, the Supreme Court of India ruled in favor of a petition filed by the National Legal Services Authority recognizing the constitutional rights of transgender individuals as well as promising them health, education, and employment benefits.[72] But to implement the 2014 verdict, the Indian government introduced the controversial Transgender Rights Bill, reserving the right to conduct mandatory medical tests to adjudicate the "authenticity" of those applying for transgender benefits. Additionally, the bill proposed the criminalization of begging, flagrantly drawing on colonial methods of *hijra* sequestration.[73] While protests by activist groups all over the country forced the Indian government to amend the bill, the very nature of the conflict and ongoing debates around the adjudicating role of the government reveals the significance of juridical (and clinical) mediation operative in the construction of transgender identity, as well as the experiences of being transgender in contemporary India.[74] Thus the scales in Pawar's film—while perhaps inspired by the recurrent use of images of "blind" Lady Justice and her familiar prop in Indian melodramas with trials and courtroom scenes—serve as a stark reminder of the vicissitudes of the mediation of the *hijra* subject in and through the law.

Existence returns us to the pecuniary consequences of this mediation in its final moments. As the dance comes to a halt with the protagonist collapsing on the ground, the film ends with a close-up of presumably a portion of her meager earnings—three coins on the ground, seen from her point of view. On one level, the ending reemphasizes the need to see *hijra* identity through its socioeconomics and the livelihood frequently associated with it. And, here, the shot also challenges the liberal desire to accord "dignity" to the *hijra* subject through the cinephilic cultural recognition and mainstreaming that KASHISH promotes. But perhaps on another level, the shot also invites us to think of the in-between state of *hijra* transgenderism as being fundamentally mediated by a system of equivalence that is dimorphic *because it is capitalist*. The coin in the middle becomes a symbol of trans dissonance against capitalist equivalence and the sex-gender binary that are, therefore, revealed to be two sides of the same coin. As noted above, *Existence* does not claim to be an ethnography. It would be difficult to ignore its melodramatic excess. Its provocation, in fact, lies in that formal excess produced through literalization. Here queer cinema seems to insist that no cinematic form or affect can release the postcolonial *hijra* subject from her identity as long as the political economy of that identity remains "grounded" in a system of exchange whose oppressiveness lies, in part, in its colonial dimorphism.

Karishma Dube's *Goddess (Devi)* is another film that troubles both the liberal politics of inclusion and queer antiessentialism, but through a more sustained aesthetic attention to the gendered and classed inequalities mediating and splitting lesbian identity in the postcolony. Shown at KASHISH 2017, the narrative of *Goddess* revolves around the eponymous protagonist, a live-in domestic worker for an affluent family in New Delhi. An erotic attraction develops between Devi and her employer's teenage daughter, Tara. But the two women are able to enjoy only a brief period of clandestine intimacy before Tara's mother fires Devi, shortly after a dinner guest outs them as lovers. The political significance of the narrative, however, is inseparable from aesthetic choices that not only foreground same-sex desire but also focalize exclusions produced

by the neoliberal mediations of queer—and more specifically lesbian—
visibility in contemporary India.

There are several moments in *Goddess* when cinematic form prompts
the spectator to see female same-sex desire as the site of heterotopic
transgression within the heteronormative household. Gendered and
classed domestic spaces—such as the kitchen and the servant's bedroom
on the terrace—are cinematically reinvented as queer spaces where the
two women express their desire for each other. An early scene in the film
suggests an ambiguous erotic spark between Devi and Tara, while they
share a smoke on the balcony in front of the servant's room. The scene
opens with a very brief shot in which Tara lights a cigarette in Devi's
mouth, turning the phallic object into a symbol of cross-class female intimacy and reciprocity. The scene does include a brief conversation—Devi
wants to know more about an altercation with which the film opens,
during which Tara angrily retaliates against a stranger's misogynist and
homophobic remark on the street. But the camera is more interested
in focusing on the space of desire suggested through the proximity of
the women's bodies, the tone of their voices, and the shared cigarette.
Tightly framed close-ups and a standard shot/reverse shot pattern in dim
lighting carve out this space within which a concerned Devi reaches out
to touch the bruise on Tara's forehead, and Tara longingly looks at Devi
as she takes a puff and coughs gently. This space of desire is reiterated in
the course of the film as the ambiguous intimacy becomes more explicitly sexual. In another brief scene in which Tara comes to sleep in Devi's
room at night, the women's bodies come even closer in another tightly
framed close-up, their mouths almost but not quite touching. And in a
later scene set in the kitchen, the normative morality of the dinner party
outside is suspended temporarily when the camera frame includes
nothing other than the display of their same-sex desire.

In all these moments, *Goddess* uses cinematic conventions to cultivate a kind of looking that isolates erotic desire from the structural
and material inequalities within which desire takes shape. In a sense,
even as these conventions make spectators aware of their technologized
gazes, they contribute to the homoerotic version of what Kevin Floyd
has called "the reification of desire." This is a reification or abstraction that capitalism enables by attributing to sexuality "a temporality
that sets it apart from social life, that represents it as independent of
other social temporalities."[75] Arguably, the spectator, and especially the
KASHISH spectator, is expected to desire this reification to a certain
extent, waiting for the moment of disruption of the heteronormative

Tara and Devi share a kiss in the kitchen in *Goddess*.

diegetic world of the film. To *want to* look, in these moments of height-ened cinematic focus on same-sex desire, is to labor with the camera, the performers, and the crew to imagine female same-sex desire as trans-gressive of dominant norms and systems of exclusion. This is where cinematic form seems to perform the worlding that Schoonover and Galt are after.

But this is not the only kind of looking that *Devi* enables. Alongside and in contrast to the formal construction of the heterotopic space of desire, the film also keeps in our view the informal and yet indispens-able aspect of Devi's labor power and her precarious status as a live-in domestic servant. That is to say, the film's intermedial subversion of its queer formalism unfolds through its own insistence on the protagonist's exceptional socioeconomic marginality, a position of servitude that lies within but also extends well beyond the queer world the film constructs. Globalization theorist Aihwa Ong has argued that neoliberalism—as the dominant technique of governmentality deployed both in advanced and developing economies—operates not by imposing a homogeneous labor regime but rather through a heterogeneous mix of regulatory and incar-ceral labor, creating highly "striated spaces of production that combine different kinds of labor regimes."[76] Neoliberalism, in Ong's view, is a

combination of technologized forms of self-management (as exemplified by a film like *Logging Out*) and "low-skilled" labor often deprived
of juridicopolitical protections. *Devi* draws our attention to this heterogeneous space of production through its narrative as well as aesthetic
focus on the classed, gendered, and disciplinary dimension of domestic
labor in the urban Indian household. Effectively, by attending to this
aesthetic focus, the spectator confronts the coevality of *and a certain dis-
continuity* between the spectatorial labor of eroticized looking—elicited
by the cinematic reification of homoerotic desire—and the labor that
Devi performs on-screen for the benefit of her employers.

A scene in the kitchen with Devi and Tara's mother, immediately
following the balcony scene, establishes the paradoxical nature of the
protagonist's labors of servitude. The scene opens with the mistress of
the house sharing her worries about her rebellious teenage daughter
with the maid while the latter does the dishes. In a sense, the cross-class
conviviality on the balcony continues in the kitchen. At the same time,
it is also clear that what makes this scene convivial is the affective labor
that Devi performs as the ever-attentive servant. She not only performs
her chores but also offers her mistress—whom she calls "Didi" ("big sister" in Bengali and Hindi)—a sympathetic ear, reassuring her that Tara
"is a good girl. In many ways, she is just like you."[77] As the mistress raises
a tall glass of water to her forehead to soothe her headache, Devi spon-
taneously responds to her discomfort by putting a few ice cubes into the
glass, bringing a smile on her mistress's face. A medium shot of Devi's
hands reaching out for the glass brings into view the affective dimension
of this physical labor that the domestic routinely performs for the household. The scene foregrounds how Devi's rapport with her mistress is
contingent on the emotional and physical work that she must perform
to be the exceptional servant, always near at hand and responsive to the
needs of Tara and her mother.

Simultaneously, the film deploys several aesthetic markers to establish
Devi's lower-class status, the undervalued nature of her domestic labor,
and, ultimately, the substitutability of her labor power. These markers,
when read from within the postcolonial Indian context, connote persistent structural inequalities that inform communicational norms and
bodily comportment within the domestic sphere. The film insists on the
everyday materiality of the domestic's exclusion from this sphere when
the camera captures Devi in a medium shot in the kitchen, drinking
from a metallic cup, as she listens patiently to her mistress's complaints.
The visual contrast between the mistress's glass and the servant's cup

highlights the normalization of discriminatory treatment and disciplinary power in the "inclusive" household. As cinematic signifiers, the cup and the glass—in relation to the social positions of the bodies that drink from them—introduce class antagonism that has been naturalized and domesticated. The signifiers function as a commonsensical representation of social difference between the employer and the servant that is fictional and yet immediately legible in the Indian context, an unmistakable marker of class boundaries within the postcolonial household.[78]

The film's most powerful signifier of servitude emerges in a later scene in which Devi, after serving tea to her mistress and Tara, walks to the dimly lit foreground on the far right toward a bucket and a mop. Even as nothing of consequence happens in the frame, the camera lingers until Devi turns into a silhouette, bends down, and wrings the water out of the mop into the bucket. Here the hierarchy between the upper-class employer and the lower-class employee is figured not only through the positions and postures of the actors but also through the sound associated with Devi's routine household chore. It is significant that Devi almost "disappears" into her labor, in the sense that her presence can be felt only through the *sound* of her labor, that of wringing water that becomes an index of her primary function and identity in the household. This acoustic index returns in the final shot of the film, which is a variation on the living room scene. As Tara joins her mother for breakfast the morning after the party, the domestic brings in tea before returning to her chore of cleaning the steps. Yet the division of labor marking the similarity or continuity between the two scenes is also predicated on interchangeability. At this moment, the spectator realizes, with Tara, that a new servant has replaced Devi. The familiar sound with which the film ends—of the mop that the new servant wrings on the steps—finally becomes an aesthetic trace of Devi's identity as replaceable and informal labor power. In this way, *Goddess* unsettles its visual mediation of lesbian desire by drawing our attention to the mediation through which the postcolonial household—and, by extension, the nation—reconciles class conflict through distinct forms of labor and erotic regulation.

The closing of the film further underscores the striated regime of labor ultimately responsible for Devi's expulsion, through the mistress's disparate responses to the lovers after the departure of the dinner guests. "We are gay now, are we?" the disgruntled mother asks Tara in English in a tone that mixes heterosexist intolerance with liberal recognition. For Tara, this brief moment of familial acknowledgment—albeit not free of the homophobia demonstrated by the violent altercation at the beginning

Devi performs her chores while her employers relax
in their living room in *Goddess*.

of the film—functions, nevertheless, as a moment of discursive naming
and visibility. In this moment, the normative household and economy
finally admit to the possibility of an alternative sexual identity. But the
same field of discursive visibility denies the domestic servant the erotic
possibility of being "gay." Instead, the rebuke that the servant receives
from the mistress in Bengali reads her same-sex desire as an inadmis-
sible perversion of her affective labors: "Aren't you ashamed of yourself
Devi? She's almost like your own child Devi!" Although Tara and Devi
are close in age, the latter's erotic transgressions are deliberately misin-
terpreted as incestuous behavior that the reproductive economy of the
family cannot tolerate.

We can, therefore, say that Dube's *Goddess* self-consciously fractures
its own lesbian "identity" between at least two kinds of mediation. On the
one hand, it elicits an identification with a utopian cinematic space of
same-sex desire. On the other hand, domestic servitude and class domination become, in the same film, indices for a politicoeconomic mediation
that includes but also remains irreducible to the formal properties of
cinema—or any mass medium, for that matter. Watching *Goddess* at the
KASHISH festival, I also had to acknowledge that the vast majority of

domestic servants in India would have neither the resources nor the leisure time to attend such a screening in the middle of a workday.[79] And by the end, the film's celebration of queer desire had morphed, for me, into a quiet but firm demand for nothing less than a subversion of the political economy that simultaneously harbors homophobia and cinematic worlding while keeping intact its neoliberal regime of labor. Film form was no longer bound to the film text or the cinephilic context within which I was encountering *Goddess*. Instead, form had quietly laid bare the festival's own strategic neoliberalism. Form had turned into an intermedial dissonance that refused representational capture, rousing me, finally, to the complicity of my own queer spectatorial labor.

Codetta

Neither an identity-based politics of cultural recognition nor cinema-bound antiessentialism, I have argued in this chapter, is sufficient to apprehend the complex mediations of queer (in)visibility in contemporary India. Instead, through my readings of four films screened at KASHISH, I have gestured toward a cinepolitics of queer dissonance, one that lays bare the intermedial and uneven production of sexual and gendered identifications and the accompanying exclusions specific to postcolonial neoliberalism. The "success" of KASHISH, then, could be said to lie not in its neoliberal vision of unity in diversity but rather in an autocritical curatorial politics that, through these films, exposes the limits of its own homoglobal and homonational vision. The same films, I have suggested, reveal the limits of queer anti-identitarianism that hopes to counter neoliberalism through a defensive valorization of cinematic form. I will conclude this chapter with my discussion of Debalina Majumder's . . . *and the unclaimed* (. . . *ebang bewarish*)—another film from India whose intermedial attention to form does not evade but digs deeper into the complicity between unequal globalization and postcolonial queerness.[80]

Majumder's documentary revolves around a letter written by a young woman named Swapna just before she and her friend (and possible lover) Sucheta died by suicide in February 2011. The two women—one in her early twenties and the other nineteen—consumed pesticide and died holding hands on the outskirts of Sonachura, a village in suburban Nandigram, about ninety miles outside of Kolkata. After the police investigation, Sucheta's and Swapna's families did not retrieve their bodies, which were then cremated by local law enforcement a week after the women died. Activists from Sappho for Equality (a Kolkata-based organization working for the rights of lesbians, bisexual women, and trans men in eastern India) traveled to Nandigram in 2011 and 2012, and subsequently released an investigative report that was circulated among LGBTQ+ groups across the country.[81] In the Indian queer imaginary, Swapna's and Sucheta's deaths came to be seen as a "lesbian suicide" that revealed how "queer lives are continuously unclaimed."[82]

Yet, it is the ex post facto claiming and labeling of the subaltern protagonists as "lesbian" that Majumder's film resists with care, while simultaneously taking on the challenging task of reconstructing the sexual and economic oppression governing the women's lives. Produced, in fact, by Sappho for Equality, . . . *and the unclaimed* can be seen as a collective meditation on the ellipses, omissions, and striations within queer politics in postcolonial India. The film combines footage from the activists' trips to Nandigram with interviews with several Kolkatans, including a social activist, a college professor, a student, and an insurance agent. Some of these interviewees self-identify on camera as transgender, lesbian, or queer, and others do not. Notably, it is the suicide letter—or, more specifically, the physical cessation and absence marked by the letter—that supplements and torques the documentary's testimonial form. The interviewees do not only recount their own experiences of being sexually marginalized but also read and respond to this letter that structures the film, to the inescapable and yet not fully retrievable circumstances of its writing. As we shall see, the letter—through which the film asks us to *listen* to the subaltern who is corporeally absent from Indian LGBTQ+ politics and unrepresentable in that political register—compels the film and its privileged viewers to take stock of a certain failure of queerness in both its identitarian and antiessentialist inflections.

Arguably, the aesthetic and political consequences of the epistolarity of Majumder's film cannot be examined without the content of Swapna's letter, the subaltern's own assessment of her situation. From Swapna's final message (which comes to us through the Sappho for Equality report and the film whose making she could not have foreseen), we learn that the women ended their lives because they were unable to tolerate their forced separation as well as the verbal and physical abuse that followed Sucheta's forced marriage. At the same time, it is impossible to determine from the letter the exact nature of Swapna and Sucheta's relationship. Written in Bengali, the five-page note makes no open declaration of the erotic desires of either woman. While Swapna repeatedly tells us that she and Sucheta "like" or "love" each other, she also explicitly denounces presumably salacious comments from her relatives and other villagers: *They used to say bad things about me and Such[eta], things which were never even possible. I never had a bad relation with her. I like-love her a lot, and she also likes-loves me a lot. We will not manage to live without each other.*[83] Somewhere between the normative and the nonnormative, Swapna's articulation of her desire in the letter remains bound to the profoundly heteropatriarchal environment within which that desire takes shape and, finally, cannot endure. Thus, there emerges a gap between the "queer" love and longing conveyed through the letter and the identitarian commitments represented by LGBTQ+ activist groups in India, including Sappho for Equality.

Furthermore, much like the letters that Dave discusses in her account of lesbian activism in India, Swapna's message prompts its readers to attend to this gap not just through patriarchal repression but also through apparent economic precarity. For alongside ambiguous female desire, Swapna recounts her experiences of growing up in extreme poverty, her inability to stay in school because of her father's insufficient income as a fisherman, and her decision to tutor teenagers in her village to make ends meet (S. Chatterjee, *Queer Politics in India*, 9). Implicit in the letter, then, is the avowal of the lack of a certain financial and cultural wherewithal that would have perhaps allowed Swapna to live independently outside the reproductive trappings of the heterosexual family. The young breadwinner's final directive to her parents toward the end of the letter cannot, therefore, be overlooked as an inconsequential pragmatic detail: *There is some pending money to be collected for tuitions—from the elder wife, 200 rupees; Papai, 20; Jayan 40; Pintu 60; Pama 70. All the money is under the mattress, take it* (S. Chatterjee, *Queer Politics in India*, 117, emphasis in the original). Desire for nonheteronormativity and the heavy burden of economic responsibility of her entire family jostle for space in Swapna's final missive to the world she knew.

Writing in the context of diasporic and exilic cinemas, Hamid Naficy notes that "exile and epistolarity necessitate one other, for distance and absence drive them both."[84] That is to say, the letter becomes a crucial medium through which the exiled subject can convey the affective weight of being away from "home," the feeling of once having been "at home" and then being displaced from it. In . . . *and the unclaimed*, Swapna's letter carries with it not so much the memory of a prior national inclusion as the impossibility of such an inclusion of the subaltern in contemporary Indian queer politics. Within the documentary's queerscape, the letter—read aloud by those who occupy a certain discursive space, however marginalized—functions as a glaring reminder of the permanent and untended physical disappearance of the subaltern queer. In other words, through our filmic encounter with the letter, we perhaps learn to view Swapna's and Sucheta's acts of suicide as "an unemphatic, ad hoc, subaltern rewriting of the social text" from which they have been always already excluded and exiled.[85]

Swapna's absent-present voice, however, has a second function within Majumder's documentary. It is through and against the subject positions indexed by the letter—positions that can only be "heard" postmortem and in absentia—that the film's interviewees convey their own varying abilities and desires to continue surviving as erotically marginalized individuals. For instance, the insurance agent Swarup/Rupa speaks of the agony of not being able to undergo transition to become female, encumbered (like Swapna and Sucheta) by an arranged marriage and economic obligations to his/her family. At the same time, his/her testimony—constructed *in relation to the letter*—also becomes the site where Swarup/Rupa reflects on the difference between his/her own position and that of the women from Nandigram: "I don't fantasize about suicide . . . but I pray for my death every day. . . . I can't leave my wife. I can't forgo my responsibility to my daughter."[86] The ability to offer a testimony, as I noted earlier, often connotes survival in the face of adversity. Swarup/Rupa's testimony, however, becomes a far more ambivalent act. It performs simultaneously a longing for physical death and a coming to terms with a kind of social death enforced by the econocultural constraints of compulsory heterosexuality. These are constraints that are not easily mitigated by legal reform in the form of the Transgender Rights Bill or the repeal of IPC 377 through a neoliberal privileging of privacy.

A contrasting yet comparable testimony comes from Sumita, a social activist who visited Nandigram as part of the Sappho for Equality team. Unlike Swarup/Rupa, Sumita speaks with confidence of having overcome an initially confusing acknowledgment of her own same-sex desire: "But once that phase was over . . . I felt that this is me. So I should explain the whole thing to the girl I was in love with. . . . I should explain it to my husband." At the same time, even as Sumita performs queer agency and self-elaboration through her testimony, she is forced to reckon with the erasure marked by Swapna's letter: "My situation and that of Swapna-Sucheta are very different . . . so very different that I cringe at the idea."

While Sumita does not elaborate on the difference, I will suggest that the classed mediations of this disjuncture come into view through the film's representation of the postcolonial urban-rural divide. Majumder's film does not, by any means, vilify rural India as the bastion of homophobia, since the heterosexist voices in the film come from both Kolkata and Nandigram. But the documentary is formally structured to foreground the social and cultural hierarchies between its participants and the geographic spaces they inhabit. In fact, the film seems to suggest that the very act of filming and documenting queerness is implicated in and thwarted by divides between the center and the periphery within the postcolonial state.

The disparity between the city and the village is visible early on, as the film transitions from Sumita recounting the trip to Nandigram to the trip itself. Visually, the shift is noticeable because we move from a semi-private urban space—a well-furnished room with a poster of Audrey Hepburn from the 1960s Hollywood film *Breakfast at Tiffany's*—to an out-door rural setting with thatched huts, muddy roads, and thick foliage. But what shapes the viewer's experience of this move from "developed" to "still developing" India is also a rhetorical shift with significant political implications. In the confines of the queer-friendly space in the city, Sumita is able to deliberate thoughtfully (in what would be considered "polished" Bengali and English) on her visit to Nandigram and, later in the film, on the complexity of her own erotic journey. As well, the dynamic between the filmmaker and the interviewee is one of familiarity and rapport. Sumita's relaxed posture and tone during a seemingly informal coffee-table conversation suggests that she is a willing participant who welcomes the presence of the filmmaker.

In contrast, once the documentary gaze shifts to the countryside, the introspective and amicable atmosphere of the earlier interview is replaced by a tense public encounter between the metropolitan activists and the villagers of Sonachura, including Swapna's parents. What stands out in these encounters is the filmmaker's decision to frequently include the urban activist and the rural interviewee in the same frame, drawing attention to their discordant ideologies and social positions. Concomitantly, what is also audible to the Bengalophone viewer is the gap between metropolitan speech and nonurban dialect, the latter not yet familiar with and perhaps even threatened by the language of urban queerspeak. For instance, reflecting (in Bengali) on his daughter's intimacy with her friend, Swapna's father Achintya expresses a hostility not just to same-sex desire but also to an Anglicized queer discourse to which he has had very little exposure: "Those who have some knowledge were saying . . . it's called 'homosex' or something like that. I never liked . . . I mean . . . I never believed it. A girl may have such relationship with another girl . . . we don't have any idea about it or its signs. We never think in that line."

I would argue that, through this antagonistic exchange between the queer activist and the villager, the film does not simply condemn rural homophobia. Rather, these are moments when the film prompts us to view homophobia through a more complex lens, through the struggle and incommensurability between two asymmetrical "language games,"[87] two discursive fields marked by undeniable differences in social mobility, cultural exposure, and subcultural capital.

This reflexivity—where documentary activism draws attention to its own socioeconomic distance from its subjects—comes to the fore in another antagonistic encounter filmed in the village. As the activists continue to interview Swapna's mother, Chandamoni, an angry neighbor asks the crew to stop filming: "Stop the camera, hey. Stop the camera. The girls of this locality are different. Our girls keep long hair, wear saris, there are many other things that they do. You don't have to teach us anything. Go and teach this to the city. You don't have to teach us. We are doing fine here." This is a significant moment in the film in that it emphasizes a communicational deadlock between the villagers and the urban activists. (An activist even runs after the villager to calm him down but fails to bring him back into the conversation.) But it is also important to note that the film includes *this* particular sound bite, one in which gendered anticolonial value coding (see this volume's introduction and chapter 3) reappears as a postcolonial defense of the rural hinterland against urban incursion. While the sociocultural repercussions of India's economic liberalization may appear to be quite distant from the subject matter of the documentary, the villager's outburst against urban intervention acquires a historically specific political overtone for viewers familiar with the antidevelopment violence and protests in Nandigram.

In 2006–2007, the West Bengal government partnered with an Indonesian corporate group to coercively acquire agricultural land to build a Special Economic Zone and industrialize the Nandigram area. But villagers from all over the region (primarily farmers and low-wage agricultural laborers) persistently resisted all such efforts of governmental and multinational expropriation. As Tanika Sarkar and Sumit Chowdhury point out, "The name has, therefore, come to signify much more than a place. Nandigram is invoked wherever peasants in India oppose the forced acquisition of their land."[88] This resistance, however, took a heavy toll—fifteen villagers died, many women were sexually assaulted, and over a hundred people "went missing" after clashes with the state police in early March 2007 (T. Sarkar and Chowdhury, "Meaning of Nandigram," 83–84).

By including a sound bite that evokes this brutal encounter with neo-liberalism spreading its fangs from the metropolis, Majumder's film subtly urges queer activism to rethink sexual and gender oppression through the politics of postcolonial development. In the ideological minefield of *. . . and the unclaimed*, then, the heteropatriarchal assertion of rural "tradition" and "authenticity" cannot be dissociated from the threats and lived experiences of economic and sexual violence and expropriation for which "globalization" has become the alibi. Willy-nilly, this is a violence in which the queer activist, filmmaker, and theorist become implicated, regardless of their positions on capitalism and queer dissidence.

Thus, like the other films discussed in this chapter, what Majumder's film also resists is the cunning of capital, refusing to capitulate to the promise of freedom from minoritizing constraints through either identitarianism or cinematic form. Instead, the film mobilizes the testimonial form to index modes of postcolonial exclusion—queer and nonqueer—that an identitarian focus on gay, lesbian, or transgender liberation cannot but fail to address. As Majumder's final interviewee starts to cry inconsolably while comparing her own social isolation to Swapna and Sucheta's inability to belong to queer India, the film cuts to a black frame. The film ends with this frame, with the voice of another interviewee encouraging the filmmaker to include the mournful crying in the film's final edited version:

> Let that cry be there. Let it go on. Let there be a heart wrenching wail in your film. A whole lot of tears will spill over your camera, frame, and the soundtrack. A whole lot will be missed too. I am drawing a map of India . . . whose outline is a chain of unclaimed dead bodies. There are countless unclaimed bodies strewn around. Countless movements. . . . Sometimes it's from the eastern frontiers of India. Sometimes from Kashmir which we have called terrorism. Sometimes it's Dandakaranya, a body of a tribal who might have died protesting some unfair . . . simply unfair takeover of their resources in the mines. Sometimes it's a body of a Muslim girl in [the] Gujarat genocide.

We should feel ashamed. Let this cry be there. Let us keep it.
A cry which will wake the unclaimed bodies up . . . which will
frighten the State.

On one level, this final moment is countercinematic, deprivileging
the visual image and the dominant discourse of queer visibility. On
another level, the ending reminds the viewer of the constructed and
performative nature of the testimonial cry that cinematic form makes
audible. Simultaneously, through the final reflections of its interviewee-
collaborator, . . . *and the unclaimed* proposes a mode of aesthetic
production and reception in which cinematic form—the black frame
and the voice together reconstructing and reinterpreting the individual
interviewee's avowal of grief—becomes the means to pluralize queer
grieving. The black frame becomes formally necessary to move beyond
the testifying body that emits the cry and toward those unclaimed and
unseen bodies whose deathly cries Indian queer politics and activism
are yet to hear. In other words, through its aesthetic-political pluraliza-
tion of the grieving voice, Majumder's film offers itself as a potential
"pre-text" for a queer resistance that is yet to come.[89]
    Finally, as the film strives to stretch itself between its medium speci-
ficity and unclaimed bodies cremated or interred in the margins of the
nation and legitimized national politics, its intermediality also calls out
instances of postcolonial oppression that are not legible to queerness
that confines itself to the *erotic*. These instances of "nonqueer" oppression include the Hindu Right's assaults on the Muslim body in the name
of nationalism, or the neoliberal state's assaults on indigenous livelihoods
to boost the national economy. "What happens to queer—as identity, ideology and theory," Oishik Sircar and Dipika Jain ask, "when it moves out
of its home base of sexuality? Does it lose salience when asked questions
that do not necessarily have any direct connections to sex and sexuality?"[90] The antineoliberal dissonant cry with which Majumder's film ends
insists otherwise. But for that new salience to emerge and be politically effective, the film suggests, queerness needs to learn to dereify
sexuality, as well as aesthetics, and to situate them both in the shifting economic and cultural asymmetries in the postcolonial field of
value production. The postcolonial queer dissonance of . . . *and the
unclaimed* is, in that sense, both profoundly mournful and optimistic.

Interdisciplinarity as Queer Optimism

Queerness is NOT yet here. . . . Queerness is a structuring and educated mode of desiring that allows us to see and feel beyond the quagmire of the present. . . . Queerness is that thing that lets us feel that this world is not enough, that indeed something is missing.
—José Esteban Muñoz, *Cruising Utopia*

Hope, often a fracturing, even a traumatic thing to experience, is among the energies by which the reparatively positioned reader tries to organize the fragments and part-objects she encounters or creates.
—Eve Kosofsky Sedgwick, "Paranoid Reading and Reparative Reading"

Several thoughtful and generous readers of this book in its earlier stages responded with a question that I could not but take seriously: "Could you possibly end with a modicum of hope?" A similar response—which I take to be a variation on the first—has been, "So what? What is the solution that *you* are offering to the mediations of identitarian violence?" These questions did not come as a surprise and were, in fact, invaluable insofar as they compelled me to confront my own doubts throughout the writing process: Was I being paralyzingly pessimistic by critiquing aesthetic utopianism, refusing to let go of "paranoid reading" in a moment where "reparative reading" is being offered as a way out of what José Esteban Muñoz, in the first epigraph to this conclusion, calls "the quagmire of the present"? Is my own critique implicitly guided by the assumption that the mere *exposure* of the cunning of capitalism will alter its aesthetic operations?[1] Given my critique of capitalism, I could

225

follow optimistic thinkers like Michael Hardt, Antonio Negri, and others and suggest that one possible solution to the cunning is the human potential to conceive of difference or "singularity" beyond the tussle between identity and nonidentity. I could look back upon forms of sociality and social exchange—such as "love" for Hardt and Negri, or "symbolic exchange" for even the infamously pessimistic Jean Baudrillard—that once defied and could, once again, perhaps allow humanity to move past the dominance of exchange value.[2] But to end *Identity* on that note would not, to my mind, be most productive, not least because I can claim to offer no quick "master plan" to get to these utopias. As well, such a closing gesture would miss the opportunity to address what some of my readers have already read (and still others might read) as paranoia, cynicism, or pessimism in my argument and method of critique in the preceding pages. My goal in these final pages will, therefore, be to reflect on that method and the stakes of an interdisciplinary optimism that is, in fact, founded on pessimism as well as a certain indeterminacy between paranoia, pessimism, and reparation. As Lauren Berlant reminds us, "Optimism might not *feel* optimistic."[3]

The dynamic relationship between optimism and pessimism surfaces in Muñoz's *Cruising Utopia*, where he defines queer utopianism as an affective disposition that looks to the past to build a better future from within an unbearable present. He writes,

> The present is not enough. It is impoverished and toxic for queers and other people who do not feel the privilege of majoritarian belonging, normative tastes, and "rational" expectations. . . . Let me be clear that the idea is not simply to turn away from the present. . . . The present must be known in relation to the alternative temporal and spatial maps provided by a perception of past and future affective worlds.[4]

While *Cruising Utopia* explicitly positions itself against the pessimism of "antisocial" queer theory—especially Lee Edelman's rejection of all futurity as heteronormative[5]—it is worth noting that Muñoz's queer optimism is also founded on a pessimism about the "impoverished and toxic" present defined by a "pragmatic contemporary gay identity" politics (11). For Muñoz, no desirable outcome can emerge from the identitarian present, which, therefore, needs to be altered through a nonidentitarian utopianism connecting the past to the future. In other words, Muñoz's hopes for a utopian future are inseparable from an indefatigable hopelessness connected to the present. This restless queer pessimism that is also hopeful can be likened to Nivedita Menon's postcolonial feminist view of "emancipation" as "not a goal we can reach" but rather "as a process without closure."[6] As an emancipatory struggle that seeks to resist the resistance that has become identitarian cooptation, Muñoz's queer utopianism thus originates, in part, in a profound skepticism about the here and now. My own skepticism in *Identity*—produced through a crossing between my archive and the ground from where I have approached and interpreted that archive—draws heavily on Muñoz's antipresentist queer politics. Beginning with Fanonian dissonance and ending with its postcolonial queer articulations, this book has argued that a more egalitarian future cannot be mapped unless we reexamine and negate the neoliberal reality through the past. In Theodor Adorno's words, there can be no hope unless it is "wrested from reality by negating it."[7] This negation can begin by reinterpreting identitarian potentialities through the lingering schizophrenic dissonance engendered by colonial matrices of power.

At the same time, this is also where my approach departs significantly from that of Muñoz, for whom the domain of the *aesthetic* becomes the primary repository of glimpses of alternatives to the present: "Often we can glimpse the worlds proposed and promised by queerness in the realm of the aesthetic. The aesthetic, especially the queer aesthetic, frequently contains blueprints and schemata of a forward-dawning futurity" (1). Notably, the aesthetic domain of *Cruising Utopia* is a socially diverse one, moving from the cultural production of the New York school of poetry to the Judson Memorial Church's dance theater to Andy Warhol's Factory (4). In Muñoz's argument, it is the reader-spectator's immersion in the soothing quotidian socialities evoked by the queer artworks and performances emerging from these spaces that yields a utopian feeling of "astonished contemplation," a reprieve from "limitations of an alienating presentness" (5). For instance, reading Frank O'Hara's poem "Having a Coke with You" alongside Warhol's silk screens of Coke bottles, Muñoz argues that these artworks enable the cultural consumer to see Coca-Cola as something far more queer than a mere commodity or product of capitalist alienation. If O'Hara's enigmatic poem about sharing a Coke with possibly a lover "signifies a vast lifeworld of queer relationality, an encrypted sociality, and a utopian potentiality" (6), Warhol's emphasis on the everydayness of the commodity through his silk screens reveals "the radically democratic potentiality" of the mass-produced beverage (7). Thus, for Muñoz, the properly aesthetic experience is synonymous with the "openness" and "indeterminacy" of pop art and performance that reinvigorate an overused commodity like Coca-Cola. Through O'Hara's and Warhol's unique and yet quotidian creations, Coca-Cola becomes a radical commodity allowing the consumer to imagine a nonidentitarian queer future that is possible but yet to arrive.

In contrast, I have argued that the tendency to seek aesthetic reprieves from identity (alongside the equally prevalent tendency to claim identity through the aesthetic) becomes an exclusionary exercise, precisely because it overlooks entirely the manifold and historically contingent aesthetic mediations of identity production under commodity capitalism. I have suggested that the problem with this mode of imaginative reconstruction—the preceding chapters have shown that Muñoz is certainly not alone here—is that it frequently defines the aesthetic in terms of an isolated encounter between the "emancipatory" cultural artifact and the cultural consumer. Instead, Identity has drawn on and contributed to a more reflexive and contextualized approach to cultural consumption and mediation, one that insists on the need to broaden the very notion of what constitutes the "aesthetic experience."

Identity's approach to mediation, then, poses a necessary challenge to Muñozian queer utopianism, and demands that cultural critique reevaluate the very means by which it aesthetically "rewrites" capitalism. Such a reevaluation of Muñoz's faith in the artistic reinvention of Coca-Cola as a commodity, for instance, could begin by considering the aesthetic lessons learned from postcolonial protests against the global beverage, where its iconic sign connotes not "democratic potentiality" but rather death-dealing drought and pollution. In March 2000, Coca-Cola opened a bottling plant in the remote village of Plachimada in Kerala, India. Within a few years, residents of the surrounding area—the majority of whom are historically oppressed indigenous groups, or adivasis—realized that the activities of the plant had contaminated the local groundwater and led to an alarming decrease in the height of the water table. Plachimada's protests against Coca-Cola entered global mass media through images of a billboard created by the Indian photographer Sharad Haksar. This billboard, which caused a national stir (and prompted Coke to sue Haksar), is remarkable in its simplicity: it depicts a series of brightly colored plastic pots, a water pump, an old rubber tire, and a plastic can, all placed in front of the well-known DRINK COCA-COLA sign painted in a white font against a red background.[8] On the one hand, it is its representational simplicity or candor—its unequivocal emphasis on the routinely experienced clash between the global citizenship promised by Coca-Cola and the scarcity produced by the same corporate giant in Plachimada—that makes the billboard a powerful aesthetic critique of queer utopianism's romance with Coke through U.S. pop art.

On the other hand, as Bishnupriya Ghosh reminds us through her meticulous reading of the same billboard, the aesthetic operations that allow Haksar to produce this cultural artifact are only partially visible to its viewers. For what makes this artifact possible is not only Haksar's (the individual maker's) aesthetic politics but, more crucially, the "mute" performative protests of the indigenous women of Plachimada not included in the billboard. These are the women who remain invisible in the much-publicized image but who, in fact, assembled their plastic water pots every day in front of the Coca-Cola sign to render visible the corporate-sponsored depletion of the water table (Ghosh, *Global Icons*, 52). Ghosh's reading alerts us to repeated psychocorporeal splittings of the indigenous women in front of the sign—or what she calls their "corporeal dynamism" (54)—that precede and provide the affective and material infrastructure for Haksar's billboard. The women's embodied act of placing their pots in front of the Coke sign represents a collective demand, while each pot reflects an individually felt and sensorially experienced feeling of "social antagonism" (or what *Identity* has called aesthetic dissonance) with that so-called global sign-as-commodity (53). In fact, for Ghosh, the women's positioning of the pots before the iconic sign reflects their own understanding of their deleterious corporeal connection with the linguistic-visual corporate sign: "In a struggle where the corporeal existence of the body is at risk, such sensuous linkage provides a phenomenological grasp of collective scarcity" (54). Thus, we can say that Ghosh's interpretation of the aesthetic origins of the indigenous demand for a better future offers an indispensable critique of Muñoz's aestheticization of Coca-Cola. Evoking above all else a locality with clean and adequate water, utopia, here, demands to be glimpsed not through the nostalgic and consumerist immersion in a Warholian "fun of having a Coke" (Muñoz, *Cruising Utopia*, 6) but rather through a minoritarian aesthetic perception of Coke's ruthless and unmistakably racialized toxification of the postcolony in the present.

Ghosh's attention to the heterogeneity of the aesthetic domain—and to the formation of ideological collectives through aesthetically mediated fragmentation—has been central to my analysis of identity politics in this book. Against the tendency in interdisciplinary critique to view aesthetic experience as primarily liberatory, and often in opposition to

norms and regulations, I have argued for the need to see identity production as aesthetic phenomena that can be at once disciplinary and
destabilizing, constraining and potentializing. In particular, my focus
has been on the aesthetic mediation of minoritizing constraints that
emerge in and through the structure of equivalence and the fetish of
the commodity form. The emergence of identity as a multiply mediated fragmentation, I have suggested, is precisely what is disavowed
by multiculturalist aesthetic claims to "minority difference" such that
"minority culture and difference also became items for the development of a new phase of global capital, a phase that would engage elite
minorities as its facilitators."[9] Antiessentialist critique in the humanities, I have further demonstrated, frequently consecrates the aesthetic
and particular aesthetic media to transcend identity but still with the
implicit intent of preserving disciplinary or interdisciplinary cultural
capital. Residual and still-emerging identitarian fragments (posing as
essences) and antiessentialist utopianism coconstitute neoliberalism's
variegated aesthetic mode of production.

Thus, it is not in spite of but rather because of its pessimistic diagnosis that *Identity* joins cautiously optimistic calls for an uncompromising
interdisciplinarity that refuses to be domesticated by the aesthetic cunning of capital. In chapter 2, I noted how scholars like Rey Chow and
Mark Chiang have argued for an interdisciplinarity that scrutinizes the
modes and costs of its own inclusion and institutionalization within the
U.S. academy. Echoing their concerns, other critics have pointed out
that while the interdisciplines (nontraditional fields of study like ethnic studies, gender and sexuality studies, and film and media studies)
took shape as a result of the social justice movements of the 1960s and
1970s, they are no longer provocateurs in the U.S. academy. The interdisciplines now need to contend with the fact that they themselves are
not "innocent of political and epistemological complicity with multiple structures of oppression."[10] Interdisciplinarity, in other words, must
determine how its institutionalized proliferation has been and continues to be the means of disciplinarization and containment. Noting the
ineluctable gap between identity-based interdisciplines and their political aspirations, Robyn Wiegman pointedly asks,

> What does it mean that practitioners are taught to read, gener-
> ate, and evaluate critical practice according to the status of the
> field's discourse outside the material locus of its production—
> that is, outside the accumulation of professional capital that

attends the reproduction of critical hegemonies within the field? What kinds of affective and analytic expectations, and . . . regulations are thus required to ensure safe passage between the field's self-defining hegemonies and the modes of critical world building it attaches to them? And what can the field *not* afford to know in order to guarantee its reproduction in the disciplinary terms on which its commitment to the political turns?[11]

The aesthetic education that *Identity* has gleaned from its archive has offered some uncomfortable but urgently needed responses to these questions. My archive's insistence on seeing identity as an intermedial wound has, in turn, allowed me to scrutinize the (disciplinary and interdisciplinary) commodification of the aesthetic through a privileged medium, whether in the literary turn to linguistic lack or ethnic difference, or cinema studies' refuge in the referential excess of the moving image. The book has, therefore, argued that image- and language-bound attempts at "reparations" rely on aesthetic hegemonies that cannot afford to know the complex and shifting intermediations of identitarian difference.

When scholars in media, literary, and performance studies uphold reparative reading, they overlook a significant delimitation and a generalization that enable the paranoid/reparative opposition in Eve Kosofsky Sedgwick's landmark essay. Sedgwick, we will recall, critiques paranoia "by setting outside the scope of this discussion" its overlap with "schizophrenia . . . delusionality or psychosis."[12] As well, as the prevalent mode of critique, paranoid reading becomes synonymous with a quest "for symmetrical relations, in particular, symmetrical epistemologies . . . 'an inescapable interpretive doubling of presence'" ("Paranoid Reading," 126). While Sedgwick is most concerned about academic knowledge production and its performative effects, her privileging of paranoia as the quest for symmetry and presence—the norm against which she delineates reparative critique—falls within the much larger cultural tendency to read identity in paranoid and neurotic terms. This approach to identity and identitarian presence, I have argued in the introduction to this book, relies on an obfuscation of the profoundly asymmetrical logic of value production. Through my archive, I have instead proposed that identity politics needs to be seen as a dynamic and discontinuous interplay between reading and being read by the mediations of capital. The schizophrenic effect of this interplay can be best described as being both "aberrantly" paranoid and reparative, wounding and capacitating, thereby demanding an interrogation of reading practices that insist that, somehow, one is "better" than the other. Thus, in constructing *Identity*, I have operated as Sedgwick's "reparatively positioned reader" who organizes seemingly disparate fragments (essences) to generate hope through skepticism and trauma ("Paranoid Reading," 146). At the same time, the fragments themselves propose that the ostensibly agentic distinction between paranoid and reparative reading cannot be sustained as soon as we attend to capitalism's schizophrenic mode of aesthetic production. The fragment necessarily signifies partial knowledge, the wound necessarily connotes painful affects and sentiments that are not fully representable. There can be no queer utopia without a relentlessly interdisciplinary and intermedial stocktaking of this injury.

NOTES

Introduction

1. Parker Bright, "Hey y'all so I am at the Whitney Biennial," Facebook, March 17, 2017, https://www.facebook.com/parker.bright.9/videos /10209898925964379/?autoplay_reason=gatekeeper&video_container _type=4&video_creator_product_type=0&app_id=6628568379&live _video_guests=0.

2. Alex Greenberger, "'The Painting Must Go': Hannah Black Pens Open Letter to the Whitney about Controversial Biennial Work," *Artnews*, March 21, 2017, http://www.artnews.com/2017/03/21/the-painting-must-go-hannah -black-pens-open-letter-to-the-whitney-about-controversial-biennial-work/.

3. Siddhartha Mitter and Christina Sharpe, "'What Does It Mean to Be Black and Look at This?' A Scholar Reflects on the Dana Schutz Controversy," Hyperallergic, March 24, 2017, https://hyperallergic.com/368012 /what-does-it-mean-to-be-black-and-look-at-this-a-scholar-reflects-on-the -dana-schutz-controversy/.

4. Randy Kennedy, "White Artist's Painting of Emmett Till at Whitney Biennial Draws Protests," *New York Times*, March 21, 2017, https://www .nytimes.com/2017/03/21/arts/design/painting-of-emmett-till-at-whitney -biennial-draws-protests.html.

5. Margaret Schwartz, *Dead Matter: The Meaning of Iconic Corpses* (Minneapolis: University of Minnesota Press, 2015), 58–59.

6. Coco Fusco, "Censorship, Not the Painting, Must Go: On Dana Schutz's Image of Emmett Till," Hyperallergic, March 27, 2017, https:// hyperallergic.com/368290/censorship-not-the-painting-must-go-on-dana -schutzs-image-of-emmett-till/.

7. For a discussion of how other artists and scholars turned to social media to argue for aesthetic resistance beyond identity politics, see Brian Boucher, "Social Media Erupts as the Art World Splits in Two over Dana Schutz Controversy," Artnet, March 24, 2017, https://news.artnet.com/art-world/art -world-split-dana-schutz-controversy-902423.

8. Emilio Spadola, *The Calls of Islam: Sufis, Islamists, and Mass Mediation in Urban Morocco* (Bloomington: Indiana University Press, 2014), 4.

9. On the distinction between human capital (comprising an individual's labor, skills, abilities, and social status) and nonhuman capital (comprising tangible financial assets and technological resources owned or traded), see Thomas Piketty, *Capital in the Twenty-First Century*, trans. Arthur Goldhammer (Cambridge, Mass.: Harvard University Press, 2017), 58–59.

10. Marshall McLuhan, *Understanding Media: The Extensions of Man* (Cambridge, Mass.: MIT Press, 1994), 8.

11. By "protestor," I do not mean only Parker Bright and other activists who physically blocked the painting to make their protest visible. I include all other viewers who, like Bright, have felt misinterpellated, commoditized, and further marginalized by Schutz's painting.

12. Fusco risks ignoring these reasons when she faults the protestors for privileging photographic mimeticism over Schutz's aesthetic abstraction, for allowing the properties of one aesthetic medium to bear upon another medium. See Fusco, "Censorship."

13. Schwartz, *Dead Matter*, 61, 65.

14. On the impact of Till's murder on the civil rights movement, see Clenora Hudson-Weems, *Emmett Till: The Sacrificial Lamb of the Civil Rights Movement* (Troy, Mich.: Bedford, 1994); and Schwartz, *Dead Matter*, 59–60.

15. Fred Moten, *In the Break: The Aesthetics of the Black Radical Tradition* (Minneapolis: University of Minnesota Press, 2003), 192–211.

16. On identity as an injury or grievance that is not only produced by the liberal state but is also perceived as something that the state alone can redress, see Wendy Brown, *States of Injury: Power and Freedom in Late Modernity* (Princeton, N.J.: Princeton University Press, 1995), 26–29; Judith Butler, *The Psychic Life of Power: Theories in Subjection* (Stanford, Calif.: Stanford University Press, 1997), 100; and Asad Haider, *Mistaken Identity: Race and Class in the Age of Trump* (London: Verso, 2018), 10–12. My theorization of identity as a wound will proceed by both including and moving beyond the mediation of the state.

17. See Mary Ann Doane, "The Indexical and the Concept of Medium Specificity," *differences* 18, no. 1 (2007): 131. On the use of *media* as a collective singular noun with the emergence of mass media in the eighteenth and nineteenth centuries, see W. J. T. Mitchell and Mark B. N. Hansen, introduction to *Critical Terms for Media Studies*, ed. W. J. T. Mitchell and Mark B. N. Hansen (Chicago: University of Chicago Press, 2010), xi.

18. Mitchell and Hansen, introduction, xx.

19. *Oxford English Dictionary*, online ed., s.v. "mediation," http://www.oed.com.exlibris.colgate.edu:2048/view/Entry/115665?redirectedFrom=mediation#eid.

20. Bright, Facebook, March 17, 2017.

21. Robyn Autry, "Another Look into Dana Schutz's 'Open Casket,'" *Black Perspectives*, May 10, 2017, https://www.aaihs.org/another-look-into-dana-schutzs-open-casket/.

22. Jodi Dean, "Faces as Commons: The Secondary Visuality of Communicative Capitalism," open! Platform for Art, Culture & the Public Domain, December 31, 2016, http://www.onlineopen.org/faces-as-commons.

23. Naomi Rea, "A Year Ago, Parker Bright Protested Dana Schutz at the Whitney. Now His Fans Are Flying Him to Paris to Protest Again," Artnet, February 21, 2018, https://news.artnet.com/art-world/parker-bright-paris-protest-1227947.

24. On this perpetual extrapolation of sameness from otherness under late capitalism, see Jean Baudrillard, *The Perfect Crime*, trans. Chris Turner (New York: Verso, 1996), 132.

25. Gayatri Chakravorty Spivak, "In a Word: *Interview*," interview by Ellen Rooney, in *Outside in the Teaching Machine* (New York: Routledge, 1993), 5.

26. Walter D. Mignolo, *The Darker Side of Western Modernity: Global Futures, Decolonial Options* (Durham, N.C.: Duke University Press, 2011), xxvii.

27. Denise Ferreira da Silva, "To Be Announced: Radical Praxis or Knowing (at) the Limits of Justice," *Social Text* 31, no. 1/114 (2013): 50.

28. Arjun Appadurai, "Disjuncture and Difference in the Global Cultural Economy," *Theory, Culture & Society* 7 (1990): 295.

29. Rey Chow, *The Protestant Ethnic and the Spirit of Capitalism* (New York: Columbia University Press, 2002), 117; Elizabeth A. Povinelli, *The Cunning of Recognition: Indigenous Alterities and the Making of Australian Multiculturalism* (Durham, N.C.: Duke University Press), 2002.

30. My claim is not that these are the only identity categories fueling capitalism but that their operations point toward a larger global logic in which minoritized differences appear to be both empowering and constraining. I should also note here that one of the many limitations of this book is that it does not examine religion, indigeneity, and disability—three highly significant sites of identitarian investments in the current world order. My only recourse is to point the reader to scholarship that also approaches these sites of differentiation through the paradox of simultaneous inclusion and exclusion. See Sadia Abbas, *At Freedom's Limit: Islam and the Postcolonial Predicament* (New York: Fordham University Press, 2014); Jodi A. Byrd, *The Transit of Empire: Indigenous Critiques of Colonialism* (Minneapolis: University of Minnesota Press, 2011); and Jasbir K. Puar, *The Right*

to Maim: Debility, Capacity, Disability (Durham, N.C.: Duke University Press, 2017).

31. Frantz Fanon, *Black Skin, White Masks*, trans. Richard Philcox (New York: Grove, 2008).

32. Frantz Fanon, *A Dying Colonialism*, trans. Haakon Chevalier (New York: Grove, 1994).

33. Theresa Hak Kyung Cha, *Dictée* (Berkeley: University of California Press, 2001).

34. Assia Djebar, dir., *La Nouba des femmes du Mont Chenoua* (1977; New York: Women Make Movies, 2002), DVD.

35. Nakshatra Bagwe, dir., *Logging Out* (Mumbai: Solaris Pictures, 2012), DVD; Karishma Dube, dir., *Devi* (2017), digital copy obtained from the filmmaker; Debalina Majumder, dir., *. . . ebang bewarish* (Kolkata: Sappho for Equality, 2013).

36. On "identity disregard," see Amartya Sen, *Identity and Violence: The Illusion of Destiny* (New York: Norton, 2006), 20.

37. For critiques of this opposition see, for instance, Rosemary Hennessy, *Profit and Pleasure: Sexual Identities in Late Capitalism* (New York: Routledge, 2000); and Chandan Reddy, *Freedom with Violence: Race, Sexuality, and the US State* (Durham, N.C.: Duke University Press, 2011).

38. Linda Martín Alcoff and Satya P. Mohanty, "Reconsidering Identity Politics: An Introduction," in *Identity Politics Reconsidered*, ed. Linda Martín Alcoff, Michael Hames-García, Satya P. Mohanty, and Paula M. L. Moya (New York: Palgrave Macmillan), 3.

39. For a useful account of the introduction of the term "identity politics" in U.S. political discourse in the late 1970s through the activism of the black feminist Combahee River Collective, see Haider, *Mistaken Identity*, 7–9. My point, however, is that this account is not sufficient to track the production of identity as a minoritizing constraint in a transnational frame under colonial and postcolonial capitalism.

40. Stuart Hall, "Who Needs 'Identity'?," in *The Media Studies Reader*, ed. Laurie Ouellette (New York: Routledge, 2013), 354, emphasis in the original.

41. Jacques Lacan, "The Mirror Stage as Formative of the *I* Function as Revealed in Psychoanalytic Experience," in *Écrits: The First Complete Edition in English*, trans. Bruce Fink (New York: Norton, 2006), 75–81. Notably, for Lacan, the neurotic longing for wholeness is what defines the "typical" ego or psychic structure. The psychic norm, in the sense of what is most common, is neurosis. On this, see Dylan Evans, *An Introductory Dictionary of Lacanian Psychoanalysis* (London: Routledge, 1996), 122.

42. Louis Althusser, *On Ideology*, trans. Ben Brewster (New York: Verso, 2008), 36.

43. Fanon, *Black Skin*, 139.

44. My use of "schizophrenia" is not meant to pathologize individuals or groups. But neither is it simply metaphorical. Reading psychoanalysts Dolto and Lacan through Fanon, schizophrenia emerges as a psychocorporeal and racializing dissonance with the universal equivalent, the feeling of being captivated by and yet severed from its ideality. I will make this use of the term clearer in chapter 1.

45. See Doane, "The Indexical," 131; and Mitchell and Hansen, introduction, xi.

46. Theodor Adorno, "On the Fetish Character in Music and the Regression of Listening," in *The Culture Industry: Selected Essays on Mass Culture*, ed. J. M. Bernstein (New York: Routledge, 1991), 40.

47. See, for instance, Walter Benjamin, "The Work of Art in the Age of Its Technological Reproducibility," in *The Work of Art in the Age of Its Technological Reproducibility and Other Writings on Media*, ed. Michael W. Jennings, Brigid Doherty, and Thomas Y. Levin, trans. Edmund Jephcott and Harry Zohn (Cambridge, Mass.: Harvard University Press, 2008), 19–55.

48. Jean-Louis Baudry, "Ideological Effects of the Basic Cinematographic Apparatus," trans. Alan Williams, *Film Quarterly* 28, no. 2 (1974–75): 45–46; and Christian Metz, *The Imaginary Signifier: Psychoanalysis and Cinema*, trans. Celia Britton, Annwyl Williams, Ben Brewster, and Alfred Guzzetti (Bloomington: Indiana University Press, 1982), 4–6. I will return to this strand of film theory in chapters 1 and 2.

49. For a definition of a technological medium as that which relies on the remediation or appropriation of older media, see Jay David Bolter and Richard Grusin, *Remediation: Understanding New Media* (Cambridge, Mass.: MIT Press, 1999), 2–19.

50. Wendy Hui Kyong Chun, *Control and Freedom: Power and Paranoia in the Age of Fiber Optics* (Cambridge, Mass.: MIT Press, 2006), 251–55.

51. Sherry Turkle, *Alone Together: Why We Expect More from Technology and Less from Each Other* (New York: Basic Books, 2011), 177.

52. John Cheney-Lippold, *We Are Data: Algorithms and the Making of Our Digital Selves* (New York: New York University Press, 2017), 5.

53. Benedict Anderson, *Imagined Communities: Reflections on the Origin and Spread of Nationalism* (New York: Verso, 2006), 24.

54. Ella Shohat and Robert Stam, *Unthinking Eurocentrism: Multiculturalism and the Media* (New York: Routledge, 1994), 102.

55. Nicole Constable, *Romance on a Global Stage: Pen Pals, Virtual Ethnography, and "Mail-Order" Marriages* (Berkeley: University of California Press, 2003), 31. See also Arjun Appadurai, *Modernity at Large: Cultural Dimensions of Globalization* (Minneapolis: University of Minnesota Press, 1996), 4–8.

56. Partha Chatterjee, *The Nation and Its Fragments: Colonial and Postcolonial Histories* (Princeton, N.J.: Princeton University Press, 1993), 6.

57. I am alert to Priyamvada Gopal's compelling argument that anticolonialism needs to be reinterpreted through radical Indian insurgencies that shaped British notions of freedom and self-determination. Without disputing the transnational legacies of these exemplary anticolonial rebellions and uprisings in India and other colonies, I am following Chatterjee to emphasize the identitarian contradictions from which anticolonialism also suffers as a mediated and capital-bound enterprise. See Priyamvada Gopal, *Insurgent Empire: Anticolonial Resistance and British Dissent* (London: Verso, 2019).

58. Shohat and Stam, *Unthinking Eurocentrism*, 103. See also Teshome Gabriel, "Towards a Critical Theory of Third World Films," in *Questions of Third Cinema*, ed. Jim Pines and Paul Willemen (London: British Film Institute, 1989), 36.

59. For a discussion of how anticolonial chromolithography, painting, and cinema produced in early twentieth-century India also reflect this tension between capitalist progress and anticolonial tradition, see Christopher Pinney, "Iatrogenic Religion and Politics," in *Censorship in South Asia: Cultural Regulation from Sedition to Seduction*, ed. Raminder Kaur and William Mazzarella (Bloomington: Indiana University Press, 2009), 29–62.

60. The term "intermedia" is usually used in the context of artistic practice that challenges boundaries between media technologies. I am, however, arguing for a subjective intermediality that conditions identity politics under capitalism. On intermedia as experimental aesthetics, see Yvonne Spielmann, "History and Theory of Intermedia in Visual Culture," in *Intermedia: Enacting the Liminal*, ed. Hans Breder and Klaus-Peter Busse (Dortmund, Ger.: Dortmunder Schriften zur Kunst, 2005), 131–38; Mary Simonson, *Body Knowledge: Performance, Intermediality, and American Entertainment at the Turn of the Twentieth Century* (New York: Oxford University Press, 2013), 17–19; and Christophe Wall-Romana, *Cinepoetry: Imaginary Cinemas in French Poetry* (New York: Fordham University Press, 2013).

61. For a useful distinction between mediation (an invisible but "vital" process of human entwinement with technology) and media (various devices and technologies), see Sarah Kember and Joanna Zylinska, *Life after New*

Media: Mediation as a Vital Process (Cambridge, Mass.: MIT Press, 2012), xv–xvii. But I am more interested in examining why and how the (necessarily capitalist) mediation of minoritizing identity becomes a very material constraint to the kind of emancipatory and life-giving potential of mediation that Kember and Zylinska celebrate.

62. Mitchell and Hansen, introduction, xx.

63. Richard Gunn, "Marxism and Mediation," *Common Sense* 2 (1987): 58, emphasis in the original.

64. Here I am challenging the distinction that Mitchell and Hansen make between Marxist thinking that overemphasizes the role of ideology leaving "little possibility for agency" and more contemporary theoretical and media studies approaches that offer a more "dynamic sense of mediation" along with a "more robust conceptualization of social agency" (introduction, xx–xxi). The dynamic mediation of anticolonial capitalism is a compelling instance where agency and ideology are not mutually exclusive. As well, on examining the complexities of capitalist mediation, it becomes difficult to idealize "media" as a "technoanthropological universal" and "minimal openness to alterity" (viii–ix, xii). Mitchell and Hansen argue that media designates a primal relationship between technology—the making of tools—and the very definition of humanity. Here, media (like Kember and Zylinska's notion of mediation) is the general environment for the proliferation of human life, collectivity, and sociality. Without dismissing this technophenomenology, *Identity* argues for the need to examine how capitalist mediation has, in fact, historically enforced differentiation and otherness *within* the category of the human.

65. Here I am drawing on Mitchell and Hansen's useful discussion of McLuhan's theory of media, especially his insistence on the distinctiveness of the domains of human action and technological materiality even as they converge in complex ways. My emphasis, however, is not on the ostensibly homogeneous collective identity of the "human" but rather on ideological apparatuses like the modern colonial state that produce the human as an explicitly racialized and hierarchical category. See Mitchell and Hansen, introduction, xii. See also McLuhan, *Understanding Media*.

66. N. Katherine Hayles, *How We Became Posthuman: Virtual Bodies in Cybernetics, Literature, and Informatics* (Chicago: University of Chicago Press, 1999), 195.

67. Spivak, "In a Word," 20, emphasis in the original.

68. Bishnupriya Ghosh, *Global Icons: Apertures to the Popular* (Durham, N.C.: Duke University Press, 2011), 94. Ghosh is drawing on Alfred Gell's anthropological study of art and, specifically, his theory of "the

distributed person." See Alfred Gell, *Art and Agency: An Anthropological Theory* (Oxford: Oxford University Press, 1998), 96–154.

69. I am drawing on Ghosh's analysis of the identitarian effects of the intermedial consumption of mass-mediated icons. See Ghosh, *Global Icons*, 12.

70. Tracy McNulty, *Wrestling with the Angel: Experiments in Symbolic Life* (New York: Columbia University Press, 2014).

71. Laura U. Marks, *Hanan al-Cinema: Affections for the Moving Image* (Cambridge, Mass.: MIT Press, 2015).

72. Karl Schoonover and Rosalind Galt, *Queer Cinema in the World* (Durham, N.C.: Duke University Press, 2016).

Chapter 1

1. Mark Robson, dir., *Home of the Brave* (1949; Chicago: Olive Films, 2014), DVD.

2. Fanon, *Black Skin*, 119.

3. See E. Ann Kaplan, "Fanon, Trauma and Cinema," in *Frantz Fanon: Critical Perspectives*, ed. Anthony C. Alessandrini (New York: Routledge, 2005), 147–58; and Kara Keeling, *The Witch's Flight: The Cinematic, the Black Femme, and the Image of Common Sense* (Durham, N.C.: Duke University Press, 2007), 39–40.

4. Michel Foucault, *The History of Sexuality*, vol. 1, *An Introduction*, trans. Robert Hurley (New York: Vintage, 1990), 43.

5. Althusser, *On Ideology*, 44–51.

6. Diana Fuss, "Interior Colonies: Frantz Fanon and the Politics of Identification," *diacritics* 24, nos. 2–3 (1994): 20. For a discussion of how Martinique "both *is* and *is not* French" as an overseas department of France, see Stuart Hall, "Cultural Identity and Diaspora," in *Colonial Discourse and Postcolonial Theory: A Reader*, ed. Patrick Williams and Laura Chrisman (New York: Columbia University Press, 1994), 396–97, emphasis in the original.

7. W. E. B. Du Bois, *The Souls of Black Folk: Essays and Sketches* (Chicago: McClurg, 1903), 3.

8. Jean Lhermitte, *L'image de notre corps* (Paris: Nouvelle Revue Critique, 1939), 17–18.

9. Lewis R. Gordon, *What Fanon Said: A Philosophical Introduction to His Life and Thought* (New York: Fordham University Press, 2015), 22, emphasis in the original.

10. Pierre Macherey, "Figures of Interpellation in Althusser and Fanon," *Radical Philosophy* 173 (2012): 13–16.

11. Lacan, "The Mirror Stage," 76. For an account of how Lacan modifies Henri Wallon's "mirror test," see Kaja Silverman, *The Threshold of the Visible World* (New York: Routledge, 1996), 14–15.

12. Jacques Lacan, "The Ego and the Other," in *Freud's Papers on Technique, 1953–1954: The Seminar of Jacques Lacan, Book I*, ed. Jacques-Alain Miller, trans. John Forrester (New York: Norton, 1991), 50.

13. For a discussion of this deconstructionist-Lacanian critique that takes root in U.S. institutions (like Johns Hopkins and Yale Universities through the 1960s and 1970s) and begins to privilege the failure of the symbolic signifier over imaginary meaning and identity, see Vincent B. Leitch, *American Literary Criticism since the 1930s* (New York: Routledge, 2010), 246–50.

14. For a discussion of Felman and Lane, see Ani Maitra, "Aberrant Narcissisms in Dolto, Lacan, and Fanon," *differences* 28, no. 3 (2017): 98–100.

15. McNulty, *Wrestling with the Angel*, 7.

16. On this antivisual thrust of psychoanalysis, see Martin Jay, *Downcast Eyes: The Denigration of Vision in Twentieth-Century French Thought* (Berkeley: University of California Press, 1994), 329–80. My own focus is on overlooked cultural and clinical accounts of subjectivation that allow us to move beyond the formalist privileging of language or the image.

17. Hennessy, *Profit and Pleasure*, 177.

18. I am deliberately invoking the sociological notion of "the symbolic" as the domain of competing cultures, tastes, and habits regulated by capitalism. On "symbolic capital" as capital that denies its status as such and appears to be economically disinterested, see Pierre Bourdieu, *The Logic of Practice*, trans. Richard Nice (Stanford, Calif.: Stanford University Press, 1990), 112–21.

19. For instance, for a slightly earlier but comparable psychoanalytic invitation to rethink the ethnicized subject through the indeterminacy of language, see Antonio Viego, *Dead Subjects: Toward a Politics of Loss in Latino Studies* (Durham, N.C.: Duke University Press, 2007); for an argument for a universalism "indifferent to difference" exemplified by art, literature, and oral storytelling, see Madhavi Menon, *Indifference to Difference: On Queer Universalism* (Minneapolis: University of Minnesota Press, 2015).

20. David Macey, "The Recall of the Real: Frantz Fanon and Psychoanalysis," *Constellations* 6, no. 1 (1999): 99–100.

21. See Homi K. Bhabha, *The Location of Culture* (New York: Routledge, 1994), 74; and Christopher Lane, "The Psychoanalysis of Race: An Introduction," in *The Psychoanalysis of Race*, ed. Christopher Lane (New York:

Columbia University Press, 1998), 14. For a variation on this argument, see Kalpana Seshadri-Crooks, *Desiring Whiteness: A Lacanian Analysis of Race* (New York: Routledge, 2000), 30–33.

22. Silverman, *Threshold*, 24–28.

23. Ranjana Khanna, *Dark Continents: Psychoanalysis and Colonialism* (Durham, N.C.: Duke University Press, 2003), 172.

24. Fuss, "Interior Colonies," 21–22.

25. While my focus is on the differences between the neurotic and schizophrenic experiences of the mirror stage, it is important to note Lacan's broader insistence on the inseparability of the three registers of the real, the symbolic, and the imaginary. On this, see Jacques Lacan, *Le sinthome: Le séminaire, livre XXIII*, ed. Jacques-Alain Miller (Paris: Seuil, 2005), 50; and Pierre Skriabine, "The Clinic of the Borromean Knot," in *Lacan: Topologically Speaking*, ed. Ellie Ragland and Dragan Milovanovic (New York: Other Press, 2004), 252–55.

26. Fuss notes that Fanon was not unaware of Lacan's 1949 essay. But that makes it all the more urgent to analyze why Fanon quotes from and cites the 1938 essay. See Fuss, "Interior Colonies," 23.

27. Françoise Vergès notes Fanon's use of Lacan's earlier version of the mirror stage. But she maintains an absolute distinction between Fanon's "empirical subject" and Lacan's "psychic subject." See Françoise Vergès, "Creole Skin, Black Mask: Fanon and Disavowal," *Critical Inquiry* 23, no. 3 (1997): 585–86, 590.

28. Jacques Lacan, "Les complexes familiaux dans la formation de l'individu," in *Autres écrits*, ed. Jacques-Alain Miller (Paris: Seuil, 2001), 37, my translation.

29. On affective identification in Lacan's 1938 essay, see Mikkel Borch-Jacobsen, *Lacan: The Absolute Master*, trans. Douglas Brick (Stanford, Calif.: Stanford University Press, 1991), 66–71.

30. On Dolto's influence on Lacan, see Shuli Barzilai, *Lacan and the Matter of Origins* (Stanford, Calif.: Stanford University Press, 1999), 130–32; and Françoise Hivernel, "'The Parental Couple': Françoise Dolto and Jacques Lacan: Contributions to the Mirror Stage," *British Journal of Psychotherapy* 29, no. 4 (2013): 505–18.

31. On this initial difference between Dolto's and Lacan's approaches to the mirror stage, see also Maitra, "Aberrant Narcissisms," 129n12.

32. Françoise Dolto, *L'image inconsciente du corps* (Paris: Seuil, 1992), 150, my translation, emphasis in the original.

33. Françoise Dolto and J.-D. Nasio, *L'enfant du miroir* (Paris: Rivages, 1987), 19–20, my translation.

34. Françoise Dolto, "The Mirror's Child," in *Freud's Tracks: Conversations from the Journal of European Psychoanalysis*, ed. Sergio Benvenuto and Anthony Molino (Lanham, Md.: Rowman and Littlefield, 2009), 196.

35. Here Dolto anticipates Silverman's theory of the maternal "acoustic mirror." See Silverman, *The Acoustic Mirror: The Female Voice in Psychoanalysis and Cinema* (Bloomington: Indiana University Press, 1988), 80.

36. Dolto, "Mirror's Child," 191.

37. Jacques Lacan, "Remarks on Daniel Lagache's Presentation: 'Psychoanalysis and Personality Structure,'" in *Écrits*, 568.

38. Jacques Lacan, "From the Cosmos to the *Unheimliche*," in *Anxiety: The Seminar of Jacques Lacan, Book X*, ed. Jacques-Alain Miller, trans. A. R. Price (Cambridge: Polity, 2014), 38.

39. Jacques Lacan, "The Other and Psychosis," in *The Psychoses, 1955–1956: The Seminar of Jacques Lacan, Book III*, ed. Jacques-Alain Miller, trans. Russell Grigg (New York: Norton, 1997), 41.

40. Jacques Lacan, "The Hysteric's Question," in *The Psychoses*, 162.

41. Jacques Lacan, "*Passage à l'acte* and Acting-Out," in, *Anxiety*, 120.

42. R. Khanna, *Dark Continents*, 172.

43. For a discussion of "disidentification" as a politically enabling individual act of oppositional reading that neither fully accepts nor strictly opposes dominant ideology, see José Esteban Muñoz, *Disidentifications: Queers of Color and the Performance of Politics* (Minneapolis: University of Minnesota Press, 1999), 11. I would, however, argue that disidentification is empowering only for those individuals who have the necessary subcultural capital to engage in it as a deliberate performative practice. In contrast, by "(dis)identification," I am referring to structural intermedial processes through which capitalism produces identity as a minoritizing constraint.

44. I am alert to Susan Sontag's caution against the dangers of drawing on the medicalized language of disease and illness for cultural critique. At the same time, I am suggesting that rereading the psychoanalytic approach to schizophrenia through anticolonial discourse can, in fact, disrupt the hierarchy between the "scientific" (or the "medical") and the "cultural." See Susan Sontag, *Illness as Metaphor and AIDS and Its Metaphors* (New York: Picador, 1990).

45. For an account of how the stigmatization of "insanity" and, specifically, schizophrenia became racialized in U.S. clinical and cultural discourse in the 1960s and 1970s, see Jonathan M. Metzl, *Protest Psychosis: How Schizophrenia Became a Black Disease* (Boston: Beacon, 2010).

46. Vergès argues that Fanon's mirror stage is locked in a white/black binary that ignores racial hybridity as well as the presence of other nonwhite groups in colonial Martinique. But the inclusion of hybridity—or of other racial markers like "red" or "brown"—does not undermine Fanon's claim: hierarchically organized images of blackness (and/or nonwhiteness) and whiteness do not bolster but act simultaneously to fragment the bodily ego of the colonized. See Vergès, "Creole Skin," 594.

47. A. L. Becker uses the term "languaging" to mean the process by which a language comes to be articulated as utterances in particular sociopolitical contexts. As a context-shaping process, languaging is to be distinguished from language, an abstract system of rules and structures. See A. L. Becker, *Beyond Translation: Essays Toward a Modern Philology* (Ann Arbor: University of Michigan Press, 1995), 8–13.

48. On the endurance of this paradigm of linguistic mimicry in the postcolonial "call center" in the twenty-first century, see Maitra, "Aberrant Narcissisms," 121–24. For a critique of linguistic mimicry as performative subversion, see Fuss, "Interior Colonies," 25.

49. Guy Debord, *The Society of the Spectacle*, trans. Donald Nicholson-Smith (New York: Zone, 1995), 13–14.

50. Jean-Joseph Goux, *Symbolic Economies: After Marx and Freud*, trans. Jennifer Curtiss Gage (Ithaca, N.Y.: Cornell University Press, 1990), 14, emphasis in the original.

51. For a critique of this myth of perfect equivalence in Goux's writings, see Gayatri Chakravorty Spivak, "Scattered Speculations on the Question of Value," *diacritics* 15, no. 4 (1985): 75–76.

52. On the subordination of use value by exchange value, see Debord, *Society of the Spectacle*, 31–32.

53. Jacques Lacan, "The Topic of the Imaginary," in *Freud's Papers*, 84, emphasis in the original.

54. Jacques Lacan, "On Narcissism," in *Freud's Papers*, 108.

55. Jacques Lacan, "The Function and Field of Speech and Language in Psychoanalysis," in *Écrits*, 248, emphasis added.

56. Jacques Lacan, "The Meaning of Delusion," in *The Psychoses*, 21.

57. Mikko Tuhkanen argues that decolonial violence in Fanon can be compared to a Lacanian "ethics of the real" that embraces symbolic ruptures without predictable outcomes. The origins of this violence, Tuhkanen contends, lie in the oppressed imaginaries of the colonized. My approach to identity politics, however, is more cautious precisely because racialized capitalism has been able to survive and produce new identitarian exclusions

through such eruptions of real revolutionary violence. Chapter 3 takes up this issue in more detail. See Mikko Tuhkanen, *The American Optic: Psychoanalysis, Critical Race Theory, and Richard Wright* (New York: State University of New York Press, 2010), 102–5.

58. Jane Gallop, *Reading Lacan* (Ithaca, N.Y.: Cornell University Press, 1985), 60.

59. See Gayatri Chakravorty Spivak, *A Critique of Postcolonial Reason: Toward a History of the Vanishing Present* (Cambridge, Mass.: Harvard University Press, 1999), 12–15; Pierre Bourdieu, *Distinction: A Social Critique of the Judgment of Taste*, trans. Richard Nice (Cambridge, Mass.: Harvard University Press, 1984); and Terry Eagleton, *The Ideology of the Aesthetic* (Oxford: Basil Blackwell, 1990).

60. See Pamela R. Matthews and David McWhirter, "Introduction: Exile's Return? Aesthetics Now," in *Aesthetic Subjects*, ed. Pamela R. Matthews and David McWhirter (Minneapolis: University of Minnesota Press, 2003), xvi–xviii; Wolfgang Welsch, *Undoing Aesthetics*, trans. Andrew Inkpen (London: Sage, 1997); and Monique Roelofs, *The Cultural Promise of the Aesthetic* (New York: Bloomsbury Academic, 2014).

61. Jacques Rancière, *The Politics of Aesthetics: The Distribution of the Sensible*, trans. Gabriel Rockhill (New York: Continuum, 2004), 12–13.

62. See Luc Ferry, *Homo Aestheticus: The Invention of Taste in the Democratic Age*, trans. Robert de Loaiza (Chicago: University of Chicago Press, 1993), 19–25; and Peter Murphy and Eduardo de la Fuente, "Introduction: Aesthetic Capitalism," in *Aesthetic Capitalism*, ed. Eduardo de la Fuente and Peter Murphy (Boston: Brill, 2014), 1–9.

63. Giorgio Agamben, *The Man without Content* (Stanford, Calif.: Stanford University Press, 1999), 6.

64. What I mean by mean by "politics" is what Rancière calls the "police order" that communally distributes the sensible to prevent the emergence of "true" politics. See Jacques Rancière, "The Cause of the Other," trans. David Macey, *parallax* 4, no. 2 (1998): 28–29.

65. See Mary Ann Doane, *Femmes Fatales: Feminism, Film Theory, Psychoanalysis* (London: Routledge, 1991), 222; Fuss, "Interior Colonies," 30–31; Gwen Bergner, "Who Is That Masked Woman? or, The Role of Gender in Fanon's *Black Skin, White Masks*," *PMLA* 110, no. 1 (1995): 75–88; and Rey Chow, *Ethics after Idealism: Theory, Culture, Ethnicity, Reading* (Bloomington: Indiana University Press, 1998), 55–73.

66. See Chow, *Ethics after Idealism*, 59–60; and Bergner, "Who Is That Masked Woman?," 82.

67. T. Denean Sharpley-Whiting, *Frantz Fanon: Conflicts and Feminisms* (Lanham, Md.: Rowman and Littlefield, 1998), 36–37; see also Gordon, *What Fanon Said*, 35–36.

68. See, for instance, Cheryl Duffus, "When One Drop Isn't Enough: War as a Crucible of Racial Identity in the Novels of Mayotte Capécia," *Callaloo* 28, no. 4 (2005): 1096.

69. Martin Jay calls for a stricter definition of the aesthetic experience, and warns us that the reduction of the artwork to spectatorial desires leads to a fascist aestheticization of politics. My point is, however, that a more normalized version of that aestheticization is part and parcel of the colonial project, with the de-aestheticized colonized subject at its receiving end. See Martin Jay, "Drifting into Dangerous Waters: The Separation of Aesthetic Experience from the Work of Art," in Matthews and McWhirter, *Aesthetic Subjects*, 3–27.

70. Chow argues that Fanon's anger against Capécia is symptomatic of patriarchal anxieties around a female sexuality that threatens to erode racial hierarchies and postcolonial discourses of national "purity." But such a critique risks overlooking the blatantly antiblack racism through which Capécia's protagonist expresses her erotic desire to transgress racial boundaries. See Chow, *Ethics after Idealism*, 69.

71. Such an interpretation would also have to acknowledge that, while reading Fanon, critics identifying as women and/or women of color would experience their identities as an aesthetic dissonance of a different kind, as Fanon repeats the violent raciosexual abstraction to which he has felt subjected by colonialism.

72. Doane, *Femmes Fatales*, 226–27; and Kaplan, "Fanon, Trauma and Cinema," 149–51.

73. I do not mean to elide important differences between the Apparatus theorists. But what I am stressing is their commonality—an attempt to theorize the ideological effects of cinema through the neurotic mirror stage. I discuss Mulvey's critique of the masculinist nature of neurotic equivalence in chapter 2. See Baudry, "Ideological Effects," 45–46; Metz, *Imaginary Signifier*, 45–49; and Laura Mulvey, "Visual Pleasure and Narrative Cinema," in *Narrative, Apparatus, Ideology: A Film Theory Reader*, ed. Philip Rosen (New York: Columbia University Press, 1986), 204.

74. As noted in the introduction, Fanon's self-representation anticipates Ella Shohat and Robert Stam's description of the "fissured" colonial spectator. See Shohat and Stam, *Unthinking Eurocentrism*, 103. Fanon's reaction can also be read alongside Manthia Diawara's later theorization of the "resistant" black spectator and bell hooks's notion of the "oppositional

gaze." See Manthia Diawara, "Black Spectatorship: Problems of Identification and Resistance," *Screen* 29, no. 4 (1988): 66–79; and bell hooks, "The Oppositional Gaze," in *Black Looks: Race and Representation* (Boston: South End Press, 1992), 115–31.

75. Joan Copjec argues that Apparatus theorists mistakenly conflate the radical Lacanian subject of symbolic indeterminacy with the cinematic subject of the imaginary and its logic of proprietorship. Effectively, Copjec seeks to preserve the language-bound subject of "the signifier" by isolating it from (the neurotic version of) the imaginary. See Joan Copjec, "The Orthopsychic Subject: Film Theory and the Reception of Lacan," *October* 49 (1989): 68–69.

76. The moment to which Fanon refers is likely where Mingo (in the final scene of the U.S. version of the film) asks Moss to shake off the openly racist comments of another white soldier who, it turns out, also mocks the white soldier's impairment: "Why don't you quit whining? . . . He makes cracks about me too."

77. Doane, *Femmes Fatales*, 227.

78. Doane, "The Indexical and the Concept of Medium Specificity," 136.

79. I differ with Kara Keeling's interpretation of this scene, in which she argues that Fanon's rejection of Hollywood's representation of blackness should be traced back to the potentiality of cinematic "affect." Keeling distinguishes between Fanon's affective response to the film and his ideologically limited reading of the scene. But by doing do so, she isolates Fanon's encounter with the visual image, thereby overlooking his encounters with other bodies and other media both inside and outside the theater. See Keeling, *Witch's Flight*, 39.

80. I return to the violence of the "tactile" narrative image and the identitarian causes of its tactility in chapter 3.

81. Rosalind Krauss, "Reinventing the Medium," *Critical Inquiry* 25, no. 2 (1999): 296.

82. Several scholars have noted the ambiguity of interracial male bonding in the film as well as the nervousness of white reviewers around this bonding. See, for instance, Michael Rogin, "Home of the Brave," in *The War Film*, ed. Robert Eberwein (New Brunswick, N.J.: Rutgers University Press, 2005), 87–88; and Robert Eberwein, *Armed Forces: Masculinity and Sexuality in the American War Film* (New Brunswick, N.J.: Rutgers University Press, 2007), 83–85. On the feminization of Moss's character in the film, see E. Ann Kaplan, *Looking for the Other: Feminism, Film, and the Imperial Gaze* (New York: Routledge, 1997), 107. On Fanon's homophobia, see Fuss, "Interior Colonies," 30–36.

83. Anna Gibbs's important formulation of the body as a sensory-motor medium (albeit in a different context of racial violence) is relevant here. Reality, for Gibbs, is not simply either internal or external. Rather, it is simultaneously both, and the body is one of the media that produces that complex view of reality. See Anna Gibbs, "Horrified: Embodied Vision, Media Affect and the Images from Abu Ghraib," in *Interrogating the War on Terror: Interdisciplinary Perspectives*, ed. Deborah Staines (Newcastle, England: Cambridge Scholars, 2007), 129. I am borrowing Miriam Hansen's influential term "vernacular modernism" to describe the "sensory-reflexive horizon" and contradictory experiences of modernity that Hollywood cinema offers and through which it is viewed. See Miriam Bratu Hansen, "Fallen Women, Rising Stars, New Horizons: Shanghai Silent Film as Vernacular Modernism," *Film Quarterly* 54, no. 1 (2000): 13.

84. See Gordon, *What Fanon Said*, 50. The appellate court in Versailles banned the controversial Banania slogan in 2011 after a lawsuit from several French antiracist nongovernmental organizations. See Malte Hinrichsen, "Racist Trademarks and the Persistence of Commodity Racism in Europe and the United States," in *Diversity in Intellectual Property: Identities, Interests, and Intersections*, ed. Irene Calboli and Srividhya Ragavan (New York: Cambridge University Press, 2015), 130.

85. Jonathan Crary, *Techniques of the Observer: On Vision and Modernity in the Nineteenth Century* (Cambridge, Mass.: MIT Press, 1992), 23, emphasis added.

86. David Macey, *Frantz Fanon: A Biography* (New York: Verso, 2012), 299–354, 585.

87. For a study on French colonial radio that also draws on Fanon's writings, see Rebecca Scales, *Radio and the Politics of Sound in Interwar France, 1921–1939* (Cambridge: Cambridge University Press, 2016), 207–57.

88. John Mowitt, *Radio: Essays in Bad Reception* (Berkeley: University of California Press, 2011), 66.

89. I am simplifying Mowitt's rigorously comparative discussion of the contributions of Walter Benjamin, Bertolt Brecht, and Jean-Paul Sartre to the field of radio studies. See Mowitt, *Radio*, 49–76.

90. Fanon also highlights the radio's role as a status symbol in the colony, its place in the chain of commodities—such as the car, the villa, and the refrigerator—defining the position of the petit-bourgeois European consumer. See Fanon, *A Dying Colonialism*, 71.

91. Macey notes that Fanon had encountered patients hearing similar voices during his tenure at Blida-Joinville. See Macey, *Frantz Fanon*, 328.

92. According to Fanon, before 1945, 95 percent of the receivers were owned by Europeans. See Fanon, *A Dying Colonialism*, 69.

93. Scales, *Radio and the Politics of Sound*, 207–9.

94. Mowitt, *Radio*, 91.

95. On this point, see also Ranjana Khanna, *Algeria Cuts: Women and Representation, 1830 to the Present* (Stanford, Calif.: Stanford University Press, 2008), 76.

96. James R. Martel, *The Misinterpellated Subject* (Durham, N.C.: Duke University Press, 2017), 2–3.

97. Alluding to this violence in Algeria, Martel notes that with misinterpellation "there is no promise of happiness, only the possibility of nondetermination and Fanon achieved that much (as did Algeria, although it quickly succumbed to new forms of determination)." By making this absolute distinction between "nondetermination" and "determination," Martel overlooks institutionalized mediations of colonial misinterpellation that shape the "nondetermination" and then acquire new forms in the postcolonial state. See Martel, *Misinterpellated Subject*, 127.

98. Raymond Williams uses the expression "structure of feeling" to mean a social and affective experience that is in flux, not quite socially legitimized, but which in analysis has its specific dominant characteristics and hierarchies. See Raymond Williams, *Marxism and Literature* (New York: Oxford University Press, 1977), 128–35.

99. See Mohamed Benrabah, *Language Conflict in Algeria: From Colonialism to Post-Independence* (Buffalo, N.Y.: Multilingual Matters, 2013), 58; and R. Khanna, *Algeria Cuts*, 75–77.

100. Martel is aware of this risk, noting that new forms of interpellation can always arise after radical acts of misinterpellation. My point, however, is that misinterpellation itself cannot be mythologized. See Martel, *Misinterpellated Subject*, 128.

101. Khanna, *Algeria Cuts*, 76.

102. Martel sees the "true lie" as "a more and horizontal local call (or at least not universal) call," which he opposes to the colonizer's lie that comes from "without." But as I have argued, Fanon's writing constantly challenges this outside/inside or interpellation/misinterpellation distinction. A psychoanalytic approach to "the call" becomes productive in that regard. As well, I agree with Mowitt's claim that Fanon anticipates Jacques Derrida's critique of phonocentrism, bringing into view the role that radio plays in organizing the sociohistorical experience that is mapped out by deconstruction. But my focus is on the signifying practices and

conditions of mediation through which the crackling of the radio becomes *real* national identity with enduring geopolitical consequences. See Martel, *Misinterpellated Subject*, 125; and Mowitt, *Radio*, 95–96.

103. I discuss this aspect of Arabization in more detail in chapter 3.

104. Derek P. McCormack, *Refrains for Moving Bodies: Experience and Experiment in Affective Spaces* (Durham, N.C.: Duke University Press, 2013), 121.

105. N. Katherine Hayles, *My Mother Was a Computer: Digital Subjects and Literary Texts* (Chicago: University of Chicago Press, 2005), 3.

106. N. Katherine Hayles, "Print Is Flat, Code Is Deep: The Importance of Media-Specific Analysis," in *Transmedia Frictions: The Digital, the Arts, and the Humanities*, ed. Marsha Kinder and Tara McPherson (Oakland: University of California Press, 2014), 31.

Chapter 2

1. On this opposition, see Ani Maitra, "CNN in North Korea: Liberal Democracy and Ethnonationalism," *Counterpunch*, December 1, 2017, https://www.counterpunch.org/2017/12/01/cnn-in-north-korea-liberal-democracy-and-ethno-nationalism/.

2. Lisa Lowe, "Unfaithful to the Original: The Subject of *Dictée*," in *Writing Self, Writing Nation: A Collection of Essays on DICTEE by Theresa Hak Kyung Cha*, ed. Elaine H. Kim and Norma Alarcón (Berkeley, Calif.: Third Woman, 1994), 36.

3. Juliana Spahr, *Everybody's Autonomy: Connective Reading and Collective Identity* (Tuscaloosa: University of Alabama Press, 2001), 119–52; and Timothy Yu, *Race and the Avant-Garde: Experimental and Asian American Poetry since 1965* (Stanford, Calif.: Stanford University Press, 2009), 100–137.

4. Cha, *Dictée*, 1.

5. For comparable readings of this theme of dictation, see Spahr, *Everybody's Autonomy*, 131–33; and Anne Anlin Cheng, *The Melancholy of Race: Psychoanalysis, Assimilation, and Hidden Grief* (New York: Oxford University Press, 2000), 159–60. We should recognize a certain *literary* echo of James Martel's theory of "misinterpellation," which I discussed in chapter 1. In both Martel and Lowe, the exposition of the oppressive nature of interpellation amounts to short-circuiting interpellation. See Martel, *Misinterpellated Subject*.

6. Michael Stone-Richards rightly points out that there is nothing in Cha's text to suggest that these two passages do not belong to two different or parallel scenes of linguistic instruction. See Michael Stone-Richards,

"A Commentary on Theresa Hak Kyung Cha's *DICTEE*," *Glossator* 1 (2009): 157.

7. As a text written in Chinese, English, French, and Korean, *Dictée* makes its readers acutely aware of their own cultural resources, compelling readers to switch between languages and recognize the limits of their linguistic abilities. This linguistic destabilization leads Naoki Sakai to interpret the text as an experience in reading as cognitive uncertainty, as a radically democratic text that teaches us to see "every language as a foreign language." But such a reading is possible only by privileging the text's literariness over its intermediality. See Naoki Sakai, *Translation and Subjectivity: On Japan and Cultural Nationalism* (Minneapolis: University of Minnesota Press, 1997), 31.

8. Shelley Sunn Wong, "Unnaming the Same: Theresa Hak Kyung Cha's *Dictée*," in Kim and Alarcón, *Writing Self*, 113.

9. L. Hyun Yi Kang, "The 'Liberatory Voice' of Theresa Hak Kyung Cha's *Dictée*," in Kim and Alarcón, *Writing Self*, 78.

10. While the contributors in *Writing Self* adopt varying methodologies to read *Dictée*, they all emphasize the *linguistic* nature of the Asian American "difference" articulated by the text. On their distinct methodologies, see Yu, *Race and the Avant-Garde*, 115–16.

11. Mark Chiang, *The Cultural Capital of Asian American Studies: Autonomy and Representation in the University* (New York: New York University Press, 2009), 93–137.

12. The birth of Asian American studies as well as other identitarian interdisciplines like African American studies and women's studies was the result of the institutionalization of student protests against racial discrimination on U.S. campuses from the late 1960s onward. On this, see Chiang, *Cultural Capital*, 7–11; and Roderick A. Ferguson, *The Reorder of Things: The University and Its Pedagogies of Minority Difference* (Minneapolis: University of Minnesota Press, 2012).

13. Kang, "'Liberatory Voice,'" 76–77.

14. Stephen Best and Saidiya Hartman, "Fugitive Justice," *Representations* 92, no. 1 (2005): 9.

15. Fanon, *Black Skin*, 5.

16. In this chapter and in the rest of the book, I use "otherness" (with a lowercase *o*) to mean a sociohistorically produced alterity, as opposed to the nonhistorical alterity that Lacanian critics often associate with the (capitalized) Other.

17. See, especially, Louis Althusser, "On Feuerbach," in *The Humanist Controversy and Other Writings (1966–67)*, ed. François Matheron, trans. G. M. Goshgarian (New York: Verso, 2003), 129–30.

18. Luce Irigaray, *Speculum of the Other Woman*, trans. Gillian C. Gill (Ithaca, N.Y.: Cornell University Press, 1985), 133.

19. Lowe argues that the presence of multiple and incomplete inter-pellations can itself become the precondition of the emergence of a "bad subject." But this view cannot explain how the bad subject resists the commodification and institutionalization of its discursive resistance within a capitalist system that produces several competing and hierar-chically organized interpellative structures. See Lowe, "Unfaithful to the Original," 55.

20. Chow, *Protestant Ethnic*, 117.

21. The Weberian exploration of the religious origins of capitalism com-plements the Marxist emphasis on the irrationality of commodity fetishism. I will come back to this irrationality later in the chapter.

22. The distinction between the self and collective society is not very stable even in Freud. But Chow's rethinking of narcissism as a collective experience echoes Fanon's emphasis on the racialization of the mirror stage through Lacan (see chapter 1).

23. On this point, see also Lowe, "Unfaithful to the Original," 44.

24. Roelofs, *Cultural Promise*, 44. See chapter 1 for my discussion of (dis)identification and aesthetic dissonance in relation to Roelofs's argument.

25. Spahr, *Everybody's Autonomy*, 121.

26. Roland Barthes, *Empire of Signs*, trans. Richard Howard (New York: Hill and Wang, 1982), 9, emphasis added.

27. For a comparable critique of Derrida's assertion that the Chinese language is "ideographic" and outside Western logocentrism, see Chow, *Protestant Ethnic*, 61–62.

28. Chandan Reddy, "Asian Diasporas, Neoliberalism, and Family: Review-ing the Case for Homosexual Asylum in the Context of Family Rights," *Social Text* 23, nos. 3–4, 84–85 (2005): 105.

29. Elaine H. Kim, "Poised on the In-Between: A Korean American's Reflection on Theresa Hak Kyung Cha's *Dictée*," in Kim and Alarcón, *Writing Self*, 4.

30. Kim, "Poised on the In-Between," 4–5, emphasis added.

31. Kim, "Poised on the In-Between," 29.

32. On the U.S. government's role in the exacerbation of divisions between North Korea and South Korea, see Kim, "Poised on the In-Between," 13.

33. Anne Harrington de Santana, "Nuclear Weapons as the Currency of Power: Deconstructing the Fetishism of Force," *Nonproliferation Review* 16, no. 3 (2009): 330.

34. Lowe, "Unfaithful to the Original," 36.

35. See Moira Roth, "Theresa Hak Kyung Cha, 1951–1982: A Narrative Chronology," in Kim and Alarcón, *Writing Self*, 151–60.

36. Fredric Jameson, *Postmodernism, or, The Cultural Logic of Late Capitalism* (Durham, N.C.: Duke University Press, 1991), 14, 31.

37. Yu, *Race and the Avant-Garde*, 103.

38. On *Dictée* being initially ignored by Asian Americanist scholars and discussed primarily in contemporary US (white) avant-garde literary circles, see Yu, *Race and the Avant-Garde*, 108–11.

39. Ben Hickman, *Crisis and the US Avant-Garde: Poetry and Real Politics* (Edinburgh: Edinburgh University Press, 2015), 140–59.

40. Steve McCaffery, "From the Notebooks," *L=A=N=G=U=A=G=E* 9–10 (1979): 31, quoted in Hickman, *Crisis*, 143.

41. Ron Silliman, "For Open Letter," *L=A=N=G=U=A=G=E*, suppl. 1 (1980): 31, quoted in Hickman, *Crisis*, 143.

42. Steve McCaffery, "Death of the Subject: The Implications of Counter-Communication in Recent Language-Centered Writing," *L=A=N=G=U=A=G=E*, suppl. 1 (1980): 8, quoted in Hickman, *Crisis*, 143.

43. Silliman, "For Open Letter," 31, quoted in Hickman, *Crisis*, 146.

44. McCaffery, "Death of the Subject," 9, quoted in Hickman, *Crisis*, 146.

45. Marjorie Perloff, "The Word as Such: L=A=N=G=U=A=G=E Poetry in the Eighties," *American Poetry Review* 13, no. 3 (1984): 15–22.

46. Hickman, *Crisis*, 143.

47. Not all Language poets shared these views. But the experimental Marxism articulated through *L=A=N=G=U=A=G=E* played a key role in establishing the countercultural status of poets like McCaffery and Silliman in the U.S. poetry scene, and, subsequently, the institutionalization of Language poetry in the U.S. academy. See Hickman, *Crisis*, 140, 155–58.

48. Ron Silliman, *Under Albany* (Cambridge: Salt, 2004), 42. See also Yu, *Race and the Avant-Garde*, 3.

49. Hickman, *Crisis*, 156.

50. Yu draws on the work of Renato Poggioli to argue that any avant-garde formation must be analyzed *sociologically*, to evaluate how certain aesthetic preferences become the basis of building a community in opposition to mainstream culture. Yu, however, seems to idealize the "aesthetic basis" of the avant-garde, a position that I critique herein through Cha's text. See Yu, *Race and the Avant-Garde*, 4–6; and Renato Poggioli, *The Theory of the Avant-Garde*, trans. Gerald Fitzgerald (Cambridge, Mass.: Harvard University Press, 1968).

51. Arguably, the forces of capitalist abstraction producing Asian Americans as an ethnic group (and Asian American studies as an ethnically demarcated field) are *not* identical to those behind the "ethnic" self-positioning of the Language group. In fact, what I am emphasizing is neoliberalism's capacity to produce conflicting and unequally valued aesthetic ideologies.

52. The Language poets (and critics like Yu) are no doubt influenced by a version of Derridean deconstruction that is quite prominent in Anglo-American literary studies. But their stance on poetic writing should not be conflated with Derrida's more complex notion of "writing" or "arche-writing." As Gayatri Chakravorty Spivak argues, for Derrida, writing is a much broader concept, "something that carries within itself the trace of a perennial alterity: the structure of the psyche, the structure of the sign." Arche-writing, then, cannot be easily opposed to history. In fact, arche-writing is the condition of possibility of the "play" of differences that governs the movement of history through naming and classification, knowledge and power. See Gayatri Chakravorty Spivak, "Translator's Preface," in *Of Grammatology*, by Jacques Derrida, trans. Gayatri Chakravorty Spivak (Baltimore: Johns Hopkins University Press, 1997), xxxix.

53. On the divide between Asian American poetry and Language poetry circles, see Yu, *Race and the Avant-Garde*, 10.

54. Derrida, *Of Grammatology*, 108.

55. Terry Eagleton, *Criticism and Ideology: A Study in Marxist Literary Theory* (London: Verso, 2006), 63.

56. Hickman, *Crisis*, 153.

57. Peter Bürger, "Avant-Garde and Neo-Avant-Garde: An Attempt to Answer Certain Critics of *Theory of the Avant-Garde*," trans. Bettina Brandt and Daniel Purdy, *New Literary History* 41, no. 4 (2010): 707.

58. Eagleton, *Criticism and Ideology*, 60.

59. The second epigraph to this chapter summarizes this key idea of "antagonistic complementarity." See David Roberts, "From the Cultural Contradictions of Capitalism to the Creative Economy: Reflections on the New Spirit of Art and Capitalism," in Fuente and Murphy, *Aesthetic Capitalism*, 11, 17–18.

60. On this paradoxical Möbius strip–like topology of capitalism, see Anders Michelsen, "The Visual Experience Economy: What Kind of Economies? On the Topologies of Aesthetic Capitalism," in Fuente and Murphy, *Aesthetic Capitalism*, 68.

61. Theresa Hak Kyung Cha, preface to *Apparatus—Cinematographic Apparatus: Selected Writings*, ed. Theresa Hak Kyung Cha (New York: Tanam, 1980), unpaginated, emphasis added.

62. Philip Rosen, preface, in Rosen, *Narrative, Apparatus, Ideology*, ix.

63. Roland Barthes, "Leaving the Movie Theater," in *The Rustle of Language*, trans. Richard Howard (New York: Hill and Wang, 1986), 348, emphasis in the original.

64. Laura Mulvey, "Visual Pleasure and Narrative Cinema," in Rosen, *Narrative, Apparatus, Ideology*, 203.

65. Laura Mulvey, "Afterthoughts on 'Visual Pleasure and Narrative Cinema' Inspired by *Duel in the Sun* (King Vidor, 1946)," *Framework* 15–17 (1981): 12–15.

66. Stone-Richards, "Commentary," 160.

67. Stone-Richards points out that, in "Erato Love Poetry," Cha's writing draws on Carl Theodor Dreyer's 1964 film *Gertrud* and formally mimics avant-garde experiments separating the sound from the image. Yet even in its adaptation of avant-garde asynchronism, *Dictée* continues to be haunted by apprehensions of linguistic competence and dominance. See Stone-Richards, "Commentary," 163; and Cha, *Dictée*, 97.

68. Cha, *Dictée*, 87. I am aware that by reading Cha alongside feminist film theory from the 1970s and 1980s, I am ignoring more contemporary theories of spectatorship that argue for more fluid models of spectatorship. I discuss some of these approaches in chapters 3 and 4. Here let me note briefly that such cinephilic assertions of agency seldom tackle the problematic of the spectator's subjection to the commodity form. The fluid oscillation between the spectator and the image, I will later argue, is the labor through which performative identities are absorbed back into capital.

69. See Thy Phu, "Decapitated Forms: Theresa Hak Kyung Cha's Visual Text and the Politics of Visibility," *Mosaic: An Interdisciplinary Critical Journal* 38, no. 1 (2005): 34; and Stone-Richards, "Commentary," 162–67.

70. Jonathan Beller, *The Cinematic Mode of Production: Attention Economy and the Society of the Spectacle* (Lebanon, N.H.: University Press of New England, 2006), 1.

71. On the commodification of the woman through and as cinema, see also Mary Ann Doane, *The Desire to Desire: The Woman's Film of the 1940s* (Bloomington: Indiana University Press, 1987), 1, 24, 33.

72. Roland Barthes, *Camera Lucida: Reflections on Photography*, trans. Richard Howard (New York: Hill and Wang, 1981), 8.

73. W. J. T. Mitchell, "Beyond Comparison: Picture, Text, and Method," in *Picture Theory: Essays on Verbal and Visual Representation* (Chicago: University of Chicago Press, 1995), 94.

74. Crary, *Techniques of the Observer*, 13; and Allan Sekula, "The Traffic in Photographs," in *Photography against the Grain: Essays and Photo Works*,

1973–1983 (Halifax: Press of the Nova Scotia College of Art and Design, 1984), 96–101.

75. See Kim, "Poised on the In-Between," 10. Again, the reader's potential inability to translate this inscription raises the issues of linguistic incomprehensibility and differential access to cultural resources.

76. For a discussion of this debate, see Kim, "Poised on the In-Between," 25; and Kang "'Liberatory Voice,'" 99.

77. See Phu, "Decapitated Forms," 18; and Spahr, *Everybody's Autonomy*, 150.

78. Spahr's reading of the frontispiece comes close to acknowledging the trace of the colonial in the postcolonial. Yet she finally reads *Dictée* as a "decolonizing" text that displaces particularism through formalism. See Spahr, *Everybody's Autonomy*, 160.

79. What Kim and Kang refer to as the "symbolic significance" of the inscription is what I would call its lingering value as an imaginary wound. See Kim, "Poised on the In-Between," 25; and Kang, "'Liberatory Voice'," 99.

80. See my discussion of Peirce in chapter 1. Remarkably, the orientation of the frontispiece also gestures toward this photographic potentiality. As Wong points out, the frontispiece deviates from its traditional function of leading into a work and, instead, moves the spectator's eye to the edges of its visual field. See Wong, "Unnaming the Same," 107–8.

81. This photograph currently hangs at the Ewha Museum in Seoul. It is highly likely that these women were Yu's classmates, four of whom also took part in the March 1 Movement in 1919. See Sohn Ji-Young, "Remembering Yu Gwan-sun, Icon of Korea's March 1 Independence Movement," *Korea Herald*, February 28, 2019, http://www.koreaherald.com/view .php?ud=20190227000831.

82. Phu, "Decapitated Forms," 30, 33.

83. For Cheng, the reader experiences this unintelligibility as a melancholic loss that cannot be named. Implicit is a Barthesian suggestion that the spectator's experience of this loss and death ultimately takes precedence over any historical consideration of the referents in the photograph. See Cheng, *Melancholy of Race*, 147; and Barthes, *Camera Lucida*, 96.

84. Earlier in her essay, Phu convincingly argues that, in contrast to Barthes in *Camera Lucida*, Cha does not privilege language over photographic referentiality. If Barthes—in spite of his interest in referential excess that escapes the photographer's intentions—ultimately withholds his mother's photograph and describes it through language, Cha includes several photographs (including her own mother's) and withholds linguistic

assistance. Yet to retrieve Cha's aesthetic politics of invisibility, Phu over-looks the referential contingencies of the photographs that she discusses. See Phu, "Decapitated Forms," 20–22; and Barthes, *Camera Lucida*, 63–73.

85. Notably, the passage immediately following this image in *Dictée* describes the piercing voice of a fortune teller excavated from historical oblivion, thereby suggesting a parallel between the prophetic voice and the vox populi. See Cha, *Dictée*, 123.

86. See, for instance, "Massacres of Civilians under and after Japanese Rule—Korea," *Zero* (blog), February 22, 2006, http://zeroempty000.blogspot .com/2006/02/massacres-of-civillians-under-and.html; T. K., "Korea and the Great War," *Ask a Korean* (blog), October 11, 2014, http://askakorean .blogspot.com/2014/10/korea-and-great-war.html; and Korea Economic Institute of America (@KoreaEconInst), "33 representatives of the Korean nation meet in Seoul in 1919," Twitter, March 1, 2019, https://twitter.com /KoreaEconInst/status/1101497447430402054.

87. Cheng argues that Cha's focus here is not the historical event of the student protest but rather its mediated representation, the false promise of an "impossible presence." I am not convinced that examining the medi-ated nature of the historical event is ethically or politically most generative if it begins and ends as a critique of the metaphysics of presence. Like Phu, Cheng conflates the labor of the referents constituting the photograph with the spectator's desire for referentiality and meaning. See Cheng, *Melancholy of Race*, 145.

88. Ariella Azoulay, "The Execution Portrait," in *Picturing Atrocity: Pho-tography in Crisis*, ed. Geoffrey Batchen, Mick Gidley, Nancy K. Miller, and Jay Prosser (London: Reaktion, 2012), 251, emphasis in the original.

89. The referent, Azoulay has compellingly argued, is not a given and needs to be reconstructed as much as the interpretations that have become attached to it. While the referent is caught up in social hierarchies shaping the photographic encounter, it is not reducible to the point of view of the most powerful figure present in that encounter, including (the discipline-bound) spectator-critic. See Ariella Azoulay, *The Civil Contract of Photography*, trans. Rela Mazali and Ruvik Danieli (New York: Zone, 2008), 24.

90. See Kang, "'Liberatory Voice,'" 80; and Stephen Joyce, "The Link and the Chain: The Individual and Communal Self in Theresa Hak Kyung Cha's *Dictée*," *Forum for Inter-American Research* 1, no. 1(2008), http://inter america.de/current-issue/joyce/.

91. Cheng, *Melancholy of Race*, 141, emphasis in the original.

Chapter 3

1. Assia Djebar, dir., *La Nouba des femmes du Mont Chenoua* (1977; New York: Women Make Movies, 2002), DVD.

2. Guy Austin, *Algerian National Cinema* (Manchester, Eng.: Manchester University Press, 2012), 20–21; Khanna, *Algeria Cuts*, 107; and Hala Salmane, "Historical Background," in *Algerian Cinema*, ed. Hala Salmane, Simon Hartog, and David Wilson (London: British Film Institute, 1976), 5.

3. Austin, *Algerian National Cinema*, 23.

4. See chapter 1. See also Fanon, *Dying Colonialism*, 87.

5. Debra Kelly, *Autobiography and Independence: Selfhood and Creativity in North African Postcolonial Writing in French* (Liverpool, Eng.: Liverpool University Press, 2005), 374.

6. On revolutionary cinema as a "hetero-biography," see Teshome Gabriel, "Third Cinema as Guardian of Popular Memory: Towards a Third Aesthetics," in Pines and Willemen, *Questions of Third Cinema*, 58.

7. Maria Lugones, "The Coloniality of Gender," *Worlds and Knowledges Otherwise*, 2008, 2.

8. Pierre Bourdieu, "Révolution dans la révolution," in *Interventions, 1961–2001: Science sociale et action politique* (Paris: Agone, 2002), 26–27, translated in Austin, *Algerian National Cinema*, 51.

9. Benrabah, *Language Conflict in Algeria*, 30.

10. Natalya Vince, *Our Fighting Sisters: Nation, Memory and Gender in Algeria, 1954–2012* (Manchester, Eng.: Manchester University Press, 2015), 85.

11. Marnia Lazreg, *The Eloquence of Silence: Algerian Women in Question* (New York: Routledge, 1994), 53–54, quoted in Austin, *Algerian National Cinema*, 62.

12. On this point, see also Neil MacMaster, *Burning the Veil: The Algerian War and the "Emancipation" of Muslim Women, 1954–62* (Manchester, Eng.: Manchester University Press, 2009), 19.

13. Assia Djebar, "Forbidden Gaze, Severed Sound," in *Women of Algiers in Their Apartment*, trans. Marjolijn de Jager (Charlottesville: University of Virginia Press, 1992), 140.

14. Spivak, "Scattered Speculations," 75. See also my discussion of the ego and the commodity form in chapter 1.

15. Austin, *Algerian National Cinema*, 10.

16. Algerian National Charter, quoted in Lazreg, *Eloquence of Silence*, 146–47.

17. Benrabah, *Language Conflict in Algeria*, 53.

18. Austin, *Algerian National Cinema*, 11.

19. Ahmed Moatissime, "Islam, arabization, et francophonie: Une interface possible à l'interrogation 'Algérie—France—Islam?,'" in *Algérie—France—Islam*, ed. Joseph Jurt (Paris: L'Harmattan, 1997), 66, translated in Austin, *Algerian National Cinema*, 11.

20. Marie-Aimée Hélie-Lucas, "Bound and Gagged by the Family Code," in *Third World—Second Sex*, vol. 2, comp. Miranda Davies (London: Zed, 1987), 4–8.

21. Benrabah, *Language Conflict in Algeria*, 63–64.

22. James D. Le Sueur, *Between Terrorism and Democracy: Algeria since 1989* (New York: Zed, 2010), 98.

23. Khanna, *Algeria Cuts*, 125.

24. Assia Djebar, *So Vast the Prison*, trans. Betsy Wing (New York: Seven Stories, 2001), 178.

25. Ruth Leys, *Trauma: A Genealogy* (Chicago: University of Chicago Press, 2000), 282.

26. Khanna, *Algeria Cuts*, xiv.

27. Réda Bensmaïa contrasts Lila's feminine mobility and freedom with Ali's masculine immobility and lack of agency. Diegetically, this opposition cannot be sustained simply because Lila actively helps Ali overcome his confinement, pushing his wheelchair and even driving him around the countryside. More important, such a literal approach to the theme of mobility in the film overlooks entirely the film's more metaphorical intimations of a postcolonial stasis through Lila's reflections. See Réda Bensmaïa, "*La nouba des femmes du Mont Chenoua*: Introduction to the Cinematic Fragment," trans. Jennifer Curtiss Gage, *World Literature Today* 70, no. 4 (1996): 878–79. For a comparable celebration of feminine freedom and the feminine gaze, see Austin, *Algerian National Cinema*, 76–80.

28. Bensmaïa, "*La nouba des femmes*," 880.

29. Austin, *Algerian National Cinema*, 51–52.

30. See John Zarobell, *Empire of Landscape: Space and Ideology in French Colonial Algeria* (University Park: Pennsylvania State University Press, 2010), 131; and Viola Shafik, *Arab Cinema: History and Cultural Identity* (New York: American University in Cairo Press, 2007), 55–56.

31. Laura U. Marks, *The Skin of the Film: Intercultural Cinema, Embodiment, and the Senses* (Durham, N.C.: Duke University Press, 2000), 139.

32. Austin, *Algerian National Cinema*, 52. Austin is drawing on Richard Dyer's description of the Western; see Richard Dyer, *White: Essays on Race and Culture* (New York: Routledge, 1997), 36.

33. Marks is drawing on Trinh T. Minh-ha's experimental documentary practice of "speaking nearby." On this, see Nancy N. Chen, "Speaking

Nearby: A Conversation with Trinh T. Minh-ha," *Visual Anthropology Review* 8, no. 1 (1992): 87.

34. For a conception of cinema as a "pre-text" that will engender further reflection and political action—spurred but not determined by film form—see Fernando Solanas and Octavio Getino, "Towards a Third Cinema: Notes and Experiences for the Development of Cinema of Liberation in the Third World," in *New Latin American Cinema*, vol. 1, *Theory, Practices, and Transcontinental Articulations*, ed. Michael T. Martin (Detroit: Wayne State University Press, 1997), 44, 54–55.

35. Marks has since become more skeptical of her own idealization of the "healing" powers of the haptic image. Yet the larger assumption that the cinematic image can move the spectator beyond identity remains intact. See Marks, *Hanan al-Cinema*, 280–82, 312–14.

36. In this context, consider also my discussion of the tactile effects of (optical) Hollywood cinema on Fanon in chapter 1.

37. Assia Djebar, "Discours de réception, et de réponse de Pierre-Jean Rémy," June 22, 2006, Académie française, http://www.academie-francaise.fr/discours-de-reception-et-reponse-de-pierre-jean-remy, my translation, emphasis added. The second epigraph to this chapter is also taken from this speech.

38. Jane Hiddleston, *Assia Djebar: Out of Algeria* (Liverpool, Eng.: Liverpool University Press, 2006), 12–13.

39. Assia Djebar, afterword to *Women of Algiers*, 176.

40. Marks, *Hanan al-Cinema*, 308.

41. Djebar, "Discours de réception," my translation, emphasis added.

42. For Lacanian critic Mladen Dolar, a fetishistic attachment to the voice as "culture" disavows the lack that marks the subject's entry into the symbolic order. What the materiality of the psychoanalytically approached "object voice" reveals is this lack. But I would argue that Djebar's vocal "fetishism" is more strategic, demonstrating how the phonic materiality of empirical and subjugated orality arises from an identitarian lack or loss that is historically specific, necessarily marked by racial and gendered violence. See Mladen Dolar, *A Voice and Nothing More* (Cambridge, Mass.: MIT Press, 2006), 31.

43. Hélie-Lucas, "Bound and Gagged," 13–14.

44. Michel Chion, *The Voice in Cinema*, trans. Claudia Gorbman (New York: Columbia University Press, 1999).

45. Gayatri Chakravorty Spivak, "Echo," *New Literary History* 24, no. 1 (1993): 30.

46. Assia Djebar, *Fantasia: An Algerian Cavalcade*, trans. Dorothy S. Blair (New York: Quartet, 1985), 178. See also Spivak, "Echo," 29.

47. Austin reads this as a collection of female voices. See Austin, *Algerian Cinema*, 80. Yet other critics have read it as a single male voice. See, for instance, Zahia Smail Salhi, "Heard/Symbolic Voices: *The Nouba of the Women of Mont Chenoua* and Women's Film in the Maghreb," in *Storytelling in World Cinemas*, vol. 2, *Contexts*, ed. Lina Khatib (New York: Wallflower, 2013), 118.

48. On these planned asphyxiations, see Frederick A. De Luna, *The French Republic under Cavaignac, 1848* (Princeton, N.J.: Princeton University Press, 1969), 51–52.

Chapter 4

1. On the complex history of the term "queer" that involves its use in gay and lesbian activism in the United States, as well as its institutionalization along with that of lesbian and gay studies, see Donald E. Hall and Annamarie Jagose, introduction to *The Routledge Queer Studies Reader*, ed. Donald E. Hall, Annamarie Jagose, Andrea Bebell, and Susan Potter (New York: Routledge, 2013), xiv–xx; Henry Abelove, Michèle Aina Barale, and David M. Halperin, introduction to *The Lesbian and Gay Studies Reader*, ed. Henry Abelove, Michèle Aina Barale, and David M. Halperin (New York: Routledge, 1993), xv–xviii; and Rosemary Hennessy, "Queer Theory: A Review of the *differences* Special Issue and Wittig's *The Straight Mind*," *Signs* 18, no. 4 (1993): 964–73.

2. Schoonover and Galt, *Queer Cinema*, 29, emphasis in the original.

3. While I reflect on the history of KASHISH since its inception in 2010 and analyze films shown between 2010 and 2017, my analysis of the festival is largely based on my attendance in 2015 and 2017.

4. "KASHISH 2018—Call for Submission," KASHISH, http://mumbai queerfest.com/2017/10/kashish-2018-call-film-submission/.

5. Jagan T, "Big Victory for Gay Rights in India," *HuffPost* blog, February 7, 2009, https://www.huffingtonpost.com/groundreport/big-victory-for-gay -right_b_225015.html.

6. AFP, "First Major Queer Film Festival in India," *Express Tribune* (Pakistan), April 23, 2010, https://tribune.com.pk/story/8633/first-major-gay-film -festival-in-india/.

7. Dhananjay Mahapatra, "Supreme Court Makes Homosexuality a Crime Again," *Times of India*, December 12, 2013, https://timesofindia .indiatimes.com/india/Supreme-Court-makes-homosexuality-a-crime -again/articleshow/27230690.cms.

8. "Supreme Court Decriminalises Section 377: All You Need to Know," *Times of India*, September 6, 2018, https://timesofindia.indiatimes.com/india/sc-verdict-on-section-377-all-you-need-to-know/articleshow/65695884.cms.

9. On the film festival as a ludic countercultural space, see Patricia White, *Women's Cinema, World Cinema: Projecting Contemporary Feminisms* (Durham, N.C.: Duke University Press, 2015), 18; and Schoonover and Galt, *Queer Cinema*, 80.

10. Solaris Pictures, homepage, http://www.solarispictures.com/.

11. KASHISH, "KASHISH 2015 Trailer," YouTube, May 20, 2015, https://www.youtube.com/watch?v=x9uI1iS0O7c.

12. Eve Kosofsky Sedgwick, *Epistemology of the Closet* (Berkeley: University of California Press, 1990), 67.

13. Rupal Oza, *The Making of Neoliberal India: Nationalism, Gender, and the Paradoxes of Globalization* (New York: Routledge, 2006), 12.

14. Abhijit Sen, "Economic Reforms, Employment and Poverty: Trends and Options," *Economic and Political Weekly* 31, no. 35/37 (1996): 2468.

15. On the role of the British government in perpetuating and exacerbating rural poverty in colonial India, see Sumit Sarkar, *Modern India, 1885–1947* (New York: Palgrave Macmillan, 1983), 30–37.

16. Stuart Corbridge and John Harriss, *Reinventing India: Liberalization, Hindu Nationalism and Popular Democracy* (Malden, Mass.: Polity, 2000), 171.

17. Naisargi N. Dave, *Queer Activism in India: A Story in the Anthropology of Ethics* (Durham, N.C.: Duke University Press, 2012), 10–11.

18. John D'Emilio, "Capitalism and Gay Identity," in *The Gender/Sexuality Reader: Culture, History, Political Economy*, ed. Roger N. Lancaster and Micaela di Leonardo (New York: Routledge 1997), 170.

19. On the role of South Asian diasporic newsletters in queer activism in India, see Nayan Shah, "Sexuality, Identity, and the Uses of History," in *Q & A in Asian America*, ed. David L. Eng and Alice Y. Hom (Philadelphia: Temple University Press, 1998), 141–42. On print media contributing to an urban gay and lesbian subculture in the U.S. in the 1940s, see D'Emilio, "Capitalism and Gay Identity," 174.

20. Karishma Dube, dir., *Devi* (2017, digital copy obtained from the filmmaker); Debalina Majumder, dir., . . . *ebang bewarish* (Kolkata: Sappho for Equality, 2013).

21. Both in 2015 and 2017, most of the screenings were held at this theater, with additional screenings at the local branch of the Alliance Française.

22. On homonationalism as the selective racialized inclusion of same-sex desiring subjects into the nation-state, see Jasbir K. Puar, *Terrorist Assemblages: Homonationalism in Queer Times* (Durham, N.C.: Duke University Press 2007).

23. See Ani Maitra, "In the Shadow of the Homoglobal: Queer Cosmopolitanism in Tsai Ming-liang's *I Don't Want to Sleep Alone*," in *New Intimacies, Old Desires: Law, Culture, and Queer Politics in Neoliberal Times*, ed. Oishik Sircar and Dipika Jain (New Delhi: Zubaan Academic, 2017), 322–27.

24. In 2018, the festival showed films from forty-five countries. See "India's Top Corporate Honchos Nadir Godrej, Radhika Piramal Inaugurate KASHISH 2018," May 23, 2018, KASHISH, http://mumbaiqueerfest .com/2018/05/indias-top-corporate-honchos-nadir-godrej-radhika -piramal-inaugurate-kashish-2018/.

25. This list is based on my survey of sponsors and partners listed in the KASHISH festival catalogs from 2010 to 2017, which can be found at "KASHISH Mumbai International Queer Film Festival," Issuu, https://issuu .com/kashish/docs.

26. See, for instance, the festival catalogs for 2012 and 2017, https:// issuu.com/kashish/docs.

27. On the dominance of the Indian queer movement by urban gay male activists, as well the divisions between gay and lesbian activism, see Dave, *Queer Activism in India*, 28, 39–40, 120.

28. See Kavita Misra, "Politico-Moral Transactions in Indian AIDS Service: Confidentiality, Rights, and the New Modalities of Governance," *Anthropological Quarterly* 79, no. 1 (2006): 33–74.

29. Lawrence Cohen, "The Kothi Wars: AIDS Cosmopolitanism and the Morality of Classification," in *Sex and Development: Science, Sexuality, and Morality in Global Perspective*, ed. Vincenne Adams and Stacy L. Pigg (Durham, N.C.: Duke University Press, 2005), 270.

30. See Paul Boyce, "'Conceiving *Kothis*': Men Who Have Sex with Men in India and the Cultural Subject of HIV Prevention," *Medical Anthropology* 26, no. 2 (2007): 181–82; Akshay Khanna, "Taming of the Shrewd Meyeli Chhele: A Political Economy of Development's Sexual Subject," *Development* 52, no.1 (2009): 49–50; and Aniruddha Dutta, "An Epistemology of Collusion: *Hijras, Kothis,* and the Historical (Dis)continuity of Gender/Sexual Identities in Eastern India," *Gender & History* 24, no. 3 (2012): 825–26.

31. Gayatri Reddy, *With Respect to Sex: Negotiating Hijra Identity in South India* (Chicago: University of Chicago Press, 2005), 25–28.

32. Cohen, "Kothi Wars," 280.

33. Dutta, "Epistemology of Collusion," 837–38.

34. Vikram Phukan, "Queering the Mainstream," *The Hindu*, May 29, 2017, https://www.thehindu.com/entertainment/movies/queering-the-main stream/article18618856.ece. I was present on this occasion.

35. On the transformation of popular Hindi cinema into Bollywood as soft power for the Indian nation-state, see Dayanand Thussu, *Communicating India's Soft Power: Buddha to Bollywood* (New York: Palgrave Macmillan, 2013), 127–54. On Bollywood's commodification of Indian (hyper)masculinity on the global stage, see Murali Balaji, "Competing South Asian Mas(k)ulinities: Bollywood Icons versus 'Tech-N-Talk,'" in *Communicating Marginalized Masculinities: Identity Politics in TV, Film, and New Media*, ed. Ronald L. Jackson II and Jamie E. Moshin (New York: Routledge, 2013), 49–64.

36. On the commodification of queer activism in the United States, see Hennessy, *Profit and Pleasure*, 129–30.

37. Godrej Consumer Production, "LGBT Inclusion at Godrej," YouTube, September 7, 2016, https://www.youtube.com/watch?v=8RWtfOljEL8.

38. Bhaskar Sarkar and Janet Walker, "Introduction: Moving Testimonies," in *Documentary Testimonies: Global Archives of Suffering*, ed. Bhaskar Sarkar and Janet Walker (New York: Routledge, 2010), 8.

39. Brinda Dasgupta, "Godrej Partners UN Initiative for LGBT Employees," *Economic Times*, October 9, 2017, https://economictimes .indiatimes.com/jobs/godrej-partners-un-initiative-for-lgbt-employees/article show/61012237.cms.

40. Arvind Narrain, "India's Vote on the UN's LGBT Rights Resolution Dilutes Human Rights Principles," *The Wire*, July 5, 2016, https://thewire .in/gender/diluting-human-rights-principles-indias-vote-on-the-resolution -on-sexual-orientation-and-gender-identity.

41. On Godrej's anticolonial image, see Arun Chaudhuri, *Indian Advertising 1780–1950* (New Delhi: Tata McGraw-Hill, 2007), 216–17.

42. KASHISH, "KASHISH 2017 Opening Night Highlight—Ms. Nisaba Godrej," YouTube, July 31, 2017, https://www.youtube.com/watch? v=_nue3ZHqSwI.

43. Vicks India, "Vicks—Generations of Care #TouchofCare," YouTube, March 29, 2017, https://www.youtube.com/watch?v=7zeeVEKaDLM.

44. Since the release of the commercial, Sawant has been interviewed by several local and international news and nonprofit organizations. See, for instance, HRC Staff, "Grab the Tissues: Vicks Ad Featuring Transgender

Mom Goes Viral in India," Human Rights Campaign, April 20, 2017, https://www.hrc.org/blog/grab-the-tissues-vicks-ad-featuring-transgender-mom-goes-viral-in-india; and Chhavi Sachdev, "'Mummy' Is Transgender: A New Commercial Is the Talk of India," NPR, April 15, 2017, https://www.npr.org/sections/goatsandsoda/2017/04/15/523974501/mummy-is-transgender-a-new-commercial-is-the-talk-of-india.

45. See, for instance, Vicks India, "Vicks VapoRub Sweet Dreams (English)," YouTube, November 20, 2015, https://www.youtube.com/watch?v=2LQK_-Bq778; and zabardast, "Vicks Vaporub," YouTube, November 15, https://www.youtube.com/watch?v=L-1zUqmwHn8.

46. Carla Herreria, "Touching Ad Normalizes Transgender Motherhood in India," *HuffPost*, April 5, 2017, https://www.huffingtonpost.com/entry/vicks-ad-india-transgender-mother_us_58e40973e4b03a26a36729df.

47. None of the child actors appearing in the commercial is the actual adoptee. See Wire staff, "How Activism, Adoption, and an Ad Changed a Trans Woman's Life," *The Wire*, July 18, 2017, https://thewire.in/gender/trans-woman-adoption-vicks-ad.

48. Oishik Sircar, "Spectacles of Emancipation: Reading Rights Differently in India's Legal Discourse," *Osgoode Hall Law Journal* 49, no. 3 (2012): 527–73.

49. Lee Edelman's argument that political interventions are frequently premised on the child as a figure of progress and futurity is relevant here. Yet the "Lacanian" solution that Edelman proposes ("Fuck the social order and the Child") becomes a variation on the aestheticized anti-identitarianism and class knowledge I have critiqued in chapter 1. See Lee Edelman, *No Future: Queer Theory and the Death Drive* (Durham, N.C.: Duke University Press, 2004), 29.

50. On the figure of the child as an accumulation strategy in the twenty-first century, see Cindi Katz, "Childhood as Spectacle: Relays of Anxiety and the Reconfiguration of the Child," *Cultural Geographies* 15, no. 1 (2008): 5–17.

51. *8th Kashish Mumbai International Queer Film Festival* (2017), 45, https://issuu.com/kashish/docs/kashish-2017_festival-catalog.

52. KASHISH, "KASHISH 2017—Panel Discussion—Gauri Sawant, Neeraj Ghaywan," YouTube, October 29, 2017, https://www.youtube.com/watch?v=UGbtmxXJXq8. Sawant uses the Hindi word *istemaal* during the discussion.

53. Wire staff, "Activism, Adoption, and an Ad."

54. Ellen Rooney, "Form and Contentment," *Modern Language Quarterly* 61, no. 1 (2000): 34.

55. Although it is beyond the scope of my discussion here, Eugenie Brinkema's argument for seeing (cinematic) form as a pure exteriority devoid of subjectivity also relies on the elision of the historical body that reads and produces form. See Eugenie Brinkema, *The Form of the Affects* (Durham, N.C.: Duke University Press, 2014), 18–25.

56. Spivak, "In a Word," 1.

57. Nakshatra Bagwe, dir., *Logging Out* (Mumbai: Solaris Pictures, 2012), DVD.

58. Judith Butler uses the term "critically queer" to suggest a mode of inquiry that views minoritized sexual and gender identities not as unquestionable categories but rather as sites that demand historicization. See Judith Butler, *Bodies That Matter: On the Discursive Limits of "Sex"* (New York: Routledge, 1993), 223–24.

59. Beller, *Cinematic Mode*, 76.

60. Harro Maat uses the term "anti-commodity" to refer to production processes that are complementary to commodity production but are generally perceived to be of little or no significance because they are of an undefined or lower value. The commodity and the "anti-commodity" can be defined only in relation to each other. See Harro Maat, "Commodities and Anti-commodities: Rice on Sumatra, 1915–1925," in *Rice: Global Networks and New Histories*, ed. Francesca Bray, Peter A. Coclanis, Edda L. Fields-Black, and Dagmar Schäfer (New York: Cambridge University Press, 2015), 337.

61. On "foregrounding" as a countercinematic technique that lays bare the ostensible transparency of the cinematic medium, see Peter Wollen, "Godard and Counter-Cinema: *Vent d'Est* (1972)," in *The European Cinema Reader*, ed. Catherine Fowler (New York: Routledge, 2002), 76.

62. *8th Kashish Mumbai International Queer Film Festival* (2017), 15, https://issuu.com/kashish/docs/kashish-2017_festival-catalog.

63. Michael Warner, *The Trouble with Normal: Sex, Politics and the Ethics of Queer Life* (Cambridge, Mass.: Harvard University Press, 2000).

64. Sharon Flynn, dir., *I'dentity* (Mumbai: Solaris Pictures, 2014), DVD.

65. On the performative nature of identity construction in queer documentary, see Christopher Pullen, *Gay Identity, New Storytelling and the Media* (New York: Palgrave Macmillan, 2009), 213.

66. B. Sarkar and Walker, introduction, 15. The authors are drawing on Derrida's concept of the archive. See Jacques Derrida, *Archive Fever: A Freudian Impression*, trans. Eric Prenowitz (Chicago: University of Chicago Press, 1993), 1–2.

67. Sandy Stone, "The *Empire* Strikes Back: A Posttranssexual Manifesto," in *The Transgender Studies Reader*, ed. Susan Stryker and Stephen Whittle (New York: Routledge, 2006), 228.

68. Stone, "*Empire* Strikes Back," 224.

69. Kiran Pawar, dir., *Astitva* (Mumbai: Solaris Pictures, 2010), DVD.

70. G. Reddy, *With Respect to Sex*, 56; Dutta, "Epistemology of Collusion," 32.

71. G. Reddy, *With Respect to Sex*, 2.

72. Ratna Kapur, "Beyond Male and Female, the Right to Humanity," *The Hindu*, April 24, 2016, https://www.thehindu.com/opinion/op-ed/beyond -male-and-female-the-right-to-humanity/article5926142.ece.

73. Sandip Roy, "Transgender Day of Rage in Kolkata Galvanizes Community to Protest Ill-Conceived Bill to Protect," *Firstpost*, December 11, 2017, https://www.firstpost.com/india/transgender-day-of-rage-in-kolkata -galvanises-community-to-protest-ill-conceived-bill-to-protect-their-rights -4253429.html.

74. Smriti Kak Ramachandran, "Centre to Reintroduce Transgender Rights Bill with Suggested Changes," *Hindustan Times*, February 19, 2018, https://www.hindustantimes.com/india-news/centre-to-reintroduce -transgender-bill-with-changes-suggested-by-mps-panel-and-rights-groups /story-V3waQoU4kEdeJl6iJHnydL.html.

75. Kevin Floyd, *The Reification of Desire: Toward a Queer Marxism* (Minneapolis: University of Minnesota Press, 2009), 54.

76. Aihwa Ong, *Neoliberalism as Exception: Mutations in Citizenship and Sovereignty* (Durham, N.C.: Duke University Press, 2006), 121.

77. Tara and her mother's use of English to communicate with each other signals the legacy of the institutionalization of English in British India to create an intermediary, comprador, and upper-caste middle class. On this legacy, see Modhumita Roy, "The Englishing of India: Class Formation and Social Privilege," *Social Scientist* 21, no. 5 (1993): 36–62. In contrast, Devi's use of the vernaculars of Bengali and Hindi situates her on the fringes of that Anglophone social sphere.

78. On the domestic sphere and domestic labor as the site of production of class difference in colonial and postcolonial India, see Raka Ray and Seemin Qayum, *Cultures of Servitude: Modernity, Domesticity, and Class in India* (Stanford, Calif.: Stanford University Press, 2009).

79. In 2017, the KASHISH delegate pass allowing admission to all screenings cost me five hundred rupees (approximately seven U.S. dollars). While quite inexpensive compared to admission charges at queer film festivals in

the United States, that would be a substantial chunk of a female domestic worker's monthly pay in urban India, which could be as low as five thousand rupees (roughly seventy U.S. dollars). For a 2016 survey of the wages of domestic workers in India, see Krishna Pokharel and Eric Bellman, "How Much Do Indians Pay Their Many Domestic Helpers?," *Wall Street Journal*, May 3, 2016, https://blogs.wsj.com/indiarealtime/2016/05/03/how-much-do-indians-pay-their-many-domestic-helpers/.

80. Debalina Majumder, dir., . . . *ebang bewarish* (Kolkata: Sappho for Equality, 2013), DVD.

81. Sappho for Equality's mission statement can be found on its website, Sappho for Equality, http://www.sapphokolkata.in/sappho-for-equality/.

82. Shraddha Chatterjee, *Queer Politics in India: Towards Sexual Subaltern Subjects* (New York: Routledge, 2018), 4.

83. Here I am following Chatterjee's translation of the letter and not the subtitled translation offered by the film. As Chatterjee points out, the Bengali phrases "bhalo basha" and "bhalo laga" (which Swapna uses to describe the women's feelings for each other) can be translated as either "loving" or "liking," suggesting romantic attraction or friendship. See S. Chatterjee, *Queer Politics in India*, 91, 118, emphasis in the original.

84. Hamid Naficy, *An Accented Cinema: Exilic and Diasporic Filmmaking* (Princeton, N.J.: Princeton University Press, 2001), 5.

85. Gayatri Chakravorty Spivak, "Can the Subaltern Speak?" in *Colonial Discourse and Post-Colonial Theory: A Reader*, ed. Patrick Williams and Laura Chrisman (New York: Columbia University Press, 1994), 104.

86. For all the interviews within the documentary, I follow the subtitled translation.

87. Jean-François Lyotard, *The Postmodern Condition: A Report on Knowledge*, trans. Geoffrey Bennington and Brian Massumi (Minneapolis: University of Minnesota Press, 1984), 10.

88. Tanika Sarkar and Sumit Chowdhury, "The Meaning of Nandigram: Corporate Land Invasion, People's Power, and the Left in India," *Focaal—European Journal of Anthropology* 54 (2009): 73.

89. I am borrowing this definition of cinema as a "pre-text" for political action from theorists of Third Cinema. See Solanas and Getino, "Towards a Third Cinema," 44, 54–55.

90. Oishik Sircar and Dipika Jain, "Introduction: Of Powerful Feelings and Facile Gestures," in Sircar and Jain, *New Intimacies*, xv.

Conclusion

1. José Esteban Muñoz, *Cruising Utopia: The Then and There of Queer Futurity* (New York: New York University Press, 2009), 1. For the oft-cited argument for the need to move beyond a suspicious "paranoid" mode of critique and toward a self-healing "reparative" mode, see Eve Kosofsky Sedgwick, "Paranoid Reading and Reparative Reading, or, You're So Paranoid, You Probably Think This Essay Is about You," in *Touching Feeling: Affect, Pedagogy, Performativity* (Durham, N.C.: Duke University Press, 2003), 123–51.

2. Michael Hardt and Antonio Negri, *Commonwealth* (Cambridge, Mass.: Belknap, 2009); and Jean Baudrillard, *Symbolic Exchange and Death*, trans. Iain Hamilton Grant (Los Angeles: Sage, 1993).

3. Lauren Berlant, *Cruel Optimism* (Durham, N.C.: Duke University Press, 2011), 2, emphasis in the original.

4. Muñoz, *Cruising Utopia*, 27.

5. See Edelman, *No Future*. For Muñoz's critique of Edelman's anti-utopianism, see Muñoz, *Cruising Utopia*, 11–12.

6. Nivedita Menon, *Recovering Subversion: Feminist Politics beyond the Law* (Delhi: Permanent Black, 2004), 20.

7. Theodor Adorno, *Minima Moralia: Reflections on a Damaged Life*, trans. E. F. N. Jephcott (New York: Verso, 2005), 98.

8. See Ghosh, *Global Icons*, 50–51.

9. Ferguson, *Reorder of Things*, 190.

10. Joe Parker and Ranu Samantrai, "Interdisciplinarity and Social Justice: An Introduction," in *Interdisciplinarity and Social Justice: Revisioning Academic Accountability*, ed. Joe Parker, Ranu Samantrai, and Mary Romero (Albany: State University of New York Press, 2010), 2.

11. Robyn Wiegman, *Object Lessons* (Durham, N.C.: Duke University Press, 2012), 17, emphasis in the original.

12. Sedgwick, "Paranoid Reading," 129.

BIBLIOGRAPHY

Abbas, Sadia. *At Freedom's Limit: Islam and the Postcolonial Predicament.* New York: Fordham University Press, 2014.

Abelove, Henry, Michèle Aina Barale, and David M. Halperin. Introduction to *The Lesbian and Gay Studies Reader*, edited by Henry Abelove, Michèle Aina Barale, and David M. Halperin, xv–xviii. New York: Routledge, 1993.

Adorno, Theodor. *Minima Moralia: Reflections on a Damaged Life.* Translated by E. F. N. Jephcott. New York: Verso, 2005.

———. "On the Fetish Character in Music and the Regression of Listening." In *The Culture Industry: Selected Essays on Mass Culture.* Edited by J. M. Bernstein, 29–60. New York: Routledge, 1991.

Agamben, Giorgio. *The Man without Content.* Stanford, Calif.: Stanford University Press, 1999.

Alcoff, Linda Martín, and Satya P. Mohanty, "Reconsidering Identity Politics: An Introduction." In *Identity Politics Reconsidered*, edited by Linda Martín Alcoff, Michael Hames-García, Satya P. Mohanty, and Paula M. L. Moya, 1–9. New York: Palgrave Macmillan, 2006.

Althusser, Louis. "On Feuerbach." In *The Humanist Controversy and Other Writings.* Edited by François Matheron. Translated by G. M. Goshgarian (1966–67), 85–154. New York: Verso, 2003.

———. *On Ideology.* Translated by Ben Brewster. New York: Verso, 2008.

Anderson, Benedict. *Imagined Communities: Reflections on the Origin and Spread of Nationalism.* New York: Verso, 2006.

Appadurai, Arjun. "Disjuncture and Difference in the Global Cultural Economy." *Theory, Culture & Society* 7 (1990): 295–310.

———. *Modernity at Large: Cultural Dimensions of Globalization.* Minneapolis: University of Minnesota Press, 1996.

Austin, Guy. *Algerian National Cinema.* Manchester, England: Manchester University Press, 2012.

Azoulay, Ariella. *The Civil Contract of Photography.* Translated by Rela Mazali and Ruvik Danieli. New York: Zone, 2008.

———. "The Execution Portrait." In *Picturing Atrocity: Photography in Crisis*, edited by Geoffrey Batchen, Mick Gidley, Nancy K. Miller, and Jay Prosser, 249–59. London: Reaktion, 2012.

Bagwe, Nakshatra, dir. *Logging Out*. Mumbai: Solaris Pictures, 2012. DVD.

Balaji, Murali. "Competing South Asian Mas(k)ulinities: Bollywood Icons versus 'Tech-N-Talk.'" In *Communicating Marginalized Masculinities: Identity Politics in TV, Film, and New Media*, edited by Ronald L. Jackson II and Jamie E. Moshin, 49–64. New York: Routledge, 2013.

Barthes, Roland, *Camera Lucida: Reflections on Photography*. Translated by Richard Howard. New York: Hill and Wang, 1981.

———. *Empire of Signs*. Translated by Richard Howard. New York: Hill and Wang, 1982.

———. "Leaving the Movie Theater." In *The Rustle of Language*, translated by Richard Howard, 345–49. New York: Hill and Wang, 1986.

Barzilai, Shuli. *Lacan and the Matter of Origins*. Stanford, Calif.: Stanford University Press, 1999.

Baudrillard, Jean. *The Perfect Crime*. Translated by Chris Turner. New York: Verso, 1996.

———. *Symbolic Exchange and Death*. Translated by Iain Hamilton Grant. Los Angeles: Sage, 1993.

Baudry, Jean-Louis. "Ideological Effects of the Basic Cinematographic Apparatus." Translated by Alan Williams. *Film Quarterly* 28, no. 2 (1974–75): 39–47.

Becker, A. L. *Beyond Translation: Essays toward a Modern Philology*. Ann Arbor: University of Michigan Press, 1995.

Beller, Jonathan. *The Cinematic Mode of Production: Attention Economy and the Society of the Spectacle*. Lebanon, N.H.: University Press of New England, 2006.

Benjamin, Walter. "Reflections on Radio." Translated by Rodney Livingstone. In *Selected Writings*, vol. 2, pt. 2, *1931–1934*. Edited by Michael W. Jennings, Howard Eiland, and Gary Smith, 543–44. Cambridge, Mass.: Harvard University Press, 2005.

———. "The Work of Art in the Age of Its Technological Reproducibility." Translated by Edmund Jephcott and Harry Zohn. In *The Work of Art in the Age of Its Technological Reproducibility and Other Writings on Media*. Edited by Michael W. Jennings, Brigid Doherty, and Thomas Y. Levin, 19–55. Cambridge, Mass.: Harvard University Press, 2008.

Benrabah, Mohamed. *Language Conflict in Algeria: From Colonialism to Post-Independence*. Buffalo, N.Y.: Multilingual Matters, 2013.

Bensmaïa, Réda. "*La nouba des femmes du Mont Chenoua*: Introduction to the Cinematic Fragment." Translated by Jennifer Curtiss Gage. *World Literature Today* 70, no. 4 (1996): 877–84.

Bergner, Gwen. "Who Is That Masked Woman? or, The Role of Gender in Fanon's *Black Skin, White Masks.*" *PMLA* 110, no. 1 (1995): 75–88.

Berlant, Lauren. *Cruel Optimism.* Durham, N.C.: Duke University Press, 2011.

Best, Stephen, and Saidiya Hartman. "Fugitive Justice." *Representations* 92, no. 1 (2005): 1–15.

Bhabha, Homi K. *The Location of Culture.* New York: Routledge, 1994.

Bolter, Jay David, and Richard Grusin. *Remediation: Understanding New Media.* Cambridge, Mass.: MIT Press, 1999.

Borch-Jacobsen, Mikkel. *Lacan: The Absolute Master.* Translated by Douglas Brick. Stanford, Calif.: Stanford University Press, 1991.

Bourdieu, Pierre. *Distinction: A Social Critique of the Judgment of Taste.* Translated by Richard Nice. Cambridge, Mass.: Harvard University Press, 1984.

———. *The Logic of Practice.* Translated by Richard Nice. Stanford, Calif.: Stanford University Press, 1990.

———. "Révolution dans la révolution." In *Interventions, 1961–2001: Science sociale et action politique,* 21–28. Paris: Agone, 2002.

Boyce, Paul. "'Conceiving *Kothis*': Men Who Have Sex with Men in India and the Cultural Subject of HIV Prevention." *Medical Anthropology* 26, no. 2 (2007): 175–203.

Brinkema, Eugenie. *The Form of the Affects.* Durham, N.C.: Duke University Press, 2014.

Brown, Wendy. *States of Injury: Power and Freedom in Late Modernity.* Princeton, N.J.: Princeton University Press, 1995.

Bürger, Peter. "Avant-Garde and Neo-Avant-Garde: An Attempt to Answer Certain Critics of *Theory of the Avant-Garde.*" Translated by Bettina Brandt and Daniel Purdy. *New Literary History* 41, no. 4 (2010): 695–715.

Butler, Judith. *Bodies That Matter: On the Discursive Limits of "Sex."* New York: Routledge, 1993.

———. *The Psychic Life of Power: Theories in Subjection.* Stanford, Calif.: Stanford University Press, 1997.

Byrd, Jodi A. *The Transit of Empire: Indigenous Critiques of Colonialism.* Minneapolis: University of Minnesota Press, 2011.

Cha, Theresa Hak Kyung. *Dictée.* Berkeley: University of California Press, 2001.

———. Preface to *Apparatus—Cinematographic Apparatus: Selected Writings*, edited by Theresa Hak Kyung Cha. New York: Tanam, 1980.

Chatterjee, Partha. *The Nation and Its Fragments: Colonial and Postcolonial Histories*. Princeton, N.J.: Princeton University Press, 1993.

Chatterjee, Shraddha. *Queer Politics in India: Towards Sexual Subaltern Subjects*. New York: Routledge, 2018.

Chaudhuri, Arun. *Indian Advertising 1780–1950*. New Delhi: Tata McGraw-Hill, 2007.

Chen, Nancy N. "Speaking Nearby: A Conversation with Trinh T. Minh-ha." *Visual Anthropology Review* 8, no. 1 (1992): 82–91.

Cheney-Lippold, John. *We Are Data: Algorithms and the Making of Our Digital Selves*. New York: New York University Press, 2017.

Cheng, Anne Anlin. *The Melancholy of Race: Psychoanalysis, Assimilation, and Hidden Grief*. New York: Oxford University Press, 2000.

Chiang, Mark. *The Cultural Capital of Asian American Studies: Autonomy and Representation in the University*. New York: New York University Press, 2009.

Chion, Michel. *The Voice in Cinema*. Translated by Claudia Gorbman. New York: Columbia University Press, 1999.

Chow, Rey. *Ethics after Idealism: Theory, Culture, Ethnicity, Reading*. Bloomington: Indiana University Press, 1998.

———. *The Protestant Ethnic and the Spirit of Capitalism*. New York: Columbia University Press, 2002.

Chun, Wendy Hui Kyong. *Control and Freedom: Power and Paranoia in the Age of Fiber Optics*. Cambridge, Mass.: MIT Press, 2006.

Cohen, Lawrence. "The Kothi Wars: AIDS Cosmopolitanism and the Morality of Classification." In *Sex and Development: Science, Sexuality, and Morality in Global Perspective*, edited by Vincenne Adams and Stacy L. Pigg, 269–303. Durham, N.C.: Duke University Press, 2005.

Constable, Nicole. *Romance on a Global Stage: Pen Pals, Virtual Ethnography, and "Mail-Order" Marriages*. Berkeley: University of California Press, 2003.

Copjec, Joan. "The Orthopsychic Subject: Film Theory and the Reception of Lacan." *October* 49 (1989): 53–71.

Corbridge, Stuart, and John Harriss. *Reinventing India: Liberalization, Hindu Nationalism and Popular Democracy*. Malden, Mass.: Polity, 2000.

Crary, Jonathan. *Techniques of the Observer: On Vision and Modernity in the Nineteenth Century*. Cambridge, Mass.: MIT Press, 1992.

Cronenberg, David, dir. *Videodrome*. 1983; New York: Criterion, 2004. DVD.

Dave, Naisargi N. *Queer Activism in India: A Story in the Anthropology of Ethics*. Durham, N.C.: Duke University Press, 2012.

Dean, Jodi. "Faces as Commons: The Secondary Visuality of Communicative Capitalism." open! Platform for Art, Culture & the Public Domain, December 31, 2016. http://www.onlineopen.org/faces-as-commons.

Debord, Guy. *The Society of the Spectacle*. Translated by Donald Nicholson-Smith. New York: Zone, 1995.

De Luna, Frederick A. *The French Republic under Cavaignac, 1848*. Princeton, N.J.: Princeton University Press, 1969.

D'Emilio, John. "Capitalism and Gay Identity." In *The Gender/Sexuality Reader: Culture, History, Political Economy*, edited by Roger N. Lancaster and Micaela Di Leonardo, 169–78. New York: Routledge, 1997.

Derrida, Jacques. *Archive Fever: A Freudian Impression*. Translated by Eric Prenowitz. Chicago: University of Chicago Press, 1993.

——. *Of Grammatology*. Translated by Gayatri Chakravorty Spivak. Baltimore: Johns Hopkins University Press, 1997.

Diawara, Manthia. "Black Spectatorship: Problems of Identification and Resistance." *Screen* 29, no. 4 (1988): 66–79.

Djebar, Assia. "Discours de réception, et de réponse de Pierre-Jean Rémy." June 22, 2006. Académie française. http://www.academie-francaise.fr /discours-de-reception-et-reponse-de-pierre-jean-remy.

——. *Fantasia: An Algerian Cavalcade*. Translated by Dorothy S. Blair. New York: Quartet, 1985.

——. "Forbidden Gaze, Severed Sound." In *Women of Algiers in Their Apartment*, translated by Marjolijn de Jager, 133–51. Charlottesville: University of Virginia Press, 1992.

——, dir. *La Nouba des femmes du Mont Chenoua*. 1977; New York: Women Make Movies, 2002. DVD.

——. *So Vast the Prison*. Translated by Betsy Wing. New York: Seven Stories, 2001.

Doane, Mary Ann. *The Desire to Desire: The Woman's Film of the 1940s*. Bloomington: Indiana University Press, 1987.

——. *Femmes Fatales: Feminism, Film Theory, Psychoanalysis*. London: Routledge, 1991.

——. "The Indexical and the Concept of Medium Specificity." *differences* 18, no. 1 (2007): 128–52.

Dolar, Mladen. *A Voice and Nothing More*. Cambridge, Mass.: MIT Press, 2006.

Dolto, Françoise. *L'image inconsciente du corps*. Paris: Seuil, 1992.

———. "The Mirror's Child." In *Freud's Tracks: Conversations from the Journal of European Psychoanalysis*, edited by Sergio Benvenuto and Anthony Molino, 185–200. Lanham, Md.: Rowman and Littlefield, 2009.

Dube, Karishma, dir. *Devi*. 2017. Digital copy obtained from the filmmaker.

Du Bois, W. E. B. *The Souls of Black Folk: Essays and Sketches*. Chicago: McClurg, 1903.

Duffus, Cheryl. "When One Drop Isn't Enough: War as a Crucible of Racial Identity in the Novels of Mayotte Capécia." *Callaloo* 28, no. 4 (2005): 1091–1102.

Dutta, Aniruddha. "An Epistemology of Collusion: *Hijras, Kothis* and the Historical (Dis)continuity of Gender/Sexual Identities in Eastern India." *Gender & History* 24, no. 3 (2012): 825–49.

Dyer, Richard. *White: Essays on Race and Culture*. New York: Routledge, 1997.

Eagleton, Terry. *Criticism and Ideology: A Study in Marxist Literary Theory*. London: Verso, 2006.

———. *The Ideology of the Aesthetic*. Oxford: Blackwell, 1990.

Eberwein, Robert. *Armed Forces: Masculinity and Sexuality in the American War Film*. New Brunswick, N.J.: Rutgers University Press, 2007.

Edelman, Lee. *No Future: Queer Theory and the Death Drive*. Durham, N.C.: Duke University Press, 2004.

Evans, Dylan. *An Introductory Dictionary of Lacanian Psychoanalysis*. London: Routledge, 1996.

Fanon, Frantz. *Black Skin, White Masks*. Translated by Richard Philcox. New York: Grove, 2008.

———. *A Dying Colonialism*. Translated by Haakon Chevalier. New York: Grove, 1994.

Ferguson, Roderick A. *The Reorder of Things: The University and Its Pedagogies of Minority Difference*. Minneapolis: University of Minnesota Press, 2012.

Ferry, Luc. *Homo Aestheticus: The Invention of Taste in the Democratic Age*. Translated by Robert de Loaiza. Chicago: University of Chicago Press, 1993.

Floyd, Kevin. *The Reification of Desire: Toward a Queer Marxism*. Minneapolis: University of Minnesota Press, 2009.

Flynn, Sharon, dir. *I'dentity*. Mumbai: Solaris Pictures, 2014. DVD.

Foucault, Michel. *The History of Sexuality*. Vol. 1, *An Introduction*. Translated by Robert Hurley. New York: Vintage, 1990.

Fuente, Eduardo de la, and Peter Murphy, eds. *Aesthetic Capitalism*. Boston: Brill, 2014.

Fusco, Coco. "Censorship, Not the Painting, Must Go: On Dana Schutz's Image of Emmett Till." Hyperallergic, March 27, 2017. https://hyperallergic.com/368290/censorship-not-the-painting-must-go-on-dana-schutzs-image-of-emmett-till/.

Fuss, Diana. "Interior Colonies: Frantz Fanon and the Politics of Identification." diacritics 24, nos. 2–3 (1994): 19–42.

Gabriel, Teshome. "Third Cinema as Guardian of Popular Memory: Towards a Third Aesthetics." In Questions of Third Cinema, edited by Jim Pines and Paul Willemen, 53–64. London: British Film Institute, 1989.

———. "Towards a Critical Theory of Third World Films." In Questions of Third Cinema, edited by Jim Pines and Paul Willemen, 30–51. London: British Film Institute, 1989.

Gallop, Jane. Reading Lacan. Ithaca, N.Y.: Cornell University Press, 1985.

Gell, Alfred. Art and Agency: An Anthropological Theory. Oxford: Oxford University Press, 1998.

Ghosh, Bishnupriya. Global Icons: Apertures to the Popular. Durham, N.C.: Duke University Press, 2011.

Gibbs, Anna. "Horrified: Embodied Vision, Media Affect and the Images from Abu Ghraib." In Interrogating the War on Terror: Interdisciplinary Perspectives, edited by Deborah Staines, 125–42. Newcastle, Eng.: Cambridge Scholars, 2007.

Gopal, Priyamvada. Insurgent Empire: Anticolonial Resistance and British Dissent. London: Verso, 2019.

Gordon, Lewis R. What Fanon Said: A Philosophical Introduction to His Life and Thought. New York: Fordham University Press, 2015.

Goux, Jean-Joseph. Symbolic Economies: After Marx and Freud. Translated by Jennifer Curtiss Gage. Ithaca, N.Y.: Cornell University Press, 1990.

Greenberger, Alex. "'The Painting Must Go': Hannah Black Pens Open Letter to the Whitney about Controversial Biennial Work." Artnews, March 21, 2017. http://www.artnews.com/2017/03/21/the-painting-must-go-hannah-black-pens-open-letter-to-the-whitney-about-controversial-biennial-work/.

Gunn, Richard. "Marxism and Mediation." Common Sense 2 (1987): 57–66.

Gutiérrez-Rodríguez, Encarnación. Migration, Domestic Work and Affect: A Decolonial Approach on Value and the Feminization of Labor. New York: Routledge, 2010.

Haider, Asad. Mistaken Identity: Race and Class in the Age of Trump. London: Verso, 2018.

Hall, Donald E., and Annamarie Jagose. Introduction to The Routledge Queer Studies Reader, edited by Donald E. Hall, Annamarie Jagose, Andrea Bebell, and Susan Potter, xiv–xx. New York: Routledge, 2013.

Hall, Stuart. "Cultural Identity and Diaspora." In *Colonial Discourse and Post-Colonial Theory: A Reader*, edited by Patrick Williams and Laura Chrisman, 392–403. New York: Columbia University Press, 1994.

———. "Who Needs 'Identity'?" In *The Media Studies Reader*, edited by Laurie Ouellette, 351–62. New York: Routledge, 2013.

Hansen, Miriam Bratu. "Fallen Women, Rising Stars, New Horizons: Shanghai Silent Film as Vernacular Modernism." *Film Quarterly* 54, no. 1 (2000): 10–22.

Hardt, Michael, and Antonio Negri. *Commonwealth*. Cambridge, Mass.: Belknap, 2009.

Harrington de Santana, Anne. "Nuclear Weapons as the Currency of Power: Deconstructing the Fetishism of Force," *Nonproliferation Review* 16, no. 3 (2009): 325–45.

Hayles, N. Katherine. *How We Became Posthuman: Virtual Bodies in Cybernetics, Literature, and Informatics*. Chicago: University of Chicago Press, 1999.

———. *My Mother Was a Computer: Digital Subjects and Literary Texts*. Chicago: University of Chicago Press, 2005.

———. "Print Is Flat, Code Is Deep: The Importance of Media-Specific Analysis." In *Transmedia Frictions: The Digital, the Arts, and the Humanities*, edited by Marsha Kinder and Tara McPherson, 20–33. Oakland: University of California Press, 2014.

Hélie-Lucas, Marie-Aimée. "Bound and Gagged by the Family Code." In *Third World—Second Sex*, vol. 2, compiled by Miranda Davies, 3–15. London: Zed, 1987.

Hennessy, Rosemary. *Profit and Pleasure: Sexual Identities in Late Capitalism*. New York: Routledge, 2000.

———. "Queer Theory: A Review of the *differences* Special Issue and Wittig's *The Straight Mind*," *Signs* 18, no. 4 (1993): 964–73.

Hickman, Ben. *Crisis and the US Avant-Garde: Poetry and Real Politics*. Edinburgh: Edinburgh University Press, 2015.

Hiddleston, Jane. *Assia Djebar: Out of Algeria*. Liverpool, Eng.: Liverpool University Press, 2006.

Hinrichsen, Malte. "Racist Trademarks and the Persistence of Commodity Racism in Europe and the United States." In *Diversity in Intellectual Property: Identities, Interests, and Intersections*, edited by Irene Calboli and Srividhya Ragavan, 130–48. New York: Cambridge University Press, 2015.

Hivernel, Françoise. "'The Parental Couple': Françoise Dolto and Jacques Lacan: Contributions to the Mirror Stage." *British Journal of Psychotherapy* 29, no. 4 (2013): 505–18.

hooks, bell. "The Oppositional Gaze: Black Female Spectators." In *Black Looks: Race and Representation*, 115–31. Boston: Sound End Press, 1992.

Hudson-Weems, Clenora. *Emmett Till: The Sacrificial Lamb of the Civil Rights Movement*. Troy, Mich.: Bedford, 1994.

Irigaray, Luce. *Speculum of the Other Woman*. Translated by Gillian C. Gill. Ithaca, N.Y.: Cornell University Press, 1985.

Jameson, Fredric. *Postmodernism, or, The Cultural Logic of Late Capitalism*. Durham, N.C.: Duke University Press, 1991.

Jay, Martin. *Downcast Eyes: The Denigration of Vision in Twentieth-Century French Thought*. Berkeley: University of California Press, 1994.

———. "Drifting into Dangerous Waters: The Separation of Aesthetic Experience from the Work of Art." In *Aesthetic Subjects*, edited by Pamela R. Matthews and David McWhirter, 3–27. Minneapolis: University of Minnesota Press, 2003.

Joyce, Stephen. "The Link the Chain: The Individual and Communal Self in Theresa Hak Kyung Cha's *Dictée*." *Forum for Inter-American Research* 1, no. 1 (2008), http://interamerica.de/current-issue/joyce.

Kang, L. Hyun Yi. "The 'Liberatory Voice' of Theresa Hak Kyung Cha's *Dictée*." In *Writing Self, Writing Nation: A Collection of Essays on DICTEE by Theresa Hak Kyung Cha*, edited by Elaine H. Kim and Norma Alarcón, 73–99. Berkeley, Calif.: Third Woman, 1994.

Kaplan, E. Ann. "Fanon, Trauma and Cinema." In *Frantz Fanon: Critical Perspectives*, edited by Anthony C. Alessandrini, 146–57. New York: Routledge, 1999.

———. *Looking for the Other: Feminism, Film, and the Imperial Gaze*. New York: Routledge, 1997.

Katz, Cindi. "Childhood as Spectacle: Relays of Anxiety and the Reconfiguration of the Child." *Cultural Geographies* 15, no. 1 (2008): 5–17.

Keeling, Kara. *The Witch's Flight: The Cinematic, the Black Femme, and the Image of Common Sense*. Durham, N.C.: Duke University Press, 2007.

Kelly, Debra. *Autobiography and Independence: Selfhood and Creativity in North African Postcolonial Writing in French*. Liverpool, Eng.: Liverpool University Press, 2005.

Kember, Sarah, and Joanna Zylinska. *Life after New Media: Mediation as a Vital Process*. Cambridge, Mass.: MIT Press, 2012.

Khanna, Akshay. "Taming of the Shrewd Meyeli Chhele: A Political Economy of Development's Sexual Subject." *Development* 52, no.1 (2009): 43–51.

Khanna, Ranjana. *Algeria Cuts: Women and Representation, 1830 to the Present*. Stanford, Calif.: Stanford University Press, 2008.

――――. *Dark Continents: Psychoanalysis and Colonialism*. Durham, N.C.: Duke University Press, 2003.

Kim, Elaine H. "Poised on the In-Between: A Korean American's Reflection on Theresa Hak Kyung Cha's *Dictée*." In *Writing Self, Writing Nation: A Collection of Essays on DICTEE by Theresa Hak Kyung Cha*, edited by Elaine H. Kim and Norma Alarcón, 3–30. Berkeley: Third Woman, 1994.

Kim, Elaine H., and Norma Alarcón, eds. *Writing Self, Writing Nation: A Collection of Essays on DICTEE by Theresa Hak Kyung Cha*. Berkeley: Third Woman, 1994.

Krauss, Rosalind. "Reinventing the Medium." *Critical Inquiry* 25, no. 2 (1999): 289–305.

Lacan, Jacques. *Anxiety: The Seminar of Jacques Lacan, Book X*. Edited by Jacques-Alain Miller. Translated by A. R. Price. Cambridge: Polity, 2014.

――――. *Écrits: The First Complete Edition in English*. Translated by Bruce Fink. New York: Norton, 2006.

――――. *Freud's Papers on Technique, 1953–1954: The Seminar of Jacques Lacan, Book I*. Edited by Jacques-Alain Miller. Translated by John Forrester. New York: Norton, 1991.

――――. "Les complexes dans la formation familiaux de l'individu." In *Autres écrits*, edited by Jacques-Alain Miller, 23–84. Paris: Seuil, 2001.

――――. *Le sinthome: Le séminaire, livre XXIII*. Edited by Jacques-Alain Miller. Paris: Seuil, 2005.

――――. *The Psychoses, 1955–1956: The Seminar of Jacques Lacan, Book III*. Edited by Jacques-Alain Miller. Translated by Russell Grigg. New York: Norton, 1997.

Lane, Christopher. "The Psychoanalysis of Race: An Introduction." In *The Psychoanalysis of Race*, edited by Christopher Lane, 1–40. New York: Columbia University Press, 1998.

Lazreg, Marnia. *The Eloquence of Silence: Algerian Women in Question*. New York: Routledge, 1994.

Leitch, Vincent B. *American Literary Criticism since the 1930s*. New York: Routledge, 2010.

Le Sueur, James D. *Between Terrorism and Democracy: Algeria since 1989*. New York: Zed, 2010.

Leys, Ruth. *Trauma: A Genealogy*. Chicago: University of Chicago Press, 2000.

Lhermitte, Jean. *L'image de notre corps*. Paris: Nouvelle Revue Critique, 1939.

Lowe, Lisa. "Unfaithful to the Original: The Subject of *Dictée*." In *Writing Self, Writing Nation: A Collection of Essays on DICTEE by Theresa Hak*

Kyung Cha, edited by Elaine H. Kim and Norma Alarcón, 35–69. Berkeley, Calif.: Third Woman, 1994.

Lugones, Maria. "The Coloniality of Gender." *Worlds and Knowledges Otherwise*, 2008, 1–17.

Lyotard, Jean-François. *The Postmodern Condition: A Report on Knowledge.* Translated by Geoffrey Bennington and Brian Massumi. Minneapolis: University of Minnesota Press, 1984.

Maat, Harro. "Commodities and Anti-commodities: Rice on Sumatra, 1915–1925." In *Rice: Global Networks and New Histories*, edited by Francesca Bray, Peter A. Coclanis, Edda L. Fields-Black, and Dagmar Schäfer, 335–54. New York: Cambridge University Press, 2015.

Macey, David. *Frantz Fanon: A Biography.* New York: Verso, 2012.

———. "The Recall of the Real: Frantz Fanon and Psychoanalysis." *Constellations* 6, no. 1 (1999): 97–107.

Macherey, Pierre. "Figures of Interpellation in Althusser and Fanon." *Radical Philosophy*, no. 173 (2012): 9–20.

MacMaster, Neil. *Burning the Veil: The Algerian War and the "Emancipation" of Muslim Women, 1954–62.* Manchester, England: Manchester University Press, 2009.

Maitra, Ani. "Aberrant Narcissisms in Dolto, Lacan, and Fanon," *differences* 28, no. 3 (2017): 93–135.

———. "CNN in North Korea: Liberal Democracy and Ethnonationalism." *Counterpunch*, December 1, 2017. https://www.counterpunch.org/2017/12/01/cnn-in-north-korea-liberal-democracy-and-ethnonationalism/.

———. "In the Shadow of the Homoglobal: Queer Cosmopolitanism in Tsai Ming-liang's *I Don't Want to Sleep Alone*." In *New Intimacies, Old Desires: Law, Culture and Queer Politics in Neoliberal Times*, edited by Oishik Sircar and Dipika Jain, 317–50. New Delhi: Zubaan Academic, 2017.

Majumder, Debalina, dir. . . . *ebang bewarish*. Kolkata: Sappho for Equality, 2013. DVD.

Marks, Laura U. *Hanan al-Cinema: Affections for the Moving Image.* Cambridge, Mass.: MIT Press, 2015.

———. *The Skin of the Film: Intercultural Cinema, Embodiment, and the Senses.* Durham, N.C.: Duke University Press, 2000.

Martel, James R. *The Misinterpellated Subject.* Durham, N.C.: Duke University Press, 2017.

Matthews, Pamela R., and David McWhirter. "Introduction: Exile's Return? Aesthetics Now." In *Aesthetic Subjects*, edited by Pamela R. Matthews and David McWhirter, xii–xxviii. Minneapolis: University of Minnesota Press, 2003.

McCaffery, Steve. "Death of the Subject: The Implications of Counter-Communication in Recent Language-Centered Writing." *L=A=N=G =U=A=G=E*, suppl. 1 (1980): 2–17.

———. "From the Notebooks," *L=A=N=G=U=A=G=E* 9–10 (1979): 31–33.

McCormack, Derek P. *Refrains for Moving Bodies: Experience and Experiment in Affective Spaces.* Durham, N.C.: Duke University Press, 2013.

McLuhan, Marshall. *Understanding Media: The Extensions of Man.* Cambridge, Mass.: MIT Press, 1994.

McNulty, Tracy. *Wrestling with the Angel: Experiments in Symbolic Life.* New York: Columbia University Press, 2014.

Menon, Madhavi. *Indifference to Difference: On Queer Universalism.* Minneapolis: University of Minnesota Press, 2015.

Menon, Nivedita. *Recovering Subversion: Feminist Politics beyond the Law.* Delhi: Permanent Black, 2004.

Metz, Christian. *The Imaginary Signifier: Psychoanalysis and Cinema.* Translated by Celia Britton, Annwyl Williams, Ben Brewster, and Alfred Guzzetti. Bloomington: Indiana University Press, 1982.

Metzl, Jonathan M. *Protest Psychosis: How Schizophrenia Became a Black Disease.* Boston: Beacon, 2010.

Michelsen, Anders. "The Visual Experience Economy: What Kind of Economies? On the Topologies of Aesthetic Capitalism." In *Aesthetic Capitalism*, edited by Eduardo de la Fuente and Peter Murphy, 63–88. Boston: Brill, 2014.

Mignolo, Walter D. *The Darker Side of Western Modernity: Global Futures, Decolonial Options.* Durham, N.C.: Duke University Press, 2011.

Misra, Kavita. "Politico-Moral Transactions in Indian AIDS Service: Confidentiality, Rights, and the New Modalities of Governance." *Anthropological Quarterly* 79, no. 1 (2006): 33–74.

Mitchell, W. J. T. "Beyond Comparison: Picture, Text, and Method." In *Picture Theory: Essays on Verbal and Visual Representation*, 83–107. Chicago: University of Chicago Press, 1995.

Mitchell, W. J. T., and Mark B. N. Hansen. Introduction to *Critical Terms for Media Studies*, edited by W. J. T. Mitchell and B. N. Hansen, vii–xxii. Chicago: University of Chicago Press, 2010.

Mitter, Siddhartha, and Christina Sharpe, "'What Does It Mean to Be Black and Look at This?' A Scholar Reflects on the Dana Schutz Controversy." Hyperallergic, March 24, 2017. https://hyperallergic.com/368012/what -does-it-mean-to-be-black-and-look-at-this-a-scholar-reflects-on-the -dana-schutz-controversy/.

Moatissime, Ahmed. "Islam, arabization, et francophonie: Une interface possible à l'interrogation 'Algérie—France—Islam'?" In *Algérie—France—Islam*, edited by Joseph Jurt, 55–75. Paris: L'Harmattan, 1997.

Moten, Fred. *In the Break: The Aesthetics of the Black Radical Tradition*. Minneapolis: University of Minnesota Press, 2003.

Mowitt, John. *Radio: Essays in Bad Reception*. Berkeley: University of California Press, 2011.

Mulvey, Laura. "Afterthoughts on 'Visual Pleasure and Narrative Cinema' Inspired by *Duel in the Sun* (King Vidor, 1946)." *Framework: The Journal of Cinema and Media* 15–17 (1981): 12–15.

———. "Visual Pleasure and Narrative Cinema." In *Narrative, Apparatus, Ideology: A Film Theory Reader*, edited by Philip Rosen, 198–209. New York: Columbia University Press, 1986.

Muñoz, José Esteban. *Cruising Utopia: The Then and There of Queer Futurity*. New York: New York University Press, 2009.

———. *Disidentifications: Queers of Color and the Performance of Politics*. Minneapolis: University of Minnesota Press, 1999.

Murphy, Peter, and Eduardo de la Fuente. "Introduction: Aesthetic Capitalism." In *Aesthetic Capitalism*, edited by Eduardo de la Fuente and Peter Murphy, 1–9. Boston: Brill, 2014.

Naficy, Hamid. *An Accented Cinema: Exilic and Diasporic Filmmaking*. Princeton, N.J.: Princeton University Press, 2001.

Ong, Aihwa. *Neoliberalism as Exception: Mutations in Citizenship and Sovereignty*. Durham, N.C.: Duke University Press, 2006.

Oza, Rupal. *The Making of Neoliberal India: Nationalism, Gender, and the Paradoxes of Globalization*. New York: Routledge, 2006.

Parker, Joe, and Ranu Samantrai. "Interdisciplinarity and Social Justice: An Introduction." In *Interdisciplinarity and Social Justice: Revisioning Academic Accountability*, edited by Joe Parker, Ranu Samantrai, and Mary Romero, 1–33. Albany: State University of New York Press, 2010.

Pawar, Kiran, dir. *Astitva*. Mumbai: Solaris Pictures, 2010. DVD.

Perloff, Marjorie. "The Word as Such: L=A=N=G=U=A=G=E Poetry in the Eighties." *American Poetry Review* 13, no. 3 (1984): 15–22.

Phu, Thy. "Decapitated Forms: Theresa Hak Kyung Cha's Visual Text and the Politics of Visibility." *Mosaic: An Interdisciplinary Critical Journal* 38, no. 1 (2005): 17–36.

Piketty, Thomas. *Capital in the Twenty-First Century*. Translated by Arthur Goldhammer. Cambridge, Mass.: Harvard University Press, 2017.

Pines, Jim, and Paul Willemen, eds. *Questions of Third Cinema*. London: British Film Institute, 1989.

Pinney, Christopher. "Iatrogenic Religion and Politics." In *Censorship in South Asia: Cultural Regulation from Sedition to Seduction*, edited by Raminder Kaur and William Mazzarella, 29–62. Bloomington: Indiana University Press, 2009.

Poggioli, Renato. *The Theory of the Avant-Garde*. Translated by Gerald Fitzgerald. Cambridge, Mass.: Harvard University Press, 1968.

Povinelli, Elizabeth A. *The Cunning of Recognition: Indigenous Alterities and the Making of Australian Multiculturalism*. Durham, N.C.: Duke University Press, 2002.

Puar, Jasbir K. *The Right to Maim: Debility, Capacity, Disability*. Durham, N.C.: Duke University Press, 2017.

———. *Terrorist Assemblages: Homonationalism in Queer Times*. Durham, N.C.: Duke University Press, 2007.

Pullen, Christopher. *Gay Identity, New Storytelling and the Media*. New York: Palgrave Macmillan, 2009.

Rancière, Jacques. "The Cause of the Other." Translated by David Macey. *parallax* 4, no. 2 (1998): 25–33.

———. *The Politics of Aesthetics: The Distribution of the Sensible*. Translated by Gabriel Rockhill. New York: Continuum, 2004.

Ray, Raka, and Seemin Qayum. *Cultures of Servitude: Modernity, Domesticity, and Class in India*. Stanford, Calif.: Stanford University Press, 2009.

Reddy, Chandan. "Asian Diasporas, Neoliberalism, and Family: Reviewing the Case for Homosexual Asylum in the Context of Family Rights." *Social Text* 23, nos. 3–4 (2005): 101–19.

———. *Freedom with Violence: Race, Sexuality, and the US State*. Durham, N.C.: Duke University Press, 2011.

Reddy, Gayatri. *With Respect to Sex: Negotiating Hijra Identity in South India*. Chicago: University of Chicago Press, 2005.

Roberts, David. "From the Cultural Contradictions of Capitalism to the Creative Economy: Reflections on the New Spirit of Art and Capitalism." In *Aesthetic Capitalism*, edited by Eduardo de la Fuente and Peter Murphy, 10–26. Boston: Brill, 2014.

Robson, Mark, dir. *Home of the Brave*. 1949; Chicago: Olive Films, 2014. DVD.

Roelofs, Monique. *The Cultural Promise of the Aesthetic*. New York: Bloomsbury Academic, 2014.

Rogin, Michael. "Home of the Brave." In *The War Film*, edited by Robert Eberwein, 82–89. New Brunswick, N.J.: Rutgers University Press, 2005.

Rooney, Ellen. "Form and Contentment." *Modern Language Quarterly* 61, no. 1 (2000): 17–40.

Rosen, Philip. Preface to *Narrative, Apparatus, Ideology: A Film Theory Reader*, edited by Philip Rosen, vii–xi. New York: Columbia University Press, 1986.

———, ed. *Narrative, Apparatus, Ideology: A Film Theory Reader*. New York: Columbia University Press, 1986.

Roth, Moira. "Theresa Hak Kyung Cha 1951–1982: A Narrative Chronology." In *Writing Self, Writing Nation: A Collection of Essays on DICTEE by Theresa Hak Kyung Cha*, edited by Elaine H. Kim and Norma Alarcón, 151–60. Berkeley: Third Woman, 1994.

Roudinesco, Élisabeth. *Jacques Lacan and Co.: A History of Psychoanalysis in France, 1925–1985*. Translated by Jeffrey Mehlman. Chicago: University of Chicago Press, 1990.

Roy, Modhumita. "The Englishing of India: Class Formation and Social Privilege." *Social Scientist* 21, no. 5 (1993): 36–62.

Salhi, Zahia Smail. "Heard/Symbolic Voices: *The Nouba of the Women of Mont Chenoua* and Women's Film in the Maghreb." In *Storytelling in World Cinemas*, vol. 2, *Contexts*, edited by Lina Khatib, 103–21. New York: Wallflower, 2013.

Salmane, Hala. "Historical Background." In *Algerian Cinema*, edited by Hala Salmane, Simon Hartog, and David Wilson, 5–7. London: British Film Institute, 1976.

Salmane, Hala, Simon Hartog, and David Wilson, eds. *Algerian Cinema*. London: British Film Institute, 1976.

Sakai, Naoki. *Translation and Subjectivity: On Japan and Cultural Nationalism*. Minneapolis: University of Minnesota Press, 1997.

Sarkar, Bhaskar, and Janet Walker. "Introduction: Moving Testimonies." In *Documentary Testimonies: Global Archives of Suffering*, edited by Bhaskar Sarkar and Janet Walker, 1–34. New York: Routledge, 2010.

Sarkar, Sumit. *Modern India, 1885–1947*. New York: Palgrave Macmillan, 1983.

Sarkar, Tanika, and Sumit Chowdhury. "The Meaning of Nandigram: Corporate Land Invasion, People's Power, and the Left in India." *Focaal—European Journal of Anthropology* 54 (2009): 73–88.

Scales, Rebecca. *Radio and the Politics of Sound in Interwar France, 1921–1939*. Cambridge: Cambridge University Press, 2016.

Schoonover, Karl, and Rosalind Galt. *Queer Cinema in the World*. Durham, N.C.: Duke University Press, 2016.

Schwartz, Margaret. *Dead Matter: The Meaning of Iconic Corpses*. Minneapolis: University of Minnesota Press, 2015.

Sedgwick, Eve Kosofsky. *Epistemology of the Closet*. Berkeley: University of California Press, 1990.

————. "Paranoid Reading and Reparative Reading, or, You're So Paranoid, You Probably Think This Essay Is about You." In *Touching Feeling: Affect, Pedagogy, Performativity*, 123–51. Durham, N.C.: Duke University Press, 2003.

Sekula, Allan. "The Traffic in Photographs." In *Photography against the Grain: Essays and Photo Works, 1973–1983*, 96–101. Halifax: Press of the Nova Scotia College of Art and Design, 1984.

Sen, Abhijit. "Economic Reforms, Employment and Poverty: Trends and Options." *Economic and Political Weekly* 31, no. 35/37 (1996): 2459–77.

Sen, Amartya. *Identity and Violence: The Illusion of Destiny*. New York: Norton, 2006.

Seshadri-Crooks, Kalpana. *Desiring Whiteness: A Lacanian Analysis of Race.* New York: Routledge, 2000.

Shafik, Viola. *Arab Cinema: History and Cultural Identity.* New York: American University in Cairo Press, 2007.

Shah, Nayan. "Sexuality, Identity, and the Uses of History." In *Q & A: Queer in Asian America*, edited by David L. Eng and Alice Y. Hom, 141–56. Philadelphia: Temple University Press, 1998.

Sharpley-Whiting, T. Denean. *Frantz Fanon: Conflicts and Feminisms.* Lanham, Md.: Rowman and Littlefield, 1998.

Shohat, Ella, and Robert Stam. *Unthinking Eurocentrism: Multiculturalism and the Media.* New York: Routledge, 1994.

Silliman, Ron. "For Open Letter." *L=A=N=G=U=AG=E*, suppl. 1 (1980): 31–34.

————. *Under Albany.* Cambridge: Salt, 2004.

Silva, Denise Ferreira da. "To Be Announced: Radical Praxis or Knowing (at) the Limits of Justice," *Social Text* 31, no. 1/114 (2013): 43–62. https://doi.org/10.1215/01642472-1958890.

Silverman, Kaja. *The Acoustic Mirror: The Female Voice in Psychoanalysis and Cinema.* Bloomington: Indiana University Press, 1988.

————. *The Threshold of the Visible World.* New York: Routledge, 1996.

Simonson, Mary. *Body Knowledge: Performance, Intermediality, and American Entertainment at the Turn of the Twentieth Century.* New York: Oxford University Press, 2013.

Sircar, Oishik. "Spectacles of Emancipation: Reading Rights Differently in India's Legal Discourse." *Osgoode Hall Law Journal* 49, no. 3 (2012): 527–73.

Sircar, Oishik, and Dipika Jain. "Introduction: Of Powerful Feelings and Facile Gestures." In *New Intimacies, Old Desires: Law, Culture and Queer Politics in Neoliberal Times*, edited by Oishik Sircar and Dipika Jain, iii–xx. New Delhi: Zubaan Academic, 2017.

————, eds. *New Intimacies, Old Desires: Law, Culture and Queer Politics in Neoliberal Times*. New Delhi: Zubaan Academic, 2017.

Skriabine, Pierre. "The Clinic of the Borromean Knot." In *Lacan: Topologically Speaking*, edited by Ellie Ragland and Dragan Milovanovic, 249–67. New York: Other Press, 2004.

Solanas, Fernando, and Octavio Getino. "Towards a Third Cinema: Notes and Experiences for the Development of Cinema of Liberation in the Third World." In *New Latin American Cinema*, vol. 1, *Theory, Practices, and Transcontinental Articulations*, edited by Michael T. Martin, 33–58. Detroit: Wayne State University Press, 1997.

Sontag, Susan. *Illness as Metaphor and AIDS and Its Metaphors*. New York: Picador, 1990.

Spadola, Emilio. *The Calls of Islam: Sufis, Islamists, and Mass Mediation in Urban Morocco*. Bloomington: Indiana University Press, 2014.

Spahr, Juliana. *Everybody's Autonomy: Connective Reading and Collective Identity*. Tuscaloosa: University of Alabama Press, 2001.

Spielmann, Yvonne. "History and Theory of Intermedia in Visual Culture." In *Intermedia: Enacting the Liminal*, edited by Hans Breder and Klaus-Peter Busse, 131–38. Dortmund, Germany: Dortmunder Schriften zur Kunst, 2005.

Spivak, Gayatri Chakravorty. "Can the Subaltern Speak?" In *Colonial Discourse and Post-Colonial Theory: A Reader*, edited by Patrick Williams and Laura Chrisman, 66–111. New York: Columbia University Press, 1994.

————. *A Critique of Postcolonial Reason: Toward a History of the Vanishing Present*. Cambridge, Mass.: Harvard University Press, 1999.

————. "Echo." *New Literary History* 24, no. 1 (1993): 17–43.

————. "In a Word: *Interview*." Interview by Ellen Rooney. In *Outside in the Teaching Machine*, 1–23. New York: Routledge, 1993.

————. "Scattered Speculations on the Question of Value." *diacritics* 15, no. 4 (1985): 73–93.

————. "Translator's Preface." In *Of Grammatology*, by Jacques Derrida, ix–lxxxvii. Translated by Gayatri Chakravorty Spivak. Baltimore: Johns Hopkins University Press, 1997.

Steiner, George. "Post-script." In *George Steiner: A Reader*, 246–57. New York: Oxford University Press, 1984.

Stone, Sandy. "The *Empire* Strikes Back: A Posttranssexual Manifesto." In *The Transgender Studies Reader*, edited by Susan Stryker and Stephen Whittle, 221–35. New York: Routledge, 2006.

Stone-Richards, Michael. "A Commentary on Theresa Hak Kyung Cha's *DICTEE*." *Glossator* 1 (2009): 145–210.

Thussu, Dayanand. *Communicating India's Soft Power: Buddha to Bolly-wood.* New York: Palgrave Macmillan, 2013.

Tuhkanen, Mikko. *The American Optic: Psychoanalysis, Critical Race Theory, and Richard Wright.* New York: State University of New York Press, 2010.

Turkle, Sherry. *Alone Together: Why We Expect More from Technology and Less from Each Other.* New York: Basic Books, 2011.

Vergès, Françoise. "Creole Skin, Black Mask: Fanon and Disavowal." *Critical Inquiry* 23, no. 3 (1997): 578–95.

Viego, Antonio. *Dead Subjects: Toward a Politics of Loss in Latino Studies.* Durham, N.C.: Duke University Press, 2007.

Vince, Natalya. *Our Fighting Sisters: Nation, Memory and Gender in Algeria, 1954–2012.* Manchester, England: Manchester University Press, 2015.

Wall-Romana, Christophe. *Cinepoetry: Imaginary Cinemas in French Poetry.* New York: Fordham University Press, 2013.

Warner, Michael. *The Trouble with Normal: Sex, Politics and the Ethics of Queer Life.* Cambridge, Mass.: Harvard University Press, 2000.

Wayne, Mike. *Marxism and Media Studies: Key Concepts and Contemporary Trends.* Sterling, Va.: Pluto, 2003.

Weber, Max. *The Protestant Ethic and the Spirit of Capitalism.* Translated by Talcott Parsons. New York: Routledge, 2001.

Welsch, Wolfgang. *Undoing Aesthetics.* Translated by Andrew Inkpen. London: Sage, 1997.

White, Patricia. *Women's Cinema, World Cinema: Projecting Contemporary Feminisms.* Durham, N.C.: Duke University Press, 2015.

Wiegman, Robyn. *Object Lessons.* Durham, N.C.: Duke University Press, 2012.

Williams, Patrick, and Laura Chrisman, eds. *Colonial Discourse and Post-Colonial Theory: A Reader.* New York: Columbia University Press, 1994.

Williams, Raymond. *Marxism and Literature.* New York: Oxford University Press, 1977.

Wollen, Peter. "Godard and Counter-Cinema: *Vent d'Est* (1972)." In *The European Cinema Reader*, edited by Catherine Fowler, 74–82. New York: Routledge, 2002.

Wong, Shelley Sunn. "Unnaming the Same: Theresa Hak Kyung Cha's *Dictée.*" In *Writing Self, Writing Nation: A Collection of Essays on DICTEE by Theresa Hak Kyung Cha*, edited by Elaine H. Kim and Norma Alarcón, 103–40. Berkeley, Calif.: Third Woman, 1994.

Yu, Timothy. *Race and the Avant-Garde: Experimental and Asian American Poetry since 1965.* Stanford, Calif.: Stanford University Press, 2009.

Zarobell, John. *Empire of Landscape: Space and Ideology in French Colonial Algeria.* University Park: Pennsylvania State University Press, 2010.